1956

SIMON HALL

1956

THE WORLD IN REVOLT

FABER & FABER

First published in 2016
by Faber & Faber Limited
74–77 Great Russell Street
London WC1B 3DA

Typeset by Faber & Faber Ltd
Printed in the UK by CPI Group (UK) Ltd, Croydon, CR0 4YY

Material from Radio Free Europe's (RFE) News and Information Department
reprinted with the permission of Radio Free Europe/Radio Liberty,
1201 Connecticut Ave NW, Ste 400, Washington DC 20036.

Quotations from Martin Luther King, Jr, reprinted by arrangement
with The Heirs to the Estate of Martin Luther King Jr,
c/o Writers House as agent for the proprietor, New York, NY.
Copyright: © Dr Martin Luther King Jr © renewed Coretta Scott King.

Excerpts from Adam Ważyk, 'Poem for Adults', reprinted
courtesy of Małgorzata and Katarzyna Ważyk.

Quotation from Howl by Allen Ginsberg. Copyright © Allen Ginsberg, 1956,
used by permission of The Wylie Agency (UK) Limited.

A CIP record for this book
is available from the British Library

ISBN 978-0-571-31232-0

FSC
www.fsc.org
MIX
Paper from
responsible sources
FSC® C101712

2 4 6 8 10 9 7 5 3 1

For my parents

CONTENTS

PROLOGUE

We can say this year more than ever before that the future
depends on the courage, the resolution and the energy of
democratic man.
  New York Times, 1 January 1956

As the last moments of 1955 ebbed away, the four hundred thousand revellers gathered in New York's Times Square raised their
eyes eagerly to the roof of the Times Tower. There, at twenty seconds to midnight, as the ball of electric lights began its seventy-
foot descent from the top of the flagpole, the crowd roared and
sounded air horns in anticipation of the New Year. About eight
seconds in, as the noise crescendoed, all 180 lights suddenly went
out, and the ball completed its journey in darkness. The six-foot-
high numerical display also failed. A faulty circuit breaker meant
that it was not until a quarter past twelve that the lights welcoming
in 1956 from all four sides of the tower were illuminated.[1]

While the celebrations in New York descended into farce, those
in Japan were scarred by tragedy. During a Shinto ceremony at the
Yahiko Shrine, some 150 miles north of Tokyo, more than a hundred people were trampled to death, and seventy-five injured. The
disaster occurred during a scramble for the traditional rice balls, or
mochi, which were being thrown to the crowd of thirty thousand.
According to one eyewitness, people near the altar 'swarmed back'
down a steep stone staircase, 'crashing into the arriving worship-
pers'. Some 'stumbled off the staircase or were crushed under the
oncoming human wave'. With only eleven police officers on duty,
panic spread quickly: 'Amid shrieks, men, women and children
fell under the trampling feet.' The pressure from the crowd also

collapsed a six-foot wall, causing further casualties. The *New York Times* reported that the 'draped bodies of the dead were placed at the entrances and the bereaved families came to claim them there'.[2]

It was an inauspicious start to a year that many predicted would be particularly challenging. In Madrid, for instance, General Francisco Franco – who would soon be entering his eighteenth year as Spain's dictator – used his New Year message to warn that 'the dangers that threaten the world are greater than ever'.[3] Meanwhile, in its first editorial of 1956, *The Times* of London called for 'courage' in the face of the 'crises' that were 'undoubtedly in store for us', while Prime Minister Anthony Eden offered assurances that 'we shall be doing everything we can to reduce tension between the nations, at every time and at every opportunity'.[4] He was, he said, looking forward 'very much' to a forthcoming summit with President Eisenhower; a meeting that, he believed, would 'be of help to the peace of the World'.[5]

The New Year did bring some grounds for optimism. Speaking from the pulpit of Dexter Avenue Baptist Church in Montgomery, Alabama, on 1 January, Rev. Martin Luther King, Jr, told his congregation that there was 'no better way' to begin the New Year than with the firm belief in a powerful God – one who was 'able to beat back gigantic mountains of opposition and to bring low prodigious hill tops of evil'. King, the rising young star of the American civil rights movement, recognised that the scale of man's inhumanity to his fellow man, together with the awful realities of modern war, caused 'each of us' to 'question the ableness of our God'. But, King said, the conviction that good would ultimately emerge victorious in its struggle against evil lay at the root of the Christian faith. As the boycott of the city's racially segregated buses entered its second month, King urged his congregation to continue with their own struggle against evil, explaining that there was no need to worry, because 'God is able. Don't worry about segregation. It will die because God is against it.'[6]

1 January also saw the world welcome a new, independent nation, as more than half a century of Anglo-Egyptian rule came to an end in the Sudan. During a ceremony on the lawn of the palace in Khartoum, attended by two thousand official guests, the new prime minister, Ismail el-Azhari, declared that 'there is no occasion in the history of the Sudan and its people greater than this . . . If this day marks the end of our struggle for independence, it is also the beginning of our task of . . . building our future progress.' Then, as the band struck up the Sudanese national anthem and cannon fired the salute, el-Azhari joined with the leader of the official Opposition to raise the blue, yellow and green tricolour of the new state as, simultaneously, the British and Egyptian flags were lowered by officers of the Sudanese armed forces.[7]

The picture in French North Africa, though, was rather less rosy. At the end of December, following a spate of attacks by Moroccan fighters, French forces had launched a major operation near the Rif Mountains, killing more than fifty rebels; they also responded forcefully to acts of sabotage and terrorism in Algeria, where, according to one newspaper report, Friday 30 December saw more than twenty rebels killed in a single province (just a few weeks later Albert Camus warned that if the European and Muslim populations could not find a way to live together in peace and mutual respect, they would be 'condemned to die together, with rage in their hearts').[8] In his annual message, written in Cairo while a guest of Egypt's Gamal Abdel Nasser, the Yugoslav leader Josep Tito argued that the people of Africa were 'striving to consolidate their independence, to govern themselves' and he condemned the 'civilising mission' of the European imperialists as little more than an excuse to 'dominate weak and underdeveloped countries'. But Tito was optimistic that an 'era of peaceful settlement of international problems has set in', and that 'war is being repudiated as a means of solving disputes . . .'[9]

There was talk of peace in Moscow too. On 31 December, the Soviet premier, Nikolai Bulganin, declared that, given sufficient goodwill and understanding, 1956 could see major progress towards 'putting an end to the Cold War . . .'[10] Later that evening, Bulganin and Nikita Khrushchev, first secretary of the Soviet Communist Party, hosted a lavish state dinner. Foreign diplomats were among the 1,200 or so guests who gathered in the Kremlin's enormous St George Hall, for a party that continued into the small hours. Alongside the food, champagne and music were speeches, numerous toasts and enthusiastic displays of dancing, led by senior Soviet officials: according to a report in the *New York Times*, Bulganin 'pranced about surrounded by a ring of girls'.[11] It was a very different scene in Key West, Florida, where President Eisenhower was recuperating from his September heart attack, spending his time painting, hitting golf balls and going for the occasional stroll. While a 'family dinner and celebration' was planned, it was 'uncertain whether the President would remain awake until midnight to greet the New Year'.[12]

The world's statesmen may have marked the New Year by warning of the difficulties that lay ahead, expressing their desire for 'peace' or holding out the promise of a better tomorrow. But they would soon find themselves swept up, and some of them even swept aside, by an extraordinary series of events – by turns dramatic, shocking and world-changing – that could scarcely have been anticipated by even the most astute and brilliant of observers.

More than a century has now passed since the renowned Italian Marxist Antonio Gramsci complained that, by venerating chronology, historians had created the misleading impression that some years were 'like mountains that humanity vaulted over, suddenly finding itself in a new world, coming into a new life'.[13] His words, though, appear to have fallen on deaf ears. For historians, the habit of identifying a particular year as especially significant, or worthy of attention, has not only endured but flourished. During the past decade alone, dozens of books have appeared that attempt to capture the essence of an era, make sense of broader political, economic and cultural forces, or explore turning points in world history, through the story of a single year.[14] But while writers have produced evocative accounts of various aspects of 1956, the year's collective drama – and contemporaries' own sense of living through momentous times – has been largely forgotten. The contrast with 1968, which is widely (and loudly) acclaimed as an international 'year of revolt', is striking. This historical absent-mindedness actually reflects a wider tendency to view the 1950s as rather drab: an era in which, we are told, the war-weary populations of Western Europe struggled to rebuild their shattered economies and shake off the constraints of economic austerity, while in the United States virtually the entire nation was supposedly enveloped by a stifling culture of conformity. When compared with the excitement of the war against fascism on the one hand, and the colourful counter-culture and vibrant protest movements of the 1960s on the other, it is hardly surprising that the 'dreary' 1950s have frequently been consigned to the margins.[15]

By the mid-1950s, however, large parts of the world were on the cusp of dramatic change, as simmering social, economic and political tensions and deepening frustration with the post-war order made for a potent mix. Ten years after the victory over Nazi Germany, the ideals for which the Allied powers had supposedly fought the Second World War were, for many, ringing increasingly hollow. The Atlantic Charter, drafted by British Prime Minister Winston Churchill and US President Franklin Roosevelt in August 1941, and subsequently endorsed by both France and the Soviet Union, had envisioned a post-war world that would be founded on the principles of self-determination, international co-operation and 'freedom from fear and want'.[16] But the reluctance of the European powers to fully relinquish their imperial ambitions, Communists' use of terror and coercion to establish the so-called 'people's democracies' in Eastern Europe, and the determination of white supremacists in both the United States and South Africa to maintain systems of racial control, made a mockery of such lofty goals. Among the subjugated, the marginalised and the oppressed, a decade's worth of frustrated hopes and disappointments were ready to erupt.

1956 saw ordinary people, all across the globe, speak out, fill the streets and city squares, risk arrest, take up arms and lose their lives in an attempt to win greater freedoms and build a more just world. Faced with an unprecedented challenge to their power, the guardians of the 'old order' fought back – often ruthlessly – in a desperate bid to shore up their authority. It was an epic contest that would transform the post-war world. High time, then, that the story of this remarkable year was told in full.

I WINTER

CRACKS IN THE OLD ORDER

1

MONTGOMERY

Right here in Montgomery, when the history books are
written in the future, somebody will have to say, 'There
lived a race of people, a *black* people, fleecy locks and black
complexion, a people who had the moral courage to stand
up for their rights. And thereby they injected a new meaning
into the veins of history and of civilization.'

MARTIN LUTHER KING, JR.

Just before nine thirty on the evening of Monday 30 January 1956,
a light-coloured car pulled up outside the white, wooden-framed
parsonage at 309 South Jackson Street in Montgomery, Alabama.
The modest residence, built in 1912, was home to Rev. Dr Martin
Luther King, Jr, the twenty-seven-year-old pastor of Dexter Avenue
Baptist Church, his wife Coretta and their two-month-old daughter, Yolanda. According to an eyewitness, the car stopped briefly
before moving away 'in a terrific hurry'.[1] Coretta was in the living room, chatting with a family friend, when she heard a 'heavy
thump on the concrete porch outside'. Nervous following a recent
series of menacing phone calls, she immediately ushered her com-
panion towards the rear of the house. A few seconds later, there was
a 'thunderous blast', followed by 'smoke and the sound of breaking
glass'.[2] A half-stick of dynamite had exploded on the south side of
the porch, ripping a hole in the floor and damaging the roof. The
windows at the front of the house also shattered, leaving shards of
glass scattered across the living room, den and music room.[3]

As worried neighbours began to arrive Coretta phoned the First
Baptist Church, where her husband, a leading figure in the eight-
week-old boycott of the city's segregated buses, was addressing a
mass meeting. She reported that the house had been bombed and

asked that people be sent over straight away, but did not think to mention that they were all unharmed.[4] Earlier that evening, King, president of the recently formed Montgomery Improvement Association, had delivered a speech to a packed audience of two thousand. Now, with the meeting drawing to a close, he was standing on a platform at the front of the church, presiding over the collection.[5] From his vantage point, King spotted an usher talking animatedly with Ralph Abernathy, the church's pastor and a good friend. Then Abernathy darted downstairs, only to reappear a few minutes later with an anxious look on his face. It was clear that something was wrong, and King soon called Abernathy over, to be told, 'Your house has been bombed.' When King enquired whether his family were all right, Abernathy responded grimly, 'We are checking on that now.'[6]

Just a few days earlier, King had experienced a profound personal and spiritual crisis. On Thursday 26 January he had been pulled over by two motorcycle officers for allegedly travelling at thirty miles per hour in a twenty-five-mile-per-hour zone. After spending several hours in a squalid jail cell, King was released. But the unpleasant experience had unnerved him – it was the first time that he had been arrested and on the way to the prison he had, briefly, feared that he might be lynched.[7] The following day, King returned home late after an MIA meeting, to be greeted by the latest in a series of threatening phone calls: 'Nigger, we are tired of you and your mess now. And if you aren't out of this town in three days, we're going to blow your brains out, and blow up your house.'[8] That night, unable to sleep, he sat at his kitchen table in despair. King was, he later admitted, on the verge of giving up: 'With my cup of coffee sitting untouched before me I tried to think of a way to move out of the picture without appearing a coward.' Around midnight, anxious and exhausted, he placed his head in his hands and prayed out loud. King later wrote that 'the words I spoke to God that midnight are still vivid in my memory':

'I am taking a stand for what I believe is right. But now I am afraid. The people are looking to me for leadership, and if I stand before them without strength and courage, they too will falter. I am at the end of my powers. I have nothing left. I've come to the point where I can't face it alone.' At that moment, I experienced the presence of the Divine as I had never experienced Him before. It seemed as though I could hear the quiet assurance of an inner voice saying: 'Stand up for righteousness, stand up for truth; and God will be at your side forever.' Almost at once my fears began to go. My uncertainty disappeared. I was ready to face anything.[9]

The bombing of his home, just three days later, would test King's newfound resolve. On receiving word of the attack, King relayed the news to the audience, explained that he had to leave straight away and suggested that they disperse quietly to their homes. 'Let us keep moving', King said, 'with the faith that what we are doing is right, and with the even greater faith that God is with us in this struggle.'[10] On arriving home, still unsure whether his wife and baby were safe, King was greeted by chaotic scenes. The traffic in the road was snarled up, a crowd of several hundred African Americans had surrounded the house and the police were struggling to maintain order. Jo Ann Robinson, an English teacher at Alabama State College and a leading community activist, described how the police 'tried in vain to move the crowd from the bombed area. The crowd was dangerously quiet, and the air was tense. One of the policemen called out, "Please go home, folks, nobody is hurt." Not a soul moved; no one spoke. The silence was accusing, maddening, threatening . . .'[11] One black man even suggested a shootout, telling a police officer, 'I ain't gonna move nowhere. That's the trouble now; you white folks is always pushin' us around. Now you got your .38 and I got mine; so let's battle it out.' With a number of men and older youths carrying knives and broken bottles, a full-scale riot was a very real possibility. Hardly surprising, then, that Mayor W. A. Gayle and Police Commissioner Clyde Sellers, who had arrived at the parsonage shortly after the bombing, were 'deathly pale'.

Striding across his damaged front porch, King entered the house and headed into the bedroom. On seeing his wife and child uninjured, he was overcome with relief.[12] Then the young preacher walked back onto the porch and appealed for calm. 'In less than a moment', he would later recall, 'there was complete silence.' After explaining that his wife and baby daughter were safe, he urged the crowd to be peaceful: 'We believe in law and order. Don't get panicky . . . Don't get your weapons. He who lives by the sword will perish by the sword. Remember that is what God said. We are not advocating violence. We want to love our enemies.' King continued, 'I did not start this boycott. I was asked by you to serve as your spokesman. I want it to be known the length and breadth of this land that if I am stopped this movement will not stop. If I am stopped our work will not stop. For what we are doing is right. What we are doing is just. And God is with us.' The crowd responded with cries of 'Amen' and 'God bless you, brother King.' Years later, Coretta described the emotional response to her husband's extraordinary speech. 'Many people out there were crying. I could see the shine of tears on their faces . . . they were moved, as by a holy exaltation.' It had certainly been a remarkable performance, under intense pressure. Then, as Clyde Sellers attempted to address the crowd, a chorus of loud, angry boos rang out, forcing King to intervene: 'Remember what I just said. Hear the commissioner.' Sellers's assurance of 'police protection for the King family' and his condemnation of the violence was followed by Mayor Gayle's announcement that he would 'work with my last breath if necessary to find and convict the guilty parties'. He also offered a $500 reward. King then urged everyone to 'go home and sleep calm'. 'Go home and don't worry,' he said. 'Be as calm as I and my family are. We are not hurt and remember that if anything happens to me, there will be others to take my place.'[13] Robinson recalled that, when King finished speaking, the crowd began to move away, 'as a great surge of water rolls quietly, calmly, obediently downstream'. As they did so a white policeman was overheard exclaiming, 'If it hadn't been for that nigger preacher, we'd all be dead.'[14]

In 1956, the United States was the most powerful and most prosperous country in the world. A post-war boom, driven by consumerism, military spending and technological advancement, had delivered unprecedented increases in GDP (it rose by 72 per cent between 1950 and 1959), full employment and rising living standards. Americans rushed to buy the latest consumer goods – including cars, fridges, televisions and washing machines – and millions of families carved out a middle-class life in the new suburban developments that sprang up across the nation. Automation and increases in productivity, together with the growth of the service and consumer sectors, meant that the United States became the world's first 'post-industrial' economy – and in 1956 'white-collar' workers (those in professional, managerial or administrative roles) outnumbered 'blue-collar' (or manual) workers for the first time.[15] The United States had also shaken off the isolationism of the 1930s to become the world's first superpower. Backed by considerable military muscle (including a vast network of overseas bases and a substantial fleet of nuclear bombers), the US affirmed its unshakeable commitment to democracy as it led the free world's response to the international Communist threat during the early years of the Cold War.[16] Yet for all her power and wealth, and her proud boasts, the United States harboured an ugly secret: millions of her own people lived as second-class citizens, cut off from the nation's economic prosperity and democratic promise. 'Jim Crow', an entrenched system of white supremacy that operated across the South, subjected African American men, women and children to countless petty injustices and humiliations. And nowhere were these daily insults more bitterly resented than in Montgomery, Alabama.

Located on a bluff overlooking the Alabama River, in the heart of the rich, fertile land of the Black Belt, Montgomery had once been a thriving centre for the sale of cotton and slaves. During the Civil War, the city served as the first capital of the Confederacy – on 18 February 1861 Jefferson Davis had taken the presidential oath of office on the portico of the imposing state capitol building.[17] In the mid-twentieth century, Montgomery's economy was heavily dependent on the surrounding agricultural counties (it had developed lumber, furniture and fertiliser industries) and two nearby US air force bases.[18] Like communities across the American South, the city's African Americans were politically and economically disenfranchised and subjected to degrading segregation. Although African Americans made up over a third of Montgomery's population of 120,000 in 1955, they constituted only about 8 per cent of the electorate. Many thousands of potential black voters were kept off the voting rolls, thanks to the combination of legal restrictions (to be eligible to vote, ownership of property worth at least $500 was required), a literacy test (administered, unfairly, by white officials), and economic coercion and intimidation.[19] The city's African Americans also suffered economically: black median family income, which stood at around $1,000 a year, was half that of the city as a whole, and a majority of black adults were 'working poor'. Most blacks found employment in the service sector or as agricultural labourers, and more than half of the black women who worked did so as domestic servants for wealthy whites.[20]

A rigid and comprehensive system of racial segregation, undergirded by law and supported by custom, left virtually no area of life untouched. Schools, hospitals, parks, restrooms, hotels, theatres, restaurants, public transport – and even drinking fountains – were all segregated.[21] Although justified by the doctrine of 'separate but equal', which had been upheld by the US Supreme Court in 1896, the Jim Crow laws were clearly intended to reinforce white supremacy. Black facilities, where they existed, were inferior, and African Americans were subjected to humiliating treatment. One black woman, who grew up in Montgomery during the 1940s and 1950s, recalled that when she had to have her tonsils removed, the black ward of St Margaret's Hospital took the form of a small house behind the main buildings. When she returned for follow-up visits, she discovered that the 'colored' waiting room also served as a janitor's closet.[22]

The system of bus segregation that operated in Montgomery was particularly iniquitous. The buses, which were run by Montgomery City Lines, had the first ten seats reserved for whites and the last ten (which sat above the engine) for African Americans. The sixteen seats in the middle section were assigned according to need. In the event that the white section became full, black passengers could be ordered by the bus driver to vacate these seats, and even an entire row, to make room for a white passenger. No black person was permitted to sit next to, or alongside, a white. The arrangement meant that as many as four black passengers might be required to stand in order to accommodate a single white traveller. Moreover, the white section at the front was completely off limits to blacks – they could not sit there even if all other seats on the bus were full and not a single white passenger was on board. Indeed, they were not even permitted to pass through it: after paying the driver at the front of the bus black passengers, often weighed down with heavy shopping bags, had to climb back off – whatever the weather – and enter at the rear. It was not unknown for particularly vindictive drivers to drive off before the black passengers had reboarded.[23] Jo Ann Robinson explained that 'there were literally thousands of times when Negroes were made to stand up over seats "reserved" for whites. In many instances not one white passenger was aboard . . . Yet thirty or forty black riders jammed the aisles where men and women, old and young, mothers with babies in their arms, or women with huge packages, stood swaying or falling over those empty seats . . .'[24] African Americans were also subjected to discourteous and offensive treatment by white bus drivers. As one black woman explained, black passengers were treated 'as rough as can be. I mean not like we are human, but like we was some kind of animal.'[25]

Montgomery's African Americans had made some progress in the decade following the Second World War: educational attainment had increased, a black hospital and public library had opened, the (modest) number of black voters had doubled, and, following a concerted campaign by the city's major black organisations, several African Americans were hired as police officers (joining a force that had a grim record of physical and sexual violence against blacks).[26] When it came to the hated system of bus segregation, though, there was little sign of change. In October 1952, black leaders had suggested that the city adopt the system that operated in Mobile, a city 160 miles south-west of Montgomery, where blacks were seated from the back and whites from the front, with the racial dividing line dependent on where the passengers met.[27] At a series of meetings with the City Commission during 1953 and early 1954, the Women's Political Council – a middle-class civic group that enjoyed a growing reputation for championing black rights – joined with other black organisations to press for a more flexible system of segregation.[28] They also raised concerns about the poor treatment of black passengers and complained that buses stopped less frequently in black neighbourhoods. Additional stops in those areas were promised and, following an appeal from the mayor, the behaviour of bus drivers improved – temporarily. However, no concessions were made on the seating arrangements.[29]

On 21 May 1954, just four days after the historic Supreme Court decision in *Brown* v. *Board of Education, Topeka, Kansas* that segregated schooling was 'inherently unconstitutional', Robinson wrote to Mayor Gayle on behalf of the WPC, reiterating demands for a more flexible seating policy and calling for black passengers to be allowed to board the bus at the front. Robinson pointed out that the patronage of African Americans, who made up three quarters of the bus passengers, was critical to the profitability of the bus company, and explained that 'more and more of our people are already arranging with neighbors and friends to ride to keep from being insulted and humiliated by bus drivers'. Although Robinson assured the mayor that the WPC remained committed to securing 'agreeable terms' in a 'quiet and unostensible manner', she also warned that 'even now plans are being made to ride less, or not at all, on our buses'.[30]

The election of Clyde Sellers to the City Commission in the spring of 1955 doomed Robinson's hopes of quiet and agreeable progress. Sellers, a businessman and former director of the State Highway Patrol, decided that he could defeat his opponent – a racial moderate who had been elected two years earlier – by appealing to white prejudice.[31] Dismissing any talk of modifying bus segregation as 'illegal', Sellers set himself firmly against any further concessions to African Americans: 'I will not', he declared, 'compromise my principles' or 'violate my Southern birthright . . . I will not be intimidated for the sake of a block of negro votes.'[32] The strategy worked brilliantly and Sellers won a crushing victory.[33]

Sellers's success coincided with fresh controversy on Montgomery's buses. On 2 March Claudette Colvin, a fifteen-year-old student at Booker T. Washington High School and a member of the local youth council of the National Association for the Advancement of Colored People (NAACP), was arrested for refusing to give up her seat.[34] Colvin recalled telling the bus driver that 'I was just as good as any white person and I wasn't going to get up'.[35] After the police were called, Colvin still refused to move and was dragged – kicking and scratching – from the bus.[36] On learning of Colvin's arrest, Robinson and E. D. Nixon (a black labour organiser and political activist) considered using the incident to launch a legal challenge to the bus segregation law. However, the allegation that Colvin had resisted arrest, and the subsequent discovery that she was several months pregnant, meant that the idea was shelved.[37] But Colvin's conviction on 18 March outraged the black community, and for several days many blacks refused to ride the buses, in an apparently spontaneous protest.[38]

At about five thirty on the evening of Thursday 1 December 1955 a middle-aged black woman left the Montgomery Fair department store in which she worked as an assistant tailor. Having visited a nearby drug store, where she purchased some aspirin, toothpaste and a few Christmas gifts, she boarded the bus for her journey home. Rosa Parks took one of the few remaining seats immediately behind the section at the front of the bus that was reserved for whites. After making several stops, the driver noticed that a number of whites were now standing and requested that the first row of black passengers vacate their seats. But, as Parks explained later, 'didn't any of us move'. 'You all make it light on yourselves and let me have those seats!' exclaimed the driver, at which the man sitting beside Parks and the two black women in the seats opposite all stood up. Parks stayed put. Asked whether she was going to stand up, she responded, 'No, I'm not.' The driver warned her that he would call the police. Parks remained in her seat. A few minutes later, two police officers boarded the bus, arrested Parks and took her to the local police station, where she was booked and placed in a cell.[39]

Born in Tuskegee in 1913, to a carpenter father and schoolteacher mother, Rosa was raised on her grandparents' tenant farm, south of Montgomery, before moving to the city in 1924 to live with cousins, so that she could attend the Montgomery Industrial School for Negro Girls (known as 'Miss White's School' after its founder). At Miss White's, Rosa became skilled at stenography, typing and sewing, and also developed a strong sense of racial pride and self-worth. She subsequently enrolled at Alabama State College's laboratory high school, eventually graduating (following a break due to her mother's ill health) in 1933. A year earlier she had married Raymond Parks, a barber ten years her senior. Aged forty-two at the time of her arrest, Rosa Parks was an integral member of Montgomery's black leadership class. In 1943 she had joined the local NAACP branch, serving as its secretary, and the following year had led the campaign to investigate the gang-rape of a young black woman by six white men.[40] In 1948 she was elected secretary of the state-wide conference and four years later agreed to serve as an adult adviser to the Montgomery NAACP youth council. As a result of her civil rights work, Parks became acquainted with key figures including E. D. Nixon, Ella J. Baker, the NAACP's director of branches, Robert L. Carter, one of the Association's leading lawyers, and the white progressives Clifford and Virginia Durr, Montgomery residents who had been prominent support-ers of Franklin Roosevelt.[41] The Durrs, with whom Parks became quite friendly, had encouraged her to attend an interracial training workshop at the Highlander Folk School in Monteagle, Tennessee, during August 1955. Parks was inspired by her experiences at High-lander – which was committed to interracial democracy and grass-roots organising – telling its director, Myles Horton, that 'I found out for the first time in my adult life that this could be a unified society, that there was such a thing as people of differing races and backgrounds meeting together in workshops and living together in peace and harmony.' While she remained pessimistic about the prospects for change in Montgomery, believing the black commu-nity to be 'timid' and unable to 'stand together', she had, she said, 'gained . . . strength to persevere in my work for freedom'.[42]

Parks shared with many of her black neighbours a deep antipathy to the system of bus segregation operated by Montgomery City

Lines: she recalled that 'having to take a certain section because of your race was humiliating, but having to stand up because a particular driver wanted to keep a white person from having to stand was, to my mind, most inhumane'.[43] Over the years Parks had been involved in a number of altercations with bus drivers and in the winter of 1943 she had been thrown off a bus by Fred Blake, the very same driver who ordered her to vacate her seat on 1 December 1955.[44]

Rosa Parks had not intended to stage a protest that cold, dark evening. She was tired and not feeling particularly well, and, as she explained later, 'simply decided that I would not get up'. Parks was, though, fired by a clear sense of injustice. In an April 1956 interview she explained that 'the time had just come when I had been pushed as far as I could stand to be pushed . . .'[45]

Parks's refusal to yield her seat gave the city's black leaders their chance to implement long-mooted plans for a one-day boycott of the city's buses. When word of her arrest reached E. D. Nixon, he contacted the police station for more information, only to be told it was none of his business. He immediately turned to Clifford Durr, who, as a qualified attorney, was able to ascertain the details. Nixon, along with Clifford and his wife, Virginia, then headed to the city jail to post Parks's bail, which had been set at $100. On the way, they discussed using Parks as a test case to challenge bus segregation. Parks's self-confidence, composed demeanour and high standing in the local community made her an ideal candidate. After securing her release the discussions resumed, over coffee, at Parks's home. Parks was initially sceptical, and her husband was worried about possible white reprisals, but she eventually agreed: 'If you think it is all right, I'll go along with you.'[46] Meanwhile, the city's leading black attorney, Fred Gray, had contacted Jo Ann Robinson to discuss the possibility of staging a boycott of the buses on Monday 5 December – the date set for Parks's trial. After further discussions, it was decided that Robinson would publicise the planned protest, while Nixon organised a meeting of the city's black leaders.[47]

That night, Robinson did not sleep. Instead, she drafted a leaflet and persuaded a colleague to open up the mimeograph room at Alabama State College. Joined by two of her most trusted students, she worked until 4 a.m. producing tens of thousands of leaflets. These explained how 'another Negro woman has been arrested and thrown into jail because she refused to get up out of her seat on the bus for a white person to sit down', warned that 'if we do not do something to stop these arrests, they will continue. The next time it may be you, or your daughter, or mother', and called on blacks to stay off the buses on Monday.[48]

Once the leaflets had been printed, Robinson and her students spent several hours drawing up a distribution schedule and, after teaching her 8 a.m. class, she called some two dozen contacts to explain the plans and recruit volunteers to hand out the flyers. Over the next few hours, tens of thousands of leaflets were dropped off at schools and black-owned businesses (including beauty parlours, barber shops and stores). 'By two o'clock', Robinson later recalled, 'practically every black man, woman, and child in Montgomery knew the plan and was passing the word along.'[49]

Meanwhile, Nixon had arranged for about seventy of the city's influential black preachers to meet in the basement of Dexter Avenue Baptist Church. The meeting, though, did not go well. Rev. L. Roy Bennett, who had been asked to preside, embarked on a lengthy monologue and, as the frustration built, ministers began to drift away. Eventually, Ralph Abernathy, the twenty-nine-year-old pastor of First Baptist Church, persuaded Bennett to give way and allow a discussion. Although some remained wary, the ministers endorsed the proposed boycott and agreed to hold a mass meeting on the evening of 5 December to discuss extending the protest.[50] Martin Luther King and Abernathy then drew up new leaflets to publicise the boycott and the mass meeting:

Don't ride the bus to work, to town, to school, or any place
Monday, December 5.

Another Negro Woman has been arrested and put in jail
because she refused to give up her bus seat.

Don't ride the buses to work, to town, to school, or any
where on Monday. If you work, take a cab, or share a ride,
or walk.

Come to a mass meeting, Monday at 7:00 P.M. at the Holt
Street Baptist Church for further instruction.[51]

Thousands of leaflets were distributed over the weekend, and
a committee persuaded the city's black taxi companies to charge
black passengers the standard bus fare of ten cents on Monday.[52]
On Saturday evening, King and other ministers visited local bars
and nightclubs to build support and the following morning, in
black churches across the city, preachers urged their congregations
to support the one-day boycott and to attend the mass meeting.[53]

Assistance in spreading the word also came from the white
press. On Friday 2 December, Nixon met secretly with Joe Azbell
of the *Montgomery Advertiser*. A 'lanky, stoop-shouldered young
man from Vernon, Texas' who 'looked like the clichéd tough-guy
reporter on the cover of a 1950s pulp-fiction paperback', Azbell
had earned his stripes on his local paper before joining the *Advertiser* in 1948.[54] Nixon informed him about the plans for the boycott
and the mass meeting, and predicted that Monday 5 December
would be a truly historic day.[55] On Sunday 4 December the front
page of the *Advertiser* carried the scoop. Azbell reported that a 'top
secret' meeting was planned for Monday evening to help prepare
an 'economic reprisal campaign' to protest bus segregation. 'Negro
sections' of town had, he wrote, been 'flooded with thousands of
copies of mimeographed or typed leaflets asking Negroes to refrain

from riding city buses Monday'.[56] Azbell's story was quickly picked up by local television and radio news, spreading the word to those black citizens who may have not heard about the protest. It also drew an official response from the city authorities: Police Commissioner Clyde Sellers took to the airwaves to promise that his officers would protect black passengers from the 'goon squads' that, he claimed, were being organised to enforce the boycott.[57]

That Sunday evening, Martin Luther King and his wife discussed the prospects for the boycott's success. Even though news of the action had reached every part of the city, and despite the support from local ministers, he 'still wondered whether the people had enough courage to follow through'. He retired to bed that night 'with a strange mixture of hope and anxiety'.[58] The Kings were up and dressed by five thirty the following day, eager to observe the early morning buses. The first three that rolled past their parsonage, which would normally have been filled with black domestics, contained not a single African American passenger. Then King jumped into his car and drove around the city, nervously examining every passing bus. Over the course of the next hour, during the height of the morning traffic, he spotted 'no more than eight Negro passengers riding the buses. By this time I was jubilant.'[59] It was the same story across the city: Robinson recalled that 'all day long empty buses passed, trailed by white-capped city cops', whose presence probably deterred any wavering blacks. Ninety per cent of black passengers supported the boycott.[60] Several hundred African Americans, including King and Abernathy, also gathered at the courthouse that morning in an unprecedented show of support for Rosa Parks – who was found 'guilty' by the judge and fined $10. Her lawyer, Fred Gray, immediately declared that the decision would be appealed.[61]

The remarkable show of mass support had convinced many black leaders that the protest should continue until the city granted meaningful concessions. As they met to discuss the mass meeting that was scheduled to begin at Holt Street Baptist Church at 7 p.m., it was agreed to form a new organisation, the Montgomery Improvement Association, to undertake the detailed planning needed to sustain the boycott. When discussion turned to the leadership of the new group, Rufus Lewis – a Second World War veteran and Alabama State College football coach – immediately proposed Martin Luther King, the pastor of his own church, as president. Lewis acted partly to block E. D. Nixon, a long-standing rival, but he also understood that King, who embodied black middle-class respectability and was an educated and eloquent preacher, might win the support of Montgomery's more conservative African Americans. As a relative newcomer (he had arrived at Dexter Avenue on 1 September 1954), King had also not yet been drawn into the factional squabbles and personal rivalries that bedevilled the city's black leadership. The nomination was quickly seconded and endorsed unanimously. After a short pause, King agreed: 'Well, if you think I can render some service, I will.' He later recalled that 'it had happened so quickly that I did not even have time to think it through. It is probable that, if I had, I would have declined.' Indeed, King had turned down a request to run for the presidency of the local NAACP branch a few weeks earlier, preferring to focus on his new job as pastor of Dexter Avenue and fulfil his parental responsibilities. After the rest of the MIA leadership was formalised and the agenda for the evening's meeting agreed, it was decided that the continuation of the boycott would be put to a popular vote. Finally, King was charged with delivering the keynote speech.[62]

King returned home, where he informed a surprised Coretta of his new role before retreating to his study. King usually took about fifteen hours to write his weekly sermon; that evening, he had less than twenty-five minutes to prepare what would be his first major public address. Feeling somewhat overwhelmed by the task at hand, King turned to prayer. Calmed, he began to prepare his remarks, but was soon wrestling with a new dilemma – how to rouse the people to action while containing their fervour within acceptable and Christian bounds. With little more than an outline sketched out in his head, King set off for the meeting.[63] It was immediately apparent that black Montgomery was out in force: around the church, cars were lined up on both sides of the street, as far as the eye could see.[64] In his report for the *Advertiser*, Joe Azbell described how, as he made his way 'along Clevelend Avenue en route to the Holt Street Baptist Church . . . I could see Negroes by the dozens forming a file, almost soldierly, on the sidewalk . . .'[65] The church itself was packed long before 7 p.m. and thousands of boycott supporters were surrounding the building. Speakers were strung up to relay the meeting to the crowds, and police officers struggled to maintain order.[66] It took King more than fifteen minutes to make his way through the throng to the sanctuary of the pastor's study; the meeting eventually began half an hour late. It was abundantly clear that, as King put it, 'the question of calling off the protest was now academic. The enthusiasm of these thousands of people swept everything along like an onrushing tidal wave.'[67]

Following a few words of introduction, the meeting began with a thunderous rendition of the hymn 'Onward, Christian Soldiers'.[68] King recalled that 'when that mammoth audience stood to sing, the voices outside swelling the chorus in the church, there was a mighty ring like the glad echo of heaven itself'.[69] After a prayer and a reading from Scripture, King stepped forward to deliver his speech. Speaking without notes, he began by explaining that they were there for 'very serious business': 'First and foremost', he said, 'we are American citizens and we are determined to apply our citizenship to the fullness of its meaning.' Conscious of the wider Cold War struggle, in which the United States claimed leadership of the 'free world' against Communist tyranny, and eager to neuter any charges that the boycott was inspired by Communists, King declared that they were 'here because of our love of democracy, because of our deep-seated belief that democracy transformed from thin paper to thick action is the greatest form of government on earth'. Then, after outlining the long-standing problems with the city's buses and praising Rosa Parks as one of Montgomery's most upstanding citizens – a 'fine Christian person' of integrity and character – King declared:

> There comes a time when people get tired of being
> trampled over by the iron feet of oppression. There comes
> a time, my friends, when people get tired of being plunged
> across the abyss of humiliation . . . There comes a time
> when people get tired of being pushed out of the glittering
> sunlight of life's July and left standing amid the piercing
> chill of an alpine winter.

King was also at pains to emphasise that the movement was peaceful, and that they did not advocate violence of any kind: 'I want it to be known throughout Montgomery and throughout this nation that we . . . believe in the teachings of Jesus. The only weapon that we have in our hands is the weapon of protest.' It was a remarkable speech, punctuated by calls of 'That's right', 'Yeah', and 'Yes sir, Teach', as well as frequent bursts of applause.[70] One observer recalled how 'Reverend King prayed so hard that night . . . you had to hold people to keep them from gettin' to him.'[71]

After a standing ovation for Rosa Parks, Abernathy presented the resolutions, which called on 'every citizen in Montgomery' to 'refrain from riding' the buses 'until some arrangement has been worked out' between the MIA and the bus company. Azbell reported that as the assembled crowd rose to their feet in a show of unanimous support for the resolution, there was a 'wild whoop of delight. Many said they would never ride the bus again.' He concluded by noting that the mass meeting 'proved beyond any doubt there was a discipline among Negroes that many whites had

doubted. It was almost a military discipline combined with emotion.'[72]

Buoyed by the success of the one-day boycott and the extraordinary scenes at the mass meeting, the MIA leaders sought to press
their advantage. They notified the city commission and the bus
company officials of their three core demands:

Courteous treatment by bus drivers.

**Seating of Negro passengers from rear to front of bus, and
white passengers from front to rear on 'first-come-first-
serve' basis with no seats reserved for any race.**

**Employment of Negro bus operators in predominantly
Negro residential sections.[73]**

On Thursday 8 December, when the MIA leaders, city commissioners and bus company officials met for the first time, the
black leaders were optimistic that a satisfactory resolution would
be reached in a matter of days.[74] But while the authorities agreed to
support the demand for greater courtesy, they refused to yield any
ground on the substantive issues. The bus company's attorney was
particularly intransigent, making it clear that Montgomery City
Lines had no plans to hire black drivers and arguing forcefully
that any changes to the seating arrangements would violate state
law.[75] Revealingly, he also warned that 'if we granted the Negroes
these demands they would go about boasting of a victory over the
white people; and this we will not stand for'.[76] Four hours of talks
failed to make any progress, and further meetings proved similarly
dispiriting.[77]

On Christmas Day, a frustrated MIA took out a half-page
advertisement in the Sunday *Advertiser* and *Alabama Journal* that
documented their long-standing grievances, outlined their proposals and offered assurances about the nonviolent and democratic

nature of the movement.[78] In the advertisement, the MIA leadership made it clear that they were not seeking an end to segregation: 'At no time, on the basis of this proposal, will both races occupy the same seat.'[79] Just a few days later Roy Wilkins, executive secretary of the NAACP, wrote privately that the Association would not be prepared to offer its support to any effort that asked 'merely for more polite segregation'.[80] By the end of January 1956, however, the boycott of Montgomery's buses had been transformed into an all-out assault on bus segregation. Although, on one level, this reflected the deeper desire of the city's blacks for equal treatment, the continuing refusal of the city authorities to offer any meaningful concessions, and the sustained and intensifying campaign by white segregationists to destroy the boycott – which culminated in the bombing of King's house on 30 January and that of E. D. Nixon two days later – had forced the MIA's hand.[81]

As we will see, stubbornness was a character trait that southern segregationists shared with many of their white counterparts in the colonial world.

2

MOLLET'S SURRENDER

To Lose Algeria is to Lose France.
FRENCH NEWSPAPER HEADLINE

On 6 February 1956 Guy Mollet, France's new socialist prime minister, travelled to Algiers, the capital of his nation's largest and most important colony, amidst an atmosphere of growing crisis. Indeed by the mid-1950s Algeria was bitterly divided and its society, which was composed of some nine million Muslims and one million European settlers – or *colons* – had reached breaking point. Despite the promise of self-determination and democracy encapsulated in the Atlantic Charter – a document that Algeria's Muslims had embraced enthusiastically – the years following the Second World War had seen economic and political power remain very firmly in the hands of the settlers, the so-called *pieds noirs*.*[1] In the absence of meaningful change, the Front de Libération Nationale (FLN) had, on 1 November 1954, launched an armed insurgency with the aim of securing an independent Algeria. As the revolt spread across the country, France quickly became embroiled in a bloody conflict. During the weeks leading up to polling day, 2 January 1956, Mollet had consistently described the conflict as a 'stupid war with no way out' and had called for 'reconciliation and peace' based on 'the freedom of the rights of man'.[2] But the fifty-one-year-old prime minister – a former schoolmaster, hero of the French Resistance and a stalwart of the country's Socialist Party – believed that an end to the insurgency was a prerequisite for peace. Only once 'terrorism and blind repression' had ended, he stated, would it be

---

* The origin of this phrase, which translates literally as 'black feet', is uncertain.

possible to hold elections and discuss potential reforms.[3]

Caught between the opposing demands of the FLN and an influential 'ultra' faction of the settler population, Mollet sought to promote a policy of 'free elections as soon as order permits'. But although he spoke of the 'indissoluble union between Algeria and metropolitan France' and promised the settlers that they could 'count on the nation', his proposals for equality for Muslim residents, democratic elections and the release of some political prisoners alarmed many French Algerians.[4] Mollet's position was not helped when, immediately after assuming office, he replaced Jacques Soustelle, the incumbent minister-resident in Algiers, with the seventy-nine-year-old Georges Catroux, a highly decorated general and a former commander in chief of the Free French forces. For Algeria's settlers, Catroux had form. He had recognised Syrian independence in 1941 and three years later, as governor-general in Algeria, had supported the extension of full French citizenship to some sixty thousand Muslims. More recently, he had satisfied a key demand of nationalists in nearby Morocco by negotiating the return of the exiled sultan, Mohammed V. Catroux's remarks about the need to respect the 'Algerian personality' and his talk of 'an equal share of rights and duties' earned him the bitter enmity of the settlers. While the new minister-resident offered assurances that he did not intend, 'under any circumstances', to turn Algeria into a nation state and was not prepared to see the French reduced to 'minority status', the *pieds noirs* were unconvinced – some 'ultras' even threatened violence against him if he dared to set foot on Algerian soil.[5]

In the days before Mollet's trip, the atmosphere in Algiers had become febrile. Ultra leaders discussed the possibility of seizing the Palais d'Été (the minister's official residence) and holding Mollet hostage; some even talked of assassinating Catroux. In the end, it was agreed to call a general strike, accompanied by mass protests, for Monday 6 February.[6]

Dismissing the concerns of Jacques Chevallier, the liberal mayor of Algiers, as well as those of his own security team and political advisers – all of whom counselled delay – Mollet flew into Maison-Blanche airport at 2.30 p.m. on 6 February. In brief remarks, delivered shortly after touching down, he acknowledged the complexity of the political situation, asserted his 'fraternal links with all the inhabitants of Algeria' and appealed for calm.[7] Mollet then headed to his waiting limousine for the journey to the city.

Just four days earlier, Algiers had witnessed a 'wild' outpouring of 'unrestrained support' for the departing Jacques Soustelle. Thousands of *colons*, from 'all classes' of the population, had packed the streets to wave French flags, sing the 'Marseillaise' and chant '*Revenez Soustelle!*' ('Come back Soustelle!'), '*Soustelle au pouvoir!*' ('Soustelle in power!') and '*Algérie Française*'. D. J. Mill Irving, the British consul-general, witnessed these 'extraordinary scenes' from the roof of a nearby office building. He reported that, when the official party arrived at the port, the 'din was deafening'. Minutes later, Soustelle was mobbed by the enthusiastic crowd, which had 'burst through the police cordons', and ultimately had to be carried to his waiting ship, the SS *El-Djezair*, atop a tank.[8]

The popular reaction to Mollet could not have been more different. The prime minister's motorcade entered a city in which the public services were paralysed by strikes, and schools, cinemas, petrol stations, businesses and shops were closed – the signs in their shuttered windows explained that this was 'on account of mourning'.[9] Black drapes hung from the balconies of buildings and, as his car swept past, pedestrians turned their backs in protest. At 3 p.m., the premier reached the *monument aux morts*, where he planned to lay a wreath. Designed by the celebrated artist Paul Landowski (whose most famous work is the giant statue of Christ the Redeemer in Rio de Janeiro), the sculpture, which was officially unveiled in September 1928, commemorated those Algerians who had lost their lives during the Great War (and,

subsequently, the Second World War). It was situated on the plateau de Glières, on the Forum – the symbolic heart of the city.
Although designed to illustrate the mutual ties between European and Muslim, the monument had quickly become a symbol of French colonial power.[10] If Mollet entertained any hopes
that by paying his respects at a site that was sacred to the *pieds
noirs* he would earn the right to a respectful hearing, they were
quickly dispelled. Thousands of settlers – including workers, students, shopkeepers and minor government officials – had gathered nearby and, as they caught sight of the prime ministerial
car, shouted out, 'Mollet to the gallows!' and 'Algeria is French!'
Undeterred, Mollet walked up the stone steps to the monument. As he stood 'bareheaded, in silence', the catcalls, whistles
and insults of the crowd swirled around. Having laid his wreath,
Mollet turned to walk back to his limousine. As he did so, the
crowd – now, in truth, more a mob – erupted in anger, unleash-
ing a volley of tomatoes, rotten fruit and clods of earth in the
direction of the prime minister. As the crowd surged forward
dangerously, the security forces (including two thousand police
militiamen drafted in from France, and troops from the Foreign
Legion), used batons, tear gas and mounted charges to protect the
French leader, who was by now 'shaken' and 'ashen-faced'. Once
he had been safely spirited away, the crowd 'swarmed' over the
war memorial and tore the prime ministerial wreath to shreds.
These were truly shocking scenes. Mollet vividly recalled the 'total
hatred' in the faces of the protesters, and several newsmen were
convinced that a lynching had only narrowly been averted.[11] With
pitched battles between settlers and security forces continuing to
rage in the streets, Mollet – by now holed up in the Palais d'Été –
requested Catroux's resignation (it had already been offered). As
news of Catroux's departure spread, car horns were sounded and
triumphant cries of '*Victoire! Victoire!*' resounded across the city.
Later that evening, as he struggled to come to terms with the day's

traumatic events, Mollet was overheard muttering, 'I should not have given in.'[12]

In the decade or so that followed the Allied defeat of the Axis powers, France sought to maintain its empire – the world's second largest – against a rising tide of anti-colonial nationalism. Among the leaders of the Fourth Republic, which was founded out of the ruins of war in 1946, there was broad agreement that retaining the nation's overseas territories was vital to France's aspirations to preserve its own 'great power' status, and to counter the formidable influence of the Anglo-American alliance. France's determination to hold onto its colonies was also reinforced by a widespread (and, as it turned out, misguided) belief that they were of critical importance to rebuilding its war-ravaged economy and to maintaining its military strength, not least by furnishing a regular and substantial supply of soldiers.[13] The political class was, though, not unmindful of the increasingly strident calls for national self-determination that were emanating from all across the empire, nor the wartime promises of greater rights for colonial subjects (promises which had persuaded some 250,000 colonial troops to take up arms for the French army in 1944–5). They therefore enacted a series of reforms that were designed to satisfy 'legitimate' demands for change but which would not, fundamentally, threaten the continuation of French rule. The empire itself was reconstituted into a 'French Union'; some of the older colonies, including the Caribbean islands of Martinique and Guadeloupe, as well as Guiana, were reorganised as *départements* (administrative units) of France itself, while others were designated 'associate states' or 'overseas territories'; Union citizenship was granted to all who lived under the French flag, which expanded the social and legal rights of colonial subjects; and the hated penal and forced labour codes were repealed. Meanwhile a major programme of capital investment was launched in an attempt to alleviate the African colonies' endemic poverty and modernise their economies. But these efforts, while by no means insignificant, neither met the aspirations of the colonised nor prevented the rise of vibrant independence movements.[14] In any case, the chronic weakness of the French Fourth Republic made more radical change almost impossible. The country's post-war constitutional arrangements, which placed power in the lower house of the National Assembly, together with the refusal of the major parties to countenance coalition with the Communists, guaranteed a series of 'patchwork' coalition governments, reliant on the support of smaller parties. The result was political instability, or *immobilisme*, that saw twenty-two different governments in twelve years.[15]

When it came to decolonisation, France proved stubbornly resistant. The country's long-established tradition of viewing the empire and France as part of a unitary, 'indivisible whole', in which a *mission civilisatrice* would gradually help to 'make French' parts of Africa and Asia, meant that, 'to the French mind', secession from the empire 'was not emancipation, it was a heresy'.[16] Various arguments were trotted out to defend the continuation of rule from Paris. Colonial peoples, it was widely claimed, were not yet ready for self-rule, and a rush to independence would simply open the door to chaos or, even worse, a Communist take-over (the latter was particularly useful in winning support from the United States, a long-standing opponent of European coloni-alism). Meanwhile, those who agitated for an immediate end to French governance were denounced as 'terrorists'.[17] When pressed, France used military force to defend its interests. An early sign of this robust approach came in Madagascar where, between March 1947 and December 1948, thousands of Malagasy lost their lives during a brutal suppression of an anti-colonial uprising. It was a similar story in Indochina, where France had first established a colonial presence during the 1880s. The years prior to the Second World War had seen the emergence of the Viet Minh, a powerful nationalist movement led by the French-educated Marxist and anti-imperialist Ho Chi Minh. When on 9 March 1945 the Japanese easily overthrew the French colonial regime, they dealt a blow to France's image of military superiority from which the country never really recovered. Although its colonial possessions, covering much of modern-day Vietnam, Laos and Cambodia, were eventually restored, French authority remained precarious. By late 1946, in the face of fierce nationalist resistance, France launched a full-scale war against the Viet Minh in a desperate attempt to maintain its position. This long and bitter struggle lasted until 7 May 1954, when, following a two-month siege of the French garrison at Dien Bien Phu, more than thirty thousand elite troops surrendered to General Vo Nguyen Giap. Two months after this national humiliation, France signed the Geneva Accords, bringing its empire in Indochina to an end. The doomed struggle to preserve it had cost more than ninety thousand French lives – most of them colonial troops or members of the Foreign Legion – some three hundred thousand Vietnamese, and vast amounts of money (much of it American).[18]

Just as France's colonial presence in the Far East was being consigned to history, a major crisis erupted much closer to home. Algeria, conquered by the French between 1830 and 1871, was the jewel of the empire and widely viewed as an integral part of the French nation. Indeed northern Algeria, where most of the settler population lived, had as early as 1848 been organised into three *départements* of France itself; from 1881 the colony was ruled not from the Ministry of Foreign Affairs but from the Ministry of the Interior.[19] A belief in the essential unity between Algeria and France was shared across the political spectrum. Pierre Mendès-France, a liberal reformer and opponent of colonialism who, as prime minister, negotiated the end of French rule in Indochina, told the National Assembly in November 1954 that 'one does not compromise when it comes to defending the internal peace of the nation' or the 'unity and integrity of the Republic'. The Algerian *départements* were 'part of the French Republic' and 'irrevocably French'; therefore 'between them and metropolitan France there can be no conceivable secession'.[20]

While official ideology may have insisted that '*l'Algérie, c'est la France*', the hard reality was that by the mid-1950s there were two, strikingly different, Algerias.[21] The Algeria of the settlers, with its beautiful French-designed cities replete with wide boulevards and sophisticated cafes, and its large – and prosperous – rural estates, was home to more than a million Europeans, most of French and Italian origin, together with some Spanish and a smattering of Maltese. Although they made up only one tenth of the population at large, the settlers dominated the country, controlling its political institutions and economy and exercising a decisive influence over its culture and society. A tiny minority of the settler population, some twelve thousand, owned the country's most fertile land, its factories and its newspapers, leaving the rest to work as shopkeepers, traders, teachers and civil servants. As a group the *colons* – many of them now second- or third-generation settlers – had developed a distinctive French-Mediterranean identity and a deep emotional attachment to their surroundings. Enjoying all the benefits of full citizenship, the settlers had an influential voice in the National Assembly in Paris and could count on the support of powerful allies in France itself (including the military). Worried – with good reason – that an end to French rule would sound the death knell for their own privileged position, the *colons* were determined to defend 'French Algeria' at all costs.[22]

The Muslim population, meanwhile, was disfranchised, impoverished and increasingly resentful. Their predicament was bleak. In 1954 there were fewer than nine hundred Muslim Algerians in post-secondary education, and little more than six thousand in secondary school – the overall illiteracy rate stood at 90 per cent. There was a large, and growing, urban population that was underfed, struggled to find work and was confined to overcrowded slums, while the rural peasantry, barely able to eke out a living, faced malnourishment, high infant mortality, disease and poverty.[23] In theory, French law allowed for all Algerians to become full citizens, irrespective of race or ethnicity. In practice, however, for most of the previous century it had been a requirement that, to qualify for citizenship, Muslims had to conform to the French civil code and renounce their right to be judged under Islamic law. In effect, they had to reject their religious faith. Unsurprisingly, very few proved willing to take so drastic a step.[24] Even when all Algerians were finally granted citizenship under the terms of the new French Constitution in 1946, there was little change on the ground. The settlers proved adept at ensuring that proposed reforms were neutered, that restrictions on the rights of the Muslim population remained in place and that their own hold on political power remained absolute. Importantly, though, Muslim Algerians were themselves increasingly dismissive of 'reform'. Viewing co-operation with the French as a form of collaboration that would simply extend – and legitimise – colonial rule, they instead demanded, and proved increasingly willing to fight for, independence.[25]

Right across French North Africa the writ of Paris was challenged by a resurgent nationalism that, by the mid-1950s, had produced an arc of anti-colonial violence that stretched from Morocco in the west to Tunisia in the east. In Morocco, which had been run as a protectorate since 1912, nationalist sentiment was centred on the sultan, Mohammed Ben Yusuf, whose status had been buoyed by a wartime meeting with Franklin Roosevelt. In January 1944 the Istiqlal Party was founded, which demanded national sovereignty under a constitutional monarchy. Although French rule over Morocco was less direct than in Algeria, and the settler population smaller and less influential, Paris proved no more amenable to demands for self-rule. Faced with growing nationalist pressure,

the government outlawed Istiqlal, stamped down on urban disorder and despatched the sultan into exile in Madagascar.[26] But
these repressive measures only aggravated the situation, triggering
a wave of arson, sabotage and terrorism against French interests;
by the summer of 1955 the situation was threatening to slide out of
control.[27] That July, a nationalist bombing in Casablanca prompted
a furious *colon* reaction that required the elite Foreign Legion to
restore order. The following month, on the second anniversary of
Mohammed V's exile, violence erupted across the country. In the
most horrific incident, which occurred on Saturday 20 August, a
group of Berber nationalists attacked French settlers in Oued Zem,
a small town of five thousand Arabs and six hundred French, some
140 miles north-east of Marrakesh. The Berber tribesmen, armed
with knives, 'ranged through the streets. French women and children were stabbed to death. Families were burnt in their homes.'
Cars were stopped at roadblocks and their unfortunate occupants
were 'hauled out, savagely mutilated, then thrust back and burned
alive'. By the time that this orgy of violence had abated, forty-nine
people lay dead. Fierce retribution followed swiftly, at the hands
of the Legion, elite parachute units and other military forces;
across Morocco, the official death toll stood at seven hundred.[28]
Six weeks later, when the 'Maghreb Liberation Army Co-ordinat-
ing Committee' and the 'Moroccan Liberation Army' launched a
fresh insurgency in the Rif and Atlas mountains, French attempts
to hold back the nationalist tide collapsed.[29] Given the enormity
of the challenge posed by Algeria, Paris acceded to demands for
the restoration of Mohammed V, whose return to Morocco on
16 November prompted scenes of jubilation across the country.
France also announced that it would begin negotiations to end the
protectorate; Moroccan independence was finally recognised on 2
March 1956.[30]

In Tunisia, meanwhile, which had been under French rule
since 1881, the nationalist movement coalesced around the Neo-

Destour Party and its popular leader, Habib Bourguiba. The man who would lead his nation to independence was born in 1901, the youngest of seven surviving children, to a middle-class family in the Islamic Holy City of Monastir, located in the Sahel, a coastal region whose richly fertile lands supported olive groves, palm trees and vineyards.[31] In 1907 the young Bourguiba was sent to Tunis to attend school – where, according to one of his teachers, he was a 'turbulent boy' but a 'serious student'.[32] Although his education was interrupted by a bout of tuberculosis in 1920, he recovered and, in 1924, headed to Paris to read law and political science at the Sorbonne. After a brief and unsatisfying career as a provincial lawyer, Bourguiba began to immerse himself in the cause that would define his life: Tunisian nationalism.[33] He first joined the reformist Destour ('Constitution') Party before founding Neo-Destour, its modernising, nationalist rival, in 1934.[34] Despite spending much of the next twenty years under house arrest, imprisoned or in exile, Bourguiba proved extraordinarily successful in transforming himself, and his party, into what he described as 'the only true spokesman, the authentic representative of Tunisian Tunisia'.[35] This achievement owed much to his skill in promoting the Tunisian cause abroad and his political acumen.[36] Bourguiba was a canny operator who sought to exploit any opportunity, including negotiations with the French over greater autonomy, to advance Tunisian nationalism and full independence.[37] This pragmatic, gradualist approach (known as 'Bourguibism') had been outlined in a January 1929 newspaper article, in which Bourguiba explained that 'we must make progress, but make it steadily'; the ultimate choice was, he wrote, either 'evolution' or 'death'.[38] Bourguiba's influence also rested on his ability to inspire ordinary Tunisians to rally around both him and his message.[39] In his trademark smart dark suit and red *shishia* hat, Bourguiba – a 'squat, ebullient man' with 'piercing blue eyes' that could 'shoot sparks' – proved a charismatic public speaker.[40] As words flowed from his mouth like a 'torrent', they

were accompanied by facial expressions and the injection of emotion or sarcasm into his voice, as his arms and hands punched the
air to add further emphasis. It proved a winning combination.[41]

At the conclusion of the Second World War Bourguiba had
issued an open letter calling for Tunisian independence; in September 1949, after returning to Tunis from exile in Cairo, he
immediately demanded free elections and a new Franco-Tunisian
partnership based on genuine equality.[42] In the summer of 1950
hopes of a breakthrough were raised when talks began in Paris,
with the aim of achieving 'internal autonomy'. Unfortunately, the
effort quickly ran into the sand. Under pressure from Tunisia's
130,000-strong settler population (who owned or controlled two
thirds of the country's agricultural output, almost all of its industry and most of its commerce), the French government replaced
its offer of autonomy with a proposal for 'co-sovereignty' (little
more than a spruced-up version of colonial rule). This was summarily rejected, and the negotiations ended acrimoniously on 15
December.[43] The failure to achieve progress through negotiations,
and the subsequent appointment of a hardliner in Tunis, saw the
situation deteriorate alarmingly. As the French clamped down on
dissent, imprisoning Bourguiba and his colleagues, the nationalists
responded with strikes, riots and demonstrations.[44] With Bourguiba's tacit approval, they also launched an armed insurgency. Small
guerrilla cells, known as *fellaghas*, sprang up across the countryside.
Composed of young militants, ex-soldiers and bandits, they carried out sabotage and deployed hit-and-run attacks on the French,
and punished alleged 'traitors' among the Arab population. The
insurgents – who numbered little more than three thousand and
were often armed only with ageing rifles – never posed a serious
threat to French military supremacy, but they were able to hold
down two army divisions and cause a good deal of trouble.[45] Over
the next few years, successive waves of violence killed hundreds of
people, on all sides of the conflict.[46]

The beginning of the end came in July 1954, when Pierre Mendès-France, the new French prime minister, issued the 'Declaration of Carthage', in which he conceded Tunisia's rightful claim to internal autonomy. In a speech broadcast across France and Tunisia, he acknowledged that 'a people whom we have schooled in the love of liberty' had been 'suffering from the belief that it was being barred from the enjoyment of the rights which we ourselves had taught them to desire'. He also voiced optimism that Tunisia would, 'in close and fruitful union with France, become a modern nation in which reason, progress and peace would triumph together'. Speaking from house arrest in the little town of Montargis, seventy miles south of Paris, Bourguiba welcomed the proposals as 'a substantial and decisive step toward Tunisia's complete sovereignty'.[47] Mendès-France, who had negotiated the end of empire in Indochina, recognised that the price of sustaining French rule was simply too high. It also made some sense for the French to extricate themselves from Tunisia (and Morocco) in order to concentrate their political and military efforts on Algeria, where the situation was growing graver by the day. By the following spring, a generous offer of amnesty had won support from almost all of the *fellaghas* and negotiations in Paris had produced an agreement on full internal autonomy for Tunisia.[48]

On 1 June 1955, tens of thousands of Tunisians gathered to celebrate 'Victory Day'. The harbour at La Goulette, a few miles east of downtown Tunis, was full of tugs, fishing boats, feluccas (traditional wooden sailing boats) and other vessels, which had travelled from all along the coast to welcome Bourguiba, the 'father of the nation' and the 'Supreme Struggler', as he arrived back in his homeland following the negotiations in Paris. Three hundred thousand people lined the route to Tunis, and the city itself was 'garlanded with flowers' and bedecked with national flags.[49] The vast throngs, drawn from across the country, included 'men from the Sahara in Bernouses, fellahs in their tunics of brown wool, mountaineers in caftans of goat hair and Bedouins in red and blue veils of the nomad'. Bourguiba was held aloft shortly after stepping foot on Tunisian soil, and 'wept and smiled as men tried to kiss him'. Amidst the celebrations, Bourguiba was keen to emphasise that the struggle was not yet over. While he counselled respect for non-Muslims and urged co-operation with the French, he exhorted his followers to 'remember our fighters, our martyrs', and made it clear that autonomy was only a first step towards statehood.[50]

In a matter of months the new Tunisian government had taken advantage of France's difficulties in Algeria to press for full sovereignty. On 20 March, following two weeks of intense negotiations with the Mollet government in Paris, the French signed a protocol that 'solemnly' recognised 'the independence of Tunisia'. French pride was assuaged, if only temporarily, by the concept of 'interdependence', under which the two governments agreed to work together to promote shared diplomatic and security interests (this enabled France to negotiate rights to a naval base and to station troops on Tunisian territory).[51] Two days after the signing ceremony, on the eve of a landslide victory for his party in elections to a national assembly, Bourguiba told a cheering crowd of fifty thousand that they could not 'be truly happy' until Algeria, their 'sister nation', 'regains her sovereignty'. It was, he said, 'inconceivable' that 'Tunisia on one side, and Morocco on the other should enjoy their independence while Algeria, which lies between them, remains under the colonialist yoke'.[52] Even as Bourguiba spoke, the liberation struggle in Algeria was taking a decisive – and deadly – turn.

The armed struggle against French rule in Algeria had begun in the early hours of Thursday 1 November 1954 – All Saints' Day – when militant nationalists launched a series of co-ordinated attacks across all three French *départements*. In Oran province, in the north-east of the country, two farms were terrorised – crops were burned and telephone wires cut – and a young Frenchman, Laurent François, was shot through the head. Sabotage was directed against railway lines, warehouses and electricity transformers, and police officers and soldiers were targeted (a number were killed). In Algiers the radio station, gasworks and a petroleum depot were bombed. The town of Arris, in the north-west, came under sustained gunfire. Cut off for several hours, its *colon* population barricaded themselves inside a local fort, in fear of their lives. In the day's most shocking incident, a bus travelling to Arris was stopped at a road-block. One of those on board, Hadj Sadok, was a rural chieftain (or *qaïd*) loyal to the French; when he challenged the rebels, he was cut down by a burst of automatic gunfire. Also caught up in this violent attack was a young French couple – the 'gangly', 'bookish' Guy Monnerot, aged twenty-four, and his idealistic twenty-one-year-old wife, Jeanine. Recently back from honeymoon, the Monnerots had taken up teaching posts at a small rural school just three weeks earlier. Guy, who suffered bullet wounds to the chest, bled to death by the side of the road; his stricken wife was rushed to hospital by the security forces, five hours after the shooting, where doctors saved her life.[53] In all, seventy separate terrorist incidents left nine people dead and four injured, and caused property damage amounting to two hundred million francs.[54]

The FLN, which had masterminded this wave of violence, also issued a manifesto calling for 'national independence' through the 'restoration of the Algerian state, sovereign, democratic and social, within the principles of Islam' and the 'preservation of all fundamental freedoms, without distinction of race or religion'. Pledging to wage the struggle for liberation by 'every means' available, it urged the French authorities to recognise Algerian statehood, free all political prisoners and open negotiations immediately on the 'basis of recognition of Algerian sovereignty', or risk further bloodshed. It also called on Algerians to rally behind the FLN: 'It is your duty . . . to save our country and give it back its liberty.'[55] Over the course of the next year the FLN (and its military wing, the Armée de Libération Nationale or ALN) became the dominant force within Algerian nationalism. One sign of the FLN's elevated status came with its invitation to the Bandung Conference of April 1955. The gathering, which the FLN attended as official 'observers', brought together the leaders of more than two dozen countries across Africa, Asia and the Middle East, to promote economic and cultural co-operation and to oppose colonialism and exploitation.[56] This was an early and very visible success for the FLN's strategy of 'internationalising' the Algerian struggle by appealing to world opinion, seeking the support of foreign allies and exploiting opportunities to embarrass and pressurise the French government on the global stage. Just a few months later, the FLN scored a second diplomatic coup when, under pressure from the Bandung countries, the UN General Assembly debated the question of Algerian independence for the first time.[57]

The second prong of the FLN's strategy was the use of armed struggle. Inspired by the Viet Minh victory in Indochina, as well as the uprisings against colonial rule in Kenya, Tunisia and Morocco, the organisation put violence at the heart of its approach. Indeed, many FLN militants viewed violence as a powerful psychological weapon which would help to cleanse Algeria from the stain of colonial rule. As one activist put it, the armed uprising would 'cure us of all our wounds, of all our humiliations . . . we were going to hold up our heads and put ourselves on the wavelength of History'.[58] Rather than attempting to seize control of territory, individual FLN cells – operating independently and in secret from each other – used sabotage, bombings and other acts of terror to foment fear and insecurity across the country, in an attempt to pressure the French into conceding Algerian independence.[59] For their part, Paris refused to yield an inch: 'The only negotiation', declared the interior minister, François Mitterrand, 'is war.'[60]

The attacks of 1 November 1954, then, marked only the start of what would become a sustained campaign of guerrilla warfare. For the remaining weeks of the year, and particularly from the spring of 1955, the FLN embarked on what one historian has described as a 'relentless . . . upward spiral' of violence: there were 196 incidents in April, 455 in May and more than nine hundred during June and July. Concentrated in the east of the country at first, the revolt gradually spread across Algeria. Much of the violence was directed against the indigenous Arab population: the FLN was determined to deter would-be informants and, by targeting Muslim police-men or administrative officials, also sought to polarise Algerian society by 'destroying all points of contact between European and Muslim'. The *pieds noirs* were targeted too: vineyards, livestock, crops and warehouses were destroyed, farmers were murdered, and French troops were ambushed and police officers attacked.[61] The FLN's willingness to use violence was illustrated starkly in June 1955 when, under growing pressure, nationalists in the North Constantine region advocated a 'total war' against the *colons*. Their strategy was chilling: 'To colonialism's policy of collective repres-sion we must reply with collective reprisals against the Europeans, military and civil, who are all united behind the crimes committed upon our people. For them, no pity, no quarter!'[62]

On 20 August, the brutal logic of this policy played out in horrific fashion. Across the Constantine region Algerian Muslims – often peasants armed only with sticks, pitchforks and knives – unleashed a terrifying wave of violence against the *colons* that engulfed some thirty towns and villages. In Philippeville, a 'happy sweet-smell-ing' port town, the relaxed Côte d'Azur atmosphere was shattered as grenades were thrown into cafes and motorists were dragged from their cars to be 'slashed to death with knives or even razors'.[63] When French paratroopers arrived, they found bodies strewn about and local Arab children running in the streets, 'wild with enthusiasm'. In one alleyway, two children were discovered 'kicking in an old woman's head': they were killed on the spot. At the nearby mining community of El-Halia, where 130 Europeans lived alongside two thousand Muslims, the violence was exceptionally savage. Just before midday, as the women of the town were preparing lunch, four armed groups, each of between fifteen and twenty men, launched a surprise attack. Guided by Muslim mine workers (fifty of whom had failed to show up for work that morning), they went from 'house to house, mercilessly slaughtering all the occupants regardless of sex or age'. When French forces arrived several hours later, they were greeted with scenes of unimaginable horror: the bodies of women and children, their throats cut and stomachs slashed open, were discovered in houses 'awash with blood'. Not even babies had been spared – some were found with their brains splattered against the walls. Some of the men, returning home from the mine, had been hacked to pieces. In all, the attacks in El-Halia claimed the lives of thirty-seven Europeans, including ten under the age of fifteen. The premeditated nature of the violence, and the participation or collusion of many local Muslims (including work colleagues) with whom relations had previously been viewed as friendly, made it all the more shocking.[64] In total, the FLN attacks killed 123 people – seventy-one Europeans, thirty-one soldiers and policemen and twenty-one Algerians.[65] The French response was unsparing. One soldier in Philippeville described how, after receiving orders to 'shoot down every Arab we met', 'for two hours all we heard was automatic rifles spitting fire into the crowd'. Early the next morning, several hundred prisoners were taken to a local football stadium and machine-gunned. Ten minutes after they opened fire, 'it was practically over'; there were 'so many' bodies that 'they had to be buried with bulldozers'.[66] Eighty were shot dead in El-Halia alone; overall, the savage backlash left up to three thousand Muslims dead.[67]

While the FLN's use of indiscriminate violence helped create a climate of mutual fear, distrust and hatred, the military and security response from the French – which was often heavy-handed and indiscriminate – pushed many ordinary Muslims into the arms of the revolutionaries. As Algerian society became increasingly divided, compromise became impossible. Algeria's minister-resident Jacques Soustelle had initially promoted a policy of 'integration' that would have involved greater Muslim political representation, enhanced educational provision and anti-poverty programmes, underpinned by the 'immutable equality' of all Algerians. But, after the bloody violence that had engulfed Constantine, he switched his attention to neutralising the FLN.[68] According to Soustelle 'it was not only the sacked houses or the poor mutilated corpses' that the violent mobs left in their wake on 20 August 1955, but also 'confidence, hope, peace. A sombre harvest of hatred sprouted in the bloodshed.'[69]

This was the grim situation that confronted Guy Mollet when he took up his position as prime minister just a few months later. On the one side stood a *colon* population that was suspicious of the nationalists, convinced that their continued prosperity and security – even their very lives – depended on the maintenance of French rule, and increasingly opposed to any talk of 'compromise'. On the other was a nationalist movement increasingly dominated by an FLN that was determined to secure Algerian independence by any means necessary.

In retrospect it is clear that 6 February 1956 was a 'red-letter day' for the *pieds noirs*.[70] Their humiliation of the French prime minister dealt a devastating blow to those who had hoped for a progressive approach. Within days Mollet announced that three hundred thousand additional troops would be sent to Algeria, bringing the total to five hundred thousand (in late 1954 the figure had been fifty thousand, just twelve thousand of whom were combat-ready), and on 12 March the French National Assembly approved the Special Powers Act, granting the government the legal right to take any measure deemed necessary for the 're-establishment of order'. It was now clear that crushing the FLN was the overwhelming priority.[71] The FLN reacted in kind. Denouncing Mollet for planning a 'total war on Algerians', and claiming that 'a ferocious and blind oppression is already raining down on our people', it declared that 'we have not taken up arms in order for free elections in Algeria, but in order that our country recovers its independence and liberty'.[72] In the weeks that followed, the FLN instigated a series of boycotts to cripple the country's economy, students and schoolchildren were urged to strike, Algerian football teams were ordered to withdraw from all French league and cup fixtures, and Muslim men were instructed to ignore efforts to draft them into the military reserve. As well as appealing to nationalism, pride and religion, the FLN mobilised support more ruthlessly: in mid-April, for instance, several hundred people in the village of Ihadjadjen, which had proved reticent in its support for the struggle, had their throats slit as a warning to others.[73] It was a suitably bloody sign of the horrors to come.

3

THE SECRET SPEECH

The Twentieth Congress was like the explosion of a neutron
bomb – it affected people while leaving structures apparently
intact. An enormous change took place . . . but above
all it was in the hearts and minds and consciousnesses of
individuals that this change was felt.

ROY A. MEDVEDEV

In February 1956, representatives of the world Communist movement gathered in Moscow for the Twentieth Congress of the
Communist Party of the Soviet Union.[1] As the proceedings got
under way on the morning of 14 February, some 1,400 delegates
filed into the main hall of the Great Kremlin Palace, which, with
its ranks of marshals and Red Army generals resplendent in their
uniforms and with a large, imposing statue of Lenin towering
over the speakers' platform at the front, made for an impressive
sight. But as he took in the scene Vittorio Vidali, a veteran of the
Spanish Civil War who was representing his native city of Trieste,
noticed that something was amiss. Although portraits of Stalin
typically adorned public spaces, shops and offices throughout the
Soviet Union and Eastern Europe, here – in the symbolic heart of
the Communist world – there was not a single one.[2] Then, after
formally opening the Congress, Nikita Khrushchev, the first secretary of the Soviet Communist Party, made a brief mention of
those 'distinguished' Communist leaders who had died since the
previous gathering, in October 1952. But his decision to include
Klement Gottwald of Czechoslovakia, who had drunk himself to
death, and Japan's Kyuichi Tokuda, whom many had never heard
of, alongside Joseph Stalin – the man who had led the Soviet

Union for the best part of three decades – struck an odd note. As they stood to pay their respects, many of the delegates 'looked at one another in surprise'. 'What a strange tribute this was, made in such a hurry', noted Vidali – almost as if Khrushchev was 'afraid' or 'ashamed'.[3]

As the Congress progressed there were further hints that Stalin was being demoted from the pantheon of Communist heroes. The Central Committee's own report, for example, broke from Stalinist orthodoxy by stating that it was possible for countries to take different roads to socialism, and by rejecting the claim – made by Stalin in February 1946 – that a new world war was inevitable. The Party also condemned 'the cult of the individual as alien to the spirit of Marxism–Leninism'. Two days later Anastas Mikoyan, the first deputy premier, explained that 'for roughly twenty years we did not really have collective leadership'; instead a 'cult of the individual flourished'. He also rubbished Stalin's 1951 tract, *Economic Problems of Socialism in the USSR*. But, in the absence of a definitive statement, confusion reigned – on a number of occasions the audience rose to their feet, or broke into loud applause, at favourable references to the late dictator.[4]

On the evening of Friday 24 February the British journalist John Rettie noticed that the windows of the Communist Party's headquarters in Old Square 'were ablaze with light into the early hours, with the great black limousines of the Party elite parked all around it'. That the building was 'humming with activity' struck him as 'very odd', given that the Congress had just ended.[5] But what Rettie did not know was that the final preparations were being made for a secret, 'closed' session, which was to be attended only by delegates from the USSR itself.

In the early hours of 25 February, with the members of the Party's Presidium (or Politburo) sitting on the stage behind him, 'red-faced and excited', Khrushchev delivered a speech 'On the Cult of Personality and its Consequences'. Lasting for four hours, with just a single intermission, it amounted to a direct and devastating assault on Stalin's reputation.[6] Khrushchev argued that, although it was 'foreign to the spirit of Marxism–Leninism to elevate one person, to transform him into a superman possessing supernatural characteristics, akin to those of a god', such a belief about Stalin had been 'cultivated among us for many years'. The result, he claimed, was a 'whole series of exceedingly serious perversions of party principles, of party democracy, of revolutionary legality'. In particular, Khrushchev condemned the way in which Stalin, whom he described as a 'distrustful and sickly suspicious man', had 'made possible the cruellest repression . . . against anyone who in any way disagreed with [him]'. Forced confessions, torture, summary execution, mass arrests and deportations had 'created conditions of insecurity, fear and even desperation' and led to 'the honest workers of the party' being victimised.[7] Khrushchev spoke with 'agitation and emotion', according to one onlooker, and he betrayed a real animus when discussing Stalin's culpability for Soviet losses during the Second World War.[8] Rather than the patriotic hero of popular legend, Stalin had in fact ignored repeated warnings about an imminent German attack during the spring of 1941, left the Soviet Union grossly unprepared for war and insisted on military operations that needlessly sacrificed hundreds of thousands of Soviet troops. Khrushchev even mocked Stalin, the supposed 'military genius', for attempting to plan operations on a globe, and denounced him as 'a coward . . . Not once during the whole war did he dare to go to the front.'[9]

Khrushchev also delivered a devastating blow to Stalin's carefully crafted image as Lenin's anointed heir by revealing that, towards the end of his life, the Bolshevik leader had described Stalin as 'excessively rude' and suggested that he be replaced as general secretary of the Party by someone with 'greater tolerance, greater loyalty, greater kindness, [a] more considerate attitude toward the comrades, [and] a less capricious temper'.[10]

For most of the speech, the delegates listened in stunned silence. At times, there were murmurs of disbelief and indignation. Some people became unwell and had to be helped out of the auditorium.[11] Dmitri Goriunov, the editor of the Communist youth movement's official newspaper, gulped down a handful of nitroglycerine pills as he took in Khrushchev's revelations, fearful that his weak heart might give out under the shock.[12] When it was all over, 'a deep stillness descended on the hall. One could not hear the chairs squeak, coughs or whisper. Nobody looked at his neighbor – either because of the suddenness of what had happened or due to confusion and fear. The shock was extraordinarily deep.'[13] As he left the Kremlin, ashen-faced and speechless, Sergei Mezentsev, the editor of *Kommunist*, the party's official journal, wondered 'what will happen next . . . what should we do?'[14]

The man who had delivered this audacious speech was one of the most complex and fascinating figures of his age. As the de facto leader of one of the world's two superpowers, Khrushchev wielded enormous power and influence – not least over questions of war and peace – yet many struggled to understand how this 'short, thick-set man', with his bald pate, 'small piercing eyes' and 'protruding ears', had managed to rise so high.[15] Within the Soviet Union, he was often disparaged as a clown or a boor; his bitter rival, the Soviet foreign minister Vyacheslav Molotov, even claimed that Khrushchev was a 'primitive man' who reminded him of 'a petty fishmonger, or a man who sold cattle'.[16] Such views were shared by powerful figures outside the Soviet Union, too. A year before the 'secret speech', a US intelligence report had claimed that Khrushchev was 'essentially a simple type with few inhibitions and little sophistication'.[17] Observing the Soviet leader during the Geneva Summit of July 1955 – which brought together the leaders of the United States, Great Britain, France and the USSR to discuss trade, arms and security concerns – the British foreign secretary, Harold Macmillan, described an 'obscene figure; very fat, with a great paunch; eats and drinks greedily; interrupts boisterously and rudely'. Indeed, he wondered how 'this fat, vulgar man, with his pig eyes and his cease-less flow of talk' could 'really be the head – the aspirant Tsar – of all those millions of people and this vast country'.[18]

There was certainly nothing in Khrushchev's origins that sug-gested greatness. Born in April 1894 in the small farming village of Kalinovka, in south-west Russia, the child of peasants, Nikita Sergeyevich Khrushchev received a basic education and worked as a shepherd before moving to the mining town of Yuzovka, three hundred miles away in eastern Ukraine, at the age of fourteen. There he trained as a fitter at a Jewish-owned foundry. In 1914, the twenty-year-old Nikita, who had gained a reputation as something of a ladies' man, married Yefrosinia Pisareva, and children soon followed (Yulia was born in 1915, Leonid two years later). Khrush-chev was, by all accounts, a dedicated and skilled metalworker, but he was drawn increasingly towards politics – particularly the struggle of industrial workers and the socialist cause. It was the onset of the Russian Revolution, though, that marked the start of Khrushchev's lifelong association with Communism. Joining the Bolsheviks in 1918, he served as a commissar in the Red Army and, when the Civil War ended in 1921, returned to Yuzovka to take up a position at the Rutchenkovo mine. After a stint at the Mining Technical College (and a brief flirtation with Trotskyism), he was appointed a district Party boss in the summer of 1925. From here, he began to rise up the ranks of Ukraine's Communist hier-archy.[19] During these years, Khrushchev endured his share of per-sonal turmoil: his first wife, Yefrosinia, died of typhus during (or perhaps shortly after) the Russian Civil War. A brief second mar-riage was followed, in 1924, by a lasting union with Nina Petrovna Kukharchuk, a talented Party activist.[20]

In 1929, Khrushchev enrolled at the Industrial Academy in Mos-cow, a flagship institution dedicated to training a new generation of socialist leaders. In the decade that followed, Khrushchev's career advanced rapidly, helped by his appetite for hard work and self-improvement, his approachable, down-to-earth personality and his engaging style of public speaking.[21] In January 1931 he was appointed Party boss for the district in which the academy was located; a year later, he became the number two in the Moscow Party, rising to the top job there in January 1934. By early 1935, he was in charge of Moscow province, with responsibility for eleven million people. Newsreel footage of a speech delivered by Khrushchev to Party activists at a lamp factory shows him relaxed and at ease, winning over the audience with his broad, infectious smile and informal style. That same year, he was awarded the Order of Lenin for his role in overseeing the construction of the capital's Metro system. Khrushchev, who had lavished praise on 'our leader of genius Comrade Stalin' at the Seventeenth Party Congress in 1934, was one of only a handful of regional leaders who were trusted to oversee the political purges that took place in the late 1930s. Declaring that the 'scoundrels must be destroyed', Khrushchev assisted in the arrest, torture and murder of many of his own comrades in the local Party: only three of thirty-eight leading Moscow officials survived and scores of other Party secretaries and functionaries fell victim to the Terror. Khrushchev – a Communist 'true believer' who was also, presumably, terrified that he would be next on the NKVD's hit-list – also signed off the arrest, exile and execution of tens of thousands of land-owning peasants (or kulaks), 'criminals' and 'traitors'.[22]

In 1938, Khrushchev's unyielding loyalty was rewarded with another promotion, as Stalin's man in Ukraine. From Kiev, the new first secretary of the Ukrainian Central Committee called for 'all enemies of the people' to be unmasked and destroyed, and he oversaw a wave of purges in which fifty thousand lost their lives. He also embarked on a campaign to modernise agriculture and improve industry. During the Soviet occupation of western

Ukraine and western Byelorussia, which followed the Nazi–Soviet Pact of 1939, Khrushchev played a pivotal role in the forced deportation of more than 1.25 million people, the arrest of five hundred thousand and the torture and death of tens of thousands more. Then, following the Axis invasion of the USSR in June 1941, Khrushchev was at the heart of the Great Fatherland War, retreating with the Red Army from Kiev to Stalingrad before returning in triumph. During these years, as a political commissar in the Red Army, he served as an influential conduit between military commanders on the front and the authorities in Moscow. Military disasters in Kiev and Kharkov (in which hundreds of thousands of Soviet troops needlessly lost their lives) were countered with victories in Stalingrad and Kursk, earning Khrushchev a clutch of medals and the rank of lieutenant general. Then, as the Red Army pushed on towards Berlin, Khrushchev resumed his duties in Ukraine, where he helped to crush a nationalist uprising and rebuilt the Party. During 1946, though, his relations with Stalin deteriorated markedly. After challenging official policies that had exacerbated a devastating famine in the region, Khrushchev found himself demoted. But he managed to weather the storm and regained his position at the end of 1947. By the autumn of 1949 his rehabilitation was complete, and he was recalled to Moscow and admitted to Stalin's inner circle.[23]

On 5 March 1953, when the dictator finally succumbed to a massive stroke, few – either inside or outside the USSR – viewed Khrushchev as Stalin's likely successor. Yet within just two and a half years, all of Khrushchev's main rivals had fallen by the wayside: Lavrentiy Beria, Stalin's chief of police, was executed following an internal coup; Georgy Malenkov, the Soviet premier, had been comprehensively outmanoeuvred; and Vyacheslav Molotov, the foreign minister, had been undermined. Khrushchev benefited enormously from the fact that his rivals consistently underestimated him. By mistaking his garrulousness, his eagerness to please and his crude mannerisms for a lack of guile, they had miscalculated badly.[24]

Khrushchev's brutal assault on Stalin has been described by one of his biographers as 'the bravest and most reckless thing he ever did'.[25] As news of the 'secret speech' emerged during the spring and early summer of 1956 it fuelled discord within the Soviet Union, sparked a wave of popular uprisings across Eastern Europe, dealt a crippling blow to Sino-Soviet relations and left Communist parties across the west bitterly divided and, in some cases, hopelessly compromised. It is hardly surprising, then, that many have wondered why Khrushchev took such a tremendous gamble.

In Washington, DC, where rumours about the 'dramatic news from Moscow' reached the American government in early March, President Eisenhower and his senior advisers struggled to find a satisfactory explanation. At a meeting of the National Security Council on 22 March, for example, Allen Dulles, the director of the CIA, suggested that the attempt to 'blast Stalin to pieces' was driven by the Soviet leadership's desire to 'gain respectability abroad by virtue of a complete break with the past'. Wondering if they might have 'permitted themselves to be pushed further than they had initially intended to go, thanks to Khrushchev's exuberant personality', he even raised the possibility that the Soviet leader might have delivered his remarks while drunk.[26]

In fact, the 'secret speech' was a key moment in a larger process of reform (often referred to as de-Stalinisation) that had been underway for several years. When Stalin died in March 1953 the new Soviet leadership inherited a daunting set of problems. One of the most pressing was the future of the Gulag,* the vast prison network of forced labour camps and internal colonies that had been established during the early 1930s and which, by 1953, held some

* 'Gulag' derives from the acronym for Glavnoe Upravlenie ispravitel'no-trudovykh Lagerie (Main Administration of Corrective Labour Camps), the administrative body that oversaw the USSR's system of forced labour camps.

2.5 million men, women and children (including five hundred thousand 'political prisoners'). The Gulag constituted an enormous economic drain on the nation – its slave labour was inefficient and unproductive, and the costs of transporting and securing the inmates were considerable. A series of uprisings beginning in the late 1940s, and culminating in major rebellions at Norilsk in May 1953 and Kengir in early 1954, crystallised the need to reform this expensive and unsustainable system.[27] The Soviet Union was also confronted with major economic challenges, not least a chronic shortage of housing and consumer goods, as well as an approaching agricultural crisis.[28] When it came to foreign relations, meanwhile, the USSR faced growing economic and political discontent within its eastern European satellite states (particularly Poland and Hungary); tensions with Communist China and Yugoslavia; and a Western alliance, led by the United States, that was firmly committed to containing any further Communist expansion (by military force if necessary) and, in the longer term, to rolling back Moscow's influence.[29]

The initial attempt to meet these challenges had been led by Lavrentiy Beria, head of the Ministry for Internal Affairs (MVD). On 27 March 1953, for instance, a mass amnesty was decreed that released all Gulag prisoners serving sentences of less than five years, pregnant women, mothers with children under the age of ten and men aged over fifty-five. It also promised to review the cases of 'political prisoners' and mooted a wider reform of the criminal justice system. The amnesty led to the eventual release of more than one million inmates.[30] In early April, Beria announced an end to certain forms of punishment and interrogation, including prolonged periods of sleep deprivation, 'cruel beatings' and the use of stress positions. In foreign policy, meanwhile, he sought a rapprochement with Yugoslavia – which had broken dramatically from Moscow in 1948. Aware that the imposition of central economic planning in Eastern Europe had resulted in inefficiencies and chronic shortages, and alarmed by evidence of growing discontent (including unauthorised strikes) over living standards, he also pushed to loosen Soviet control over the Eastern European satellites. He even contemplated abandoning East Germany's Communist government in exchange for reparations and a unified, demilitarised and neutral Germany.[31] But Beria was no liberal. As Stalin's chief of secret police, he was thoroughly implicated in the worst excesses of the Terror and fully deserved his monstrous reputation. However, by breaking with the policies of the past and incriminating Stalin, he hoped to improve his own standing and strengthen his hold on power. The release of so many former Gulag inmates, many of them petty criminals, into the major cities, for example, gave Beria a perfect excuse to use MVD troops to maintain order (troops that, if it proved necessary, could be used to strike at his political opponents).[32]

The process of reform continued after Beria's 26 June arrest and subsequent execution. Accused of being an 'enemy of the people', he was shot by a three-star general on Christmas Eve, following an internal coup that had been orchestrated by Khrushchev. The security services were shaken up, with a new Committee for State Security (KGB) placed under the control of the Party's Central Committee to prevent it from becoming the tool of a single individual. Unlike its predecessor, which had enjoyed the power to convict and punish, the KGB's remit was restricted to investigation and arrest. The government was reorganised to devolve powers to individual ministers, and reforms to agriculture and industry were proposed. In May 1955, Khrushchev led a Soviet delegation to Belgrade for successful talks with Josep Tito, one of Stalin's most bitter enemies.[33]

Despite the increasingly obvious breaks with Stalinist policy, the Soviet leadership had not yet moved to reassess Stalin himself. By 1956, the issue had become pressing. For one thing, the release of tens of thousands of Gulag inmates, including political prisoners demanding rehabilitation, meant that a detailed picture of the Stalinist repression was beginning to spread among the general population.[34] Convinced that the truth would come out eventually, Khrushchev argued that it would be far better for the Party leadership to confront the issue head on. As he told his Presidium colleagues, 'If we do not speak the truth at the congress, then we will be forced to tell the truth after some time.' 'But', he warned, 'then we will not be reporting; we will be people under investigation . . . we will be accused as accomplices . . .'[35] There were other motives at work, too. Since some within the leadership circle, notably the foreign minister Vyacheslav Molotov and Lazar Kaganovich, the first deputy chairman of the Council of Ministers, were more culpable than Khrushchev for the bloodbaths of the 1930s, attacking Stalin promised to weaken his rivals and strengthen his own position.[36] Khrushchev also seems to have been genuinely shocked by some of the revelations that had emerged after Stalin's death, and it has even been suggested that he viewed the 'secret speech' as a way of repenting for his own sins and 'reclaiming his identity as a decent man by telling the truth'.[37] Finally – and most importantly – in seeking to remove the 'stain' of Stalinism, Khrushchev saw an opportunity to return to the Leninist principles that had fired his own enthusiasm for the Bolshevik cause in the first place. A return to Leninism would, he believed, reinvigorate the Communist system, allowing it to reach its full potential, demonstrate its superiority over capitalism and improve the social, cultural and economic lives of ordinary citizens.[38]

Khrushchev's proposal that Stalin's crimes be discussed at the Twentieth Party Congress met with opposition from some of his colleagues, who feared for their own reputations.[39] In the end, though, Khrushchev prevailed.[40] The process of drafting the speech began on 15 February, and was not completed until late on the evening of the 24th. The final text drew heavily on a Presidium report, commissioned at the start of the year, which revealed that seven hundred thousand of the 1.9 million citizens arrested for anti-Soviet activity between 1935 and 1940 had been shot, and exposed as fabrications the numerous plots and conspiracies that had allegedly been uncovered during the Great Purge (a massive campaign of repression waged against the Party, the government, the army, the intelligentsia and others during the second half of the 1930s). Evidence that Stalin had personally approved the widespread use of torture was laid bare. Khrushchev also incorporated suggestions from Presidium colleagues, material furnished from former political prisoners, wartime generals and other senior figures, and his own ideas.[41] The final version of the 'secret speech' was, though, limited in the scope of its criticism. First, Khrushchev focused on the years after 1934, thereby ignoring the massive human suffering that had accompanied the forced collectivisation of agriculture and the top-down attempts to modernise the Soviet economy – policies that had been necessary, Khrushchev believed, despite the terrible human toll. Second, sympathy was reserved for Communist victims of the Terror. Khrushchev concentrated his remarks on the several thousand 'innocent' Party officials who had been purged (many of whom had blood on their hands), ignoring the millions of ordinary citizens who had perished. Given Khrushchev's goal of relaunching the Soviet project, this limited approach is unsurprising. After all, a full and frank exposé of the past would not only have undermined his own position and that of most, if not all, of his colleagues, but would have likely proved fatal to the USSR itself.[42]

Towards the end of the 'secret speech', in remarks that drew 'thunderous applause', Khrushchev declared that 'we cannot let this matter get out of the party, especially not to the press', and he warned against giving 'ammunition to the enemy'. 'We should not', he said, 'wash our dirty linen before their eyes.'[43] But although the speech was neither published in the Soviet media nor acknowledged officially by the Party leadership until the late 1980s, its contents were quickly disseminated.[44] Before they left Moscow, a select group of Eastern European leaders was given access to the speech, while edited transcripts were subsequently sent to various foreign party leaders (one copy ended up in the hands of the CIA). Details about the 'closed' session were also leaked to the press; on 17 March a number of British newspapers reported the break with Stalin, and in June the *New York Times* and the London *Observer* published a lengthy transcript of the speech itself.[45] Within the USSR, the Presidium approved Khrushchev's suggestion that an edited copy of the text be distributed to regional, city and district Party committees. They would be tasked with organising meetings at which the speech would be read out to the Party rank and file, as well as members of Komsomol, the Communist youth organisation, in order to inform them of its contents. It was also directed that 'non-party activists including workers, white-collar personnel and collective farmers' be invited along.[46] According to one estimate, as many as thirty-five million people (roughly one in six of the population) heard about the contents of the 'secret speech' in the meetings that were held in factories, government buildings, offices, schools and universities and on farms across the Soviet Union during March.[47]

One of them was Roy Medvedev, who would go on to achieve fame as a political writer and dissident. In early March Medvedev, who was the principal of a school near Leningrad, suddenly received an urgent instruction. 'I was told to assemble all the teachers at 4 p.m. in the club of the nearby brickworks on the following day.' There the teachers joined with factory workers, farm managers and regular Party members to hear an official from the district committee read out Khrushchev's speech. It was made clear that there would be no opportunity to ask questions, and 'we were not allowed to take notes'. Medvedev, whose own father had perished in a labour camp in 1941, explained how the audience 'paid close attention and listened in silence, almost in horror'. At the end, 'for several moments there was not a sound in the room. And then we all silently left.'[48]

Although many local Party leaders discouraged discussion, others allowed questions from the floor, which often prompted wider debate.[49] A report sent to the Central Committee noted that the three most popular questions asked at Party meetings were: 'Why was Khrushchev's report so limited in its contents?' 'Why was there no self-criticism or open discussion of the report?' and 'What guarantees are there that there will not be another cult?' Other common enquiries included: 'Are not other Presidium members also guilty?' 'How could the newspapers lie for so long and now change track so easily?' 'Why did Khrushchev wait so long to tell us about these terrible events?' and 'Why did members of the Central Committee cry over Stalin's grave?'[50] Sometimes the discussions reflected particular concerns. In Ukraine, for instance, people wondered whether the Nazi–Soviet Pact had been a mistake, and asked about those who had been deported (this, clearly, was an episode that Khrushchev was not at all keen to revisit), while at Moscow's Institute of Law the Soviet legal system was singled out for condemnation. Meanwhile, letters poured in to the Communist Party's Moscow headquarters demanding that Stalin's body be removed from the Mausoleum in Red Square, where it lay next to Lenin's.[51] The KGB noted reports of busts and portraits of Stalin being smashed or defaced, and there was even an attempt to have the late dictator declared an 'enemy of the people'.[52] This outpouring of criticism began to alarm senior officials; one recorded that 'demagogic and even harmful speeches are taking place at meetings of various party organisations, and they do not always receive a decisive rebuff and political evaluation'.[53]

The most dramatic of all the discussions took place towards the end of March at Moscow's prestigious Thermo-Technical Institute. At a meeting of the local Party cell, a group of four young academics subjected Khrushchev's revelations to some particularly trenchant criticism. R. G. Arvalov, a junior fellow, asked why there had been no discussion of the 'secret speech' at the Twentieth Congress. He also suggested that, to prevent such abuses of power in the future, the workers should be armed. Arvalov's colleague, the physicist Yuri Orlov, claimed that 'power belongs to some heap of scoundrels' while the Party was 'shot through with the spirit of slavery', and he called on all Communists to ensure that the mistakes of the past would not be repeated.[54]

Not everyone was enthusiastic about the break with Stalin.[55] Although most seem to have reacted, at least initially, with a mixture of shock and confusion, others leapt to the dictator's defence. Some simply refused to accept that Stalin had been responsible for the widespread use of torture, forced confessions, mass repression and other crimes; others argued that his achievements outweighed any failings.[56] Mikhail Gorbachev, then a young Komsomol official in Stavropol in southern Russia, noticed that while the younger and better-educated participants welcomed Khrushchev's speech, others either refused to believe the revelations or simply did not see the point in raking over them.[57] Some questioned Khrushchev's motives, wondering – as one Party member put it – why he had kept 'quiet back then', only to 'pour all this muck on Stalin now that he's dead'.[58]

The most intense displays of loyalty came from Stalin's native Georgia, which continued to hold its most famous son in high regard.[59] Like others throughout the Soviet Union, the citizens of this Caucus Republic had been indoctrinated over many years to believe in the myth of Stalin as a 'great leader' and hero of the Communist movement. They thus struggled to come to terms with the shattering of an entire world view. Many Georgians also viewed Khrushchev's revelations as an insult to national pride and a violation of their cultural tradition of revering the dead.[60] It made for a potent mix. Beginning on 5 March – the third anniversary of the former dictator's death – Tbilisi erupted in pro-Stalin demonstrations that lasted for several days. Wreaths were laid at Stalin's official monument on the banks of the Kura River, and tens of thousands of people – including students, shopkeepers, schoolchildren and workers – took to the streets, carrying portraits, waving flags, singing songs and shouting, 'Glory to the Great Stalin!' and 'Down with Khrushchev!'[61] Some were armed with sticks, knives and daggers, and violent clashes broke out: several truck drivers who refused to hand their vehicles over to the protesters were beaten up, and one was even thrown into the river; police officers were attacked and journalists threatened. The protesters demanded that local newspapers publish articles celebrating Stalin's life and work, and that films glorifying Stalin's military record be screened in the cinemas. Others called for Khrushchev to be removed from office. There was even talk of Georgia seceding from the Soviet Union.[62]

With barricades on the streets, many business and government services paralysed and clashes between protesters and the security forces becoming more serious, the city was spinning out of control. According to one senior military commander, by the evening of 9 March 'there was no order. The city was in complete anarchy. Transportation, cars, trucks, taxis, buses and trolley cars were all in the hands of the mob' and 'Cars were driving around the city incessantly honking their horns.' Just before midnight, an angry crowd approached the communications building, where a delegation of protesters had been detained while seeking to telegraph their demands to Moscow. One Party journalist described how the crowd, which was pressing forward in an attempt to storm the building, was at first 'beaten off with gun butts', but when the protesters fought back using 'everything available: fists, knives, rocks, belts', the troops opened fire, killing seven people and injuring several more.[63] In the hours that followed, there were clashes across the city, including at the *Kommunist* newspaper offices and in a park near to the Stalin Monument. Tanks and motorised infantry were deployed to restore order. When it was all over, three hundred were dead, one thousand injured, and hundreds had been arrested.[64]

Back in the Kremlin, the Soviet leadership was unnerved. The pro-Stalin riots in Georgia, and what one historian has described as a 'wave of criticism, "truth-telling" and questioning on a scale that had not been seen in Soviet public spaces for many years', provided a stark illustration of how Khrushchev's revelations could generate social instability and weaken the authority of the Party.[65] Back in December, Kaganovich had warned that any public examination of Stalin's mistakes would 'raise doubts about the correctness of our whole course'.[66] Now even Khrushchev worried that he had struck too powerful a blow.[67] Concerned that the very foundations of the USSR were threatened, the leadership moved to rein in the criticism.[68] All Party organisations were warned against tolerating 'hostile outbursts', while a *Pravda* editorial called for an end to 'excessive liberalism' and criticised those who had seized on the 'secret speech' to make 'anti-party assertions' and 'slanderous fabrications'. At the end of June the Central Committee made it clear that blaming the nature of the Soviet system for the problems associated with the 'cult of personality' would not be tolerated.[69] In the end, an unremitting campaign (which saw thousands jailed for 'crimes against the state') helped to turn the tide.[70] But the task of restraining dissent would prove much harder, and would exact a far higher cost, in the Soviet Union's Eastern European empire.

4

MASSIVE RESISTANCE

The time has now come when the white people in Alabama
have but three choices remaining. We can sell our homes and
move out of Alabama, we can stay here and be humiliated, or
we can take up our shotguns.
STATE REPRESENTATIVE W. L. MARTIN

On 12 March 1956, Walter F. George, president *pro tempore* of the
United States Senate, rose to his feet and, speaking in his trademark
'slow, formal manner', introduced the 'Declaration of Constitutional Principles' from the floor of the chamber. The document,
which was soon dubbed the 'Southern Manifesto', constituted a
fierce attack on the Supreme Court's 1954 ruling, in *Brown* v. *Board
of Education, Topeka, Kansas,* that racially segregated schools were
unconstitutional. With its fondness for ritual and formality and
its near-veneration of courtesy and respect, the Senate of the 1950s
bore more than a passing resemblance to a gentlemen's club. It was
not surprising, then, that George – who was arguably the South's
greatest living orator – was heard in an atmosphere of hushed
solemnity. But there was no doubting either the significance of
the moment or the highly charged nature of his carefully chosen
words. The Southern Manifesto was nothing less than a segregationist rallying cry.

George, born on 29 January 1878 in Webster County, where his
father eked out a living as a tenant farmer, was a true son of the red
clay soil of Georgia. Having worked a series of odd jobs to fund his
education, he graduated from law school in 1901, was appointed
an associate justice on the Georgia Supreme Court in 1917 and
won his first election to the Senate in 1922. By 1956, as chairman

of the influential Foreign Relations Committee, George was one of the nation's most powerful politicians. Although George had little time for the vituperative, race-baiting rhetoric that was popular with some of his southern colleagues, he was none the less committed to white supremacy. As he put it, southerners had been 'very diligent and astute in violating the spirit' of any laws that 'would lead the Negro to believe himself the equal of a white man. And we shall continue to conduct ourselves that way.'[1] George was, then, more than happy to lend his considerable prestige to the defence of Jim Crow.

Although the 'Declaration' had been finalised during meetings held in George's Senate office, the text itself was shaped primarily by his fellow Georgian Richard Russell, South Carolina's Strom Thurmond and Virginia's Harry F. Byrd – three of the South's most vocal defenders of segregation.[2] The language used in the Manifesto reflected their uncompromising world view: the *Brown* ruling was attacked as a 'clear abuse of judicial power' that 'encroach[ed] upon' the 'rights of the states and the people'. Moreover it was alleged that the ruling, together with the actions of civil rights agitators, was 'creating chaos and confusion' across the South and 'destroying the amicable relations between the white and Negro races'. Saluting those states that had declared their intention to resist integration, supporters of the Manifesto pledged themselves to 'use all lawful means to bring about a reversal' of the *Brown* decision and to 'prevent the use of force in its implementation'.[3]

Signed by all but three of the South's senators and more than seventy members of the House of Representatives (including the entire delegations of Alabama, Arkansas, Georgia, Louisiana, Mississippi, South Carolina and Virginia), the Southern Manifesto sought to marshal white southerners behind the banner of outright opposition to desegregation. Support for the document became a political litmus test: as Alabama congressman Carl Elliott put it, 'You were either with them or against them. And if you were against them, you were gone.' And by sending a strong signal of the white South's absolute determination to resist the *Brown* decision, the Manifesto's architects hoped to deter the federal government from taking decisive action to enforce the ruling.[4]

The Southern Manifesto occupied a central place in what became known as 'Massive Resistance': a sustained political campaign, launched in early 1956, to prevent racial integration and to stymie, if not destroy, the nascent civil rights movement.[5] The Manifesto's release also contributed mightily to a significant all-round hardening of the South's racial politics.[6] During the preceding months several southern state legislatures had attacked the *Brown* decision and pledged defiance. In South Carolina, for example, lawmakers had denounced the ruling as a 'deliberate, palpable, and dangerous attempt to change the true intent and meaning of the Constitution'.[7] In legitimising their opposition, segregationists relied heavily on the doctrine of 'interposition'. Rescued from obscurity by James J. Kilpatrick, the talented young editor of Virginia's *Richmond News Leader* and the 'intellectual swordsman' for the cause, this theory held that the legislatures of individual states had the right to intervene to protect the liberties of their citizens if the federal government exceeded the bounds of its legitimate authority.[8]

Buoyed by their newfound enthusiasm for nineteenth-century constitutional theory, southern politicians passed numerous laws and devised imaginative legal remedies in the pursuit of Massive Resistance. Many states, for example, enacted measures that enabled local school districts to maintain segregated systems by using a set of complicated criteria to assign pupils without explicitly mentioning race. State governors were also authorised to shut down any school that integrated, and to divert public funds to support private all-white schools. The NAACP, America's oldest and largest civil rights organisation, was also targeted. State prosecutors, for example, tried to force it to hand over its membership lists. Aware that to do so would be to expose individuals to the risk of harassment, dismissal from their jobs or even physical violence, the Association refused. But this only brought further sanctions. The organisation was banned from operating altogether in Alabama, and found itself fighting expensive and draining rearguard actions in several other states.[9]

Away from the rarefied atmosphere of the US Senate or the Southern Statehouse, it turned out that Massive Resistance had rather more to do with intimidation than interposition. On the ground, in cities and small towns across the South, the fight to defend Jim Crow was waged by the so-called White Citizens' Councils. The first of these Councils had been founded in Indianola, Mississippi, in July 1954, and within two years there was a South-wide network of more than ninety organisations with as many as 250,000 members.[10] The Councils drew most of their support from the professional classes – bankers, lawyers, doctors, local politicians and business owners; the 'quintessence of the civic luncheon club', as one investigative journalist put it. They also took care to couch their opposition to integration as a defence of states' rights against the excessive power of the government in Washington. Their weapon of choice was economic coercion (refusing people credit or firing them from their jobs), which they used both to suppress white dissent and to intimidate civil rights activists, black voters and parents who sought to send their children to integrated schools.[11] Despite their public commitment to exclusively peaceful and legal means and their carefully crafted image of respectability, the boundary between economic pressure and outright violence became easily blurred, while the Councils' own rhetoric whipped up racial animosity.[12]

White southerners' opposition to civil rights was motivated by numerous concerns. Like their counterparts in South Africa or Algeria, many, particularly in rural counties where blacks formed a substantial proportion of the population, were simply unwilling to give up the economic and political power, and the status, that they enjoyed as a result of institutionalised white supremacy. Support for states' rights and fears about the dangers of unchecked federal power were also important, as was the view that integration was part of a Communist conspiracy to destabilise the South by fomenting social chaos. Others simply could not conceive of an end to a way of life that had persisted for more than half a century, and which drew on a deeply rooted culture of black subjugation. Pointing to the violent Mau Mau revolt in Kenya, segregationists also argued that any weakening of white control would inevitably lead to violence and chaos.[13]

Massive Resistance was, to some degree, driven by political elites who were concerned that ordinary white southerners might be insufficiently committed to defending the status quo. Certainly, in the months immediately after the *Brown* decision, many had appeared to resign themselves to a measure of token desegregation.[14] But there was no doubting that whites supported segregation in vast numbers – opinion polls showed that 90 per cent of whites in Alabama, Georgia, Louisiana, Mississippi and South Carolina were opposed to integration.[15] Central to this support for Jim Crow were widespread and ingrained fears about miscegenation, or race mixing. Writing in April 1956, Ralph McGill, the liberal editor of the *Atlanta Journal-Constitution*, explained that 'deep in the instincts of many Southerners is a fear of what might happen "when the children all drink out of the same bucket"'. 'Many of these people' were, he said, 'entirely sincere when they say that [integration] means a "mongrelised" race'. That the 'reasoning is not always sound' did not, as McGill pointed out, 'detract from the strength of its belief or fear'.[16]

From its headquarters on West 40th Street, New York, the NAACP's executive secretary, Roy Wilkins, observed the emergence of Massive Resistance with growing alarm. Swatting aside arguments about constitutional principle, Wilkins declared that southern obstructionists were simply determined to prevent African Americans from enjoying first-class citizenship, no matter what.[17] The fifty-five-year-old former journalist, whose career in the upper echelons of the Association had begun in 1931 and who had taken over the leadership the previous spring, had good reason to be worried.[18] Although the Southern Manifesto was designed to co-ordinate resistance to the civil rights movement across the South, the early months of 1956 had provided plenty of evidence that, at a local level, segregationists were already on the march. Indeed, the hardening of the racial climate in the South had come into sharp relief just a few weeks earlier, during the attempt to desegregate the University of Alabama at Tuscaloosa.

Tuscaloosa, a city of fifty-six thousand on the banks of the Warrior River in west-central Alabama, took its name from a defeated sixteenth-century Native American chieftain. As late as 1910, its population had numbered less than ten thousand. During the early twentieth century, though, it had moved away from a heavy reliance on the cotton trade to become something of an industrial and manufacturing centre. By the 1950s, in addition to the Goodrich rubber factory, which employed a thousand people, there was a paper mill, a chemical works, an oil refinery and a foundry. Coal mines dotted the area to the north and east of the city, while small farms predominated to the south and west. African Americans made up about 30 per cent of the city's population. The University of Alabama, located about one and a half miles east of the city centre, had educated most of the state's prominent politicians, and while its faculty may not have been particularly distinguished, the university was a good deal better than its reputation as 'the country club of the South' suggested. The campus, which occupied a large plateau near the river, boasted a large central quadrangle, majestic oak trees and inspiring neoclassical architecture.[19]

In February 1956 this place of extraordinary beauty and charm was convulsed by a racial conflagration that pitted the champions of African American equality against the defenders of Jim Crow. At the end of January the university had announced that, for the first time in its 125-year history, it would admit an African American student.[20] Autherine Lucy (known to friends and family by her middle name, Juanita), had been born on 5 October 1929, the youngest of ten children, and raised on her father's farm in southwest Alabama. Lucy had attended Selma University for two years before transferring to Miles Memorial College in Birmingham in 1949, with the intention of pursuing a career in teaching. A committed Christian, she worshipped regularly at her local Baptist church. She also joined the NAACP and, despite her natural shyness, was elected president of the local YWCA. At Miles she had struck up a close friendship with Pollie Anne Myers, whom she had met while taking a class in public speaking.

Born on 14 July 1932 on a cotton plantation near Montgomery, Myers had moved to Birmingham aged five. After graduating from high school in 1949, she had worked at a restaurant to save money for college. She supported herself at Miles by working for Ruby Hurley, a leading NAACP activist, maintaining a newspaper clippings file. Myers, who harboured ambitions to become a journalist, also wrote for the *Birmingham World*, whose editor, Emory Jackson, was a fierce proponent of black equality. Soon Myers was involved in the emerging civil rights movement, and she served as president of the state NAACP Youth Council in 1951–2. At five feet eight inches tall, Myers was a chic, confident and tenacious young woman – in many ways the opposite of the rather unassuming and reserved Lucy. In the early summer of 1952, Myers asked Lucy if she would like to attend the University of Alabama. At first Lucy was startled by the suggestion and even thought that her friend might be joking. On learning that she was serious, she agreed, and the two young women made a pact to apply together.[21]

After being denied admission on the grounds of race, the pair turned to the courts for redress. When a lengthy legal battle, supported by the NAACP, resulted in a favourable ruling from a federal court, the university agreed to admit Lucy. However, it rejected Myers on the grounds of her 'conduct and marital status', having discovered that at the time of her original application she had been pregnant and unmarried (she had since wed, and was in the process of divorcing, Edward Hudson, a convicted felon).[22] The university authorities hoped that, deprived of the support of the more forceful and politically active Myers, Lucy would reconsider her own decision to enrol.[23] They were to be disappointed.

Lucy, who had spent the four long years of the court challenge teaching English at a high school in Carthage, Mississippi, struck reporters as being sincere in her avowed desire to study at the university, make friends and contribute to campus life.[24] As she put it, she simply wanted 'a chance to learn', after which she would 'give [her] services in Alabama'.[25] Lucy may have been shy, but she was not naïve. The twenty-six-year-old was well aware that her admittance to Alabama's flagship school represented a significant victory for the black freedom struggle.[26] And while she may have answered the journalists' questions 'with a soft, musical tone in her voice', throughout the entire episode she displayed remarkable depths of courage and determination.[27]

Having successfully registered to study library science at the School of Education, Lucy attended her first classes at the magnificent Tuscaloosa campus on 3 February, a dreary Friday morning. Because the university had denied her room and board in a campus dormitory on the grounds that housing her would exacerbate racial tensions, she was forced to commute from Birmingham, sixty miles away, where she was living with her sister Ethel and her husband in a smart, white-painted duplex. Wearing a fashionable orange dress, a raincoat and a hat, Lucy arrived at Eugene A. Smith Hall just after 9 a.m. for an introductory lecture in geography and geology. Sitting alone in the middle of the front row, she did not notice the student who walked out in protest at her presence. At her second class, an introduction to children's literature, a couple of girls took seats next to her and later, in the bookstore, she received messages of luck and support. In her afternoon class on political science, she was particularly intrigued by the performance of Professor Charles Farris, who delivered the lecture while sitting cross-legged on the desk and smoking a cigarette.[28] Aside from some 'yowling and parading' from a small group of male students, it had all passed off relatively peacefully.[29] However, late the next night, 4 February, while Lucy was fast asleep back in Birmingham following a second, incident-free day at the university, a thousand people attended a demonstration on campus at which a cross was burned, before marching downtown, shouting, 'Keep 'Bama white! To hell with Autherine!'[30]

One of the leaders of the protest was a nineteen-year-old second-year student called Leonard Wilson. Intense and serious, Wilson was a committed white supremacist who, during his final year of high school, had argued for sending Alabama's black citizens to Africa. Now, addressing the crowd from the base of the city's flagpole, which had been erected to honour Tuscaloosa's war dead, he made a number of monkey jokes before delivering a defiant speech in favour of segregation. He ended by urging demonstrators to assemble on the Monday morning in order to protest against Lucy's attendance at the university.[31]

Monday 6 February was to be a 'day of fury and violence'.[32] After eating breakfast, Lucy, who had received assurances that the recent disturbances were little more than inebriated college students blowing off steam, was picked up at about seven thirty by a black businessman, Henry Nathaniel Guinn, for the drive to Tuscaloosa. Even at the best of times Lucy was not particularly talkative, but today the journey in Guinn's Cadillac was made in silence.[33] Arriving on campus, Lucy noticed that the atmosphere was 'strangely quiet'. As the car approached Smith Hall, an imposing yellow-brick building at the north-east corner of the quadrangle, the crowd of angry-looking students waiting outside seemed distracted. Indeed, they did not notice Lucy until she reached the top of the steps that led to the front entrance. At this point, the tension built precipitously and within minutes she could hear cries of 'Lynch the nigger!' Realising the potential danger she now faced, Lucy became extremely nervous. When the class ended, Sarah Healy, the university's Dean of Women, suggested that they leave by the rear entrance to try and avoid the attentions of the hostile mob – which, swelled by workers from the nearby rubber plant, now numbered three thousand. However, Lucy and Healy, along with another official and several plainclothes police officers, were met with a 'barrage of rocks, eggs, mud balls and curses' and, as Lucy was bundled into a waiting car, several people were hit. A further volley of stones cracked the windscreen and several windows. Lucy was by now overcome by terror.

On arriving outside Graves Hall for her next class, Lucy's car came under attack once again. A large rock shattered the rear window and, as she got out, Lucy was hit on her left arm and an egg splattered on her pretty green coat. From inside the building, she could hear the frightening rhythmic chants of 'Kill her, seize her, kill her, seize her, burn her, lynch her!' Eventually, shortly after 1 p.m., she was spirited away from campus, thankful to be alive.[34]

Late that night, the university announced that its Board of Trustees had agreed unanimously that, for her own safety 'and for the safety of other students and of faculty members', Lucy was to be suspended from classes temporarily.[35] Although she called for swift reinstatement 'to prove that violence does not rule', Lucy was not permitted to resume her studies. With racial moderates reluctant to speak up for desegregation, and with O. C. Carmichael, the university's president, failing to offer clear leadership, the hardliners on the board took control. After a federal court ordered her readmission on 29 February, the trustees expelled Lucy permanently on the grounds that she had made 'baseless, outrageous, and unfounded charges' against university officials. (A lawsuit filed on 10 February, later withdrawn, had accused the trustees of having 'intentionally permitted' the riot as a subterfuge for excluding her.)[36]

The NAACP was bewildered by the dramatic turn of events. As Roy Wilkins explained, 'since 1950 more than 2,000 Negro students have been enrolled in previously all-white southern universities and colleges without incident' and the 'procedure at Alabama was no different than . . . elsewhere'.[37] But the surprise did not hide their anger. The president of one local branch claimed that 'organized terrorism' was now 'casting its dark spectre' over the entire nation, and Wilkins described the university's 'surrender' to the mob as a 'disgrace'.[38] He also blamed the riot on the emerging Massive Resistance campaign, arguing that 'the continued preaching of defiance of law by the highest public officials' had 'created a climate in which hoodlums commit violence'.[39]

Many Americans shared the NAACP's outrage. Labour activists, religious leaders and college students joined with liberal politicians, editorial writers and ordinary citizens to express their horror at what had transpired.[40] One New Yorker spoke for many when, in a letter to President Eisenhower, he condemned the 'open violence of the Ku Klux [Klan] elements' that 'should shock every decent, democratic-minded American'. Such 'open defiance' of the law would, he argued, 'only encourage these racist elements to increase their terror . . . in the future'.[41] Some white southerners, too, stood against the mob. From its editorial page, the *Tuscaloosa News* condemned the trustees for their 'abject surrender', while the university's Student Government Association passed a resolution condemning the violence. Five hundred students (from a total enrolment of seven thousand) signed a petition calling for Lucy's reinstatement.[42]

The Cold War loomed large over the Autherine Lucy affair. In the aftermath of the Second World War, with arguments rooted

in scientific racism discredited by the Holocaust, southern segregationists had, along with their counterparts in South Africa,
turned to anti-Communism as a more respectable and effective
means of justifying the racial status quo. White southerners frequently pointed to the American Communist Party's support for
racial equality, and the involvement of individual Communists or
Communist sympathisers in civil rights activity, as proof that the
black freedom struggle was part of a 'red' conspiracy. Segregationists argued that demands for African American equality were part
of a systematic programme to destroy America. The fomenting of
racial animosity and social tension would, they claimed, destabilise
the nation and render it 'ripe for revolutionary changes'. Defending Jim Crow was thus framed as a necessary counterpart to the
effort to contain Communism abroad. It was, then, predictable
that segregationists blamed the Soviet Union and her allies for the
disturbances at the University of Alabama. In an article published
on 14 March, for example, the *Tuscaloosa News* pointed out that
'the trouble on the University of Alabama campus is the kind of
thing Communists can use, and do use, to help themselves all over
the world', while the Citizens' Council newspaper proclaimed that
'The Comrades Love Lucy'.[43] Nevertheless, even as southern segregationists accused the NAACP of being, at best, an unwitting ally
of the Communists and fumed that Lucy was a paid plant – or
perhaps even a dupe of the East German security services – civil
rights supporters and their liberal allies voiced their own Cold War
concerns.[44]

At a moment in history when the United States, as the leader
of the 'free world', was seeking to win over the hearts and minds
of newly emerging nations in Africa and Asia, high-profile incidents of racial violence threatened its credibility. A central concern
among many of those liberal politicians and editorial writers who
deplored the outbreak of violence in Tuscaloosa was the damage
that the episode might inflict on American prestige overseas. They

were right to be worried: the Autherine Lucy case became an 'international cause célèbre'. Radio Moscow 'seized on' the incident with glee as evidence of American hypocrisy, and the riot generated prominent and critical newspaper coverage across Europe, as well as in Latin America, Egypt, Nigeria and India – where one newspaper claimed that American race relations were 'even worse than in the Union of South Africa'.[45]

For the South African government itself, the crisis held out a distant hope that the United States might adopt a 'less doctrinaire approach' when it came to the difficulties of 'other multi-racial societies', but in the short term it shared in the concern – widespread among many US allies – that racial difficulties might undermine the United States's international leadership.[46] Opponents of apartheid drew a rather different lesson. The ANC's Alfred Hutchinson wrote as a 'comrade-in-arms' to Lucy, saluting her courage, pledging solidarity and claiming that she had 'dealt a blow to the monster of racism and advanced the struggle of freedom by yet another step'. 'Everywhere', Hutchinson said, 'the fires of freedom are alight', 'new suns are rising and . . . our dawn cannot be far away'.[47]

Understandably, civil rights leaders sought to turn Cold War concerns to their advantage. Lucy herself hit back at segregationists' allegations that she had, in some way, aided America's enemies. In a message that was broadcast around the world by the US government's official radio station, Voice of America, she explained that throughout her long struggle to gain admittance to the University of Alabama she had conducted herself 'in the American spirit'.[48] The mob, plainly, had not. Speaking from Montgomery, meanwhile, Martin Luther King declared that until 'we in the South . . . respect the laws, the finer law of the land, we will never have the type of democracy that will make our nation the leader of the free world'.[49]

Those hoping that strong executive leadership, at either the state or federal level, might resolve the crisis would be left frustrated.

Alabama's governor, 'Big' Jim Folsom, sat out the crisis in Florida on a drinking and fishing excursion. Although he had enjoyed a reputation as a racial moderate, Folsom – under growing pressure from hardline segregationists – rebuffed calls to use state troopers to enforce desegregation: it was, he said, 'normal for all races not to be overly fond of each other'.[50] President Eisenhower also refused to intervene. Born in Texas and raised in a small segregated town in Kansas, the president had some sympathy with white southerners. He privately remarked that opponents of the *Brown* decision were 'not bad people. All they are concerned about is to see that their sweet little white girls are not required to sit . . . alongside some big overgrown Negroes.' Although personally uncomfortable when it came to questions of race, Eisenhower was committed to a society where 'every person [would be] judged and measured by what he is, rather than by his color, race or religion'. But he counselled a patient and gradualist approach to achieving this goal, arguing that 'the fellow who tries to tell me that you can do these things by *force* is just plain *nuts*'.[51]

Eisenhower's approach was also shaped by his strong conviction that the government's room for manoeuvre was heavily circum-scribed by America's federal system. While, in his press conference of 8 February, he described the riot as 'an outbreak that all of us deplore', the president expressed his hope that 'we could avoid any interference with anybody else as long as that State, from its governor on down, will do its best to straighten it out'.[52] The White House was clear that 'the problem at the University of Alabama is not within the jurisdiction of the federal government' and that, as a consequence, any intervention would be 'interpreted as a violation of the constitutional rights of the individual states'.[53] Accordingly, Eisenhower was content to leave the matter to Alabama's political leaders, university officials and the federal courts to resolve. With legal efforts to overturn Lucy's expulsion ending in failure, the university was ultimately able to maintain an all-white student body until 1963. There was no doubt that the segregationists had claimed a significant victory in Tuscaloosa, and their success would inspire further, bitter fights over school desegregation later in the year. But they would not always prevail. As events in Montgomery revealed, their uncompromising approach could be counterproductive.

The bombing of Martin Luther King's house on 30 January, and the home of the labour organiser and veteran NAACP activist E. D. Nixon two days later, had come amidst a 'get tough' campaign by the city's leaders. Frustrated by the failure of negotiations to end the boycott, and angered and embarrassed when an attempt to cut a deal with three non-MIA ministers unravelled publicly, Mayor W. A. Gayle adopted an inflexible stance. On 23 January, in remarks that were broadcast on local television, he declared that 'we have pussyfooted around on this boycott long enough and it is time to be frank and honest . . . The Negro leaders have proved that they are not interested in ending the boycott but rather in prolonging it so that they may stir up racial strife.' According to Gayle, the real issue facing white Montgomery was not a narrowly focused question of seating practices on the city's buses, but 'whether the social fabric of our community' would endure or 'be destroyed by a group of Negro radicals who have split asunder the fine relationships which have existed between the Negro and white people for generations'. Announcing defiantly that 'the white people are firm in their convictions that they do not care whether the Negroes ever ride a city bus again', Gayle declared that until the MIA was ready to end its boycott there would be no further discussions.[54] The following day Gayle and his fellow commissioner Frank Parks announced that, like their colleague Clyde Sellers, they had joined the White Citizens' Council.[55]

One of the first targets of the 'get tough' policy was the MIA's car pool. The system, which provided African Americans with transport to and from their places of work, was vital to the boycott's continued success. Involving a highly sophisticated pick-up and drop-off schedule that was maintained by a group of talented administrators, and backed up by a major fundraising effort to help cover insurance premiums and the costs of fuel and repairs, it relied on dozens of drivers (and their vehicles). It was, in sum, a terrific example of black Montgomery's ingenuity and organisational capability. During the last week of January, police officers had begun to arrest African Americans who were waiting at designated pick-up points across the city and charge them with 'loitering'. Volunteer drivers were also singled out – stopped and questioned about their licences, their insurance coverage and their places of work; many were given tickets for alleged traffic violations. Under such pressure, some dropped out quietly, while the MIA had to make repeated assurances to the others that it would provide them with legal, financial and moral support.[56]

A Citizens' Council rally, held at Montgomery's Coliseum on the evening of 10 February, provided a focus for hardening white opinion. According to the *New York Times*, some 'ten thousand stamping, cheering Alabamians' jammed into the auditorium, 'waving Confederate flags and rising to cheer whenever the band broke into "Dixie"', the de facto national anthem of the South. The atmosphere was more akin to an evangelical revival than a political meeting. Sam Englehardt, a state senator and leader of the Central Alabama Citizens' Council, opened the rally by declaring that 'segregation is an institution of the South we don't intend to see scrapped', while Senator James Eastland of Mississippi called for whites to establish a united front to avoid being 'crushed'. Meanwhile Police Commissioner Clyde Sellers's suggestion that any African American desiring desegregation should 'go where there is desegregation' drew widespread support from the crowd, who began chanting 'Let him go, let him go.' Sellers ended his address with a defiant shout: 'Let our battle cry be states' rights and white supremacy.'[57]

At the rally – which drew people from every walk of life – a handbill was circulated which declared that 'when in the course of human events it becomes necessary to abolish the Negro race, proper methods should be used. Among these are guns, bows and arrows, sling shots, and knives.' The flyer went on to claim that in every stage of the bus boycott white citizens had been 'oppressed and degraded because of black, slimy, juicy, unbearably stinking niggers' and warn that 'if we don't stop helping the African flesh eaters, we will soon wake up and find Reverend King in the White House'.[58] There is no evidence that this notorious document was in any way sanctioned by the Citizens' Council, and doubtless many thousands of Montgomery's whites were appalled when they read about its contents in the pages of the *Montgomery Advertiser*. Although an extreme example, the fact that the flyer was distributed at all at such a public meeting gives a flavour of the increasingly hostile racial climate.[59] Within weeks of the boycott beginning, membership of the local Citizens' Council had mushroomed to fifteen thousand.[60]

While the organisation was committed to purely legal and peaceful tactics, there is little doubt that its defiant rhetoric and uncompromising support for white supremacy inflamed racial tensions.[61] Jo Ann Robinson, one of Montgomery's most prominent black leaders, noticed that after the 'get tough' policy was launched, 'whites began staring at Negroes as they passed by in crowded cars. Some would harass blacks who walked along the streets', with cries of 'Walk, nigger, walk.' Rotten fruit, eggs, and balloons filled with water, or even urine, were thrown at black pedestrians.[62] The ugly mood was captured by one elderly citizen: 'I have heard the word "nigger" used more in the last 11 weeks than in my whole life.'[63]

In mid-February, the city turned to the courts to break the boycott. The first target was the talented young black attorney Fred D. Gray, who had studied law at Case Western Reserve University in Cleveland, Ohio, before returning to his native Montgomery, where he soon became active in the burgeoning civil rights revolution. A member of the NAACP and an ordained minister, Gray served as chief counsel to the MIA.[64] On 8 February, it was announced that Gray's draft status had been raised to 1-A (available for unrestricted military service), after the summary withdrawal of his ministerial deferment. Ten days later, he was indicted by a grand jury on a trumped-up charge of having failed to obtain the consent of a plaintiff in a lawsuit. If convicted, he faced being disbarred.[65] Then, on Tuesday 21 February, around a hundred MIA activists (including about two dozen ministers) were indicted under a hitherto obscure state anti-boycott law that carried a punishment of up to six months in prison and a fine of $1,000. In their written report, the grand jurors blamed the NAACP for stirring up 'distrust, dislike and hatred' in Montgomery. 'We are committed to segregation by custom and by law', they stated, and 'we intend to maintain it'.[66]

But those white segregationists who were expecting that the steady stream of intimidation, harassment and outright violence would undermine or even break the boycott were to be proved wrong. As Martin Luther King told his supporters at the end of January, the 'get tough' policy of the city fathers would fail because 'a man's language is courage when his back is against the wall'.[67] Rather than cower before the forces of Massive Resistance, Montgomery's black citizens responded with bravery and determination; indeed, they appear to have drawn considerable strength from their opponents' hostility. Rufus Lewis, the head of the MIA transportation committee, noticed that when King's house was bombed, the entire black community reacted 'as though *their* house was bombed'. While the attack was intended to intimidate, it had the opposite effect: 'It roused the Negroes in the community to stand up, not to run and hide.'[68] It also helped convince the MIA to launch a direct assault on segregation, rather than continue to find a compromise. Accordingly, on 1 February, Fred Gray filed suit in federal court asking that the bus segregation law be declared unconstitutional.[69]

Given her key role in the initiation of the boycott and the subsequent day-to-day running of the car pool, Jo Ann Robinson was an obvious target for segregationists. The harassment began with a series of traffic tickets; next came the menacing phone calls. By the time that a brick had been thrown through her picture window, Robinson feared for her safety. Then, one evening, she heard a disturbance outside, in the vicinity of the carport where her brand new Chrysler was parked. When she peered out of the window, Robinson caught sight of two police officers. The next morning she discovered that her car had been 'eaten up with acid. I had holes as large as a dollar, all over the top of the car, all over the hood and the side of the car.' Robinson was reduced to tears, but soon turned her ordeal into a source of pride: 'I said, "Well, you know, these are beautiful spots." Everyone wanted to know what ate that car up, and I had pleasure in saying, "Well, the *police* threw the acid on it and burned it up, but it became beauty spots."'[70]

The mass indictment of the MIA's leaders proved to be a catastrophic error of judgement on the part of the segregationists. Not least, it generated widespread publicity for the protest (for the first time, the *New York Times* published a front-page story about the boycott, and ABC television provided prominent coverage). Messages of support and financial contributions poured in from around the country, many from religious groups angered by the targeting of Montgomery's black ministers.[71] Ultimately, by turning the leaders into martyrs, the mass indictment actually helped unify the black population.[72] On 22 February the MIA staged a rally outside the county courthouse as many of those who had been indicted arrived, voluntarily, wearing their Sunday best or clerical collars. The atmosphere was akin to that of a public holiday as the smiling indictees 'laughed and joked' and 'slapped each other on the back'. It was even said that some MIA activists were upset to discover that they had not been deemed important enough to be indicted.[73] Given the very real dangers that a southern jail held for black Americans, these were truly remarkable scenes. According to one observer, while Montgomery's whites were astounded by the show of defiance, the city's black population was thrilled.[74] The following afternoon, African Americans began gathering at the First Baptist Church, singing hymns and reciting prayers, in advance of a mass meeting. At 7 p.m., with the emotional crowd on the verge of pandemonium, the indicted leaders made their way to the front of the church, roared on by about five thousand men, women and children, some of the women even holding out their babies to touch the leaders as they passed by.[75] As Martin Luther King put it, a once fearful people had been transformed: 'Those who had previously trembled before the law were now proud to be arrested for the cause of freedom.'[76]

The extraordinary impact of the mass indictment was still visible a week later. During a mass meeting at the Holt Street Baptist Church a succession of ministers took to the platform to declare that they were not afraid to go to jail, and that the boycott must continue. As one preacher told the cheering crowd: 'we are no longer afraid no matter what the enemy might do . . . We are only concerned about making a contribution that the world will always remember.'[77] Another declared that arresting the leaders would not end the boycott, because 'This is your movement . . . you are the leaders.' As King himself proclaimed: 'We have a new zeal, [a] new stamina to carry on.' Explaining that the protest had now reached far beyond Montgomery, he told the crowd that men and women across the nation were 'saying one thing – "You've gone too far; you can't turn back now."'[78]

II SPRING

A YEARNING FOR FREEDOM

THE LINE

5

THE LONG WALK

The attack on Stalin has produced disbelief, uncertainty, confusion, embarrassment, and anger.
US INTELLIGENCE REPORT, 30 March 1956

On 25 April 1956 Harper & Bros, the prestigious New York publishing house, released *The Long Walk*, the purportedly true story of an audacious escape from the Soviet Gulag.[1] The book was written by Slavomir Rawicz, a former Polish army officer who, in November 1939, had been captured by the Russians and accused of espionage. After a harsh interrogation by the secret police and an obligatory show trial, he had been sentenced to twenty-five years' forced labour. In his memoir, Rawicz provided a detailed description of the horrors of the Soviet police state, including the brutal beatings and torture that he had experienced: on one occasion, molten tar was poured onto his hand in an attempt to extract a confession; on another, for two days guards took turns to tap the same spot on the crown of his head every two seconds. Rawicz was also forced to endure six months in the *kishka* (which translates as 'the intestine' or 'the gut'):

> A chimney-like cell into which one stepped down about a foot below the level of the corridor outside. Inside a man could stand and no more. The walls pressed round like a stone coffin. Twenty feet above there was the diffused light from some small, out-of-sight window . . . we excreted standing up and stood in our own filth. The *kishka* was never cleaned.[2]

After an evocative account of life in a Siberian labour camp, Rawicz described how, in April 1941, he and six companions made their daring break for freedom. Having successfully tunnelled under the wire fence of Camp 303, near Yakutsk (about four hundred miles south of the Arctic Circle), the escapees spent almost a year walking four thousand miles before reaching the safety of British India. Their journey took them through some of the most demanding and inhospitable terrain imaginable, including the blistering heat of the Gobi desert and the treacherous mountain passes of the Himalayas.[3] Three of the party never made it. Rawicz's remarkable book was one of the publishing sensations of the year. Writing in the *Manchester Guardian*, R. L. West declared: 'I have read no modern tale of adventure that can compare with this, either for excitement or for the inspiration of its dogged heroism.'[4] Meanwhile, the *New York Times* described Rawicz as a man 'with something of a poet's sensibility – but . . . a poet with steel in his soul'.[5] *The Long Walk* was not just a terrific read. Its meditation on the horrors of Stalinist oppression and emphasis on man's innate yearning for freedom gave it a powerful contemporary resonance – particularly in light of developments in Eastern Europe, where, in the aftermath of Khrushchev's 'secret speech', an oppressed citizenry sought to push back against the constraints on their own liberty.

On 22 March Allen Dulles, the director of the CIA, told a meeting of President Eisenhower's National Security Council that Khrushchev's denunciation of Stalin posed a particular problem for Communists in Eastern Europe. 'What', he asked, 'would the leadership in the satellite states now do?' – since, as he pointed out, 'These men were almost all the creatures of Stalin.'[6] Dulles's question was a pertinent one. Not only did the Communist regimes in places like East Germany, Poland and Hungary owe their very existence to the USSR (which had furnished them with critical military and political support after 'liberation' by the Red Army during 1944–5), their leaders had demonstrated tremendous personal loyalty to Stalin. Moreover, in order to solidify Communist rule they had embraced Stalinist methods – including agricultural collectivisation, the nationalisation of businesses, factories, mines and banks, a relentless focus on rapid industrialisation, central planning, press censorship, attacks on the church and civil society, the purging of rivals and the use of police terror. A number, including Poland's Bolesław Bierut and Hungary's Mátyás Rákosi, had even developed their own personality cults that aped that of the Soviet dictator. In the two weeks leading up to Rákosi's sixtieth birthday in 1951, for example, half a million Hungarians attended special evening classes to study the heroic life of their leader, while a similar number participated in public meetings or reading groups dedicated to the same theme. Meanwhile, the walls of Hungary's classrooms, shops, factories, offices, public buildings, libraries, cinemas and hospitals were adorned with portraits of 'the people's wise father'.[7]

As news of the 'secret speech' began to filter out across the Eastern Bloc, Party activists, workers, students and others responded by seeking more information, asking probing questions and – tentatively at first – demanding change. At the Štětí paper mill in Czechoslovakia, for instance, Party activists 'wanted to know why the facts were only disclosed now', three years after the dictator's death (they were told that it had taken this long 'to "investigate" the case of Comrade Stalin').[8] At the large Skoda plant in Pilsen, a Party official was unable to respond to workers' demands that he 'comment and explain the debunking of Stalin', only promising that they would receive answers 'after two weeks or so . . .'.[9] In Hungary, meanwhile, many citizens praised the 'condemnation of Stalin', while others seized on the chance to 'sneer at Communism and the Communists'.[10] It was in Poland, though, where the full force of the speech was felt most immediately.[11]

Poland's Bolesław Bierut, one of Europe's 'little Stalins', was – literally – finished off by the 'secret speech', which was read to him as he lay in a Moscow hospital, having been taken ill with pneumonia during the Twentieth Party Congress. The shock of Khrushchev's denunciations caused a heart attack, from which the

Polish leader never recovered; he finally succumbed on 12 March.[12] His successor, Edward Ochab, described Khrushchev's speech as 'like being hit over the head with a hammer', but he believed that the Polish leadership 'had no right to conceal what had happened at the Twentieth Congress' or try to 'pass over' Stalin's crimes in 'deathly silence'. Although aware that 'complications would inevitably ensue', he judged it better to 'tell the bitter truth the way we saw it' and hope that, after the Party and society had come to terms with the shock, they would 'emerge into clear waters'.[13] Ochab and some of his more liberal-minded colleagues also viewed Khrushchev's demolition of Stalin and Bierut's death as a golden opportunity to burnish their own reformist credentials, and thereby renew public support for the Party.[14]

On 21 March, the leadership of the Polish United Workers' Party (PZPR) launched a mass campaign to familiarise the party *aktyw* (activists) with Khrushchev's speech, distributing fifteen thousand copies of a Polish translation of the text.[15] During late March and April thousands of meetings took place across the country, which were open to non-Party members as well, to enable the speech to be read out and discussed. At these gatherings, which often lasted for several hours, Poles expressed their confusion and doubts.[16] For many, the 'demolition' of Stalin's image and reputation was a major shock. As one previously loyal Polish Communist put it: 'I feel lost and betrayed; I believed in Stalin for so many years. I am in despair, for we have been turned into idiots and dummies. It turns out that everything that happened before was wrong and false. I no longer believe anything.'[17]

For others, open discussion of the 'secret speech' presented an opportunity to ask pointed questions and engage in vigorous debate.[18] At a 'heated' meeting at the Szczecin Technical University on 26 March, for instance, Party activists demanded a 'guarantee against a reversion to Stalinist methods' and criticised Soviet control of the Polish armed forces (the defence minister, Konstantin

Rokossovsky, was a marshal of the Soviet Union). When activists began to question the legitimacy of Poland's own Communist leadership, the meeting quickly spun 'out of control'. It eventually broke up at 2 a.m. Workers at the Gdańsk shipyard, meanwhile, poured scorn on Khrushchev's explanation that Stalin had acted alone, asking, 'How was he able to decide everything? Where were other members of the Politburo?' Others voiced nationalist concerns by describing the PZPR's heavy reliance on Moscow as a violation of Poland's sovereignty.[19] The prime minister, Józef Cyrankiewicz, even found himself heckled at a meeting of Polish architects.[20] Alarmed by the scale of dissent, the Central Committee restricted access to the full text of Khrushchev's speech to Party functionaries, but by then it was too late. Unofficial copies changed hands on the black market for significant sums.[21] As one young Pole put it, 'The people have regained confidence and are not afraid to speak up to the authorities when they think that they are right.'[22]

Throughout the spring Poland was consumed by what British diplomats characterised as an 'orgy of public criticism'.[23] Nowhere was this more evident than in the press (Polish newspapers were viewed as so subversive that the authorities in Hungary and Czechoslovakia quickly banned them).[24] Articles appeared criticising the secret police and condemning the 'distortions' of Stalinism that had 'demoralised' and 'humiliated' the people. There was also open discussion of the persecution of those who had served in the Armia Krajowa (Home Army), which had led Polish resistance to the Nazi occupation and had subsequently been denounced by the Communists.[25] As the spring wore on, bold demands for reforms to the entire political and economic system came to the fore. For example, in the 15 April edition of *Po prostu* ('Frankly Speaking'*) – a leading weekly for 'students and young intelligentsia', with a

---

* *Po prostu* is hard to translate literally: 'Saying it Straight' or 'Saying it Simply' are good alternatives.

print run of 150,000 – Jerzy Urban argued for a much greater role for 'the people'. 'The dictatorship of the proletariat', he explained, 'does not exist when it is ruled by professional functionaries in the name of the proletariat. The people's democracy does not exist without actual rule by the people . . .' Other writers complained that in Poland, rather than the people's rule, there had instead been a 'dictatorship of the bureaucracy', or a 'dictatorship over the proletariat'.[26]

There was evidence of dissent elsewhere, too. During the May Day parade in Łódź, some students held aloft banners proclaiming 'Down with tyrants!' and 'Down with despots!' Later that month, during the annual student festival in Kraków, hundreds marched through the streets, demanding changes to the constitution. Tram windows were smashed, and some students even attempted to break into the radio station in an effort to broadcast jazz music.[27] Across Poland, discussion clubs, theatre groups and satirical reviews blossomed, and writers and artists spoke out.[28] Jan Kott, a leading theatre critic and intellectual, lamented the fact that 'whenever the facts stood in the way, the facts were changed. If genuine heroes were obstacles, they evaporated', while the poet Antoni Słonimski charged Communist apparatchiks with having 'warped' the nation's cultural life by zealously imposing the Party line on all forms of art.[29]

At the secret police headquarters in Warsaw, reports started to trickle in that citizens were refusing to pass on information, and even previously reliable informants would no longer co-operate. Some Poles were expressing their hostility openly. With the security services subject to harsh criticism for their abuse of power (including torture, fabrication and the imprisonment of thousands of innocent people), and undermined by the amnesty granted to thousands of political prisoners, morale plummeted.[30] One young Pole, a technician from a small town in the south of the country, gloated that the security officers were 'going around as if they were castrated'.[31] From the Party rank and file, meanwhile, came demands for greater transparency and democratic elections for all Party posts, and, despite the PZPR's sustained campaign to marginalise the Catholic Church, thousands of devout Poles took advantage of the more relaxed atmosphere to celebrate holy days, press for religious freedoms and display Christian symbols openly.[32]

As peasants vented their frustration with agricultural co-operatives, collective farms and harsh production quotas, a dangerous combination of coal shortages, discontent over living standards and low wages fed discontent among Poland's industrial workers. The Central Committee reported that there was 'much bitterness' and 'cursing of the people's government', with many blaming the Party for their predicament.[33] Workers also used the official criticism of the 'cult of personality' as a way of challenging factory officials, who were accused of aloofness, dictatorial behaviour and rank incompetence.[34] The difficulties faced by ordinary Poles were exacerbated by the existence of so-called 'yellow curtain' shops: reserved for senior Party, military and security officials, they contained goods that most citizens could only dream about. In this more liberal climate, tram passengers were overheard making quips about 'shops for the cult of personality', or making highly charged comparisons with the 'Meinl' stores that, during the Nazi occupation, had been 'for Germans only'.[35] That April, *Po prostu* carried a sharply satirical article that described a woman, dressed in a mink coat, exiting a military car to purchase goods from a shop that was 'stuffed with meat and other luxuries' as, across the street, a crowd of women were forced to queue in the bitter cold outside a municipal shop, whose shelves were virtually bare.[36]

For many Poles, their hopes of a better future – within a reformed and genuinely Polish version of socialism – came to centre on the figure of Władysław Gomułka, the former general secretary of the PZPR. Gomułka had been demoted in 1948 and, three years later, arrested and imprisoned on charges of 'rightist-nationalist' deviation. A supporter of Tito, Gomułka had broken further with Stalinist orthodoxy by urging the encouragement of private industrial enterprise and opposing agricultural collectivisation. Although he had been released from prison at the end of 1954, this was only made public in April 1956 (though it had, apparently, been common knowledge for many months).[37] But while Ochab announced that Gomułka's conviction for espionage and subversion had been a product of an 'atmosphere of espionage mania', he maintained that his expulsion from the Party had been justified due to his embrace of 'false ideological conceptions'.[38] Nevertheless, calls for Gomułka's full rehabilitation, and even his return to power, would prove unstoppable. As an anonymous letter, mailed to *Trybuna Ludu* ('The People's Tribune'), put it:

> The nation does not want Bolshevism, it doesn't want the Sovietisation . . . of Poland. We want to walk on our own Polish road . . . Comrade Wiesław [Gomułka] must be rehabilitated and paid the honour and respect he is owed . . . Down with Bolshevism and Moscow! Long live an independent and truly people's Poland.[39]

The reaction to the 'secret speech' elsewhere in Eastern Europe was, for the time being at least, rather less dramatic. Walter Ulbricht faced relatively little opposition in East Germany, where (until the construction of the Berlin Wall in August 1961) critics of the regime were able to flee to the West – 316,000 did so in 1956 – and where the failed workers' uprising of June 1953 served as a powerful deterrent; Soviet tanks had brutally crushed the million-strong revolt.[40] Elsewhere, though, there was plenty of confusion, anger and uncertainty, as well as outright opposition to the Communist authorities.[41] On 16 April Bulgaria's 'little Stalin', Vulko Chervenkov, tendered his resignation as prime minister. Just ten days before he had been censured for having encouraged his own 'cult of personality'. Although he had tried to remain in office,

Moscow, eager to improve its relations with Yugoslavia, withdrew its support for a man who had been one of Tito's fiercest critics (they also ensured that a Yugoslav delegation was in Sofia to witness Chervenkov's humiliation first-hand).[42]

Meanwhile Hungary's Mátyás Rákosi, who had taken considerable pride in his sobriquet of 'Stalin's best pupil', was furious, warning the future Soviet leader Yuri Andropov, 'You shouldn't have hurried. What you have done at your Congress is a disaster, I don't know what will come of it, either in your country or in mine.'[43] On returning from Moscow, Rákosi prepared to ride out the storm. When briefing the Hungarian Central Committee about the Twentieth Party Congress, he chose to emphasis his own (newly discovered) enthusiasm for 'Leninist collective leadership', and passed quickly over Khrushchev's sustained critique of the 'cult of personality'.[44] The comrades duly passed a resolution which, while acknowledging that tweaks to economic policy might be required and that more could be done to 'democratise' the Party, affirmed that their overall approach was fundamentally 'correct'.[45] They also made a point of condemning the 'right-wing distortions' that, they claimed, had been introduced during Imre Nagy's short-lived premiership (from June 1953 to April 1955). During this period, as part of the so-called 'New Course', Nagy had attempted to switch the emphasis away from rapid industrialisation and onto living standards, announced an end to the forced collectivisation of agriculture and encouraged a more liberal approach to cultural and press freedoms.[46] Rákosi also attempted to keep news of the 'secret speech' from the Hungarian people. When details began to leak out (through the press, the radio and word of mouth), he sanctioned the publication of a heavily redacted edition, widely ridiculed on the street as a 'children's version'.[47] None of this prevented Party organisations from being inundated with requests to implement the new line from Moscow, as well as complaints about living standards, bureaucracy and press censorship.[48]

On 28 March, during a Party meeting in the northern city of Eger, Rákosi – under mounting pressure – announced the posthumous rehabilitation of László Rajk, the former interior minister. Rajk, who had helped found the Államvédelmi Osztálya (ÁVO, later reorganised as the ÁVH), Hungary's secret police, had been one of Rákosi's most powerful rivals. In October 1949 he was executed, following a brutal interrogation and show trial, as an imperialist, a Titoist spy and an enemy of socialism. Now, Rákosi explained, it had become clear that these charges had been fabricated. In a move that cost him the support of senior security officers, he sought to pin the blame on Gábor Péter, the former chief of the secret police.[49] Rákosi's personal authority continued to drain away. On 30 March, at a meeting of the Writers' Association, one young literary critic accused the Hungarian leader of being a 'Judas whose hands are stained with blood'.[50] Just a few days earlier, at a meeting of Party activists in Budapest's Thirteenth District, György Litván, a twenty-seven-year-old history teacher, turned to the platform where Rákosi was sitting and told him directly: 'Comrade Rákosi, the Hungarian people no longer trust you.' That Litván was not arrested, never mind thrown in jail or even hanged, spoke volumes.[51] Indeed, many ordinary Hungarians were openly disparaging their once-feared leader as 'the bald-headed murderer'.[52] On 18 May, in a speech in Budapest, Rákosi was forced to admit to past mistakes, and accepted some culpability for Rajk's execution. But he continued to warn against 'rightist views', and sought to blame recent dissent on domestic reactionaries, internal enemies and Western propaganda.[53] With many of his own Party activists now calling openly for 'the trial of the assassins', he appeared to be fighting a losing battle.[54]

Two days after Rákosi's partial atonement, the Majáles – a student carnival celebrating the arrival of spring – was staged in Prague for the first time since 1948. The Czechoslovak Union of Youth (CSM), a Communist organisation, had been pushing hard for the festival's reinstatement as part of an effort to boost their own credibility with students, and the authorities eventually relented. That afternoon, under cloudy skies, the city's population lined the two-mile parade route to cheer some five thousand students and admire the colourful floats. The parade, led by its 'King' and 'Queen', set off from the Old Town Square just after 1 p.m. Many of those taking part had donned fancy dress and masks and were carrying placards and banners. They headed down Pařížská Street, Prague's most fashionable boulevard, before making their way past the Dvořák Embankment, on the right bank of the Vltava River. As the students headed over the beautiful Čechův Bridge, with its Art Nouveau styling, a giant, seventeen-thousand-tonne marble monument to Stalin – which had been unveiled just a year earlier – loomed ominously over them. Once on the left bank of the river, the parade entered the Julius Fučík Park of Culture and Rest for a post-parade party.[55]

The Majáles, whose origins could be traced back to the Middle Ages, was traditionally used to send up professors, celebrate student life and carry out lighthearted pranks.[56] But this year it had a distinctly political edge. Sydney Gruson of the *New York Times* described how one group of students, wearing top hats and beautiful silks, marched behind a placard labelled 'The Theory'; they were followed by a second group, dressed in rags, who held aloft a banner reading 'The Practice'. The lack of press freedom was lampooned by a dozen or so 'gagged and blindfolded boys and girls', representing the editor and reporters of *Mladá Frontá*, the CSM's own newspaper.[57] A series of placards, meanwhile, provocatively referred to the show trials of 1952: 'What is better?' 'That the small criminals are hanged and the great ones go scot free?' 'Or that the great ones are hanged and the small ones take their place?'[58] There was also some barbed commentary on the new fashion for blaming all of Communism's woes on the 'cult of personality': one student, carrying a poster proclaiming 'Small cult', was followed by two shorter students who held posters that read 'Smaller cult' and 'Tiny cult'.[59] The students also shouted out slogans including: 'Nowadays we eat less than before, but we do it with more pleasure!' and 'Don't build students' dormitories, but build monuments for the glorification of personalities!' By all accounts the crowds seemed to lap up the anti-establishment mood: when a group of law students, loyal to the regime, passed by with a placard reading 'We thank the working class for having an opportunity to attend the university', it was widely presumed to be ironic, and drew laughter and sarcastic cheering.[60]

This very public display of dissent, while highly unusual, was not exactly unexpected. According to one observer, just a week earlier students in Bratislava had taken 'even more liberties'. Their Majáles parade had featured one group weighed down with chains, following behind a coffin labelled 'Academic freedom'; another contingent marched with a banner proclaiming: 'The principle stands firm, but the house tumbles down!' Most provocative of all, Soviet soldiers were ridiculed as ignorant drunkards.[61] Students had, in fact, been holding noisy meetings in universities across Czechoslovakia, venting their criticisms of living conditions, the quality of the curriculum and constraints on academic (and other) freedoms.[62] The most important of these gatherings took place on the evening of 26 April, when hundreds of students at Prague's Charles University attended a meeting of the local CSM chapter. The atmosphere inside the packed lecture hall was electric as, over the course of several hours, a series of resolutions were debated and then endorsed unanimously. Along with a call for comprehensive reforms to the education system and curriculum, the students demanded greater worker involvement in economic decision-making, insisted that Party organisations and leading officials be 'subject to full scrutiny and control from below', and urged that the National Assembly be made more accountable to the people. Calling for a climate in which discussion and criticism would be actively encouraged, the students also demanded greater press freedoms, access to foreign newspapers, an end to the jamming of foreign radio broadcasts, and the easing of travel restrictions. They also decried the continued existence of an official 'index' of prohibited books. Criticising the 'practice of mechanically adopting the Soviet experience' (which had, they asserted, caused 'great harm' to the country), they further requested that the 'Soviet national anthem and the Soviet flag be present only on occasions which directly involve the Soviet Union'. Perhaps most daring of all, the students directly attacked the regime and its leader, Antonín Novotný, the general secretary of the Communist Party of Czechoslovakia (KSČ): they disputed his insistence that the Central Committee was properly the ultimate source of authority, demanded a full and transparent investigation into the 1952 show trials and called for measures to guarantee that such gross violations of justice would 'not be repeated'.[63] A partial report of the meeting was published in *Mladá Fronta* on 28 April, and copies of the resolution were mailed to a range of newspapers, Party organisations and government ministers. In the absence of any official response, and after failing to persuade any newspaper to publish the resolution, some of the students took it upon themselves to spread the word; within days, similar resolutions were adopted at a number of universities, including in Ostrava and Plzeň.[64] The regime, though, stood firm. On 12 May the minister of education even told a student delegation that they should count themselves lucky not to have been beaten up by the police, and four days later motorised units were used to snuff out student protests in Bratislava.[65]

Faced with growing dissent not just from students, but also from writers, academics, artists, rank-and-file Party members and some workers, the leadership held fast.[66] Their resolve strengthened by the alarming reports emerging from Poland and Hungary, they sought to pin the blame for any internal discontent on 'enemy agents', 'criminals' and 'scum' who, they claimed, were being smuggled into Czechoslovakia from military bases in West Germany.[67] This uncompromising approach had been adopted in the immediate aftermath of Khrushchev's 'secret speech', which saw the leadership in Prague stress that the more liberal line from Moscow should not be taken too far. They had warned, for instance, that 'Our enemies would like to persuade us that with the lessening of international tension, peaceful co-existence should also find its expression in the field of ideology. They would like us to demobilise ideologically so that they could defeat us.'[68]

Novotný had also made it perfectly clear that the Central Committee's hold on power was not up for discussion: it 'decides and must decide the most important questions of the Party and state'.[69] This conservative line continued to be applied. At the KSČ's annual congress on 11 June, for instance, Novotný declared that the comrades' approach to building socialism did not need to be altered 'in any way', warned newspapers against flirting with 'incorrect ideas' and condemned student reactionaries.[70] In his own speech four days later, the Czechoslovak vice premier denounced student protestors for using 'anti-Stalinism' as cover for their efforts to undermine the Communist system: 'It begins with a demand for freedom of the press', he said, 'and ends with freedom for capitalism.'[71] Shortly after the congress had concluded, the education minister tightened the rules permitting children of the 'intelligentsia' and 'bourgeoisie' to attend universities: students from such backgrounds, he explained, were behind the 'most aggressive and most unjustified' of the recent 'provocations'.[72]

Amidst rumours of mass arrests and expulsions, and with the troublesome Charles University chapter of the CSM disbanded 'temporarily', the student rebellion had been subdued by the start of the summer holidays.[73] In proving more capable than their Polish and Hungarian counterparts at holding the line, Czechoslovakia's leaders benefited from the fact that Communism enjoyed a far greater degree of public support there than elsewhere in the

Soviet bloc (the KSČ had won 38 per cent of the popular vote in the free elections of 1946 – a contest in which the total vote for Socialist parties reached 69 per cent; in contrast, the Hungarian Communists had managed just 17 per cent). Czechoslovakians also enjoyed a higher standard of living than was the case in many of the other 'people's democracies'. Moreover, since he had come to power shortly after Stalin's death, Novotný was better able than many of his peers to claim that his leadership marked a genuine break from Stalinism.[74]

While it caused a series of crises for Communist parties in the West, outside of the Soviet bloc the repercussions of Khrushchev's 'secret speech' were felt most strongly in the People's Republic of China.[75] The Chinese had neither been consulted in advance of the speech nor invited to listen to it at the Twentieth Party Congress. Although China's leader, Mao Zedong, had had a number of run-ins with the Soviet dictator, he nevertheless viewed Khrushchev's denunciation of the 'cult of personality' as an attack on his own authority (reportedly, he never forgave Khrushchev for the assault on Stalin).[76] In the immediate aftermath of the 'secret speech', then, Mao sought to differentiate his own leadership style from that of Stalin. And in April, during a keynote speech, the founder of the People's Republic claimed that, while a certain level of discipline was necessary, if it was too rigid, 'initiative will be stifled'. Mao therefore called on the Chinese Communist Party to 'let a hundred flowers bloom and a hundred schools of thought contend'.[77] China appeared to be on the threshold of an exciting new era of cultural, intellectual and political reform.

6

RETREAT FROM EMPIRE

The old concepts of Empire, of conquest, domination and
exploitation are fast dying in an awakening world.
KWAME NKRUMAH

On 19 April 1956 the legislative assembly in Accra, the capital of
the Gold Coast, published detailed proposals for an end to British
rule in the West African colony. A new constitution would see
'supreme legislative power' vested in a national parliament, to be
elected every five years, with the government taking full responsibility for defence and foreign policy, in addition to internal affairs.[1]
Subject to a plebiscite, the new state would also incorporate British Togoland – thirteen thousand square miles of territory to the
east, which was administered by Britain under the auspices of the
UN.[2] The newly independent country would be known as Ghana:
a name that, by conjuring up the great medieval empire of western Africa, was intended to inspire a new generation of Africans
as they remade the continent in their own image.[3] A few weeks
later Alan Lennox-Boyd, the secretary of state for the colonies,
informed the House of Commons that 'If a general election is held
[in the Gold Coast], Her Majesty's Government will be ready to
accept a motion calling for independence . . . passed by a reason-
able majority in a newly elected Legislature, and then to declare a
firm date for this purpose.'[4]

In the years following the Second World War, the sun began to
set on an empire that, at its height, had covered a quarter of the
world's surface. With colonies, dependencies, protectorates and
self-governing dominions stretching across North America and the
Caribbean, the Pacific, the Mediterranean, Africa, Asia, the Far East

and Australasia, more than four hundred million people had lived under the Union Jack. Barely two decades after the defeat of Nazi Germany, it had virtually all been swept away – a remarkable development in world history, and one over which historians have puzzled ever since.[5] Economic forces certainly played a part. Britain's parlous position in 1945, for instance, resulted in policies designed to increase the supply of vital foodstuffs, raw materials and commodities from the colonies. This so-called 'second colonial occupation' inflamed (and helped to unify) local opposition to British rule and strained the fragile systems of colonial governance. Moreover, Britain's relative economic decline during the post-war era meant that the increasingly untenable burden of maintaining the empire, and the limited rewards of being associated with it, became ever more obvious.[6] At the international level, meanwhile, the superpower rivalry between the USA and the USSR (both of whom had ideological objections to colonialism) and the growing influence of the United Nations (whose Charter affirmed the principle of 'equal rights and self-determination') augured a new era in which formal empire became something of an international liability.[7] The British were, for a time, able to convince the Americans that the empire represented a bulwark against Communism. But the rising tide of anti-colonialism could only be resisted for so long. The choice, then, was 'to scuttle first or await the inevitable collision with an iceberg'.[8]

Probably the most important factor in the 'end of empire' – at least when it came to determining the pace of events on the ground – was the rise of anti-colonial nationalism. Taking advantage of Britain's military and economic difficulties, exploiting the weak and perennially under-resourced structures of colonial government, and seizing on the rhetoric of self-determination and democracy that was now in vogue, a succession of nationalist leaders overcame significant obstacles – notably ethnic and religious divisions and the arbitrary borders of most colonial states – to mobilise mass support for a rapid end to colonial rule.[9] Their efforts proved contagious, encouraging a domino effect that saw almost all of Britain's significant overseas possessions gone by the mid-1960s – far sooner than the planners in Whitehall had ever imagined.

The Gold Coast, which the British had begun to colonise during the early nineteenth century, was a beautiful, captivating land of three distinct regions: the Colony, a densely populated coastal area (it took in the cities of Accra, Cape Coast and Sekondi) whose arid scrubland featured cotton trees and coconut palms; the central Asante region, with its tropical forests and cocoa farms; and the burnt savannah of the Northern Territories, whose inhabitants eked out a living through subsistence farming.[10] By the mid-twentieth century, this West African colony was one of the most advanced in the empire.[11] Thanks to the export of cocoa, as well as gold and diamonds, the Gold Coast's economy had prospered; it boasted a significant urban population, a well-developed system of mission and state schools and a burgeoning rail and road network.[12] In contrast to most of the other African colonies, a large proportion of the Gold Coast's population of four million spoke similar dialects, practised similar customs and shared a common culture.[13] There was also no entrenched white settler population to complicate matters. The Gold Coast, then, faced fewer obstacles to decolonisation than would be the case elsewhere.

In London, policymakers knew that the Second World War had both stirred the political consciousness of Africans (especially returning soldiers) and delivered an international climate that was hostile to colonialism. They also understood that the social and economic development of the colonies required the participation of the indigenous population. They therefore developed a 'new' policy for the African colonies to promote and strengthen 'efficient, local, representative government' and to enable them to gradually take on 'full responsibility for local affairs'. What today we would understand as 'independence' was not initially on the table, although 'internal self-government' was believed possible within perhaps twenty or thirty years.[14]

In the Gold Coast, the governor, Sir Alan Burns, encouraged a series of political reforms culminating in a new constitution, introduced in 1946, that allowed for an elected majority on the legislative council for the first time. But Burns's confidence that 'the people' were 'really happy . . . and satisfied' with this outcome was quickly dispelled. In 1947, Dr J. B. Danquah, an Oxford-educated lawyer, founded the United Gold Coast Convention to demand 'self-Government in the shortest possible time'. At the end of February 1948, riots broke out in Accra. Triggered by economic grievances (namely high inflation and shortages of consumer goods) and lasting for several weeks, they left twenty-nine dead, more than two hundred injured, and the country in a state of emergency. Then, in June 1949, Danquah's fiery young lieutenant, Kwame Nkrumah, broke away to form the Convention People's Party (CPP). Its aim was to 'fight relentlessly to achieve and maintain independence for the people of Ghana', and Nkrumah rallied his forces under the less deferential slogan of 'Self-government Now!'[15]

The renowned African American writer Richard Wright described Nkrumah as 'slightly built, a smooth jet black in color; he had a largish face, a pair of brooding, almost frightened eyes, a set of full lips. His head held a thick growth of crinkly hair and his hands moved with a slow restlessness, betraying a contained tension.'[16] Born in September 1909 in Nkroful, a village of mud huts and bamboo compounds in the south-west of the country, just a couple of miles from the coast, Nkrumah trained as a teacher at the elite Prince of Wales College at Achimota, in Accra, before moving to Lincoln University, Pennsylvania, to study theology (working his way through college as a bellhop and dish washer, and by selling fish on street corners). Then, in May 1945, he moved to London to study law and quickly immersed himself in the anti-colonial and pan-African cause.[17] In 1947, after a twelve-year absence, he returned to his homeland and put his talents at the disposal of Danquah's UGCC. But Nkrumah, a Christian Marxist who was captivated by the vision of a proud, united and independent Africa that had been championed by Marcus Garvey, the Jamaican-born black nationalist and charismatic president of the Universal Negro Improvement Association, in the years following the first world war, and inspired by Mahatma Gandhi's pioneering use of nonviolent resistance against the British Empire, quickly became disillusioned with the respectable, middle-class 'stooges' (as he called them) of the UGCC, and their gradualist approach to ending colonial rule. They, in turn, viewed Nkrumah as a dangerous zealot. After being expelled from his post as UGCC secretary in June 1949, he immediately set up a rival organisation that pitched its appeal squarely at the masses.

There is no doubt that the British would have preferred to negotiate with Danquah and his fellow moderates, and in private they disparaged Nkrumah as 'our little local Hitler'.[18] But a successful campaign of civil disobedience in January 1950 and a strong performance in that year's municipal elections showed that the CPP was a force to be reckoned with. In the general election of 1951, it won thirty-four of the thirty-eight seats available in the National Assembly. Nkrumah directed the election effort from his jail cell (where he was serving a three-year sentence for his role in promoting mass protests), smuggling out instructions written on toilet paper; he achieved a personal mandate by defeating his UGCC rival in Accra by 20,780 votes to 1,451.[19] No wonder, then, that Sir Charles Arden-Clarke, who had succeeded Burns as governor in August 1949, concluded that there was little choice but to work with Nkrumah.[20]

At 1 p.m. on 12 February 1951, the CPP leader walked through the gates of the James Fort prison to be greeted by a rapturous crowd. Carried aloft to an open-topped car, he was then driven to the nearby arena for a rally. Several years later, Nkrumah wrote that he found it 'difficult even now to describe all I experienced as this car moved at a snail's pace like a ship being dragged by an overpowering current in a sea of upturned faces'. The sight of thousands of supporters, and the 'deafening clamour of their jubilant voices made me feel quite giddy'. The following morning, Nkrumah strode into the courtyard of Christiansborg Castle, the fortified seventeenth-century trading post that served as the seat of the colonial government. It was his first ever visit, and 'the glaring white stone of the battlements, the impressive forecourt and the beauty of this imposing building with the roaring surf battering against its foundations, seemed to me like a new world'.[21] Once inside, he was promptly invited to become Leader of Government Business. A year later the post was upgraded, and Nkrumah became the colony's prime minister.[22] After a second general election victory in 1954 (this time the CPP secured seventy-two out of 104 seats in the General Assembly) and the appointment of an all-African cabinet, full self-government for the Gold Coast appeared within reach.[23] Ironically, the biggest obstacle to the end of empire now came from within the colony itself.

Early on the morning of 19 September 1954, tens of thousands of Asante men, wearing traditional mourning dress, began to gather at the source of the sacred Subin River in Kumase, the historic heart of the Asante Empire. Just before noon, the ancient battle cry rang out, *Asante Kotoko, woyaa, woyaa yie* ('Asante Porcupine, we are moving forward, no moving back'), before, to the beat of ceremonial drums, a giant flag was unfurled: green symbolising the region's lush forests, gold the mineral resources, and black the Asante's revered ancestors. At the flag's centre, beneath a cocoa tree, stood a cocoa pod, the basis of the region's wealth, and a porcupine, symbol of the once formidable Asante military. By the day's end, the vast crowds had endorsed plans to form the National Liberation Movement in order to 'save Gold Coast from dictatorship'. The NLM's principal demands were for the price paid to farmers for their cocoa, which Nkrumah's government had recently frozen at seventy-two shillings per 60 lb load, to be doubled, and for the Gold Coast to adopt a new, federal constitution that would guarantee autonomy for the regions.[24] Although discontent over the cocoa price had provided the immediate catalyst, the NLM's emergence reflected deeper concerns over economic exploitation and corruption, and real anxieties about the centralisation of power in Accra.[25] Indeed, the Gold Coast's charismatic leader was widely distrusted by the Asante, whose king, the Asantehene, believed, as one British report put it, that 'Dr Nkrumah was a madman and that once he had secured power in an independent Gold Coast a number of his more eminent opponents in Asante would have their throats cut'.[26]

Against a backdrop of serious street violence – including the firebombing of cars and homes – and ominous talk of secession, a compromise was eventually forged. Although there would be no federal constitution (both Nkrumah and the British believed that a unitary government would be more efficient and effective), the regions were promised a greater say. Nkrumah – with great reluctance – agreed to a further general election to resolve the constitutional crisis and secure a popular mandate for independence.[27]

The election campaign of 1956 was fiercely fought. The NLM denounced the CPP as 'thieves, rogues, traitors . . . and gangsters'. Its rallies in the Asante heartlands attracted enthusiastic audiences of 'young men, elders, market women, farmers, petty traders, teachers and clerks', and featured emotional proclamations of loyalty to the Asantehene and the Golden Stool (his sacred throne) and raucous celebrations of Asante military prowess.[28] Meanwhile the CPP's pitch to the electorate was clear:

ALL YOU HAVE TO DO is to ask yourself two questions:

(1) Do I want FREEDOM and INDEPENDENCE NOW – THIS YEAR – so that I and my children can enjoy life in a free and independent sovereign state of Ghana thereafter?

(2) Do I want to revert to the days of imperialism, colonialism and tribal feudalism?[29]

The only way to secure independence – and defeat the 'saboteurs' and 'tribalists' who wanted to break up the country – was, proclaimed Nkrumah and his supporters, to vote for the CPP.[30] It was a message that Nkrumah would reprise throughout the campaign: speaking at a giant election rally in Accra, for example, he told his countrymen that they had reached 'the end of the road. Whether we go through the golden gate to freedom, or whether we remain behind is now a matter for you to decide.'[31]

On Tuesday 17 July the people of the Gold Coast went to the polls. *The Times*'s colonial correspondent painted an exotic picture for his readers back home, describing how 'in the ports and towns of the south, with their two-storied houses with verandas . . . the majority of the men voters will come in European suits, or at any rate shorts and singlets, though there will be plenty of "market mammies" in their attractively coloured "cloths"'. In contrast, in the 'mud and wattle villages' of the Asante 'the cocoa farmers will throng in wearing the bright togas that set off so well their muscular torsos', and in the more remote parts of the north (where some ballots had been distributed by canoe) 'white-clad Muslims' would join with 'naked pagans' to cast their vote.[32] Despite fears of violence, election day itself was orderly and peaceful. Turnout was modest: about half of the country's registered voters placed their ballot paper in the box bearing the relevant party symbol (a red cockerel for the CPP, a green and yellow cocoa tree for the NLM) before having their thumb marked with indelible ink.[33] The CPP performed strongly, even securing 43 per cent of the popular vote in Asante, and ultimately winning seventy-one out of the 104 seats in the new General Assembly – which promptly passed a resolution calling for independence.[34]

At noon on 18 September 1956, Kwame Nkrumah rose in the Assembly chamber to announce that the secretary of state for the colonies had just published an official despatch confirming that 'Her Majesty's Government will, at the first available opportunity introduce into the United Kingdom Parliament a Bill to accord Independence to the Gold Coast and, subject to Parliamentary approval, Her Majesty's Government intends that full independence should come about on the 6th March, 1957.' 'The whole of the Assembly', Nkrumah recalled, 'was for a few seconds dumbfounded. Then all at once the almost sacred silence was broken by an ear-splitting cheer.' Many of his fellow parliamentarians were in tears. Amid chaotic scenes, the prime minister was carried into the streets, where jubilant crowds were already gathering to celebrate. It was, Nkrumah later wrote, 'the most triumphant moment of my life'.[35]

British imperial power was coming under pressure elsewhere during 1956 too. The year had begun with the granting of formal independence for the Sudan. Technically a province of Egypt, this Anglo-Egyptian 'co-dominium' had been a de facto British colony since 1899. On 1 January 1956, following complex diplomatic negotiations that had seen Egypt withdraw its own sovereignty claims, the Republic of Sudan was born (even as the flags were being lowered and the congratulatory telegrams read, simmering tensions between the broadly Arab, Muslim north and the African, part-Christianised south augured bitter conflicts to come).[36] Then, on 1 March, Jordan's twenty-year-old King Hussein dismissed Lieutenant General Sir John Bagot Glubb from his post of commander of the Arab Legion. Glubb, who was denounced by the Egyptians as an 'imperialist scorpion', personified Britain's influence in the Middle East and his forced departure (which was widely, though erroneously, blamed on Egypt's General Nasser) was a humiliation for Sir Anthony Eden's government.[37] But one of the bloodiest challenges to empire during the early months of 1956 would come from the Mediterranean island of Cyprus.

At 3 p.m. on Friday 9 March, Makarios III, Archbishop of Cyprus and spiritual head of the Cypriot Orthodox Church, was driven from his palace to Nicosia airport to catch a flight to Athens, where he was due to attend a series of meetings with Greek supporters of the Cypriot cause. Just over an hour later, as he walked onto the tarmac, the archbishop suddenly found himself surrounded by British troops, ushered to a specially screened-off area on the runway and then bundled into a Hastings Mark II transport aircraft. After a refuelling stop in Aden, Makarios's plane touched down in Nairobi, where a military convoy was on hand to escort the prelate to the Kenyan port city of Mombasa. Transferred into the custody of the Royal Navy, Makarios was then taken aboard the frigate HMS *Loch Fada* for the final nine-hundred-mile leg of his journey to Mahé, the largest island of the Seychelles archipelago, in the Indian Ocean. He would spend the next year under house arrest at Sans Souci, the country residence of the colony's governor (the British cabinet had vetoed an earlier plan to house Makarios in a more modest residence when they discovered, to their horror, that it was named La Bastille).[38] In his radio address explaining the decision to exile the archbishop, Field Marshal Sir John Harding, Cyprus's governor, accused Makarios of having 'remained silent while policemen and soldiers have been murdered in cold blood, while women and children have been killed and maimed by bombs . . . His silence has understandably been accepted among his community as not merely condoning but even as approving assassination and bomb-throwing.'[39]

Ceded to the British by the Ottomans in 1878, Cyprus, long neglected by its rulers, had by the 1950s become a key strategic asset. The island's airfields enabled RAF bombers to reach targets – including oilfields – in the south of the USSR, and the Crown Colony also gave the British a vital foothold in the Middle East during a period when their influence there was being squeezed.[40] The British were, uniquely, confronted with a demand not for straightforward self-determination, but rather for *enosis* – union – with Greece.[41] This scenario was deemed unacceptable in London, not least because it would set a dangerous precedent for other colonies (notably Gibraltar and Hong Kong) and inflame the island's substantial Turkish minority and the government in Ankara.[42] Britain, in fact, was caught between two NATO allies: Greece, which supported *enosis* and championed the Cypriot cause at the United Nations, and Turkey, which served as an important bulwark against the spread of Communism in the Middle East, and which was keen to see the rights of the Turkish Cypriot population protected.[43] The British also feared that, given Greece's chronic political instability, *enosis* might result in London suddenly being faced with a government in Athens that was hostile to her military and strategic interests on the island.[44]

There could, though, be no doubting the strength of support for *enosis* among Greek Cypriots, who made up about 80 per cent of the population. In January 1950, a plebiscite organised by the Orthodox Church saw more than 215,000 men and women (some 96 per cent of the adult Greek population) vote in favour of a union with Greece. The Cypriot Church, which had been founded by St Barnabas the Apostle in AD 45, occupied a privileged and influential position in the life of the island. In the fifth century it had been awarded autocephalous status by the Roman Emperor Zeno, which gave it independent jurisdiction on both spiritual and temporal matters and granted special privileges to the archbishop: he was permitted to carry a sceptre rather than the traditional pastoral staff, to wear the imperial purple under his vestments, and to sign his edicts in vermilion. On 28 June 1950, at the age of just thirty-nine, Makarios III was elected as the new archbishop and swiftly became the spiritual and political leader of the campaign for *enosis*.[45]

The son of a goatherd, Makarios (born Michael Christodoulou Mouskis) had entered the famous Byzantine monastery at Kykkos in 1926, before going on to study at the University of Athens and then at a seminary in Boston. Youthful, energetic and cosmopolitan, the Ethnarch cut a magnetic figure; the English poet James Fenton wrote that 'the robes, the head-dress, the beard, the smile, assured him of world-wide fame; he might hardly have needed a voice to add to his accomplishments. Yet the voice alone would have made him a hero. It was distinctive enough in English . . . in Greek it was music of the most heady kind.' Makarios was, moreover, a committed evangelist for *enosis*; on assuming the throne of St Barnabas he had promised that he would 'not let my eyes close to sleep until the golden wings of the sun arise to announce the longed-for day of national liberation'.⁴⁶ Unfortunately for the British, however, the campaign for *enosis* was not to be restricted to the spiritual front.

On April Fool's Day 1955, EOKA (the National Organisation of Cypriot Fighters) began its campaign for the 'liberation of Cyprus from the British yoke', bombing government buildings in Nicosia, Limassol and Larnaca.⁴⁷ The organisation was led by Colonel George Grivas, an extreme anti-Communist and fanatical supporter of *enosis*. Described by one journalist as 'a dull, competent, obstinate and somewhat courageous professional soldier', Grivas – fifty-six years old, five foot six and a half inches tall, with a 'strong, broad face', trademark moustache and beret, and 'large ears set low' – had been born in the Famagusta district of Eastern Cyprus in 1898, before moving to Greece during his teens.⁴⁸ Commissioned into the Greek army, he had fought in the Balkans during the Great War, in Asia Minor during 1921–2 and on the Albanian front during 1940. A shadowy figure, Grivas had first come to national prominence during the resistance to the Nazi occupation (his exact role remains murky) and then, during the Civil War that erupted in 1944, he had led a far-right paramilitary unit dedicated to the restoration of the Greek monarchy. Following a failed attempt at a political career, Grivas had switched his focus to *enosis* and begun to formulate plans for a guerrilla campaign that would eject the British from the land of his birth.[49] The attacks of April 1955 marked the start of a sustained terrorist campaign – an armed rebellion that, as the revolt's leading historian has explained, lay in the clash between Britain's determination that Cyprus had to be exempted from the 'process of imperial retraction' and a belief among Greek Cypriots that, as the heirs of Hellenic civilisation, they were 'exceptionally qualified to determine their own future'. Cypriot resentment at Britain's refusal to countenance self-determination was only heightened by the process of imperial retreat elsewhere – most notably, of course, in the Gold Coast.[50] The British, determined to crush the revolt, deployed thousands of troops and imposed a series of repressive measures including detention without trial, the banning of strikes and assemblies, censorship, the jamming of radio broadcasts, the use of curfews, the shutting down of 'troublesome' schools and the liberal use of the death penalty. These policies, though, simply made things worse.[51]

The deterioration of the situation on the ground provided a suitably grim backdrop to the last-ditch talks between Governor Harding, Archbishop Makarios and Alan Lennox-Boyd at the end of February 1956. Lennox-Boyd, six feet five inches tall, was elegant, charming and exuberant, blessed with formidable powers of recall and a drive that was matched, it seemed, only by his extraordinary tolerance of alcohol. Appointed colonial secretary at the end of July 1954, Lennox-Boyd – who had first been elected to the House of Commons in October 1931 and had seen active service in the Royal Navy during the Second World War – was, according to his contemporary Michael Foot, 'a real Tory without prefix, suffix, qualification or mitigation'.[52] Yet in office this 'Imperial diehard' proved surprisingly pragmatic; on the eve of the talks in Nicosia, he urged Sir Anthony Eden to concede that any revived national assembly for the island would contain a Greek-elected majority. Fearing a negative reaction from within his own party, the prime minister refused this 'sweetener', thereby dooming the summit. The negotiations, which took place in the drab official residence of the Anglican Archdeacon, quickly broke down; Lennox-Boyd's final words to the archbishop were 'God save your people.'[53]

The British, convinced that Makarios was complicit in EOKA's campaign of terror, now moved to deport him. Their reasoning was not entirely spurious: after all, in July 1952 he had joined with Grivas in swearing a 'Holy Sacred Oath' in support of *enosis* and, while Makarios was careful never to explicitly endorse violence, he had declared that 'we shall accept assistance even from unclean hands'.[54] Nevertheless, for all the British claims that Makarios had played a leading role in the 'foundation and major operational planning of EOKA', or that Grivas was merely the prelate's 'henchman', the relationship was far more ambiguous. The EOKA bombs that rocked Nicosia on 29 February, just as the talks were getting under way, were probably intended as much to remind Makarios of the dangers of 'selling out' as to intimidate the British.[55]

The archbishop's deportation may have delighted large parts of the Conservative Party and the right-wing press in Britain, but it caused outrage elsewhere.[56] Dr Geoffrey Fisher, Archbishop of Canterbury, expressed his deep unease at the imprisonment of a fellow church leader, explaining that many around the world viewed the British action as a 'sacrilege'. Meanwhile Earl Attlee, the former prime minister, noted wryly that 'the rebels of the past generally tend, sooner or later, to be the Prime Ministers of the British Commonwealth'.[57] In the United States, one journalist's warning that 'advice from the land of Autherine Lucy' was unlikely to 'go down too well in Britain' was largely ignored. Many Americans took the view that the British were engaged in a 'last-ditch stand of "colonial imperialism" in the Mediterranean'.[58] New York's mayor expressed solidarity with the Cypriot cause, the labour leader George Meany demanded self-determination for Cyprus and, in off-the-record comments that caused dismay in London, State

Department officials briefed that the British had made a 'grave mistake' that would likely worsen the situation.[59]

There was also strong criticism from the Danish, Dutch and Spanish press, while the Norwegian daily *Arbeiderbladet* accused Britain of engaging in old-fashioned colonialism.[60] Soviet coverage was surprisingly restrained, possibly because Khrushchev and Bulganin were shortly to begin an official visit to Britain. In Poland, however, the tone was sharply critical. *Trybuna Ludu* denounced the 'brutal deportation' of Makarios, delighted in the apparent difference of opinion with the United States and portrayed Britain as hypocritical: having condemned the Polish government for placing Cardinal Stefan Wyszyński under house arrest, now London had a prelate under lock and key![61]

The reaction in the eastern Mediterranean was far more visceral. In Heraklion, Crete, the British Consulate was sacked, and there were angry demonstrations in Athens, where the offices of British European Airways were attacked, and Thessaloniki, where a mob of two thousand students set wooden barricades alight and fought running battles with the police. Cyprus, meanwhile, was immediately paralysed by a general strike, and British troops unleashed tear gas and baton charges against several hundred protesters in Limassol after being pelted with stones. Meanwhile EOKA, which now promised to 'fight to death for free Cyprus or destroy it completely, under whose ruins will be buried both the British and ourselves', stepped up its campaign of violence – targeting houses occupied by British families and attacking soldiers and military bases. EOKA also dealt ruthlessly with suspected collaborators. In the little village of Dhora, for example, 'three masked men walked into a coffee shop and ordered all the customers to stand with their hands on the wall. Three men were picked out and told: "You are traitors and must pay the price." Two of them were shot dead, but the third escaped with a bullet through the hand.'[62]

Grivas's aim was to 'strike and strike again at the enemy and

never give them a moment of relaxation wherever they might be
. . . we must be everywhere in attack, and nowhere when attacked
ourselves.'[63] EOKA carried out bombings, shootings, ambushes
and sabotage all over the island, targeting the island's police force
(increasingly reliant on seconded British officers and recruits from
the local Turkish population) along with the British military.[64] Grivas's forces, never more than two hundred active fighters, were audacious too.[65] On 3 March, an EOKA bomb had destroyed a Hermes
aircraft at Nicosia airport – only an unforeseen delay in its scheduled
departure prevented the deaths of sixty-eight passengers.[66] Two and
a half weeks later, an attempt to blow up the governor by placing a
bomb underneath his bed narrowly failed. When, on 10 May, two
EOKA fighters were hanged in the courtyard of Nicosia Central
Prison, Grivas retaliated by executing two British corporals that they
had taken hostage.[67]

As in Algeria, both sides committed appalling atrocities as the
conflict intensified. On 8 July, for example, George Kaberry, a customs official who had been on the island for five months, and his
wife were ambushed as they drove to the Kyrenian coast for a picnic.
As their car approached a sharp bend on an isolated, tree-lined pass,
they came under fire from EOKA gunmen armed with automatic
weapons, shotguns and hand grenades. The thirty-one-year-old
Marjorie, who was pregnant with her first child, was killed instantly;
her husband died at the side of the road.[68] On 23 October, a large
bomb hidden beneath a water tap at the edge of Lefkonico High
School's football field was detonated at the end of an army rugby
game (the signal was given by two young girls, waving their hand-
kerchiefs). Two young soldiers were disembowelled in the resultant
explosion and four more were left badly injured. The British reacted
to this attack with undisguised fury.[69] Grivas recalled that troops:

> rushed through the village beating and kicking everyone
> they met, smashing windows and ransacking shops . . .

Then they arrested every man they could find and herded them into the village square [where] they were made to stand against the wall with their hands up, while they were kicked or punched or struck with rifle-butts.[70]

Throughout the 'Cyprus Emergency' the British, as elsewhere in the empire (most notoriously Kenya, where much of the country was turned into a police state in the attempt to crush the Mau Mau), routinely resorted to repressive measures, including collective punishment, reprisals, harsh interrogation techniques and even torture.[71] Alan Staff, who served with the Parachute Regiment, described taking part in an operation near Trapeza, on the north of the island, where his unit discovered five EOKA fighters hiding in a barn, together with shotguns, bombs and ammunition: 'Well, we just guarded these blokes and were getting quite matey when the police arrived, Special Branch, and they were bastards. They really knocked those blokes about; I could hear them crying. None of us liked this but I have to admit that the terrorists talked . . .'[72] Although such tactics degraded EOKA's effectiveness as a fighting force, they also fuelled resentment against the British and solidified popular support for Grivas, embodied in the popular phrase, 'We are all EOKA now!'[73]

The struggle to end British rule in Cyprus would last for four years and claim the lives of more than five hundred people (230 of them civilians), with a further twelve hundred injured, many of them seriously.[74] As the French were discovering in North Africa, the attempt to hang on to empire could be a painful and bloody business.

CAPTION:

The flag-draped coffins of some of the young French soldiers who lost their lives during an FLN ambush near Palestro, Algeria, May 1956.

Credit: Pages François

7

THE PALESTRO MASSACRE

For every resistance fighter guillotined, a hundred Frenchmen
will be slaughtered indiscriminately.
    FLN, June 1956

On 18 May 1956 a platoon of twenty-one French reservists was
on a routine patrol in the rugged countryside near Palestro, fifty
miles south-east of Algiers. After passing through the village of
Djerrah and entering one of the area's steep, wild gorges, the unit
was ambushed by a group of FLN militants commanded by Ali
Khodja – a charismatic figure who had deserted from the French
army in 1955. Within minutes, seventeen soldiers had been killed
– most shot at close range – and four taken prisoner. When the
patrol failed to return to base that evening, the alarm was raised
and a search party despatched. On reaching the site of the ambush
they made their grim discovery: at least two of the corpses had
been mutilated – the testicles cut off and the disembowelled
bodies stuffed with stones.[1] In response, General Jacques Massu,
commander of the 10th Parachute Division, sent seven battalions,
together with several helicopters, to find the missing soldiers and
hunt down those responsible. In subsequent clashes more than a
dozen rebels were killed, as well as fifty Muslim villagers. Hundreds
more were arrested. Khodja, though, managed to evade justice. Of
the four missing conscripts, one was rescued and one cut down by
'friendly fire'; the bodies of the other two were never found.[2]

The violence that occurred in and around Palestro that spring
day was not particularly remarkable.[3] By this stage in the conflict,
terrorism, sabotage and murder were occurring on a daily basis.
On 6 May, for instance, the following were reported:

In Algiers three Moslems shot dead, French policeman wounded, and bomb thrown in hospital.

16 soldiers killed, 14 wounded, and 9 missing in two rebel ambushes near Sabdou, Oran Department; 40 rebels killed in military counter-attack.

5 Cars burnt by rebels, 4 passengers kidnapped.

20 rebels killed at Gesto, near Tunisian border.

International train derailed by terrorists near Oran – no injuries.[4]

Over the next few days, dozens of farms were attacked, thousands of vines and fruit trees destroyed, more than forty military posts targeted and sixty civilians killed (seventeen of them French).[5]

Thanks to the sensationalist coverage of the rescue mission, however, the Palestro massacre was transformed into a cause célèbre, outraging French public opinion and driving the authorities to adopt ever tougher countermeasures. The loss of the platoon certainly helped to bring home both the scale and the horror of the war – it was the French army's biggest single loss of life thus far, and the young reservists, who had been in Algeria for barely two weeks, were almost all family men from suburban Paris. The brutal manner of their deaths and the appalling defilement of their bodies were shocking.[6] The incident also occurred at a particularly sensitive time, with opinion polls showing that 63 per cent of the French public now believed that Algeria was the nation's 'most important problem' (up from just 25 per cent at the turn of the year), and significant anti-war sentiment bubbling to the surface.[7] On the very day that the young soldiers lost their lives, two thousand people had gathered in Grenoble to block a train that they believed was carrying reservists bound for Algeria (it was in fact packed with commuters). When the police fired tear gas to clear the tracks they were met by a hail of bricks and stones. Ninety people, including sixty policemen, were injured in the clashes, with twenty-three arrested.[8] Ominously, disgruntled reservists were in the vanguard of anti-war protest: denouncing Mollet and other senior politicians, calling for 'peace', confronting the police and flouting military discipline.[9] Criticism also came from influential writers and intellectuals. In an editorial for *L'Observateur*, for example, Claude Bourdet warned that a hundred thousand young Frenchmen were threatened with 'being thrown into the "dirty war" of Algeria, with losing the best years of their lives, perhaps with being wounded, indeed killed, for a cause few of them approve'.[10] Claude Gérard – a journalist, former Resistance leader and recipient of the Légion d'Honneur – actually spent ten days with rebel forces, and afterwards spoke warmly of their cause. In an interview with the London *Observer*, she explained, 'I felt I was watching the birth of a nation. I love my own country too much to blame them for loving theirs and for sacrificing their lives for it.'[11] Both were soon arrested: Bourdet charged with spreading 'demoralisation', Gérard with attacking the 'security of the state'.[12]

The French authorities now seized on Palestro as a way to encourage patriotic unity in the face of FLN 'barbarism'. Robert Lacoste, Algeria's new minister-resident, was clear about which 'side was practising extermination'. The fifty-seven-year-old socialist used the outrage to crack down on the FLN, proclaiming that 'the war we are waging . . . is that of the Western world, of civilisation against anarchy, democracy against dictatorship.'[13] Lacoste, who had served with distinction in both the Great War and the French Resistance, possessed a 'bullish, no-nonsense' temperament.[14] Although committed to reforming Algeria – with the ultimate aim of creating a new, Franco-Muslim society rooted in the values of tolerance, mutual respect and political equality – Lacoste, like most of his colleagues, was convinced that first the FLN 'extremists' had to be defeated.[15] But this approach failed to recognise either the overwhelming preference of Algeria's Muslims for a fully independent Arab state or the settlers' stubborn refusal to countenance any compromise.[16] French efforts to win over Muslim 'hearts and minds' were also undermined by the FLN's determination to bear down on any Muslim who advocated co-operation. In early summer, for example, a band of FLN fighters infiltrated the town of Saint Lucien in the Kabylia, on Algeria's northern coast, where sixteen Muslim farmers had recently agreed to participate in a French programme of land redistribution. By the time they left, four of the farmers were dead, the other twelve had withdrawn their co-operation and the government project lay in ruins.[17] But it was the increasingly harsh counter-terrorism measures, adopted in the attempt to pacify the country, which ultimately doomed efforts to find a liberal 'solution' to the Algerian question.[18]

By the end of the spring France was involved in a full-scale war, with 350,000 troops ranged against some twenty thousand FLN fighters. At $1.7 million a day (the equivalent of $14 million today), the cost was eye-wateringly high – in part because the attempt to pacify Algeria relied on the resource-intensive strategy of 'quadrillage'.[19] Under this system small fortified posts, sometimes garrisoned by as few as ten men, were placed at every key point in a given area – villages, agricultural centres, major road junctions and commanding features – typically at distances of two or three miles. Quadrillage was designed to reassure the *pieds noirs* that both they and their property would be protected. Meanwhile, regular patrols were mounted to 'show the flag', befriend the local Muslim population and show that they would be supported if they defied the FLN.[20] Army units, supported by helicopters and light aircraft, launched regular attacks on FLN units, and a series of major security measures – including checkpoints in towns and on all major roads, curfew and regular 'stop and search' – were imposed across Algeria.[21]

The French army was, though, not fighting a conventional war but an insurgency. This produced a distinctive environment, where the traditional demarcation between the battle front and the home front collapsed, and where the 'enemy' – mobile, elusive and often invisible – could blend into the local civilian population. Reservists – usually unable to speak Arabic or Berber and unnerved by reports of previously 'friendly' Muslims suddenly turning on Europeans – were actively encouraged to regard every Arab as a possible rebel, and high-profile incidents of FLN savagery provoked a desire for retribution. Indeed, French soldiers often found themselves condoning, or engaging in, acts of terrible barbarity.[22]

Torture, for instance, was endemic. Common techniques for interrogating suspected FLN prisoners included beating their feet until they were raw, and then placing them in cold water; the forced ingestion of water (often using a hose), until both the stomach and lungs began to fill up; repeatedly forcing the head of a prisoner into a trough until they were half drowned; and applying electrodes, typically powered by a portable army signals magneto, to sensitive areas of the body (ear lobes, fingers, the mouth and, of course, the genitals).[23]

By the summer, word of French brutality had reached Roderick Sarell, Britain's new consul-general in Algiers. Fifty-seven years old and a graduate of Oxford, Sarell had joined the consular service in 1936 and enjoyed a series of postings across the Middle East and North Africa. At the end of August, Sarell had a 'distressing' meeting with a Catholic priest, who read from letters from soldiers stationed across Algeria. Not only did the soldiers' testimony corroborate long-standing rumours about the use of torture, they painted a deeply troubling picture of French military behaviour more generally. Sarell heard how 'groups of farm houses in which there were suspects were mortared, and how the troops made a habit of looting the villagers' possessions without distinction of guilt'. Another letter recounted how two young soldiers, out on patrol, had 'come on a shepherd sitting harmlessly with his back to them. They had discussed whether to pick him off, and decided to toss up. He was unlucky and was shot.' In another letter, an officer was quoted saying that 'in his unit at least rape was only committed in secret'. 'Running through the letters', Sarell explained, 'was a feeling of pointlessness and of disillusionment with the realities of the "pacification" campaign.'[24] While recognising the difficulties that confronted the French troops, Sarell feared that such conduct would erode France's moral status, and prove counterproductive.[25]

Sarell was right to be concerned. Burning down entire villages, summary executions, mass arrests, torture and looting failed to win round Arab opinion. After one particularly brutal French attack, which left several Muslim women dead, an FLN fighter proclaimed it a victory for the nationalists: 'They hate the French a little more now. The stupid bastards are winning the war for us.'[26] Yet, in their determination to pacify the country, the French persisted in turning the screw.

Just days after the Palestro massacre, for instance, some six thousand troops and fifteen hundred gendarmes raided the Casbah in Algiers, a hotbed of FLN support. Combing through its winding, densely populated streets, they arrested almost five thousand people and seized significant quantities of arms as well as FLN literature. While this complex operation was conducted with little bloodshed, it inevitably caused a good deal of distress and anger among Algerian Muslims.[27] Three weeks after the raid on the Casbah, Muslim rage reached new heights. On 19 June, two FLN operatives – Ahmed Zabane and Abdelkader Ferradj – were dragged into the stone courtyard of Algiers's imposing Barberousse prison. Each, in turn, had his hands and feet bound and his head locked into position, before the blade of the guillotine descended. It completed its grim journey with a thud that was audible inside the notoriously overcrowded jail. They were the first FLN prisoners to be executed; dozens more would follow.[28]

The *pieds noirs* had long been calling for the sentences on Zabane and Ferradj to be carried out (Zabane had killed a gamekeeper, while Ferradj had participated in an ambush that claimed the lives of a European woman and a seven-year-old girl). In the bitter aftermath of Palestro, these demands reached fever pitch. Although the case of Ferradj was particularly sensitive – during his capture he had sustained injuries that had cost him an eye and left him crippled – Lacoste dismissed the appeals of the Archbishop of Algiers and others who urged clemency. But while the executions delighted most Europeans, the FLN viewed them as a declaration of war.[29] In one handbill, distributed in the immediate aftermath of the executions, the FLN claimed that it had been left with no choice but to meet 'violence with violence' and issued a chilling threat: 'For every resistance fighter guillotined, a hundred Frenchmen will be slaughtered indiscriminately.'[30]

The nationalists immediately sought to make good on their promise. By 24 June they had carried out more than twenty attacks in Algiers, killing ten and injuring dozens more. On the early evening of 20 June, for instance, a dozen or so rebels, working in pairs and armed with pistols, roamed through the Bab el Oued neighbourhood, killing three Europeans and injuring fourteen, including a teenage girl.[31] The following day, Marcel Garbagnati, a twenty-year-old student, was shot dead while driving his motor scooter around the city.[32] These reprisals – random and indiscriminate – pushed the city toward the abyss.

On the night of 10 August a powerful bomb, which had been planted by *pied noir* ultras in the heart of the Casbah, destroyed several houses on the rue de Thèbes, claiming the lives of seventy Muslims, including women and children. Six weeks later, the FLN replied in kind. Saadi Yacef – twenty-nine years old, the son of a baker, and a keen footballer – had established an extensive and elaborate FLN network in the Casbah. On the evening of 30 September, he sent three young women – Zohra Drif, Djamila Bouhired and Samia Lakhdari – on a deadly mission. Drif, a law student at the University of Algiers, was incensed by what she viewed as French intransigence and had been outraged by the executions of Zabane and Ferradj. 'Of all the horrors of war', she explained, this was 'the most atrocious'. She also noted that, while Muslim citizens were subject to the indignities and inconveniences of the curfew, stop and search and other 'counter-terrorism' measures, 'the European population, in its tranquil quarters . . . lived peacefully, went to the beach, to the cinema, to *le dancing*, and prepared for their holidays . . .' Attractive and light-skinned, the three women removed their veils, tinted their hair and donned pretty summer dresses in order to help them pass more easily through the city's numerous security checkpoints. They placed their 1 kg bombs, with the automatic timers set for 6:30 p.m., carefully in beach bags, covering them up with towels, sun lotion and beachwear. Lakhdari then headed to the Cafétéria on the fashionable rue Michelet. It was a favourite among European students, and several young couples were already dancing to the mambo music that blared from the jukebox. Simultaneously, Drif made for the Milk-Bar on place Bugeaud, which was packed with European families relaxing after a day at the beach. The sight of young children sipping on their milkshakes gave her pause, but she steeled herself by recalling those who had died in the rubble on the rue de Thèbes. At twenty past six, after paying her bill, she departed, leaving her bag hidden underneath a table. Minutes later, both bombs detonated. The scenes at the Milk-Bar – where the glass which covered the walls had shattered, sending large splinters across the crowded room – were particularly gruesome. The attacks left three people dead, with another fifty injured; a dozen people, including some children, had limbs amputated. The bloody toll would have been even higher if not for a faulty timer on the third device, which had been left in the waiting area at Air France's downtown offices.[33]

Even as the violence spiralled out of control, some held out hope that a negotiated settlement might still be possible. Any remaining prospects for a deal were, though, firmly extinguished by the extraordinary series of events that took place on Monday 22 October.

Late that afternoon, a chartered DC-3, operated by the Moroccan airline Air Atlas, took off from a refuelling stop in Palma de Mallorca, en route from Rabat to Tunis. Aboard were four senior members of the FLN's leadership in exile, including Ahmed Ben Bella.[34] Ben Bella, born in Oran Province on Christmas Day 1918, was tall and athletic – as a young man he had been a talented footballer (he played for Olympique de Marseilles during the 1939–40 season). He was also a courageous soldier who had had 'no qualms' about taking up arms for the French during the Second World War, explaining that 'her war was a just one . . . It was a fight against Fascism, and I had a good idea what Fascism meant.' Awarded the Croix de Guerre in 1940, Ben Bella also served with distinction for the Free French and was presented with the Médal Militaire (that army's highest honour) by none other than Charles de Gaulle. After the war Ben Bella, who had chafed against colonial rule from an early age, was drawn towards Algeria's nationalist scene and, in 1954, was one of the 'historic nine' founders of the FLN. Charismatic, fearless and blessed with a razor-sharp intellect, Ben Bella became the organisation's putative military chief and one of its most prominent figures.[35]

On 22 October, Ben Bella and his comrades were travelling to a summit meeting in Tunis that had, with the discreet encouragement of Paris, been convened by Morocco's Mohammed V and Tunisia's Habib Bourguiba. The intention was to discuss proposals for Algerian independence within the framework of a North African federation – a sort of 'Maghreb Commonwealth' which would work to forge a co-operative relationship with France, and which would respect the rights of the European settlers.[36]

For the French military authorities, though, the plane's valuable cargo presented an irresistible target.[37] On hearing intelligence reports that the FLN leaders were not, as had originally been planned, travelling in the same aircraft as the Moroccan sultan, they hatched an audacious scheme. With the support of Max Lejeune, the hawkish armed forces minister – but acting without the approval, or it seems the knowledge, of Guy Mollet – they radioed the French pilot, Gaston Grellier, with orders to 'proceed to Algiers'. Although he demurred at first, Grellier – an officer in the French reserve – was eventually won round. In order to avoid arousing suspicion as the plane changed course, he summoned the plane's twenty-two-year-old stewardess, Claudine Lambert, and asked her to distract the passengers' attention: 'Be a big girl,' he told her, 'tonight you are entering history.'[38] Thomas Brady, a *New York Times* correspondent who was aboard the flight, described how Lambert 'chattered gaily with the Algerians' and kept her cool as the plane, accompanied by a fighter escort, made its descent into Algiers, asking the passengers to 'please fasten your seatbelts and extinguish your cigarettes. We are arriving in Tunis.' Only after touching down, shortly after 9 p.m., was the deception revealed: the tarmac was covered with tanks, armoured cars and military personnel carrying submachine guns.[39] Ben Bella was incandescent – 'This', he shouted, 'is how you can trust the French!' He then 'jumped up, boiling with rage' and reached for the revolver that was in his coat pocket. A comrade, placing a hand on his arm, cautioned him: 'No, no . . . You must not give them such a beautiful excuse.' When a gendarme appeared in the cabin, Ben Bella conceded that the game was up. In turn, the FLN leaders jumped to the tarmac, with their hands over their heads, and were promptly arrested. Charged with treason, they would spend most of the next six years in prison.[40]

In the European neighbourhoods of Algiers, news of *le coup de l'avion* was met with undisguised jubilation. One newspaper reported that strangers, swept up in a 'wave of enthusiasm', had been 'accosting and congratulating each other on the streets'. There was a palpable sense that France had finally seized the initiative: as one radio commentator put it, 'At last France has dared!'[41] Alain Savary, minister for Morocco and Tunisia, resigned from the cabinet in protest and the former prime minister, Pierre Mendès-France, warned that the imprisonment of the FLN leaders was likely to prove counterproductive – 'I have never considered these men spokesmen for Algeria', he said, 'but I am afraid they are going to be now.'[42] It was to no avail. French public opinion was overwhelmingly supportive, which was one reason why Mollet, despite his initial fury, refused to free the prisoners.[43] Reluctant to break with the military, he also believed that the 'decapitation' of the FLN would weaken the organisation. He was wrong. With the leading 'external' figures immobilised, the position of FLN hard-liners in the provinces – who dismissed all talk of compromise – was strengthened immeasurably.[44]

It is of course impossible to know whether the planned summit in Tunis would have led to a settlement. The combination of a weak French government and an increasingly assertive faction of *pied noir* hardliners, together with internal divisions among the FLN, did not augur well.[45] Ben Bella, though, insisted that the outlook had been 'hopeful' and that an agreement had been within reach before the military had intervened. By accepting the fait accompli, Mollet's government had, he claimed, 'buried' any chance of peace, thereby condemning Algeria to many more years of unnecessary 'bloodshed' and 'suffering'.[46]

The interception of the plane – a brazen violation of international law – certainly cost Paris diplomatic support. The Moroccan government condemned an 'act of pure piracy' and Tunisia recalled her ambassador from Paris. A general strike in Tunis saw thousands take to the streets, chanting 'Free Ben Bella!', while huge crowds in Casablanca waved Algerian flags and roared 'Free Algeria!' and 'Lacoste to the gallows!' Feelings ran strongly throughout the Middle East and North Africa – the governments of Iraq, Syria, Saudi Arabia, Sudan, Egypt and Libya all condemned the interception of the plane and called for the release of the FLN prisoners, while thousands took to the streets of Cairo, Tripoli and other cities, to show solidarity with the Algerian freedom struggle. At the United Nations, the Arab League and a group of twenty-four nations from Africa and Asia lodged official protests with Secretary General Dag Hammarskjöld.[47]

Meanwhile in Washington, the Eisenhower administration – which had welcomed the diplomatic efforts to solve the Algerian crisis – was appalled. While it expressed to the French government its concerns that the incident would damage Western interests throughout the region, the administration declined to call for the prisoners' release on the basis that it had no 'legal right' to intervene. In private, though, the Americans worried that the French government was veering out of control.[48]

The wider diplomatic and geopolitical consequences of Paris's desire to crush the nationalist uprising in Algeria became all too apparent just days later, when France joined with Britain and Israel to deliver what they hoped would be a mortal blow to Egypt's leader – and vocal FLN supporter – Gamal Abdel Nasser.[49]

8

PART OF A GREAT STRUGGLE
ALL OVER THE WORLD

> Now this determination on the part of the Negro to struggle
> and to struggle, until segregation and discrimination have
> passed away, springs from the same longing for human
> dignity that motivates oppressed peoples all over the world.
> MARTIN LUTHER KING, JR

On the evening of 17 May 1956, Martin Luther King, Jr, preached the sermon at the Cathedral Church of St John the Divine, on Manhattan's Upper West Side. Work on the magnificent neo-Gothic structure had begun in December 1882, yet the building remained – and remains today – a work in progress (it is known to locals as 'St John the Unfinished'). Nevertheless the church, with its six-hundred-foot-long nave, intricate stone carvings, vaulted ceilings, imposing west doors (made from three tons of bronze) and Great Rose Window, offered an inspiring setting for the ecumenical service of prayer and thanksgiving that was being held to commemorate the second anniversary of the *Brown* school desegregation ruling.[1]

When the service began at half past seven, twelve thousand people had packed into the aisles to hear the rising young star of the black freedom struggle. King began his sermon with a disquisition on evil – which was, he said, 'a stark, grim, and colossal reality' that projected its 'nagging, prehensile tentacles into every level of human existence'. 'In a sense', King explained, 'the whole history of life is the history of a struggle between good and evil.' But, fortified by his faith, the MIA president reminded the congregation that evil was 'ultimately doomed by the powerful, insurgent forces of good'. After all, while Good Friday might 'occupy the throne for a day', it ultimately had to 'give way to the triumphant beat of the drums of Easter'. Referring to the struggle of the ancient Israelites against the Egyptians, King noted that God had parted the waters of the Red Sea, enabling the Israelites to escape from slavery and leaving their oppressors vanquished. The MIA president then drew a striking parallel with the contemporary world, declaring that 'good, in the form of freedom and justice' was battling 'evil, in the form of oppression and colonialism'. The 'great struggle of the twentieth century', King stated, was between the 'exploited masses' of Africa and Asia who were 'questing for freedom' and the old colonial powers who sought to maintain their domination. Gradually, he explained, the 'forces of freedom and justice' were winning. Turning his attention to the United States, King argued that African Americans' struggle to overcome the vicious and cruel system of segregation would prove similarly triumphant. Jim Crow was, King asserted, 'caught in the rushing waters of historical necessity. Evil in the form of injustice and exploitation cannot survive.'

King ended his sermon with a message of love and forgiveness, arguing that segregationists could be redeemed, since 'man, by the grace of God, can be lifted from the valley of hate to the high mountain of love'. He also commanded those struggling against evil to 'have love, compassion and understanding goodwill for those against whom we struggle, helping them to realise that as we seek to defeat [evil] we are not seeking to defeat them but to help them, as well as ourselves'. The ultimate prize, as King described it, was a 'world where all men will live together as brothers' in dignity and mutual respect.[2]

Back in February, when the MIA had filed a federal lawsuit seeking an injunction against bus segregation in Montgomery, the fate of the protest had effectively been placed in the hands of the courts. Some within the movement, including King himself, had

[146]

briefly wondered whether or not to continue with the boycott. But asking the city's African Americans to return to the segregated buses and await a court ruling would have been a grievous affront to their dignity and handed a moral victory to their opponents. Moreover, the organisational potential of the MIA would have been squandered, as would any hopes of attracting national attention and political support, or of using the example of Montgomery to encourage sustained black protest elsewhere in the South. In reality, the strength of support among the rank and file meant that the question was almost certainly academic. As Jo Ann Robinson put it, 'The leaders couldn't stop it [even] if they wanted to.'[3]

As the MIA dug in for a protracted legal battle, the boycott was sustained by the hard and often mundane work of grassroots organisers. In addition to the mass meetings that were held to boost morale and maintain unity, MIA volunteers helped to raise money to fund, and undertook the complex day-to-day operation of, the car pool that transported black residents of the city to and from their places of work. They published and distributed a regular newsletter, wrote press releases, operated a speakers' bureau and contributed to the running of an office – where there was a constant need to answer correspondence, complete paperwork and stay on top of the bookkeeping. The MIA also organised a block-by-block canvassing effort as part of a campaign to increase black voter registration in the city. The organisation, along with the NAACP, provided legal representation for boycott supporters and fought the Montgomery City Commission's efforts to have the car pool declared illegal. MIA volunteers formed a welfare committee, largely run by women, which offered assistance, including food, clothes and money, to supporters who faced economic reprisals (typically eviction or dismissal from their jobs).[4]

It is fair to say that Martin Luther King did not possess a great love for administration; he was more than happy to delegate the day-to-day running of the boycott to others.[5] His most meaningful contributions to the struggle flowed, instead, from his role as the boycott's principal spokesperson. Over the years much ink has been spilled in justified praise of King's mighty oratory, which proved such a formidable weapon for the civil rights movement. Virginia Durr, for example, reported that 'my wash lady tells me every week about how she hears angel's wings when he speaks, and God speaks directly through him . . .'[6] King's charismatic leadership certainly helped to empower tens of thousands of Montgomery's African American citizens, encouraging them to believe that they could make a difference and that they would succeed.

As his sermon at St John the Divine demonstrates, one of the ways that King sought to do this was by framing the boycott as a battle between 'good' and 'evil' in which, with God on their side, the forces of 'justice' would ultimately prevail. King also argued that the struggle in Montgomery had a significance that resonated well beyond the city itself; that it promised no less than a rebirth of American democracy, and offered an inspiration to people around the world. As King put it at one of the regular MIA mass meetings, 'We want it to be known throughout the length and breadth of this land – to Asia and Africa – let the world know – that we are standing up for justice.' The Lord, said King, was 'using Montgomery as his proving ground' and 'It may be that here in the capital of the Confederacy . . . the ideal of freedom in America and in the Southland can be born.'[7]

King's conviction that the bus boycott represented a key moment in world history was shaped by his keen sense of contemporary international affairs. During his very first speech as MIA leader, he had drawn a contrast between the 'great glory' of American democracy, where the 'right to protest for right' was sacrosanct, and the grim reality of life behind the Iron Curtain. He had also roused the audience that night by claiming that, in standing up for their rights, they would inject a 'new meaning into the veins of history and of civilization'.[8] As the boycott progressed, King expanded upon this theme by drawing repeated parallels with the struggle against colonialism in Asia and Africa.

In the years since the end of the Second World War a number of countries – including India, Pakistan, Burma, Sri Lanka, Indonesia and Egypt – had secured their independence from European rule, and pressure was building precipitously elsewhere, particularly across Africa, for an end to control by foreign powers. In April 1955, delegates from twenty-nine countries from across Asia and Africa, representing half of the world's population, had met in Bandung, Indonesia, in a striking display of the growing power of the newly independent, non-white nations. Challenging the bipolar framework of the Cold War, these 'nonaligned' states (they offered allegiance to neither Washington nor Moscow) denounced racial discrimination, called for the peaceful resolution of disputes and affirmed the right of all peoples to self-determination and national independence.[9] Like countless other African Americans, King took heart from these events. He was drawn especially to the successful fight against British rule in India and the struggle to end colonialism in the Gold Coast/Ghana.[10] Black leaders throughout the twentieth century, most notably Marcus Garvey and W. E. B. Du Bois, had sought to connect the question of civil rights in the United States with the global struggle of people of colour for dignity and self-determination, and King followed enthusiastically in this tradition. Indeed, one of his key contributions to the freedom movement was to anchor the bus boycott firmly within the global context. As King pointed out, the overwhelming majority of the world's people were non-white and, until very recently, most of them had been exploited by European colonialism. But 'today many of them are free . . . And the rest are on that road.' 'We', said King, 'are part of that great movement.'[11] In July, at a gathering of Baptists in Green Lake, Wisconsin, King explained that African Americans' determination to fight on until segregation and discrimination were swept away 'springs from the same longing for human dignity that motivates oppressed peoples all over the world. This is not only a nation in transition, but this is a world in transition.' All across Africa and Asia, King noted, those who had previously been 'exploited economically, dominated politically, segregated and humiliated by some other power' were in the process of gaining their freedom. The struggle of African Americans for first-class citizenship rights was, declared King, 'a part of this *great* struggle all over the world'.[12]

Internationalising the bus boycott in this way did not simply help inspire Montgomery's black citizens during their long, tiring months of protest against segregation. It also provided a marvellous opportunity to exploit America's position as the self-styled 'leader of the free world' in its struggle against Soviet Communism. King, like other black leaders, was well aware that segregation and racial discrimination in the South threatened to undermine America's international reputation, and provided the USSR with invaluable propaganda with which to discredit her claims to support 'freedom' and 'democracy'. The Cold War also offered civil rights activists a chance to rebut segregationist claims that they were little more than Communist dupes. In fact, in King's skilful hands the boycott actually became a valuable weapon in America's fight against Communism. In an article published in June, King argued that in Montgomery it was not simply the dignity of African Americans that was at stake, but the very reputation of the United States itself. The 'deep rumblings of discontent from Africa and Asia', King explained, 'are at bottom expressions of their determination not to follow any power that denies basic human rights to a segment of its citizens. So in order to save the prestige of our nation and prevent the uncommitted peoples of the world from falling into the hands of a communistic ideology we must press on.'[13] The boycott, then, was a profoundly patriotic act. As King put it, 'Because of our love for *America*, we cannot afford to slow up.'[14]

The Montgomery bus boycott certainly achieved significant

international attention. As well as widespread coverage in the foreign press, supporters from around the world wrote to King offering encouragement and advice.[15] In May, for example, Bishop Henri Varin de la Brunelière, of the Caribbean island of Martinique, gave his assurance that 'the colored people of the USA and you especially, Reverend dear Pastor, have our deepest sympathy' in 'your heroic struggle'.[16] As they learned of foreign newspaper accounts of the boycott or received letters from overseas, King and his associates took considerable comfort from the fact that their protest was resonating with people all over the world.[17] The boycott's international dimensions were not lost, either, on American commentators. On the evening of Friday 24 February, in a television broadcast for ABC news, the award-winning journalist Edward P. Morgan argued that what was happening in Montgomery 'thrusts beyond the city limits, girdles the globe and comes home again'. The US government, he noted, was about to stage an exhibition in India to showcase the virtues of America's economic, social and political system. While acknowledging that it 'may arouse interest there', he explained that 'another exhibit has preceded it: the press accounts of the Montgomery story. It needs no prophet to foretell which . . . will make the deeper impression on the disciples of Gandhi who have now become the free citizens of India.'[18]

Morgan's reference to Gandhi draws attention to another of King's signal contributions: the adoption of nonviolence as the central weapon in the struggle for civil rights. King had, of course, stressed the Christian beliefs of the boycott's supporters, as well as their commitment to peaceful, democratic forms of protest, from the very start of his leadership of the MIA. On the evening of 30 January, when his own house was bombed, he had offered a powerful example of his personal commitment to peaceful methods – defusing a volatile and potentially violent situation by urging his supporters to put away their weapons, imploring them to love their enemies and reminding them of the teachings of Jesus: 'He who lives by the sword will perish by the sword.'[19] But at this point King had neither adopted nonviolence as a way of life nor developed a systematic and coherent ideology of nonviolent resistance. Just two days after the attack on his home, he applied (unsuccessfully) for pistol permits for the guards who had been organised to protect the parsonage. Astonishingly, given his later reputation, he even suggested that it might be 'good to shed a little blood'. In confidential remarks, King raised the possibility that if one or two white men lost some blood then the federal government might well feel compelled to intervene.[20] During the spring of 1956, though, King came to fully embrace philosophical nonviolence and endorse key Gandhian principles, including: an insistence that the means of protest should be as pure as the ends; that nonviolence had to be practised spiritually, as well as physically; and that activists' willingness to endure violence and abuse in service of a just cause would help to achieve a greater good.

On his journey to nonviolence, King received invaluable assistance from Bayard Rustin and Glenn Smiley, veteran pacifists and longtime exponents of nonviolent protest. Rustin, who was African American, was a chain-smoking, guitar-playing, folk-singing Quaker, a homosexual and a socialist, who had, during the 1930s, been a member of the Young Communist League. He served a prison term as a conscientious objector during the Second World War and, together with fellow members of the Fellowship of Reconciliation (an anti-war and social justice organisation founded in 1915), pioneered the use of nonviolent methods in the struggle for civil rights during the 1940s. In 1948, he spent several weeks in India, learning more about nonviolent resistance from some of Gandhi's associates. On 21 February 1956, the forty-three-year-old Rustin had arrived in Montgomery, excited by the possibilities that the nascent protest offered for mobilising mass nonviolent action across the South. Although he would go on to have a long and fruitful association with King, Rustin was persuaded to leave Montgomery after little more than a week, amid growing fears that his presence there might be used by segregationists to discredit the movement – though he continued to offer advice from afar.[21]

Rustin's sojourn overlapped briefly with that of his friend and colleague Glenn Smiley. A white native of Texas and a Methodist minister, the forty-five-year-old Smiley, who served as FOR's national field secretary, was committed to developing local non-violent actions, promoting greater understanding of nonviolent theory and emphasising interracial reconciliation. Smiley had arrived in Montgomery on 27 February and, in his first meeting with the MIA leader, had asked King about his familiarity with the teachings of the Mahatma.[22] King, who had studied Gandhi briefly while a college student, 'was very thoughtful, and he said, ". . . I know who the man is. I have read some statements by him, and so on, but I will have to truthfully say . . . that I know very little about the man."' Smiley, who had noted the presence of weapons in King's house, emphasised that a central precept of the Gandhian approach was an absolute refusal to retaliate in the face of evil and handed King some relevant literature. Soon after, he wrote to colleagues, conveying his belief that King had been called by God to 'lead a great movement here and in the South' and had the potential to become a 'Negro Gandhi'.[23] Yet Smiley also noted that King was 'young and some of his close help is violent'. The MIA president accepted the presence of bodyguards, for example, and his home was 'an arsenal'. King 'saw the inconsistency, but not enough. He believes and yet he doesn't believe. The whole movement is armed in a sense, and this is what I must convince him to see as the greatest evil.' Smiley was certain that if King could '*really* be won to a faith in non-violence', then there was 'no end to what he can do'.[24] Smiley continued to tutor King in the nonviolent method, in late-night discussions that were often accompanied by plates of soul food (pig's ear sandwiches became a particular

[153]

favourite), as the MIA leader sought to discover whether or not he was truly able to 'apply nonviolence to my heart'.²⁵

King's greater understanding of nonviolent resistance was not simply an intellectual odyssey; the accumulated experience of everyday protest also proved vital. 'As the days unfolded', he recalled, 'I came to see the power of nonviolence more and more.' The lived experience of a nonviolent protest was itself transformative: 'Nonviolence became more than a method to which I gave intellectual assent; it became a commitment to a way of life.' Theoretical questions, meanwhile, were resolved through the business of decision-making and practical action.²⁶ King also took heart from the ways in which those around him developed a deeper appreciation of this protest technique. In a letter to Lillian Smith, the acclaimed southern novelist and white liberal, King confessed that it was 'gratifying to know how the idea of non-violence has gradually seeped into the hearts and souls of the people'.²⁷

At the outset of the boycott, King had talked in very general terms about how the movement was dependent on spiritual or moral forces, and had described activists as walking with love in their hearts.²⁸ But during the spring, in a series of published writings and speeches, King addressed the concept of nonviolence with increasing sophistication. In an article published in the May edition of *Fellowship*, FOR's official journal, King explained that love – which he defined as 'understanding, good will toward *all* men' – was the movement's principal weapon. 'No matter what sacrifices we have to make', he said, 'we will not let anybody drag us so low as to hate them.' Whereas retaliatory violence would simply 'intensify the existence of evil and hate in the universe', love constituted a 'transforming power that can lift a whole community to new horizons of fair play, good will and justice'.²⁹ Speaking at San Francisco's Civic Auditorium on 27 June, during the NAACP's annual convention, King told his audience that the essence of nonviolent resistance was a refusal to 'cooperate with the evil of segregation'. Rejecting retaliatory violence on the grounds that it would be both impractical and immoral, he instead advocated the use of Christian love: 'a love that seeks nothing in return . . . a love that loves the person who does the evil deed, while hating the deed that the person does'. Central to the nonviolent approach was a conviction that 'the universe is on the side of right and righteousness'. 'We have this strange feeling down in Montgomery', King explained, 'that in our struggle we have cosmic companionship.'[30]

A few weeks later, King elaborated further on many of these themes, emphasising in particular that nonviolent protest, which was frequently dismissed by its critics as merely 'passive', was neither submissive nor a method of surrender. 'The nonviolent resister', King insisted, 'is just as opposed to the evil he is protesting against as a violent resister.' While 'passive physically', the method was 'aggressive spiritually', not least because practitioners were seeking actively to persuade their segregationist opponents to change their ways. The ultimate goal of nonviolent protest was not to defeat or humiliate the oppressor but to win his understanding, and even friendship, through a process of reconciliation. The key to nonviolence – its 'regulating ideal', as King put it – was Christian love, which, through its redemptive qualities, had the power to change not merely individuals but social systems, and even entire nations.[31]

King drew on the Indian independence movement to illustrate this latter claim. Simplifying the long and ultimately successful struggle against the Raj just a little, King explained that a 'little brown man' had 'looked out at the British empire' with its 'vast and intricate military machinery' and decided to confront it with 'soul force'. This method, claimed King, had enabled Mohandas K. Gandhi to 'free his people from the political domination, the economic exploitation, and the humiliation that had been inflicted upon them'. Truly, nonviolence was a 'powerful weapon' and 'we', King declared, 'must be willing to use it'.[32] He predicted that it would provide the key to destroying segregation right across the American South.[33]

King would be proved spectacularly right. Nonviolent resistance would be at the heart of the civil rights movement's signature campaigns during the decade that followed. To be sure, King was not the first civil rights leader to advocate the nonviolent approach. During the 1940s, for instance, the black labour leader A. Philip Randolph had sought to promote 'Non-Violent Good Will Direct Action', while the Congress of Racial Equality had experimented with nonviolent protests to challenge racial discrimination at a number of restaurants in Chicago.[34] But King's historic achievement was to popularise nonviolence. Before the Montgomery bus boycott, support for Gandhian nonviolence was restricted to a small band of militant pacifists and socialists. In the skilful hands of King, though, an idea that had operated in the margins of American political culture became respectable – even mainstream. This shift owed much to King's ability to ground nonviolent theory firmly in Christian teaching and to fuse it with patriotic rhetoric and symbolism. The MIA president readily acknowledged that he had himself come to Gandhi 'through Jesus'. 'Christ furnished the spirit and motivation', King explained, and 'Gandhi furnished the method.'[35] Drawing on Christian teaching, in particular Jesus's command to 'Love your enemies, bless them that curse you, do good to them that hate you, and pray for them which despitefully use you, and persecute you', King couched nonviolent resistance in terms that his deeply religious southern black audiences understood readily. This message of love and forgiveness also resonated strongly with northern white liberals, whose political support would prove vital.[36] King further strengthened its appeal by arguing forcefully that nonviolence was being used to realise America's founding promise of freedom and equality. Nonviolent resistance to Jim Crow segregation, then, provided a means of strengthening American democracy.[37]

Even at the height of the civil rights movement in the early 1960s, only a small (albeit influential) minority of activists embraced nonviolence as a way of life. Most civil rights protesters appear to have adopted it, instead, as a tactic. While prepared to use nonviolence, particularly in public, so long as it proved effective, these activists were also willing to use other methods, including armed self-defence, as and where appropriate.[38] Moreover, not everyone in the movement was convinced by nonviolence in any form. Even some of King's closest colleagues in Montgomery remained sceptical. E. D. Nixon, who had done so much to launch the boycott, 'never agreed with it . . . I told Rev. King, "There isn't any use in your telling me that if a man slaps me, I'm not to slap him back. I know that before I could think about what you said, I'm going to have knocked the guy's block off."' Nixon, who was regularly targeted by white supremacists, even took to sitting on his front porch with a Winchester rifle, in order to protect his home and family from further attack.[39] Nevertheless, the public use of nonviolent tactics and the projection of a nonviolent image – both within the United States and to the world – enabled civil rights activists to present a compelling moral case and to win widespread, and decisive, public and political support.

By the summer of 1956, King had developed an unshakeable belief in both the righteousness and the revolutionary potential of nonviolent resistance. Convinced that violent methods could only ever result in bitterness and bloodshed, he viewed nonviolence not just as the solution to the problem of segregation in the United States but as the key to defeating injustice and tyranny everywhere. Fired by this faith, King urged oppressed peoples the world over to wage their struggle with the weapon of love.[40] In the months ahead, though, those seeking to win their freedoms outside the United States would turn more readily to the gun than to Gandhi.

III SUMMER

A SPIRIT OF REBELLION

9

BREAD AND FREEDOM

Every provocateur or maniac who will dare raise his hand
against the people's rule may be sure that . . . the authorities
will chop off his hand.
JÓZEF CYRANKIEWICZ, Polish prime minister

Poznań, on the banks of the Warta River, halfway between War-saw and Berlin, is one of Poland's oldest cities – its magnificent Cathedral of St Peter and St Paul was founded in 968. The historic capital of Wielkopolska ('Greater Poland') had remained fiercely committed to its Polish identity, despite more than a century of Prussian occupation and an attempt by the Nazis to eradicate any vestige of non-German culture.[1] By the mid-1950s this important centre for manufacturing and trade had been rebuilt following the massive damage suffered during its liberation by the Red Army. Away from its industrial suburbs, with their dark red brick build-ings, the city centre boasted large open spaces, a beautiful old town square and an imposing stone palace ('the Castle') that had been built by the Germans in 1910 and which housed the offices of the local government. Half a mile to the south-west lay the grounds of the International Trade Fair, whose white, futuristic buildings conjured up images of progress and modernity. With a large and highly disciplined working-class population, Poznań was viewed as 'the vanguard city of communist Poland'.[2] At the end of June 1956, however, it found itself at the cutting edge of popular opposition to the 'People's rule'.

At 6.30 a.m. on Thursday 28 June, amidst mounting anger over low wages and poor conditions, the workers at Poznań's ZISPO Metal Works downed tools. As the plant's siren was sounded, shattering the early morning calm, thousands assembled at the factory's brick gates before heading north to the city centre, two miles away. As they walked along Górna Wilda Street, many of the protesters, just off the night shift, wore 'black greasy working clothes' while others 'carried hammers over their shoulders' or waved Polish flags and banners. Amid the singing of patriotic songs and hymns, chants of 'We want bread!' rang out. When the procession passed by St Martin's Church, two priests appeared on the steps to deliver a blessing.[3]

Swelled by thousands of recruits from factories across the city, as well as high-school and university students, housewives and children, the demonstrators cut an impressive sight as they poured into Stalin Square, close to the Castle and the headquarters of the Provincial Committee of the Polish United Workers' Party (PZPR).[4] A British diplomat, Donald Boswell Gurrey, who was in town for the city's famous trade fair, reported that by 9 a.m. the square was already 'packed with people', perhaps as many as twenty thousand, with 'fresh lorry loads' of demonstrators arriving 'at every moment'. The crowd were 'singing a hymn . . . and the whole atmosphere was one of seriousness and determination'. As Poles stood on their balconies or in their windows, applauding and cheering, people continued to head towards the square in their thousands, carrying banners that read 'We demand bread for our children!' and singing the Polish national anthem ('Poland is not yet lost').[5] The scale of the protests was extraordinary, and as many as one hundred thousand people – more than a quarter of the population – took to the streets during this tumultuous day.[6]

At 9.10 a.m. a group of fifteen people claiming to be representatives of the crowd entered the Castle for a meeting with Franciszek Frąckowiak, chairman of the Municipal National Council. But when they demanded that a government delegation be despatched immediately to Poznań, and that both prices and production targets be lowered, Frąckowiak demurred, claiming that he lacked sufficient authority, and telephoned local PZPR headquarters. When he was put through to Wincenty Kraśko, head of the propaganda section, one of the delegates – a university student – grabbed the receiver and shouted, 'Either we get someone here from Warsaw or you pay with your head.' Meanwhile, more protesters from the square outside had entered the building: some placed a white flag of surrender in a window; others climbed onto the roof of the tower and, to roars from the crowd, raised a Polish flag. The delegation soon moved on to the Communist Party offices across the street for discussions that proved similarly fruitless, and when Kraśko addressed the crowd, in an attempt to defuse the situation, his bureaucratic language and evasions caused uproar. Catcalls and loud booing soon drowned him out.[7]

At the outset, the demonstrators had focused on economic issues – there were constant chants of '*Chleba, chleba, chleba!*' ('Bread, bread, bread!'), as well as demands for higher wages and lower prices.[8] Gurrey had encountered the crowd shortly after quarter to nine, as he attempted to drive from his hotel to the trade fair. On being stopped by the protesters, he 'asked what was up and was told they were on strike. I asked why. Two of them – middle-aged men – struck their stomachs and spoke the Polish word for "bread".'[9] Demands for greater religious freedom had also begun to circulate, with workers appealing for the release of Cardinal Stefan Wyszyński, the Primate of Poland, who had been held under house arrest since September 1953, and requesting the return of religious instruction into the schools.[10] Soon, though, overt opposition to the regime itself bubbled to the surface.

Peter Wiles, a Fellow of New College, Oxford, was in Poznań with a delegation of visiting economists when the protests broke out. Wiles, an expert on Communist economies, had 'lost no time' in venturing into the city centre to observe the protests, despite the objections of his official guides (who had 'offered all short of physical opposition' to try and dissuade him).[11] Arriving on the scene at 10 a.m. he noticed that, while the 'lorry loads of workers' who were still arriving were 'demanding only more bread, more wages, etc.', the atmosphere in Stalin Square itself increasingly resembled 'that of a popular revolution'. By this point many trams had been overturned and one, draped with Polish flags, served as a make-shift podium, from which a succession of speakers harangued the crowd.[12] 'We want freedom!' and 'Down with Soviet occupation!' were shouted out, or scrawled on placards and banners, and the protesters talked freely, claiming that only 5 per cent of Poles supported the Communist regime and insisting that 'the people' had now 'risen against' the Russians.[13] There was also excited talk that other cities were in revolt.[14]

The protesters' mood was also becoming more aggressive. When the strike had begun, it had the air of a holiday. People marched with 'smiles on their faces', according to one secret police report, and waiters at the Europejskii Café had offered refreshments to those at the head of the column, rushing out with 'trays of drinks and appetisers' as the crowds arrived in the city centre. There had, though, been ugly hints of what was to come. When one plant director tried to prevent his workers from joining the strike, for instance, his furious employees poured oil over him.[15] Several hours into the protests, the anger had built precipitously. At about 10 a.m., amidst shouts of 'Down with the Russkis!' and 'Let's destroy the Communist shits!' a group of workers forcibly entered the headquarters of the PZPR Provincial Committee and chased out its employees. The protesters collected up all of the red banners that they could find and threw them into the street, along with portraits of various Communist leaders (in a sign of respect, Lenin alone was spared this indignity; his portrait was turned against the wall). Busts of eminent figures, including the late Bolesław Bierut, were smashed. A banner reading 'Death to the Betrayers!' was hoisted over the building, and blackboards were placed in the windows, bearing the slogans 'We want freedom!' and 'We demand a free

Poland!' Outside, as the crowd cheered their support, some burned their Party membership cards on a bonfire.[16]

Other symbols of authority soon came under attack. Amid rumours that a delegation of ZISPO workers had been arrested, a group marched to the Młyńska Street jail, where they overpowered the guards, released the inmates and destroyed files, furniture and equipment. They also helped themselves to weapons. A second group forced their way into the offices of the public prosecutor and were soon setting fire to documents in the street.[17] Others headed to the city's fairgrounds, site of the Twenty-fifth International Trade Fair, where they tore down the Soviet flag and raised banners proclaiming 'Down with this phony Communism!' and 'Russians get out!' Meanwhile, red banners and Soviet flags were destroyed all across the city and the city's radio station was 'sacked': jamming equipment was hurled out of the sixth-floor windows to the streets below, where the crowd took evident enjoyment in stamping on the wrecked machinery. 'Now', said one striker, 'we shall be able to listen to the BBC at last.'[18]

Initially, the strikers faced little resistance – both the police and the local Citizens' Militia were reluctant to maintain order, and some troops fraternised with the strikers, even handing over their weapons. When two trucks of Militia arrived at the Castle, they were greeted with enthusiastic cries of 'The Militia is with us, the Militia is with the nation!'[19] However, when thousands of protesters began to converge on the Provisional Office of Public Security – an imposing structure, built in the Constructivist style, on Kochanowski Street – the situation quickly deteriorated. The headquarters of the hated secret police was an obvious target for the demonstrators, who suspected that the missing ZISPO workers were being held in its underground cells (in fact the rumour about the arrested workers was false). At about 10.15 a.m. a group of protesters, headed by a contingent of children aged between ten and fourteen, arrived at the Security Office building, carrying

Polish flags and singing patriotic songs. Stopping in front of the headquarters, they chanted, 'Down with the Communists' flunkeys!' and 'Down with the nation's butchers, you shits!' before attempting to force open the doors.[20]

At first, the security forces sought to disperse the crowd by using water hoses, but the protesters proved determined. Creating a barricade out of overturned trams, tree branches and broken equipment from the nearby radio station, they responded with a hail of stones and rocks, and shouts of 'Down with the Communists!' and 'Your time is come. Today we will be rid of you!' Further attempts were made to force open the doors. Some time around eleven o'clock, shots rang out from a second-floor window.[21] One British observer explained how 'for a second everyone froze in his tracks. Then everyone tried to run in the same direction – away from the firing . . . many . . . got trampled. I heard screams of women and men . . .'[22] Several people were hit, including a number of children; according to one account, the body of a sixteen-year-old boy was carried aloft as a Polish flag 'dipped in his blood, was escorted by a proud and pretty Polish girl'.[23] The secret police headquarters was now under siege as the protesters, armed with Molotov cocktails and guns, responded in kind, and 'small arms fire, ranging from sporadic to continuous' continued throughout the afternoon.[24] Observing the situation from an apartment block in Roosevelt Street, some four hundred metres away, a German reporter noticed how 'again and again the frightened crowd would run into the archways to hide from the bullets'. At about twelve thirty, two tanks which had been commandeered by a group of protesters on nearby Dąbrowski Street 'rumbled through the streets wet from the rain' before coming to a halt outside the Security Office. A woman attached a flag to the turret of one of the tanks, and the crowd delivered an emotional rendition of '*Boże, coś Polskę*' ('God Save Poland'). Using its top-mounted machine guns (there was no ammunition for the cannon), the tank then opened fire on the building.[25] Meanwhile, a number of workers had taken up positions on the rooftops of nearby buildings, from where they exchanged fire with Security Office guards. Across the city, overturned trams, cars and even furniture were used to erect makeshift barricades, and both of the town's railway stations were closed down in an effort to prevent military reinforcements from entering the city.[26]

Although only a minority took up arms, there was plenty of excitement about the attack on the Security Office and the fact that the workers had risen up against the Communist Party.[27] But there was a vengeful element at work, too: the crowd outside the Security building denounced the 'fascists' inside and threatened to burn them alive, and secret police came under attack across the city. The most notorious incident occurred at the main railway station, where Corporal Zygmunt Izdebny was cornered by a mob. As they kicked the twenty-five-year-old to death, they boasted of their intention to 'stamp out all the Security Office employees like bed bugs'.[28]

In Warsaw, news of the disturbances had reached Edward Ochab, first secretary of the PZPR Central Committee, shortly before 10 a.m. During a private meeting, the defence minister, Konstantin Rokossovsky, warned that local forces might prove insufficient and, asking to be given a 'free hand', suggested that army units should be sent in. Ochab agreed immediately, and the decision was rubber-stamped retrospectively by the Politburo.[29] Rokossovsky deployed overwhelming firepower, sending thousands of troops (both army regulars and soldiers from the Internal Security Corps) and hundreds of tanks to crush the uprising.[30] As air force jets swooped low over the city, tanks, infantry trucks and armoured vehicles poured into Poznań.[31] At times, the events seemed distinctly surreal. One British businessman, for example, 'described . . . his astonishment at seeing two tanks', one of which had joined the rebels, 'firing at each other with spectators lined up along the pavement rather as though they were at Wimbledon watching a tennis match'.³² And some of the young men who were firing on the Security Office 'seemed to be very pleased with themselves, even posing for photographs while aiming at their targets'.³³ The situation was, though, deadly serious. While some soldiers used tear gas to disperse the protesters, others fired directly into the crowds. One eyewitness saw five people lying dead in Stalin Square and 'another one collapsing under machine-gun shots a few yards away from me'.³⁴ Others were crushed to death. In one gruesome incident an eighteen-year-old university student was run through with a bayonet as he attempted to surrender. Even when troops fired into the air the effects could be fatal, as 'children who had climbed trees to escape tanks, or for a better view, fell dead like sparrows'. Throughout the afternoon makeshift ambulances – little more than trucks daubed with red crosses – shuttled back and forth, ferrying the dead and the injured.³⁵

As the scale of the military assault became clear, protesters desperately sought out Western observers, shouting out in French and German, 'This is our revolution! Tell people abroad about it. The Soviets must go . . .'³⁶ From the start, the strikers had greeted foreign visitors with enthusiastic displays of friendliness. When a car with a foreign licence plate was stopped on University Bridge, near to Stalin Square, for example, the driver was hoisted into the air as the crowd shouted, 'Long live!'³⁷ Similarly a British trade delegate recounted that when the strikers saw his car was flying the Union Jack they cheered and clapped. On arriving at his hotel in the early afternoon, he was approached by several workers, who urged him to 'please tell people in your country what is happening here. We want bread, we cannot live any longer under these conditions . . . This tears the mask off the Party which is supposed to be our friend . . .'³⁸ As one revolutionary put it, 'Tell the men in the West that Poland wants to be free. The dead bones of June 28 will rest one day in a shrine of marble, and millions will remove their hats before them.'³⁹

Armed only with Molotov cocktails, grenades and small arms, the insurgents were outgunned. Although fierce fighting continued in and around the Security Office, the resistance elsewhere had petered out by 4 p.m.[40] The sound of gunfire and the occasional explosion punctuated the night, but by daybreak order had been restored.[41] The toll, though, was a heavy one: seventy-three killed, including sixty-four civilians, and four hundred wounded.[42] More than six hundred people were rounded up, and many of them subjected to brutal treatment. One eighteen-year-old girl had seen her own father, an electrician, cut down by gunfire. Arrested for participating in the uprising, she was held in the notorious Kochanowski Street jail, and later recalled how one of her cellmates was taken away for interrogation, only to return with all the teeth in her upper jaw removed. The corridors of the jail echoed with the sound of 'inhuman screams and howling', akin to that of 'slaughtered animals'.[43]

The Poznań uprising was triggered by deep-rooted economic discontent. A BBC correspondent, travelling around Poland just a few weeks earlier, had reported that 'complaints about the low standards of living were bitter and universal'.[44] But while life was tough across the nation, the 380,000 residents of Poznań had particular reason to feel aggrieved. The level of per capita investment, at 368 złotys, was dramatically lower than elsewhere (the figure was 572 in Łódź and 1,147 in Kraków), and Poznań province had been at the forefront of efforts to collectivise agriculture and establish industrial co-operatives. Indeed, Poznańians, with their proud tradition of efficiency, appear to have been particularly outraged by the waste, chaos and incompetence that characterised Stalinist economic planning. By 1956 the monthly salary of an industrial worker in Poznań was significantly lower than the national average, the price of everyday necessities (such as bread, fruit and sausages) was high, and medicines cost so much that, it was said, hardly anybody in Poznań could afford to buy them.[45] The city also faced a chronic housing shortage, which caused particular hardships for younger workers who were forced to live with their parents in overcrowded and dilapidated apartments.[46]

These difficulties were compounded by detrimental changes to bonuses, production targets and working conditions that affected workers in many of Poznań's industrial enterprises during the early months of 1956. At the Metallurgical Works, for instance, productivity bonuses were abolished, tram workers were denied the cold weather payments that their counterparts in other cities received as a matter of course, and workers at the Rolling Stock Company had their coal allowances slashed. Meanwhile, at the giant ZISPO works – which produced high-quality ship engines, locomotives and train carriages as well as machine tools and other metal products – the fifteen-thousand-strong workforce faced the abolition of bonuses, the raising of productivity targets, and cramped, unsafe and often foul-smelling working conditions. All this on top of revelations that, over a period of several years, more than five thousand of the plant's employees had been cheated out of eleven million złotys in overpaid taxes (the equivalent of two months' wages, annually, for each worker affected).[47] It was little wonder that ZISPO's workforce was so belligerent.

Efforts to mitigate the situation had failed. More than four thousand petitions were submitted to the ZISPO management, and negotiations took place with Communist Party officials, government representatives and factory managers. All proved fruitless. As discontent smouldered, workers engaged in silent protests, work stoppages and mass rallies. Discussions were also held with workers in other factories to co-ordinate action. Attention naturally focused on the International Trade Fair, scheduled to open on 17 June: as one ZISPO worker put it, 'Let the foreigners see that there is poverty in Poland, and not enough to eat.'[48]

The ongoing effects of Khrushchev's 'secret speech' were also at work. In the months prior to the uprising the Polish press had reported extensively on the criticisms aimed at the government by writers and intellectuals; mass meetings, held in towns and villages all over Poland, had seen unprecedented attacks on the Communist Party, and letters of complaint had flooded into newspapers and local Party offices.[49] In this more liberal climate, Poznań's workers expressed their own grievances publicly.[50] At an open meeting at the ZISPO plant to discuss the Twentieth Party Congress, the writer Piotr Guzy had urged the workers to defend their interests 'with greater courage' and 'without fear'; secret police reports provided plenty of evidence of the workers' newfound willingness to speak out.[51] In fact, the Poznań uprising offered a stark illustration of the difficulties involved in de-Stalinisation. The more open, critical atmosphere that emerged in the wake of the Twentieth Party Congress raised expectations and emboldened dissent. It was an explosive mix that proved difficult to contain. As the *Manchester Guardian* put it:

> freedom in small doses is a tricky prescription. Between
> consent freely given and the consent of the prison cell
> lies a no man's land in which the Polish Government
> has just struck a mine . . . we now see how hard it is for
> communism to slip out of the Stalinist mould, even though
> its leaders may wish it. By now, the outer air is a killer.[52]

On 27 June a ZISPO delegation had returned from Warsaw, following talks with the minister of metal industry. They believed that they had won important concessions, including the reimbursement of the overpaid taxes, improvements to work norms and the reinstatement of some bonuses. But at mass meetings held across the plant, many workers were sceptical. Later that day, when the minister himself spoke to the workers of the railway carriage factory, the mood worsened. Using convoluted language, the minister appeared to row back from the earlier agreement, prompting boos and shouts of 'lies, down with him . . .' When he ended his speech, declaring 'things are not so bad – just get back to work!' a strike was a certainty.[53]

The violent suppression of the Poznań demonstrations was met with predictable howls of outrage in the West. The British government (itself by no means averse to using lethal force when it came to keeping colonial subjects in check) was distressed at the 'considerable loss of life', while in Washington the State Department declared that it was 'profoundly shocked by the shooting' and offered its sympathy to the families of those who had been killed. Arguing that the demonstrators had been 'merely expressing their . . . grievances', the Americans called for 'the peoples of Eastern Europe', including the Poles, to be given the 'right to choose the form of government under which they live'.[54] Given that many of those who took to the streets – and lost their lives – were ordinary workers, trade union leaders were understandably quick to join the chorus of criticism. The International Confederation of Free Trade Unions, an anti-Communist labour organisation that had been founded in 1949, and which represented tens of millions of workers (including those affiliated with Britain's TUC and America's AFL-CIO), 'saluted the fighting spirit of the Polish workers, their unflinching courage, and their burning love for freedom'. It also paid 'homage to the true heroes of labour who fell dead or wounded when the communist masters ordered the police and the army to fire on the workers'.[55]

There was condemnation from the press, too, with the *New York Times* declaring that 'the first barrage of Communist bullets stripped off the mask from those who claim that the Communists represent and rule for the working class. It was the proletarians of Poznań who took to the streets to voice their demands and it was the proletarians whose lives were taken . . .' The brutal response of the authorities had demonstrated the 'moral and political bankruptcy of Polish communism . . .'[56] Writing in the French daily

Franc Tireur, meanwhile, Charles Ronsac predicted that Poland's Communist leaders would 'not be able to hide a genuine outburst of working class feeling . . .'[57] That, though, did not stop them from trying.

On the evening of 29 June, as troops continued to mop up pockets of resistance, Prime Minister Józef Cyrankiewicz broadcast from a Poznań radio station. Explaining that he was in 'great pain' because this 'beautiful city, known for its diligence, patriotism, and love of order' had witnessed 'murderous . . . and bloody riots', the forty-five-year-old former Auschwitz inmate blamed 'provocateurs' and 'imperialistic agents' for the trouble. He also praised the 'heroic soldiers, militiamen, and members of the security forces' for their bravery, and claimed that they had 'avoided using weapons until the last moment when they were shot at by the aggressors'. The Polish leader also issued a chilling threat to anyone contemplating further resistance: 'Every provocateur or maniac who will dare raise his hand against the people's rule may be sure that in the interest of the working class . . . in the interest of our Fatherland, the authorities will chop off his hand.'[58]

Claims about foreign imperialists working in concert with domestic reactionaries were repeated across the Polish press. The Communist youth newspaper *Sztandar Młodych* ('Flag of Our Youth'), for instance, claimed that Poznań had been 'intentionally chosen by the provocateurs' who wanted to 'take advantage of the presence of numerous foreigners' in order to undermine confidence in the Party and to discredit the nation before the eyes of the world.[59]

There was, in fact, no evidence at all that 'nests of agents' had organised the uprising. In fact, Party members supported the strike in large numbers, and even provided some of its leaders. Although Moscow remained keen on the line that 'subversive imperialist activity' was behind the trouble, in Poland such claims were not taken seriously (except, perhaps, by a few officials).[60] Even as Polish politicians and journalists pointed the finger of blame at 'bandits' and reactionaries, they also acknowledged that the country's economic situation was 'not easy' and that there were 'shortcomings in the life of the workers'.[61] A report on the riots, published in *Trybuna Ludu* on 30 June, for example, conceded that the 'economic demands of workers were to a large extent justified, and their grievances were understandable'.[62] In his 29 June radio broadcast, Cyrankiewicz had admitted that workers in many of Poznań's factories had legitimate grievances and that mistakes would have to be 'immediately corrected'. Now the government moved to address the workers' concerns. On 10 July, it announced that some 6.5 million złotys in taxes were to be repaid to the ZISPO employees. Meanwhile various officials, at both national and local level, were dismissed from their posts.[63]

Although the United States had no involvement in the Poznań uprising, it did attempt to exploit it. Washington's official policy was to encourage 'determined resistance to dominant Soviet influence over the satellites in Eastern Europe and to seek the eventual elimination of that influence' by developing 'feasible political, economic, propaganda and covert measures' to 'create and exploit troublesome problems for the USSR, complicate control in the satellites, and retard the growth of the military and economic potential of the Soviet bloc'.[64] When news of the riots broke on the evening of 28 June, it generated considerable excitement. Just before six o'clock John Foster Dulles, the secretary of state, spoke on the telephone with his brother Allen, the CIA director. As the latest reports from the ticker were read out to him, Foster responded, 'When they begin to crack they can crack fast. We have to keep the pressure on.'[65] Dulles was keen to generate maximum leverage from the uprising, believing that it presented the West with an 'excellent opportunity' to exert 'psychological pressure on [the] Soviet orbit'.[66] In an attempt to embarrass the Polish and Soviet leadership, the American government made an offer, via the International Red Cross, of 'appropriate quantities of wheat, flour, and other foods' to help 'relieve the critical situation in the Poznań area' where recent disorders had apparently been 'marked with demands by the population for bread'. It was rejected out of hand.[67] Radio Free Europe – the US-funded broadcaster – also sought to exploit the uprising, not just in Poland (where listeners were told that Poznań had illustrated the 'bankruptcy of Communist rule') but throughout Eastern Europe.[68] Broadcasts to Hungary, for example, pointed out that workers there had 'similar reasons for dissatisfaction and despair', claimed that a 'Poznań revolt' was stirring in Hungarian intellectual life, and drew parallels with what they called 'Hungary's Poznań', when on 25 June 1919 workers in the nation's capital had risen up against the short-lived Communist regime of Béla Kun.[69] In truth, these efforts had little practical effect, other than to encourage the regime's opponents to believe that, in the event of a serious challenge to Communist rule, meaningful support from the West might be forthcoming.

The Poznań uprising sparked a wave of dissent across Poland.[70] Flyers and graffiti – pledging solidarity with the workers of Poznań, expressing anti-Russian sentiment and demanding greater political and economic freedoms – appeared in towns and cities all over the country, while anonymous letters and manifestos were sent to newspaper editors, radio stations and local Communist Party offices. Dissent was also voiced at several of the rallies and mass meetings that, ironically, the authorities had themselves encouraged in order to denounce the 'provocateurs'. Meanwhile, workers in factories and farms across Poland demanded pay rises or reductions in the price of goods, calculating that the authorities would be likely to offer concessions rather than risk further disorder. There were increasingly bullish demands for more radical reforms and a growing clamour for the return to power of Władysław Gomułka – the 'national' face of Polish Communism, who had been expelled from the Party in 1948 for challenging Stalinist orthodoxy.[71]

The shockwaves from Poznań were also felt some four hundred miles south, in Hungary. In the immediate aftermath of the revolt, the Hungarian interior minister had placed both the police and the ÁVH (State Protection Agency) on high alert. In Csepel, an industrial suburb south of Budapest, for example, police patrols were doubled while in Győr, in the north-west of the country, leave was cancelled for guards at the power station, gasworks and other key facilities, arms were distributed and reinforcements were deployed.[72] Unnerved by growing evidence of unrest that spring, Hungary's Mátyás Rákosi was determined to hold the line. On 30 June, the Central Committee of the Hungarian Workers' Party denounced the 'demagogic' and slanderous attacks that had recently been made on the Party by 'enemies of the working people'. With one eye firmly on the recent disturbances in Poland, it further declared that the 'Poznań provocation is a warning to every Hungarian worker and every honest patriot firmly to oppose attempts at troublemaking and to help the unfettered development of those forces which . . . lead our People's Democracy to new successes'.[73] It was a desperate attempt to steady the ship.

10

THE PETŐFI CIRCLE

The source of our troubles is lack of freedom.
TIBOR DÉRY

In mid-July 1956 the veteran Soviet leader Anastas Mikoyan – one of Khrushchev's key lieutenants and the de facto number two in the Kremlin – was sent on an urgent mission to Budapest, amid intense concern about the stability of Hungary's Communist government. Moscow was right to be worried. In a top-secret report for his Presidium colleagues, filed on 14 July, Mikoyan painted an alarming picture: 'One can see how day after day the comrades are further losing their grip on power. A parallel centre is forming from enemy elements operating actively, decisively, and self-confidently.' He reported that 'hostile elements' were agitating among the workers, the intelligentsia and disaffected Party members, steadily building support and expanding their influence, and all without fear of punishment or reprisal. Mikoyan described a leadership in disarray: there was no unity on either 'issues of principle' or 'practical questions of party management', discipline had 'fallen apart' and control of the press and radio had been surrendered. The Hungarian comrades had even admitted that power was 'slipping away'. When Mikoyan had suggested that Mátyás Rákosi, Hungary's veteran leader, should voluntarily step aside, there was much support. Indeed, some of Rákosi's colleagues on the Central Committee were reported to have expressed 'a certain pleasure'.[1]

On 18 July, Rákosi announced his resignation as first secretary of the Hungarian Workers' Party (MDP). In his official statement he cited his age and poor health (he was sixty-five and was suffering from high blood pressure) but also admitted to a number of 'mistakes', particularly concerning the 'cult of personality' and the 'violation of socialist legality'. Rákosi explained that in the aftermath of Khrushchev's 'secret speech', it 'became clear to me that the weight and effect of these mistakes were greater than I had thought'; they had 'caused serious harm to our socialist development as a whole'. He also accepted that his attempts to atone for these errors had been sluggish, inconsistent and weak.[2] This humiliating and unceremonious ejection from power must have been a bitter pill to swallow for a man who had once compared his own achievements with those of Stephen I, the revered eleventh-century king-saint who had founded the nation. In an anguished telephone call with Khrushchev, Rákosi had begged for more time, warning that 'if I go, everything collapses'. Flown to Moscow for urgent 'medical treatment', he would see out the remaining fifteen years of his life in Kirghizia (modern-day Kyrgyzstan).[3]

The pressure on Rákosi had been building steadily for months. Khrushchev's dramatic revelations at the Twentieth Party Congress, and the desire to secure a rapprochement with Yugoslavia, meant that Rákosi's reputation as 'Stalin's best pupil' and his bitter personal enmity with Josep Tito had become serious liabilities. Among ordinary Hungarians, meanwhile, the first secretary's standing had never been worse. One journalist wrote that he was 'universally detested and despised', both 'in and out of his party'; Khrushchev recalled that, by the summer, Rákosi's name had 'acquired the connotation of something despicable'.[4] Certainly, one did not have to look hard to find evidence of either opposition to his leadership or dissatisfaction with his government.[5]

In particular, the pages of Hungary's major newspapers and magazines bristled with criticism.[6] The 7 June edition of *Nok Lapja* (the leading women's weekly) carried an article by Tibor Tardos, a journalist who was fast acquiring a reputation as a dissident. In 'Alone in Budapest' he described the everyday lives of four young women who worked at a lamp factory. The girls, who lived 'scat-

tered in the big city, far away from parents, [and] from any kind
of education', were forced to rent a bed from a rather fearsome
landlady because there was no sign that the hostel promised in
their factory's five-year plan would ever be built. Their dream was
simply to 'have a home, to have supper every day'. Tardos casti-
gated the 'silly journalists' who, in innumerable articles, painted a
rosy picture of Communist Hungary as 'the best of all worlds', and
he attacked Rákosi's relentless drive to transform Hungary into a
land of 'iron and steel', whatever the cost.[7]

The Party's day-to-day control over industry was also denounced.
Writing in a May edition of *Partelet* ('Party Life') László Sárkány
drew attention to the 'discord between the factory manager and
the party secretary, which stems from the fact that the latter does
not possess adequate technical and economic knowledge'. This
meant that, all too often, 'when there is an argument, instead of
convincing, he issues orders'.[8] Workers in Diósgyőr, an industrial
city in the north-east, were described by another observer as being
increasingly impatient with officials who displayed 'a bureaucratic
insensibility and dryness of heart'. One Budapest steel worker
explained that, more than the economic disappointments, it was
the lack of personal freedoms that really grated. 'Many times', he
explained, 'I have been obliged to accept the opinion of others, one
which perhaps I don't share.' Moreover, 'As that opinion changes,
it's demanded that mine change equally.' And this, he declared,
made him feel 'sick': 'I'm a man . . . I too have a head which I use
to think.' While he remained committed to socialism, he nevertheless yearned to be treated as an 'adult who lives and knows how
to think. I want to be able to speak my thoughts without having
anything to fear – and I want to be heard as well.'[9]

Rural life was no better. A May edition of *Beke es Szabadsag*
('Peace and Freedom') carried a lengthy article by Tamás Aczél. A
gifted writer, Aczél had been appointed as editor-in-chief at the
Party's in-house publishing company at the age of just twenty-

nine; within two years he had been lauded by both Hungary and the USSR (winning, respectively, the Kossuth Prize and the Stalin Prize). In November 1955 he had played a leading role in the so-called Writers' Revolt, which saw the Hungarian Writers' Association, the body responsible for ensuring that published poetry and prose did not deviate from the Party line, attack the 'anti-democratic methods which cripple our cultural life'.[10] Aczél, who spent a week in an unnamed village on the Great Hungarian Plain, reported that although the co-operative stores, selling old clothes and other items, were 'fairly well stocked', the villagers faced difficulties in obtaining some basic supplies: 'Fat, for instance, is available only rarely and in small quantities'; wine – if available at all – was priced exorbitantly; and the village market was 'small and rather empty'. Politically, the villagers seemed apathetic. Many, including some of the most talented and intelligent, had decided that silence was the prudent option. As one villager explained, 'Why should I speak up, Comrade? Who knows which of my sentences will be challenged in a year from now?' Aczél cited many examples of villagers who had been rebuffed, slighted or sidelined by the Party for offences real or imagined. The result was 'a feeling of defencelessness, of precariousness' that 'pervades everything'. Aczél denounced the indifference of local officials, who considered themselves 'infallible and judge the living and the dead without appeal'. Given the 'chasm' between Party functionaries and the masses, Aczél argued that reforms were desperately needed that would not only 'bring home to the workers the right to criticise, but also create a climate where criticism can thrive'.[11]

By the summer of 1956, much of the opposition to the Rákosi regime was focused around the Petőfi Circle – a debating club, named in honour of the poet and hero of the 1848 revolution Sándor Petőfi, that had been founded in the spring of 1955 by DISz (the League of Working Youth). The Party leadership had even encouraged the group, believing that it would act as a kind of safety valve for dissent. In the event, things worked out rather differently. Although the Petőfi Circle was affiliated formally with a youth organisation, its leaders were mostly young professionals, rather than students, and about 80 per cent were Party members. While many had become disillusioned with the regime, they had not given up on Communism itself (as the historian Anne Applebaum has pointed out, 1956 was not 1989; 'not everybody was yet convinced Communism was doomed to fail'). Most of those drawn to the Petőfi Circle were motivated by the belief that, as one of its leaders put it, 'socialism could be improved and that Marxism could be reborn'.[12] Although there were no formal connections to Imre Nagy, the Circle had a strong ideological affinity with the former prime minister and the liberal reforms of his so-called 'New Course'. While Nagy himself never attended a Petőfi Circle debate, he was kept abreast of its discussions, and some of his key lieutenants, notably Géza Losonczy and Miklós Vásárhelyi, served as unofficial go-betweens.[13]

During its first year, the Petőfi Circle's discussions – on history, economics, science, literature and Soviet art – sometimes involved no more than a dozen people and were pretty unremarkable. But by the middle of 1956 the Circle was providing a platform for what one Western analyst described as 'some of the most outspoken criticism of Communist rule heard anywhere in the Soviet orbit to date'.[14]

News of Khrushchev's 'secret speech' liberated Budapest's intellectuals, transforming the Petőfi Circle into a centre of anti-regime sentiment. Drawing ever larger and more boisterous crowds – including regular workers' delegations from Budapest's main factories – it had, by the early summer of 1956, become the focal point of an emerging movement for political reform. In May, a public discussion on political economy turned into an 'all-out denunciation' of Rákosi's 'megalomania' and saw bitter attacks on his entire economic approach (including forced industrialisation, low wages and the imposition of unrealistic production targets). A few weeks later a debate on historiography, of all things, attracted an audience of thousands, who heard impassioned denunciations of the falsifications and distortions that littered official accounts of the nation's past. The Communist authorities were accused of perverting the writing of history, rendering it little more than cheap propaganda. On 14 June György Lukács, the distinguished Marxist philosopher, was scheduled to address the group. So many people turned up to hear him that Lukács, puffing away on a cigar, personally marched the crowd from the cramped Kossuth Club to more spacious accommodation at the nearby Karl Marx University of Economics. There the seventy-one-year-old man of letters disparaged the 'assembly-line production of philosophers unable to do anything but spout the Marxist line' and extolled 'independent thinking'.[15]

Four days later, during a debate on socialist legality, a thousand-strong crowd of 'old warriors' (including veterans of the Spanish Civil War) and 'young intellectuals' heard Júlia Rajk – the widow of the purged Communist leader László Rajk – deliver the most electrifying speech so far. After requesting permission to speak, the forty-four-year-old, who had been released from prison only six months earlier, walked slowly to the podium. Speaking in a firm, steady voice, her face gaunt and lined, she declared, 'I stand before you deeply moved after five years of prison and humiliation.' Holding back tears, she explained that 'not only was my husband killed, but my little baby was torn from me' – for years 'I received no letters and no information about the fate of my little son.' Then, in remarks clearly aimed at Rákosi and his associates, she declared that 'these criminals have not only murdered László Rajk. They have trampled underfoot all sentiment and honesty in this country. Murderers should not be criticised – they should be punished.' Promising not to rest until 'those who have ruined the country, corrupted the Party, destroyed thousands, and driven millions into despair receive their just punishment', she issued a rousing call to arms: 'Comrades, help me in this struggle!' Her remarks were met with 'stormy applause' and a thunderous standing ovation; the next day, Rajk's extraordinary speech was the talk of Budapest.[16]

Then, on 24 June, the Communist Party's official newspaper, *Szabad Nép* ('The Free People'), having studiously ignored the Petőfi debates for months, published a remarkable editorial describing the Circle as a 'shaft of sunlight' which was challenging the 'tragic distortions' and 'inhuman' methods that had previously been employed by the Communist Party, thereby helping to sweep away the 'rigid dogmas' of the past. The paper even suggested that senior Party officials and government ministers would benefit from attending the group's discussions.[17]

The excitement provoked by news of Júlia Rajk's intervention and the publicity afforded by the *Szabad Nép* editorial guaranteed a massive crowd for the Petőfi Circle's next debate, on press freedom, scheduled for the evening of 27 June. By late afternoon, a crowd of several thousand had already begun to gather outside the Officers' Club – an imposing turn-of-the-century building on Váci Street, one of Budapest's main thoroughfares. Inside, the eight-hundred-seat auditorium was already packed with an audience of some sixteen hundred students, workers, white-collar professionals, intellectuals, army officers and Party officials. Speakers who arrived late – including Márton Horváth, the editor of *Szabad Nép* – had to struggle through the hordes. The unseasonable humidity, meanwhile, added to everyone's discomfort. The debate began at six thirty, half an hour early, with loudspeakers rigged up to relay proceedings to the crowd on the street outside – which now numbered six thousand. A succession of speakers took to the floor to denounce the government and make the case for reform. Tibor Tardos claimed that many Hungarians viewed the dogmatic and bureaucratic leadership of the country as 'alien to our people and our ideals', while Tibor Méray declared that a 'purifying storm of history' was needed to cleanse the nation.[18] But it was fifty-one-year-old Tibor Déry – the veteran Communist and celebrated writer – who made the evening's most controversial remarks.[19] After attacking Communist luminaries including Horváth ('one day he's extreme right, and other days extreme left; one never knows where he stands') and the former minister of culture József Révai ('he knows what he says isn't the truth, but he goes ahead and says it anyway'), Déry – his voice thin but clear – turned his focus onto the system itself. He warned that 'As long as we direct our criticism against individuals instead of investigating whether the mistakes spring from the very system – from the very ideology – we can achieve nothing more than to exchange evil for a lesser evil.' While 'trusting' that 'we will get rid of our present leaders', Déry argued that 'we must seek in our socialist system the mistakes which not only permit our leaders to misuse their power, but which also render us incapable of dealing with each other with the humanity we deserve'.[20] Déry was, though, not championing the cause of liberal democracy. While he declared that 'the source of our troubles is lack of freedom', he made it clear that he understood 'freedom as the freedom of the individual restrained through the obligations to the socialist society. Restricted economically, emotionally and intellectually.'[21] But this was explosive stuff all the same.

By now, the atmosphere in the Officers' Club was one of 'absolute pandemonium'. At one point Horváth implored his comrades to refrain from attacking the Party, only to be shouted down with cries of 'We are the Party!' During another altercation, he was forced to admit that press freedom did not exist in Hungary.[22] Although participants were careful not to criticise the Soviet Union, when one journalist declared that 'our fight for the truths revealed by the Twentieth Congress' would take place not in Moscow but 'right here in Budapest', the audience responded with 'long, loud rhythmic applause'.[23] Finally, in the early hours of the morning, Géza Losonczy took up the cause of the former prime minister, prompting enthusiastic chants of 'Long live Nagy!' and 'Return Nagy to the Party!' After nine hours of emotional debate the delegates – dripping with sweat and hoarse from shouting – headed home, exhausted.[24] Within hours, the atmosphere in Budapest was transformed. *Time* magazine's Simon Bourgin observed: 'The events of the night before had, in a way, electrified the town, and people were talking of nothing else. Many people said to me that this was "the second Hungarian revolution", that this was "the way things were going to be from now on".' Others, though, were more cautious – noting that 'for the first time people had spoken up' and had not been thrown into jail – yet.[25]

Mátyás Rákosi was determined to restore discipline. Concerned by the growing, and very public, criticism of his leadership, and alarmed by the workers' revolt that broke out in Poznań on the morning of 28 June, the Hungarian leader decided to crack down. On 30 June the Central Committee, meeting in emergency session, passed a resolution condemning the Petőfi Circle – which was accused of expressing 'bourgeois and counterrevolutionary views', slandering Party officials and exaggerating the Party's mistakes.[26] They also blamed Imre Nagy and his supporters for organising 'open opposition' to the 'People's Democracy'. Tibor Tardos and Tibor Déry were expelled from the Party, and *Szabad Nép* was chided for its 'erroneous' editorial of 24 June. Referring to recent developments in Poland, the resolution declared that the 'Poznań provocation is a warning to every Hungarian worker and every honest patriot firmly to oppose attempts at troublemaking', and urged them to support the country's leaders.[27] Rákosi also drew up a list of four hundred people – rumoured to include Party officials, Nagy and his close associates, and leading critics of the regime – for immediate arrest. But the planned crackdown never materialised. The Soviets had by now concluded that the first secretary was a liability and they summarily withdrew their support.[28]

If, at this fateful moment, Imre Nagy had been returned to power, history might have turned out very differently.[29] As it was, Moscow gave the green light for Ernő Gerő to succeed Rákosi. The fifty-seven-year-old had been a devoted supporter of Stalin and was scarcely more popular than his predecessor. Although, on taking office, he declared that there would be 'no second Poznań' in Hungary, Gerő was incapable of restoring unity at the top of the MDP, never mind in the country at large. Even his closest colleagues described him as 'coarse', 'impatient' and unable to tolerate criticism.[30] His appointment was disastrous.[31]

According to Támas Aczél, the summer of 1956 'belonged to the writers of Hungary'. The Opera House staged a hugely successful production of *The Miraculous Mandarin* by Béla Bartók (whose music had been banned under the Rákosi regime); *Szabadsaghegy* (*Freedom Mountain*), a play which exposed the gilded life of Hungary's Party elite, was staged by a leading theatre company; and Tibor Déry published an allegorical novella, *Niki*, exploring the fate of an innocent man suddenly imprisoned, seen through the eyes of his dog.[32] When border controls with Austria were relaxed, limited group excursions to Vienna became possible for the first time in many years. The delegations of writers, journalists and artists who visited Budapest's great rival were struck by the city's relaxed and open atmosphere, its beautiful shops, its abundance of fresh fruit, food and consumer goods, and the high standard of living enjoyed not just by capitalist businessmen but by ordinary workers. Tales of such delights quickly spread back home: a joke, popular on the streets of Budapest that summer, hinted at a disquiet and cynicism that was never far from the surface:

Two Hungarians meet on the beautiful Kahlenberg
Mountain, near Vienna. One sniffs the air, his face twisted
in a strange grimace. The other asks him what he is doing.

'Can't you smell?' the first man asks. 'Don't you smell how it stinks here?'

'No, what kind of smell is it?'

'The smell of rotting capitalism!'[33]

The leading members of the Writers' Union, meanwhile, were openly dismissive of the Party's attempt to rein them in. Their journal, *Irodalmi Újság* ('Literary Gazette'), saw its circulation rocket tenfold to thirty thousand – at which point a Party apparatchik declared that, due to paper shortages, the print run could be increased no further. Popular demand was so great, however, that the paper was reported to be changing hands for up to thirty times its cover price of one forint; fights broke out at news-stands when supplies ran low, and some people even typed out articles for friends.[34] Aczél recalled how 'Time and again strangers stopped writers on the street to congratulate them on a new poem or article; literature had become, at last, common property.'[35]

This new spirit of freedom was not confined to Budapest. Although the Petőfi Circle suspended its programme until after the summer holidays, it had spawned imitators in the provinces, including the Kossuth Circle in Debrecen, Hungary's second city.[36] It was also reported that, at factory meetings across the country, workers who were asked to support attacks on Déry and Tardos requested copies of their alleged 'anti-Party' speeches to read first. On 12 August, an editorial in *Szabad Nép* acknowledged that 'the unprecedented crisis brought on by the intellectuals now manifests itself among workers and peasants'.[37] There were ample grounds to believe that this was true. At many workers' meetings, for example, there were demands for tax cuts and wage increases. Meanwhile the countryside saw growing opposition to agricultural collectivisation. Peasants – emboldened by a recent Party announcement that force would no longer be permitted when setting up co-operative farms – now simply refused to join such enterprises voluntarily, while others requested formal permission to withdraw from existing ventures.[38]

Most worrying of all, for the government, were reports of growing unrest among the industrial working class. In early September, for instance, workers at the automobile factory in Csepel, a heavily industrialised district of Budapest, downed tools in a long-running dispute over pay.[39] Employees at the neighbouring plants that made up this flagship industrial park followed suit. As the striking workers sat next to their machines, eating their lunch, they studiously ignored the orders of local Party bosses and functionaries. Then, after two hours, they resumed their labours. A few weeks earlier, workers disgruntled about chronic shortages of consumer goods had broken shop windows in the district. That such open dissent was emanating from a solidly working-class population, previously famed for their commitment to the socialist cause, made it all the more significant.[40] Wherever they looked, Party bosses saw signs of trouble. As one Party official put it, 'Everyone felt that there was something fateful in the air.'[41]

11

ANGRY YOUNG MEN

I wear blue jeans and dig rock 'n' roll. I am not a delinquent.
ROSEMARY CALDWELL, letter to *Time* magazine, 9 July 1956

This kind of music is excessively stimulating only to the
maladjusted or to people of a primitive type.
HARLEY STREET PSYCHIATRIST, *Daily Express*, 12 September 1956

On Saturday 7 July 1956, a Fats Domino concert at San Jose's Palomar Gardens erupted into a full-scale riot. The black, white and Latino teenagers who made up the audience had been jostling since 9 p.m. as they waited for the headline act. Just before midnight, the New Orleans pianist Antoine 'Fats' Domino – whose exuberant style and southern drawl would help make him America's most successful black rock 'n' roll star – finally made his way through the crowd and onto the stage. During his opening number, first beer bottles and then a string of firecrackers were thrown onto the dance floor. The Palomar's owner, Charles Silvia, described how, in the ensuing chaos, 'everybody was at each other. Boys fought boys, and even girls. Girls were slugging boys and scratching one another.' Some girls attempted to flee via a restroom window. Dozens of tables and chairs were broken, and as many as a thousand bottles were smashed. Thirty police officers – who had, by complete chance, been attending the annual policemen's ball a few blocks away – rushed to the scene to offer their assistance (thereby missing an eagerly anticipated appearance by Joan Beckett, the recently crowned Miss California); it took the authorities an hour to restore order. Ten youths were arrested, and two policemen and a number of revellers required medical attention. Although the local police chief blamed excessive alcohol consumption for the trouble, the newspapers lost no time in pointing the finger at the 'pulsating rhythms' of Domino's music: the Palomar had become the site of America's first official 'rock 'n' roll riot'.[1]

San Jose was no one-off. In September, for example, a riot at the naval station club in Newport, Rhode Island, prompted the base commander, Rear Admiral Ralph D. Earle, Jr, to ban rock 'n' roll for at least a month, and that November two people were stabbed at another boisterous Fats Domino concert, this time in Fayette-ville, North Carolina. The authorities in Boston, Jersey City and other cities cracked down – banning rock 'n' roll concerts, refusing to co-operate with promoters and even ordering the removal of the offensive records from local jukeboxes.[2] Nor was the trouble restricted to the United States: in March, fans of the American singer Johnnie Ray had smashed windows and attempted to storm onto the tarmac at Brisbane airport as their hero touched down for the latest leg of his Australian tour, while screenings of the hit film *Rock Around the Clock* prompted teenage riots in towns and cities all over western Europe, as well as in Sydney, Brisbane and Auckland.[3] On the evening of Monday 11 September, for example, hundreds of raucous teenagers and 'Teddy boys' took to the streets of Elephant and Castle, in the London borough of Southwark, hurling bottles and attacking parked cars following a screening of the movie, while in Oslo three consecutive nights of rioting led to dozens of arrests.[4] Little wonder that some local officials attempted to head off any possible trouble: in the United Kingdom, some eighty councils – including Brighton, Birmingham and Belfast – banned the film outright.[5]

There was actually very little in *Rock Around the Clock* that could be considered at all incendiary. The seventy-seven-minute musical, distributed by Columbia Pictures, told the story of a small-time dance band manager who, after stumbling across a local rock 'n' roll band at a teenage dance, decides to promote the new music as the 'next big thing'. The movie – the world's first film targeted at the teenage market to prove a box-office hit – grossed $2.4 million worldwide, eight times its production costs. It featured Bill Haley and the Comets, whose 1954 record '(We're Gonna) Rock Around the Clock' had sold two million copies by the end of 1955 and become an anthem of youth rebellion.[6] Yet the thirty-four-year-old Haley, with his 'chipmunk cheeks and a spit curl plastered on his forehead', and his strict edicts to band members prohibiting drinking or dating while on tour, was an unlikely rebel.[7]

In fact, the disorder sparked by the movie may well have been overstated. In Britain, the Cinematograph Exhibitors' Association complained bitterly about the local authority bans – which they blamed on excitable chief constables, irresponsible journalists and council leaders who had not even bothered to watch the 'innocuous' movie for themselves. As they pointed out, the film had been shown in hundreds of cinemas with 'very little trouble' and, although the audiences at some venues had 'exhibited high spirits', the accounts in the press of rioting youth had been greatly overdone. They even suggested that members of the press had stoked up the trouble in the first place, encouraging teenagers to put on a show for the cameras and then making sensationalist claims that encouraged 'copy-cat' incidents.[8]

Nevertheless, a succession of sociologists, psychiatrists and 'experts' were soon lining up to denounce this latest musical 'fad'. Rock 'n' roll, with its innovative blend of African American and white musical traditions – notably rhythm and blues, country and pop – and its powerful, repetitive beat, had emerged in the mid-1950s, thanks to the talents of innovative record producers (such as Sam Phillips in Memphis), the entrepreneurial spirit of independent record labels, the influence of pioneering disc jockeys (including the legendary Alan Freed), and the enormous power and popularity of local radio stations – whose executives, aware that adults were increasingly turning to television as their primary source of entertainment, decided to reorient their programming around popular music for teenage audiences.[9] But while rock 'n' roll would go on to enjoy commercial and critical success, in 1956 many commentators were unconvinced.[10] In June 1956, for instance, the readers of *Time* magazine learned that the defining characteristics of rock 'n' roll were:

> an unrelenting, socking syncopation that sounds like a bull whip; a choleric saxophone honking mating-call sounds; an electric guitar turned up so loud that its sound shatters and splits; a vocal group that shudders and exercises violently to the beat while roughly chanting either a near-nonsense phrase or a moronic lyric in hillbilly idiom.[11]

Meanwhile, the editors of the British jazz weekly *Melody Maker* were dismissive. 'Instrumentally and vocally', they declared, the 'Rock-and-Roll technique' represented the very 'antithesis of . . . good taste and musical integrity'.[12] The American singer Frank Sinatra soon added his voice to the criticism, claiming that rock 'n' roll was 'phony' music, 'sung, played and written for the most part by cretinous goons', which constituted 'the martial music of every side-burned delinquent on the face of the earth'.[13]

Indeed, the public debate revolved around claims that rock 'n' roll threatened the moral fabric of Western civilisation itself.[14] Francis J. Braceland – one of America's most eminent psychiatrists – described rock 'n' roll as a 'cannibalistic and tribalistic' form of music, likened it to a 'communicable disease' and declared it a sign of 'adolescent rebellion'.[15] The boisterous, high-spirited teenagers who flocked to rock 'n' roll concerts, the boys in their trademark leather jackets and fashionable 'ducktail' haircuts, the girls in their skirts or blue jeans, shrieking and gyrating to songs with highly suggestive lyrics, certainly stoked public fears about teenage 'delinquency' and errant sexual behaviour (rock 'n' roll, after all, took its name from a popular African American euphemism for sexual intercourse).[16] It was a similar story in Britain, where the Bishop of Woolwich, the Rt Rev. Peter Stannard, called for *Rock Around the Clock* to be banned on the grounds that its 'hypnotic rhythm and wild gestures' encouraged teenagers to lose 'all self-control'.[17]

During 1956, no single artist better personified the spirit of rock 'n' roll – nor caused greater alarm among the guardians of the status quo – than a certain Elvis Aaron Presley.[18] Born in the little town of Tupelo, in northern Mississippi, in 1935, Presley had moved to Memphis in 1948 when his father, Vernon, found work in a local paint factory. With his bushy sideburns, pomade quiff, upturned collar and love of outrageous clothes, Elvis was a rebel – but one who also conformed to conventional mores: he regularly attended the local Pentecostal Church with his mother and was, throughout his career, unfailingly polite. After graduating from high school, Elvis scraped a living as a truck driver, machinist and cinema usher, but he dreamed of becoming a star. He had learned to thrash out a few basic chords on a guitar that had been given to him by his beloved mother, Gladys, and his musical tastes were strikingly ecumenical, although he had a particular fondness for gospel music and the blues. In the summer of 1953, Elvis had recorded a couple of covers at Sam Phillips's Sun Studios, where he was judged a 'good ballad singer', but his big break came a year later. Standing alongside the guitarist Scotty Moore and bass player Bill Black in Phillips's cramped recording studio, Elvis had struggled through a couple of nondescript numbers before, instinctively, turning to a 1946 blues song, 'That's All Right'. The effect on Sam Phillips, who was listening from inside the control room, was electrifying: it was, he later said, 'like someone struck me in the rear end with a brand new supersharp pitchfork'. 'That's All Right' and its B-side, a version of the hillbilly classic 'Blue Moon of Kentucky', proved regional hits, popular with fans of both rhythm and blues and country music. Before long, the nineteen-year-old Elvis was performing live on stage, where his quivering legs and upturned lip drove audiences wild.[19] In December 1955, RCA paid $45,000 to buy out his contract at Sun Records; within months, Elvis Presley was rock 'n' roll's first global superstar.[20]

RCA released 'Heartbreak Hotel' on 28 January 1956; by the end of March it had stormed to the top of the pop, country *and* rhythm and blues charts, selling almost a million copies in the process. It hit the British charts in May.[21] Guided by the brilliant if controversial 'Colonel' Tom Parker, a carnival hand turned manager-promoter, Elvis quickly set about exploiting the growing power of television (by the end of the decade, almost 90 per cent of American families owned their own set).[22] On Tuesday 27 March he appeared on *The Milton Berle Show*, performing 'Heartbreak Hotel' and 'Blue Suede Shoes' to a cheering studio audience. But in the aftermath of Elvis's appearance, which had delivered a major ratings boost to NBC, a storm of newspaper criticism erupted over his 'suggestive' and 'vulgar' 'grunt and groin antics'.[23] When he appeared on *The Ed Sullivan Show* later that year, the audience reacted to even the smallest hint of bodily movement. Eager to avoid controversy, when Elvis drove the audience wild by launching into a raucous rendition of 'Ready Teddy' by the black artist Little Richard (renowned for his brash, flamboyant style, sexual energy and suggestive lyrics), the producer ordered the cameras to zoom in so that viewers at home could see only the top half of the singer's body. Elvis's performance, which was watched by a staggering 82.6 per cent of the total television audience, was a triumph.[24]

On 3 June, when announcing a blanket ban on rock 'n' roll music at all public gatherings, the Santa Cruz authorities justified their actions on the grounds that the music was 'detrimental to both the health and morals of our youth and community'. The ban had been prompted by a concert the previous evening, which, according to local police lieutenant Richard Overton, had seen the crowd 'engaged in suggestive, stimulating and tantalizing motions induced by the provocative rhythms of an all-negro band'.[25] As Overton's comments indicate, much of the opposition to rock 'n' roll music – especially in the United States – was prompted by fears about interracial socialising (and, particularly, interracial sex). It was, then, no surprise that southern segregationists were among its loudest critics. In incendiary comments that spring, the Alabama firebrand Asa 'Ace' Carter claimed that the roots of rock 'n' roll could be traced to 'the heart of Africa, where it was used to incite warriors to such frenzy that by nightfall neighbors were cooked in carnage pots!' The 'basic, heavy-beat music of the Negroes', Carter warned, 'brings out animalism and vulgarity'. The popularity of black artists with multiracial audiences left segregationists apoplectic; some claimed it was all part of an NAACP plot 'to mongrelize America'.[26] On 10 April, four white men attacked the popular African American singer Nat King Cole – a jazz pianist and singer rather than a rock 'n' roll artist – as he performed on stage in Birmingham, Alabama. At one level Cole was a convenient proxy, but the fact that he was touring with a white singer, June Christy, provided added provocation. The following month, segregationists holding placards that declared 'Jungle Music Promotes Integration' and 'Jungle Music Aids Delinquency' picketed a genuine rock 'n' roll concert at the city's auditorium (they were particularly exercised by the presence of both black and white artists on the bill). As segregationist pressure mounted, the local authorities moved to ban mixed-race shows, while in Louisiana segregationist politicians went further, passing a state law that prohibited 'all interracial dancing, social functions [and] entertainments'.[27] Nor were the racial anxieties surrounding rock 'n' roll restricted to Dixie: in Inglewood, California, white supremacists warned that interracial dancing would result in 'total mongrelisation', while teachers in Boston heard that rock 'n' roll 'enflames and excites youth like jungle tom-toms'. Meanwhile, on the other side of the Atlantic, where Britons were adjusting to the consequences of mass immigration from the West Indies, the *Daily Mail* wondered whether rock 'n' roll was 'the Negro's revenge'.[28]

The battles over rock 'n' roll were, though, just one manifestation of a wider cultural and generational revolt. The prevailing sense of dissatisfaction with the status quo was captured in *Invasion of the Body Snatchers*, released in February. Directed by Don Siegel and based on an earlier novel by Jack Finney, it told a story of an alien invasion of the little town of Santa Mira, California. Gradually, the town's citizens were being replaced with emotionless replicas that hatched from mysterious extraterrestrial pods and displayed a hive mentality. The movie brilliantly tapped into Americans' deep fears about possible Communist infiltration while also offering a parable about the dangers of mindless conformity (whether suburban or socialist).[29]

Nor was the year's cultural rebellion restricted to the West. Across Eastern Europe, for instance, the guardians of the status quo faced youthful subcultures that proved every bit as worrying as the rock 'n' roll fans in America or the Teddy boys in Britain. Eastern Europe's young rebels may have gone by different names – the *bikiniarze* in Poland, the *potapka* in Czechoslovakia and the *jampecek* in Hungary – but they shared a taste for unconventional fashion (drainpipe trousers and brightly coloured shirts for the boys, wide, loud-patterned skirts for the girls and thick rubber-soled shoes for both) and a commitment to 'outlaw' music, above all jazz. In fact, jazz was banned in the 'people's democracies' on the grounds that it was symptomatic of the corrupt, decadent, individualistic culture of the West. Some young zealots had even taken to smashing up the offending records with hammers. Although the post-Stalinist thaw saw an easing of cultural restrictions (notably in Poland and Czechoslovakia), listening to jazz retained its association with dissidence.[30] In Hungary, for example, the *jampecek* – with their 'tight trousers, checkered coats, and colourfully-decorated neckties', distinctive street slang and love of

American jazz music, which they sought out in coffeehouses and dancehalls and listened to illicitly on the BBC and Radio Free Europe – were condemned as 'hooligans' by newspaper editors, and faced harassment (or worse) from the secret police, precisely because their attempt to carve out an alternative social and cultural sphere was seen not merely as incompatible with the wider 'social-ist' project but as an attempt to resist Communism itself.[31]

In fact, throughout 1956 writers, poets and artists were at the forefront of efforts to secure social and political change across the 'people's democracies', using the opportunities afforded by Khrush-chev's 'secret speech' to push back against Stalinism, demand greater cultural freedom and criticise the regimes under which they worked. In his 'A Poem for Adults', for example, Adam Ważyk por-trayed a Poland in which students were 'shut off in textbooks with-out windows' and where the language had been 'reduced to thirty magic formulas'. In its most famous verse, Ważyk wrote that:

> *They drink sea water,*
> *crying:*
> *'lemonade!'*
> *returning home secretly*
> *to vomit.*[32]

First published in the summer of 1955, 'A Poem for Adults' was roundly condemned by Party officials, but enjoyed renewed suc-cess – both in Poland and across Eastern Europe – in the aftermath of the Twentieth Party Congress, as its denunciation of inhumane bureaucratic structures and attack on the betrayal of socialist prin-ciples resonated ever more strongly.[33] In Hungary, meanwhile, Tibor Déry's 'Behind the Brick Wall' – a short story about Buda-pest factory workers, forced to steal to supplement their meagre wages and increasingly resentful at their treatment at the hands of faceless bureaucrats – was one of several dissident stories, poems and plays that proved popular during the summer of 1956.[34]

The year's contribution to a wider cultural revolution was further strengthened by the publication of Allen Ginsberg's 'Howl'. With its references to illicit drugs and 'deviant' sexual practices, and its denunciation of modern capitalist society, the poem – which had first been performed in San Francisco the previous October – quickly became one of the most famous works by the so-called Beat generation of writers. 'Howl', which begins in the stepped triadic style before moving into a unique extended form in which the length of the lines are determined by the poet's own breaths, was the culmination of Ginsberg's attempt to 'write what I wanted to without fear, let my imagination go . . . and scribble magic lines from my real mind'.[35] Its opening lines would become some of the most famous words of poetry ever committed to paper:

> *I saw the best minds of my generation destroyed by madness,*
>   *starving hysterical naked,*
> *dragging themselves through the negro streets at dawn looking*
>   *for an angry fix,*
> *angelheaded hipsters burning for the ancient heavenly connection*
>   *to the starry dynamo in the machinery of night . . .*[36]

Ginsberg's masterpiece, which would make him an icon of the 1960s counterculture, encapsulated what the respected poet Richard Eberhart described as the new generation's exuberant, youthful desire to 'kick down the doors of older consciousness and established practice' in favour of 'what they think is vital and new'.[37]

Another young artist who was eager to kick in the doors of the establishment was the British playwright John Osborne, whose *Look Back in Anger* debuted at the Royal Court Theatre that May. Set in a cramped attic bedsit, it told the story of the dysfunctional relationship between Jimmy Porter, a working-class anti-hero, and his young wife, Alison – who bears the brunt of Jimmy's tantrums, hurtful taunts and pent-up frustrations. Although the early reviews were terrible (the play was described as 'putrid bosh' and 'self-pitying snivel'), Osborne's fortunes were transformed by a couple of glowing notices in the *New Statesman* and the *Observer*, whose theatre critic, Kenneth Tynan, gushed that 'all the qualities are there, qualities one had despaired of ever seeing on the stage – the drift towards anarchy, the instinctive leftishness, the automatic rejection of "official" attitudes, the surrealist sense of humour . . . the casual promiscuity, the sense of a crusade worth fighting for . . .' *Look Back in Anger* was, Tynan declared, 'the best young play of its decade'.[38]

In October, the BBC broadcast a twenty-five-minute extract on television, and a month later the play was shown in its entirety on the new commercial network, ITV. Meanwhile, audiences flocked to the Royal Court – drawn, in part, by breathless talk in the gossip columns about the 'Angry Young Men'. The term, which was coined by the theatre's press officer, was soon being applied to a range of contemporary artists, writers and filmmakers (including the existentialist Colin Wilson and novelist Kingsley Amis) who, as one historian has put it, 'sought to loosen the grip of a conservative establishment on the throat of British culture'. *Look Back in Anger* was hailed as a revolutionary cultural watershed and Osborne lauded as the voice of a new generation: a playwright who had, in the words of one commentator, 'captured the young imagination and with it the fish-sweatered noctambules from Espresso-land' and the 'bed-sitter *avant-garde* from . . . Notting Hill'.[39]

Writing in the autumn edition of *Sight and Sound*, the director and film critic Lindsay Anderson claimed that the enthusiastic response of many young people to *Look Back in Anger* could be traced to Osborne's attack on the establishment's 'sacred cows'.[40] It was an anti-establishment tone that would resonate even more strongly in the aftermath of Suez.

12

A COUP DE MAIN

We Egyptians will not allow any coloniser, any despot, to
dominate us.
GAMAL ABDEL NASSER

Shortly after four o'clock on the afternoon of Thursday 19 July 1956,
Ahmed Hussein, Egypt's ambassador in Washington, strode into
John Foster Dulles's office for an urgent meeting. Hussein, who had
recently returned from Cairo, was in good spirits, but the secretary
of state was the bearer of bad news: he had, he said, reluctantly concluded that it would not be feasible for the United States government to provide a $56 million loan to help with the construction of
a High Dam at Aswan. Dulles explained that the United States was
concerned that the economic sacrifices that would be required of the
Egyptian people, together with the diversion of national resources
while the project was completed, would generate resentments that
might sour relations between the two countries. He also made it
clear that American public opinion had turned against the project
and, as a result, he doubted that the administration could procure
the necessary funds from Congress, even if it wished to do so. Hussein was stunned and implored the Americans to reconsider. It was
to no avail. The withdrawal of Western support (Britain rescinded
its proposed $14 million contribution the following day) caused a
$200 million financing deal with the World Bank, the details of
which had been worked out meticulously over many months, to
collapse, throwing the entire project into considerable doubt.[1]

The Anglo-American decision was a bitter pill for the Egyptians.
The High Dam promised to be the biggest civil engineering project in the world, at 365 feet high and three miles wide – seventeen

times the size of the Great Pyramid at Giza – with a reservoir large enough to store 45,890 billion cubic feet of water. But it was not simply a prestige project; it was also seen as central to the country's efforts to modernise its economy. The High Dam would enable the flow of the River Nile to be regulated throughout the year, opening up seven hundred thousand acres of land to irrigation and reclaiming a further 1.3 million acres for settlement. It would also produce an initial 720,000 kilowatts of hydro-electricity, with capacity for that to be doubled.[2]

News that the US and Britain had withdrawn their support was greeted with shock and anger in Cairo, and seen as a deliberate slight against Egypt's president, Gamal Abdel Nasser.[3] The Egyptian leader heard the news while flying back to Cairo from a state visit to Yugoslavia, accompanied by the Indian prime minister, Jawaharlal Nehru. Nasser would later claim that the American decision had come as no surprise: 'I was sure that Mr Dulles would not help us.' But what stung was the 'insulting attitude with which the refusal was declared'. For Nasser, the fact that the State Department publicly cast doubt on the 'willingness and ability' of the Egyptians to pull off the project was a 'slap in the face'.[4] On 24 July, while attending a ceremony to open a new refinery and oil pipeline north of Cairo, Nasser broke his silence. Mounting a robust defence of his country's economic record, he launched a vitriolic attack on the United States – 'I look at Americans and say: May you choke to death on your fury!' 'We, the 22,000,000 Egyptians', he continued, 'will not allow any colonizer, any despot to dominate us either politically, economically, or militarily. We shall yield neither to force nor to the dollar.'[5] But while Nasser's ire may have been directed at Washington, he was already planning an audacious strike against his real enemy, Great Britain.

Although Egypt had nominally won its independence from the empire in 1922, it had remained a de facto British possession. The country's monarch, King Farouk – described by one historian as a 'gourmand, libertine, kleptomaniac, drug-trafficker and buffoon' – epitomised the Egyptian government's impotence while, as late as 1954, the British maintained a sizeable military presence in the land of the pharaohs. A narrow strip of land, 120 miles long, stretching from Port Said in the north to Suez in the south, housed a vast network of airfields, ports, railway stations, roads, hospitals, barracks, storage depots, ammunition dumps and other facilities that, at its height, was home to some eighty thousand troops. The purpose of this vast garrison, which cost £50 million a year to maintain, was to protect the Suez Canal.[6] Conceived by the brilliant French diplomat Ferdinand de Lesseps and opened to great fanfare in 1869, the canal, which linked the Red Sea to the Mediterranean, was one of the world's most important trade routes: by 1955, two thirds of the oil that fuelled western Europe's economy, together with other vital goods, passed through this famous waterway. The canal's operation, meanwhile, was overseen by an Anglo-French joint-stock company, whose concession to run the canal was due to expire in 1968.[7]

In July 1952, after months of nationalist unrest and violence, the Free Officers Movement – appalled by the abject poverty of the *fellahin* (or peasantry), outraged by the corruption and incompetence of the government and determined finally to end the country's subservience to the British – had overthrown King Farouk and established a new military government. Within two years Colonel Gamal Abdel Nasser, the dashing and ambitious son of a postal clerk from Alexandria, had outmanoeuvred his rivals and established himself as Egypt's undisputed ruler. He bore down on opposition parties, most notably the Muslim Brotherhood, enacted major agricultural and social reforms and declared Egypt a republic. Nasser, according to one historian, 'radiated energy. Tall and muscular, he moved like a panther. His olive-skinned countenance, white teeth gleaming between aquiline nose and prognathous jaw, was spellbindingly expressive . . . he behaved like the embodiment of the national will.'[8] He quickly became the darling of the Arab world – the personification of anti-colonial nationalism and regional self-confidence, following decades of subservience to the West.[9] On 23 June 1956 Nasser, who was the first native Egyptian to rule the country for more than two and a half millennia, was elected president with more than 99 per cent of the vote (his was the only name on the ballot).[10] A week earlier, he had led the national celebrations to mark the departure of the last British troops from Egyptian territory. A three-day public holiday had been declared to mark the start of a 'bright new era' in which Egypt would 'no longer . . . be under the domination of the imperialists'.[11] Great celebrations took place in Cairo and Alexandria and in villages along the banks of the Nile. The main ceremony, though, was staged in Port Said. As Nasser made his way in an open car to Navy House – the imposing yellow stucco building that had served as British headquarters – he was greeted by vast, screaming crowds, who swarmed around his motorcade. At one point, the Egyptian leader was reported to have 'completely disappeared from sight' as his countrymen, desperate to embrace their hero or shower him with kisses, surged forward. A dishevelled Nasser finally emerged and took his place in front of Navy House. As nine MiG fighter jets flew in formation overhead and a frigate, surrounded by five torpedo boats in the harbour, fired off a salute, he first kissed and then raised the green Egyptian flag, with its white crescent and three stars, declaring: 'Citizens, we pray that God may forbid any other flag to fly over our land.'[12]

Nasser had, right from the start, insisted on a complete British withdrawal: 'We cannot feel free and sovereign until they go.'[13] There were actually good reasons for Britain to vacate the Canal Zone: the cost of maintaining the base was prohibitively expensive; the continued presence of British troops in the face of popular hostility was counterproductive; and the realities of the

Cold War nuclear arms race, together with Britain's decline as a manufacturing power, had contrived to reduce the canal's strategic importance. The British, though, concerned (as ever) about their international standing and anxious about talk of 'imperial decline', had departed reluctantly – encouraged on their way by an Eisenhower administration that was keen to distance the United States from European imperialism.[14] Speaking in June 1953 following a twenty-day tour of the Middle East and south Asia, John Foster Dulles had made it clear that America had no intention of preserving or restoring the 'old colonial interests'. Instead, it would pursue its 'traditional dedication to political liberty' by encouraging an 'orderly development of self-government'.[15] In October 1954, following months of protracted negotiations, Britain finally signed the Suez Base Agreement, consenting to withdraw its forces within twenty months, while retaining the right to return 'in the event of an armed attack by an outside Power' on any member of the Arab League or Turkey.[16] Now, declared Nasser, Britain and Egypt would be able to work together 'on a solid basis of mutual trust and confidence'.[17]

It was not to be. Over the next eighteen months, Anglo-Egyptian relations deteriorated precipitously. The formation of the Baghdad Pact in 1955 – a security agreement signed by Turkey, Pakistan, Iran, Iraq and Britain as a bulwark against the Soviet Union – was viewed by Nasser (with some justification) as little more than a front for Western imperialism. Almost immediately the Pact became a major target for Egyptian propaganda and drew London into its own counterproductive media offensive. Britain and then the United States also proved reluctant to sell Egypt much-needed arms (the country was engaged in a tense standoff on its border with Israel, with whom it had fought a disastrous war in 1948–9). Nasser turned instead to Moscow, which arranged for large quantities of weapons – including tanks, fighter jets and bombers – to be supplied via Czechoslovakia. This sparked panic in Western capitals that Egypt might be lost to the Communists – a concern that was further heightened when, in May, Nasser recognised the People's Republic of China. Britain also (wrongly) blamed Nasser for King Hussein's decision, on 1 March 1956, to summarily dismiss General Sir John Glubb from his post as commander of Jordan's Arab Legion – a move that weakened British influence in the region and humiliated the Eden government.[18]

By the spring of 1956, London's patience had run out. Writing to President Eisenhower on 5 March, Sir Anthony Eden urged him to 'accept . . . that a policy of appeasement will bring us nothing in Egypt'.[19] The British cabinet had come to the view that Nasser, intent on leading the Arab world, was prepared to accept Soviet help, and that there was no longer any basis on which 'friendly relations' with Egypt could be established. Britain now sought to 'do our utmost to counter Egyptian policy and to uphold our true friends in the Middle East'.[20] Eden, though, seemed determined to go further. The prime minister – suave, cultured, fiercely intelligent, vastly experienced and with an unmatched reputation for statesmanship and good judgment – was clearly rattled by Nasser.[21] On the evening of 12 March Anthony Nutting, the minister of state at the Foreign Office, was dining at London's Savoy Hotel when he was interrupted by an urgent call from Number 10. Eden, who had just read a memorandum outlining a long-term plan to isolate Egypt, was furious: 'What's all this nonsense about isolating Nasser or "neutralising" him, as you call it? I want him destroyed, don't you understand?'[22] MI6, meanwhile, cooked up wild schemes to assassinate Egypt's new pharaoh, including one that involved piping nerve gas into his office.[23] Nutting – a rising star of the Conservative Party, protégé of Eden and negotiator of the October 1954 agreement with Nasser – now came to the conclusion that the prime minister had 'completely lost his touch' and, perhaps affected by illness (a botched gall bladder operation in April 1953 had proved ruinous to Eden's already frail health), 'began to behave like an enraged elephant charging senselessly at invisible and imaginary enemies in the international jungle'.[24] Unfortunately, all Eden's fears were about to be confirmed.

'Alexandria at the end of July', wrote the Egyptian journalist Mohamed Heikal, 'is a holiday city, and with its long palm-lined beaches, its brilliantly lit cafés and shops, a place of beauty and excitement.' On the evening of Thursday 26 July – four years to the day since King Farouk's expulsion – the atmosphere in the country's second city was 'electric' as President Nasser stood before a crowd of 250,000 in Liberation Square.[25] During a speech that lasted for the best part of three hours, and which was beamed across the Middle East and North Africa by Cairo's 'Voice of the Arabs' radio station, Nasser explained that the Egyptian people had been 'striving, struggling and fighting' to throw off imperialism and foreign exploitation. After recounting the recent controversy over the High Dam, Nasser turned his attention to the Suez Canal. Although it had been 'dug . . . with our skulls, bones and blood', Egypt, Nasser claimed, received just $3 million a year while the Suez Canal Company – which operated as a 'state within a state' – pocketed some $100 million (the actual figure was $35 million). But now all that would end. Nasser announced that earlier that day he had signed a decree nationalising the Suez Canal Company, whose revenues would be used to finance the High Dam. 'The people of Egypt alone', declared Nasser, 'shall be sovereign in Egypt. We shall march forward united and in solidarity . . .'[26] Even as he spoke, Egyptian soldiers were occupying the company's offices and installations along the canal.[27] The ovation, which lasted for ten minutes, was deafening, and when Nasser attempted to exit the square, the crowds – singing, dancing and chanting 'Long live Nasser, Lord and Saviour of the Arabs!' – repeatedly blocked his way.[28]

Nasser's audacious gambit stunned even members of his own government. It united the country, and Egyptians of all political leanings and social classes poured onto the streets in jubilation. Even his opponents expressed admiration.[29] The following morning, Nasser arrived back in Cairo in triumph. The British Embassy noted that his train from Alexandria had 'stopped at all stations en route, where he is reported to have addressed tumultuous crowds'.[30] In the capital, a crowd of a hundred thousand showered the president with flowers and roared their approval. Standing outside his office, a defiant Nasser proclaimed, 'Egypt is exercising her sovereignty in full, and will not allow any State or any gang to diminish [it].' Boasting that the 'Egyptian people are today one hand, one heart, one hope and one aim', he declared that 'the Suez Canal Company has become our property . . . and we shall defend this with our blood'.[31]

Nasser's actions were wildly popular across the Arab world. Congratulatory telegrams were despatched from the region's capitals, glowing newspaper editorials appeared, imams preached approving sermons and spontaneous public demonstrations of support broke out.[32] Jordan's King Hussein offered his country's 'wholehearted congratulations and compliments to her sister State' and declared that 'the shadow of exploitation is fading from the Arab world', while crowds took to the streets of Amman and East Jerusalem to cheer Nasser and condemn Western imperialism.[33] The response was mirrored in Syria, where the press were unanimous in their approval, and support flowed in from Lebanon and Sudan too. Even Nasser's most bitter regional rivals felt compelled to offer public endorsement (privately, they continued to denounce the Egyptian leader as a dangerous troublemaker).[34]

Nationalisation of the canal was also greeted with enthusiasm across much of North Africa. There was 'delight' on the streets of Morocco, amidst widespread admiration for Nasser's open defiance of the old colonial masters. In the northern port city of Tétouan, for instance, the local newspaper declared that Egypt had finally broken free from its chains: 'Today Colonialism is drawing its last

breath; tomorrow it will be dead.' A British assessment of the popular mood stressed that, as far as ordinary Moroccans were concerned, Egypt could 'do no wrong'.[35] Meanwhile Jacques Chevallier,
the liberal mayor of Algiers, informed the British consul-general
that, among the Arab population, there had been a 'swelling of
pride in Nasser's activities'.[36]

A chorus of approval also rang out from the Communist world.
In Beijing, the *People's Daily* offered warm support to the Egyptian people in their 'struggle for sovereignty and independence'.
The Egyptians had, the paper claimed, written a new page in their
history and struck a powerful blow for the cause of anti-colonialism everywhere.[37] Mao's government, meanwhile, commended the
nationalisation of the canal as a 'righteous action taken by Egypt
in defence of its own sovereignty and independence'.[38] In Moscow,
despite serious disagreements with Nasser, who had an awkward
habit of throwing local Communists into jail, *Pravda* emphasised
Soviet sympathy for all those struggling to cast off the yoke of
colonialism and declared that 'military threats, economic pressure or political blackmail' would not prevent national liberation
movements from achieving ultimate victory.[39]

In Britain and France, however, it was a very different story.
'GRABBER NASSER', screamed the headline of Britain's *Daily
Mirror*, while the *Daily Telegraph* suggested that Nasser's decision
'should have been announced late on Saturday night, as was the
way in Hitler's and Mussolini's day'.[40] The parallel with the 1930s
was pursued on the other side of the Channel too, where *France-
soir* thundered that Nasser was a 'full-blooded Hitler'.[41]

Sir Anthony Eden had been hosting a dinner at Downing Street
for King Feisal of Iraq and his prime minister, Nuri es-Said, when, at
10.15 p.m., the duty secretary informed him that Nasser had nation-
alised the canal. As the guests were departing, Nuri advised Eden
to 'hit, hit now, and hit hard. Otherwise it will be too late.' At 11
p.m., the prime minister gathered his senior advisers in the Cabinet

Room for an impromptu meeting: Selwyn Lloyd, the foreign secretary, Lords Salisbury and Kilmuir (the Lord President of the Council and Lord Chancellor respectively), the Earl of Home (secretary of state for Commonwealth Relations) and Sir Dermot Boyle, chief of the Air Staff, who had been at the dinner, were joined by the First Sea Lord, Earl Mountbatten, and Sir Gerald Templer, chief of the Imperial General Staff, as well as the French ambassador and the American chargé d'affaires. Eden dominated the meeting and, according to notes taken by his press secretary, was clear that military action would be necessary and that Nasser would have to be removed. The Egyptian leader, Eden declared, could not be allowed 'to have his hand on our windpipe'. But when he turned to his military chiefs for options, their response was rather disheartening. Mountbatten explained that the Mediterranean Fleet, which was anchored off Malta, could set sail within hours and would be able to land 1,200 Royal Marine Commandos at Port Said within three or four days. However, this daring mission would secure only a portion of the canal, while leaving the Marines dangerously exposed. A full landing force, with the requisite air and naval support, capable of taking control of the entire Canal Zone, would not, Eden was told, be ready for at least six weeks.[42]

Nevertheless, Eden's view that Nasser had to be stopped commanded broad political and public support – at least for now. Speaking in the Commons on the morning of 27 July, the Labour leader Hugh Gaitskell deplored the 'high-handed and totally unjustifiable step by the Egyptian government'.[43] Nasser was widely viewed as a menace who threatened to destabilise the entire Middle East, while the seizure of the canal not only dented Britain's prestige, it threatened vital national interests including the security of her oil supplies. The arguments were set out clearly at the first cabinet meeting after the crisis broke. Eden and his ministers accepted that they would 'be on weak ground in basing our resistance on the narrow argument that Colonel Nasser had acted illegally' since, technically, 'his action amounted to no more than a decision to buy out the shareholders'. Instead, the case had to be made on 'international grounds': the Suez Canal was a 'vital link between the East and the West' and an 'international asset of the highest importance'. Moreover, Eden and his colleagues doubted whether the Egyptians had the necessary technical expertise and resources to run the canal efficiently or to undertake the improvements (such as widening and deepening the waterway to accommodate more modern ships) that would be necessary over the next ten years. In light of Nasser's recent behaviour, they were also understandably sceptical that the Egyptians would 'recognise their international obligations in respect of it' (the Convention of Constantinople, signed in 1888, guaranteed that the canal 'shall always be free and open, in time of war as in peace, to every vessel of commerce or of war, without distinction of flag').[44] The cabinet thus concluded that 'every effort must be made to restore effective international control over the Canal' and accepted that 'our essential interests in this area must, if necessary, be safeguarded by military action . . .'[45] The military chiefs were promptly tasked with drawing up a plan to retake the canal, and a cabinet sub-committee, known as the Egypt Committee, was established to oversee planning and co-ordinate policy. On 2 August, thousands of military reservists were called up.[46]

The French also viewed the nationalisation of the Suez Canal Company as intolerable. Speaking late on the morning of 27 July the French foreign minister, Christian Pineau, told reporters that his government considered it 'quite impossible for us to accept the unilateral action decided by Colonel Nasser . . . [which] did considerable injury to French rights and interests'.[47] France had long harboured suspicions of Nasser's brand of Arab nationalism and, while the government in Paris also worried about the risk to oil supplies, its main focus was on the danger that Nasser posed to French interests in North Africa – particularly Algeria. Nasser's vocal support for the FLN (he allowed their leadership-in-exile to operate from Cairo) and the belief that he was furnishing the rebels with arms hardly endeared him to the French. Many leading politicians apparently convinced themselves that if Nasser was destroyed the FLN insurgency would collapse, and Pineau told the Americans that 'one successful battle in Egypt would be worth ten in North Africa'.[48] Mollet's Socialist government was keen on military action.

In the White House, however, it was seen rather differently. On 31 July President Eisenhower received the latest report from Robert Murphy, the deputy under-secretary of state, who had been despatched to London at the start of the crisis. The previous day, Murphy had lunched with Eden, Pineau and Harold Macmillan, the Chancellor of the Exchequer, in Downing Street where, Macmillan recalled, 'we did our best to frighten [him] all we could . . . We gave him the impression that our military expedition to Egypt was about to set sail.'[49] Murphy duly informed his superiors that 'the British government has decided to drive Nasser out of Egypt. The decision, they declared, is firm.' He also described how Macmillan had 'stressed that if [Britain] had to go down now, the Government and . . . British people would rather do so on this issue than become perhaps another Netherlands'.[50] Eisenhower, who believed that such action would be 'extremely unwise', was appalled. It was a view widely shared. The CIA's Allen Dulles, for example, warned that the entire Arab world would unite behind Nasser, and the Treasury secretary George Humphrey declared that 'it looked as though [the British] were simply trying to reverse the trend away from colonialism, and turn the clock back fifty years'.[51] Although the Americans were concerned by Nasser's decision to nationalise the canal, they did not view the seizure of the waterway – in and of itself – as 'sufficient reason for military action'.[52] John Foster Dulles, Eisenhower's somewhat brusque secretary of state, was immediately despatched to 'persuade the British from their course'.[53]

On arriving in London on 1 August, Dulles handed Eden a letter from President Eisenhower. Although Eisenhower recognised the 'transcendent worth of the Canal to the free world' and understood that 'eventually the use of force might become necessary in order to protect international rights', he argued that resorting to military action at this point would be imprudent. Indeed, he warned that it might have 'the most far reaching consequences' for the transatlantic relationship. The president was clear: military action 'should not be undertaken until every peaceful means of protecting the rights and the livelihood of great portions of the world have been thoroughly explored and exhausted'.[54]

Four days later, Eden replied. The British government sought not only to compel Nasser to 'disgorge his spoils' and restore international oversight to the canal, but to replace the Egyptian regime with a government 'less hostile to the West'. Nasser, Eden explained, had 'embarked on a course which is unpleasantly familiar' and was seeking to use the canal to 'further his ambitions from Morocco to the Persian Gulf'. 'I have never thought Nasser a Hitler', he explained, 'but the parallel with Mussolini is close. Neither of us can forget the lives and treasure he cost us before he was finally dealt with.' If Nasser succeeded in retaining his 'loot', or if he managed to drive a wedge between the Western powers, then, Eden warned, 'the consequences . . . would be catastrophic and . . . the whole position in the Middle East would . . . be lost beyond recall'. The British people, though not 'eager to use force', were 'grimly determined that Nasser shall not get away with it this time because they are convinced that if he does their existence will be at his mercy. So am I.'[55]

CAPTION:

South African women march on the Union Buildings in Pretoria,
to oppose the extension of the pass laws, 9 August 1956.

© Drum Social Histories / Baileys African History Archive /
Africa Media Online

13

THE WOMEN'S MARCH

'Now that you have touched the women you have struck a
rock.'

SOUTH AFRICAN PROTEST SONG

On Thursday 9 August 1956, twenty thousand women marched on
the Union Buildings, the imposing seat of the South African government in Pretoria, to protest against the extension of the hated
pass laws. It took more than two hours for the women, led by
Sophie Williams, Rahima Moosa, Lilian Ngoyi and Helen Joseph,
to file through the beautiful terraced gardens and into the magnificent neoclassical amphitheatre.[1] Reporting on the demonstration
for *Fighting Talk*, the influential anti-apartheid monthly, Phyllis
Altman, a teacher and labour activist, wrote that 'Only a camera
could record the richness of the scene: the gay headscarves, Pondo
women in their ochre dresses; Indian women in bright saris;
women from Bethlehem in the Free State wearing embroidered
ANC shawls; other delegates wearing skirts in black, gold and
green.' The route was lined with volunteers, dressed in distinctive
green blouses, who directed the protesters, and the women – some
with 'old faces, lined by life'; others 'young' and 'made-up in European style' – struck a solemn and dignified note.[2]

As they marched, the women carried with them mimeographed
leaflets stating that they represented women 'from every part of
South Africa' and 'of every race', who were 'united in our purpose
to save the African women from the degradation of the passes'.
'*We shall not* rest', they declared, 'until all pass laws and all forms
of permit restricting our freedom have been abolished' and 'until
we have won for our children their fundamental right to freedom,

justice and security'.[3] To loud cries of 'Mayibuye I Afrika' ('Let Africa return to its people'), an interracial delegation then entered the building to present copies of the petition, containing some one hundred thousand signatures, to South Africa's prime minister, J. G. Strijdom – the so-called 'Lion of the North' and an implacable defender of apartheid.[4] According to the ANC's Frances Baard, they were told that 'Strijdom was not there and that we were not allowed in anyway because we were black and white together . . . but we knew that he was just too scared to see us!'[5] Eventually, five of the women were permitted to enter the prime minister's office, which they promptly 'flooded' with thousands of petition pamphlets, placing them 'on his desk, and on the floor' until 'the room was full of them'.[6]

On returning to the amphitheatre, Lilian Ngoyi – a forty-five-year-old seamstress and trade union organiser, and the first woman elected to the executive committee of the African National Congress (ANC) – called for thirty minutes of silence to symbolise their defiance. Only the chimes of the clock (identical to those of Big Ben) and the occasional crying of a baby interrupted the silence as the women stood as one in the hot afternoon sun, raising aloft their right thumbs in the iconic freedom salute.[7] Then twenty thousand voices joined together in 'magnificent four-part harmony' to sing the ANC anthem, 'Nkosi sikelel' iAfrika' ('God Bless Africa'). The effect was electrifying and many wept openly. 'The singing', reported Phyllis Altman, 'reached the sky and then I knew . . . Nothing will defeat these women, these wives, these mothers.'[8] The women also performed a song composed especially for the occasion: 'Heyi Strijdom! [W]atint a bafazi; watint'imbokotho uzokufa!' ('Strijdom beware! Now that you have touched the women you have struck a rock, and you will die!')[9] When it was over the women, still singing, made their way down the terrace steps, through the gardens and out onto the main road, before heading home. They departed, Helen Joseph noted, 'with the same

dignity and discipline with which they had come'.[10] But there
was a palpable sense of elation at their achievement. Maggie Ree-
sha, an activist from the black Johannesburg suburb of Sophia-
town, recalled: 'The women had done it! Women from the ghettoes
. . . from the farms, from the villages, young and old, had dared to
invade the very citadel of oppression in order to express their indignation and detestation for apartheid . . .'[11]

The women's march, which had been organised by the Federation
of South African Women (FEDSAW) and the Women's League
of the ANC, took place during a period of growing resistance
to apartheid, a system of institutionalised white supremacy that
was designed to control all aspects of the lives of South Africa's
non-white people – from where they lived and worked to where
(and whether) they were educated, and even where they died.[12]
Rooted in scientific racism, and justified as a way to guarantee
the survival of 'western, Christian civilisation' in an Africa where
anti-colonial nationalists were clearly on the march, apartheid
('apartness' in Afrikaans) was introduced by the National Party
after its sensational victory in the general election of 1948.[13] Sanctioned by a range of new laws and enforced by the state's formidable security agencies, it replaced the more informal systems
of segregation and racial discrimination that had characterised
South Africa since the Dutch had first established a colony on
the Cape of Good Hope in 1652. During the late 1940s and early
1950s, South Africa's first apartheid government enacted measures that made various rights and privileges dependent on one's
place in a strict racial hierarchy, with whites (both Afrikaners and
those of English descent) firmly at the top, black Africans (known
as 'natives' or 'bantu') at the bottom, and 'Coloureds' (those of
mixed ancestry) and Indians (originally brought to South Africa
by the British to work as indentured servants) somewhere in
between. Having classified the entire population according to

race, the National Party government then proceeded to heavily circumscribe black educational and employment opportunities and mobility, prevent blacks from joining trade unions or participating in strikes, outlaw interracial marriage and interracial sexual relations, confine racial groups to separate territorial areas of the country, restrict access to various public amenities (including beaches, public transport and parks), suppress dissent – ruthlessly if necessary – and ensure that only white South Africans would enjoy economic and political power.[14]

Among black Africans – who, in 1956, made up two thirds of South Africa's population of 13.9 million – the pass book was one of the most loathed features of apartheid.[15] Long used as a means of regulating the movement of blacks, the whole pass system had been reorganised on a national basis in 1952. All black men aged sixteen and over were issued a 'reference book' (known colloquially as a 'dompas'), which contained a photograph, together with address, date of birth, marital status, record of employment and tax payments, a list of any criminal convictions and details of any influx control endorsements, which were used to regulate the movement of blacks into urban areas. The failure to produce the documentation on demand, or to have the correct permits in hand, was a criminal offence – punishable by fine, imprisonment and even deportation to rural 'reserves' or farm colonies. Ostensibly designed to control and regulate the right of blacks to live and work in 'white areas', the pass system undermined the dignity of black Africans and reinforced the country's official racist ideology.[16] Pius Langa, who became a senior judge in post-apartheid South Africa, experienced 'the frustration, indignity and humiliation' of the pass system first-hand. He was 'merely one of tens of thousands who peopled those seemingly interminable queues at the end of which . . . bad-tempered clerks and officials might reward one with some endorsement or other'. He recalled, at the age of seventeen, 'having to avert my eyes from the nakedness of grown men in a futile attempt to salvage some dignity for them in those queues where we had to expose ourselves to facilitate the degrading [physical] examination'.[17]

White officials exercised enormous power over the day-to-day lives of individual blacks, who, with good reason, quickly came to fear the sudden revocation of residency and work permits. Ezekiel Mphahlele, a university graduate and schoolteacher, explained how the 'big man' in the influx control office could 'send a man packing in twenty-four hours to quit the city. He it was who was supposed to . . . issue a heavily prescribed permit to look for work; to register every employer and his worker or workers so as to control the black man's movements everywhere and at all times.' Mphahlele recalled how his book was marked with a stamp that showed he had permission to look for work in Johannesburg. 'When I found employment, my boss would have to sign his name in the book every month and write "discharged" if and when he should kick me out or I should decide to leave. But this would only be after another rubber-stamp had come down to give me permission to stay in Johannesburg.' Indeed, if he later 'failed to get "suitable" employment and the big man got tired of renewing my permit to look for work, down would come his stamp sending me to Pretoria, my place of birth, there to go through the same process'.[18]

Hundreds of thousands of black South Africans were soon falling foul of the pass laws, with 330,000 convicted for violations of curfew, registration and other regulations during 1955 alone. Blacks, in fact, faced a 'nightmare' – a constant fear of 'the policeman or plain-clothes detective at the next corner, of the roving pick-up van; humiliated and wearied by queuing day after day at the pass office where men are herded like cattle for dipping; afraid above all of that dreaded purple stamp across their pass books: "Not to be employed in the urban area of —"'. For its critics, the pass system – with its elaborate surveillance systems and restrictions on black mobility – constituted a modern form of slavery.[19]

Faced with an avalanche of oppressive, racist legislation, apartheid's opponents fought back. The ANC, founded in 1912, had emerged during the Second World War as a 'modern, mass campaigning organisation' dedicated to securing first-class citizenship for South Africa's blacks. Inspired by the success of Gandhi in India, it launched a programme of boycotts, unofficial strikes and non-cooperation. In 1952, the ANC joined with the South African Indian Congress (SAIC) to launch the so-called 'defiance campaign', which involved mass rallies, 'stay-at-homes' and civil disobedience. As one of apartheid's leading historians has explained, 'The hope was that by inviting arrest and imposing intolerable burdens on the state's capacity to police its own regulations, the system would be rendered inoperable.' More than eight thousand were arrested, the ANC enjoyed a dramatic spike in its membership (which reached a hundred thousand by the end of the year), and public statements and demonstrations of support came from black leaders in the United States. But the campaign was, in many ways, a failure. Participation was patchy, and nonviolent protest too often spilled over into displays of popular anger and even rioting. The authorities responded ferociously: in one notorious incident, police officers gunned down 250 blacks as they attended a mass meeting in the coastal city of East London.[20]

Three years later three thousand delegates representing the ANC, the SAIC, the Coloured People's Congress, the multiracial South African Congress of Trade Unions and the Congress of Democrats (a coalition of white liberals and former members of the recently outlawed Communist Party) convened in Kliptown, near Johannesburg, for the Congress of the People. On 25 June they ratified the Freedom Charter, which demanded full racial equality (economic, political, legal and social) within a genuinely democratic South Africa.[21] It would remain the manifesto of the anti-apartheid movement until the country's first free, multiracial elections in April 1994.

In the face of continued protests by the ANC and its allies, the National Party government, spurred on by a comfortable victory in the 1953 election, worked to further entrench the apartheid system – creating sweeping new police powers, enacting a brutal programme of forced population transfers, gutting black educational provision and extending racial segregation.[22] Then, in September 1955, H. F. Verwoerd, the minister for native affairs – and an unabashed apologist for white supremacy – announced that from January 1956 African women would, for the first time, be issued with pass books.[23]

Black women, who understood all too well that new restrictions on their freedom of movement would make it much more difficult to find the menial or unskilled jobs on which they – and their families – relied, were alarmed. They also feared that they would be prevented from living with their husbands in urban areas – a move that would strike at the heart of family life.[24] Moreover, there were concerns that black women would be exposed to sexual abuse at the hands of unscrupulous white officials. As one anti-pass leaflet put it, 'a man only has to come into any home or stop a woman on the street and say he is a policeman or detective and the law of the country empowers him to take away that woman and to touch any part of her body . . . under the pretext that they are searching for a pass'.[25] The pass system would, declared its critics, not simply 'bring as much misery' to African women 'as it has to the men', it would be 'far worse'. FEDSAW, which had been founded in April 1954 to co-ordinate campaigns for equal rights and equal opportunities for women as well as men, irrespective of race, warned: 'In this year 1956 we are faced with the carrying out of a law that will arrest women indiscriminately in the street, remove mothers from their families, leave infants and young children without care, imprison pregnant and nursing mothers, and humiliate all African women.'[26]

Faced with this threat, the political consciousness of black women was stirred: as the popular black magazine, *Drum*, put it, the extension of the pass laws had 'started pots and pans rattling' in kitchens all over South Africa.[27] Anti-apartheid activists quickly sought to channel the widespread fury at the proposed changes in the pass laws into a co-ordinated mass movement. Writing in *Fighting Talk* in January, for example, FEDSAW's national secretary, Helen Joseph, declared that the 'coming year' would 'be a vital one for the liberation movement'. If the 'women [and] the mothers of South Africa' could wage a 'courageous and determined' campaign against the extension of the pass laws, then there was a real possibility of rendering 'passes for women inoperable' and, more broadly, of striking a 'mortal blow' against apartheid itself.[28] With thousands attending meetings, rallies and demonstrations during the early months of the year, there was every sign that a genuine mass movement was in the offing.[29] In January, for example, six thousand attended a giant rally in Port Elizabeth and in March two thousand attended an anti-pass conference in Johannesburg. That same month, three hundred women marched to the offices of the Native Affairs Commission in Germiston, in the north of the country, where they declared that 'even if the passes are printed in real gold we do not want them'.[30] Then, as dawn broke on 9 April, several hundred women in Winburg, in the Orange Free State, marched to the local magistrate's court and, in a spontaneous and public display of defiance, burned their newly issued pass books.[31] Between January and July more than fifty thousand women participated in almost forty anti-pass demonstrations right across the country – and it was amidst this extraordinary upsurge of activism that the decision was taken to stage a national demonstration in Pretoria.[32]

In South Africa, black women were in the vanguard of the struggle against white supremacy. It may have been a male ANC leader, Walter Sisulu, who had called for 'continuous campaigning among the people' against the pass laws but it was South Africa's women who were the backbone of the anti-pass movement.[33] Like their counterparts in the American South, these women sought to combine a commitment to nonviolent protest (including the use of peaceful marches, non-cooperation and civil disobedience) with a politics of 'respectability' that used their gender, and especially their status as wives and mothers, as a basis for political organising. By conforming to middle-class standards of behaviour and dress (thereby challenging pervasive negative white stereotypes about black women), emphasising the importance of the family, and organising and protesting as women and as mothers, these courageous and determined activists crafted a 'bold and respectable brand of political resistance'.[34] As the popular cry 'Give us your pants, the women will wear them!' illustrates, these women also offered a provocative challenge to the patriarchal views of many black men.[35]

The women's march of 9 August was hailed by FEDSAW as 'a rock, a monumental achievement by the most oppressed, suffering and downtrodden of our people – the women of South Africa'.[36] The protest certainly came to resonate powerfully among anti-apartheid activists, and 9 August was subsequently declared 'national women's day' (marked since 1994 by an official public holiday in South Africa). More tangibly, the anti-pass protests also seemed to be having an effect on the government's ability to implement its policy. By September 1956 a mere twenty-three thousand reference books had been issued, and officials had refrained from attempting to distribute passes in ANC strongholds.[37]

Such success, however, proved short-lived. Indeed, even as FEDSAW and its allies were plotting the next stage of their campaign against the pass laws, the National Party government was putting the final touches to an extraordinary measure that was intended to cripple the entire anti-apartheid movement. It was an inflexible and uncompromising response from South Africa's white supremacist leaders – but one that would not have been out of place nine thousand miles away in Dixie, where the defenders of Jim Crow were equally determined to hold the colour line, whatever the cost.

14

MOB RULE

No self-respecting white man would abide by the Communist-dominated court decision. They will use force, violence, anything and everything they can to keep their children from becoming mixed with the niggers.

WHITE CITIZENS' COUNCIL LEADER, Mansfield, Texas

The effigy, its head and hands painted black, its body daubed with splodges of red paint, could be seen swinging from a wire rope at the intersection of Broad and Main Streets in Mansfield – a little prairie town of fifteen hundred people (one quarter African American), in Tarrant County, Texas, twenty miles south-west of Dallas. Pinned to the straw-filled figure, which had appeared during the night of Tuesday 28 August, were signs that read 'THIS NEGRO TRIED TO GO TO A WHITE SCHOOL' and 'WOULDN'T THIS BE A HORRIBLE WAY TO DIE'. There was 'lynch talk' on the streets, and one African American woman, returning home from a shopping trip, noted that 'You could feel the way they looked at a Negro . . . they wanted to kill one.'[1] Over the next few days, as the new school year began, Mansfield was one of several southern towns to witness ugly racial clashes as the defenders of Jim Crow sought to defy court-ordered integration. As this dramatic battle for civil rights played out, President Eisenhower ensured that the federal government remained firmly on the sidelines.

A year earlier the families of three black teenagers, acting with the support of their local NAACP branch and the Association's national officials, had filed a lawsuit to desegregate Mansfield High School.[2] The town's African Americans certainly had good reason to feel aggrieved at the quality of the educational provision on offer. Mansfield Colored School, which taught children aged six to fourteen, had no lunch programme, lacked adequate teaching materials and, despite being located on a busy road, had 'no fence to restrain children from darting on the road while playing'. Moreover, African Americans were excluded completely from Mansfield High and forced to attend one of two black schools in Fort Worth, fifteen miles away. Because the local school board refused to provide a bus, the black teenagers had to use the Trailways public service, which dropped them twenty blocks from the school and left them with a two-hour wait for the first bus home.[3] At the end of June 1956 the US Fifth Circuit Court of Appeals ruled that the 'plaintiffs have the right to admission to, and to attend, the Mansfield High School on the same basis as members of the white race'. The court was also clear that the local school board's refusal to admit students 'on account of their race or color' was 'unlawful'. On Monday 27 August the court order decreeing the immediate desegregation of Mansfield High was issued.[4]

For segregationists, the prospect of black and white children sitting alongside one another in the classroom was anathema. Back in October 1955, more than a hundred people had attended a rally at the town's Memorial Hall to hear Howard A. Beard, a local White Citizens' Council leader, fulminate against the 'Communistic' NAACP and stir up fears about miscegenation. School integration, he declared, would mean that 'our children will be guinea pigs and our days as a national race will be numbered . . . once mixed they can never be unmixed, and this [is] the surest and most certain way to destroy us.' 'If we don't organize', warned the Fort Worth salesman, 'it will be our children who will pay the price . . . for our cowardice.' Fired up by Beard's rhetoric, the audience pledged themselves unanimously to preserve Jim Crow and promptly founded their own Citizens' Council chapter to lead the fight against the integration of Mansfield High. Beard assured the crowd that desegregation could be stopped in its tracks. All it would take, he explained, was 'grits, guts and gunpowder'.[5]

In the summer of 1956, as court-ordered integration loomed over the town, Mansfield's diehard segregationists turned to fear and intimidation in their effort to hold the colour line. On 22 August a cross was burned in the heart of the black neighbour-hood (a second cross was burned the following day); the father of one of the black plaintiffs was told that if his son enrolled at the previously all-white school, he would be evicted from his property; the president of the local NAACP received a series of threatening telephone calls warning him to 'get out of town'. Meanwhile, the Citizens' Council decided to hold a rally on the school grounds, to dissuade any African American student from registering for the new school year.[6]

During the early hours of Thursday 30 August – the first day of registration – a second effigy was hoisted atop the flagpole that stood proudly outside Mansfield High. By 8 a.m. a crowd of whites – mostly men, with some women and children – were gathering on the school field. Many carried signs, stating 'NIGGER STAY OUT, WE DON'T WANT NIGGERS, THIS IS A WHITE SCHOOL', 'A DEAD NIGGER IS THE BEST NIGGER' and 'COONS EARS $1 A DOZEN'. There was plenty of talk about 'mongrelisation' and the need to 'drive the NAACP out of town'. A number of the men were rumoured to be carrying weapons, and there were angry exchanges with the county sheriff when he warned against taking the law into their own hands. The crowds, which numbered as many as four hundred, spent most of the day milling about; one teenage girl doubtless spoke for many when she explained, 'If God had wanted us to go to school together He wouldn't have made them black and us white.' Meanwhile, at the behest of 'radical elements', the city's merchants and shopkeepers closed their businesses in a show of support (though several did so only reluctantly).

The next day the crowd was larger and the mood more ugly.

An observer from the Tarrant County district attorney's office was roughed up, watching journalists were jostled, and hate literature was passed out claiming that 'the Jews were behind the NAACP and that school desegregation was a communist plot to mongrelize the white race'. Citizens' Council leaders sought to intimidate business owners into cutting off credit to African Americans, and vigilantes began patrolling Mansfield's streets to ensure that 'anyone suspected of being sympathetic to the Negro cause' was quickly 'escorted out of town'.[7] A third effigy now hung above the school's front porch. Not a single black child had yet attempted to register at Mansfield High.[8]

Nor would they.

On the afternoon of 31 August, Allan Shivers, the state's Democratic governor, announced that he was despatching the Texas Rangers to Mansfield to 'see that order is kept'. But the state's elite law enforcement officers would not be used to protect black schoolchildren, nor would they enforce the court ruling. Instead, Shivers despatched the Rangers, with their distinctive, wide-brimmed hats, to maintain segregation. Citing concern for the 'general welfare', he urged school board officials to transfer out of the district any pupil, 'white or colored', whose attendance or attempted attendance at Mansfield High School 'would reasonably be calculated to incite violence', and ordered the Rangers to 'arrest anyone, white or colored, whose actions are such as to represent a threat to the peace . . .' Shivers also had a clear message for the authorities in Washington: 'If this course is not satisfactory . . . to the federal government, I respectfully suggest further that the Supreme Court, which is responsible for the [desegregation] order, be given the task of enforcing it.' The governor's willingness to defy the federal court, and the strength of local white resistance, guaranteed that – for now – segregation remained. The doors of Mansfield High would stay closed to African Americans until September 1965.[9]

*

Eight hundred miles away in Clinton, Tennessee, twelve African American teenagers did manage to attend classes at the previously all-white high school, but they had to run a gauntlet of hate that was, if anything, even worse than that in Mansfield. Clinton – a small mill town, nestled in the Cumberland Mountains of east Tennessee – was a relatively prosperous community which prided itself on being a calm, well-ordered kind of place, with a strong civic ethos: 'Welcome to Clinton. A Wonderful Place to Live', boasted the sign that greeted visitors. Clinton's population of 3,700 or so included more than two hundred African Americans, who were concentrated into the segregated west-side neighbour-hood of Foley Hill (known to whites as 'Nigger Hill'). The nearby Oak Ridge atomic energy centre provided unskilled employment for many of the town's black men, while African American women were likely to work as domestic help in the homes of the local white middle-class. In the absence of local provision, Clinton's black teenagers had to travel to Knoxville, fifteen miles away, to attend high school. However, in January 1956, following a five-year legal fight, the courts finally ordered the Anderson County School Board to desegregate its three high schools, including Clinton High, by the autumn.[10]

As the new school year dawned, there was good reason to believe that the desegregation of Clinton High would be completed peacefully. Over the spring and summer David J. Brittain, the school's thirty-nine-year-old principal, had organised a series of meetings to prepare teachers and students for desegregation, while the local newspaper had printed details of the school's new policies on sports and social events to calm white fears about inter-racial 'mixing'. On Monday 20 August, seven hundred students – including twelve African Americans – had attended Clinton High, without incident, to register formally for classes. The town's white citizens were by no means enthusiastic about integration, but they did appear resigned to it. As the editor of the *Clinton Courier-News* explained, 'We have never heard anyone in Clinton say he wanted integration . . . but we have heard a great many people say: "We believe in the law. We will obey the ruling of the Court. We have no other lawful choice".'[11] Then, at this critical moment, a twenty-six-year-old native of Camden, New Jersey, entered the fray.

Newsweek's Bill Emerson later wrote that John Kasper was 'to some people an almost spectral figure, a satanic rabble rouser licked about with flame, and smoking hate', while for others he was 'a sort of Citizens' Council version of Moses come to set his people free'.[12] An acolyte of the modernist poet and notorious anti-Semite Ezra Pound, Kasper – who earned a degree in English and Philosophy at Columbia University – had abandoned a PhD in order to run a right-wing bookstore in New York's Greenwich Village. (During this time, he enjoyed friendships – and, it is said, intimate relationships – with African Americans of both sexes.) Drawn increasingly to the conspiratorial world-view of the political far right, Kasper had cut his teeth as a militant anti-Communist before forging a career as one of America's most notorious race-baiters.[13] In Clinton, he would whip up a storm of racial animosity that threatened to run out of control.

Kasper, who had arrived in Clinton late on the evening of Friday 24 August, immediately set to work – first phoning around local whites to recruit support, and then handing out provocative, racist literature on the streets (one leaflet included pictures of an African American man kissing a white woman).[14] On the Saturday afternoon, a delegation of Clinton's civic leaders, including the newspaper editor, the mayor and the chief of police, tried to persuade Kasper to leave town. The following evening, after holding a small rally, Kasper was arrested on charges of vagrancy and attempting to incite a riot. On Monday, 715 white students, together with a dozen African Americans, attended their first classes at Clinton High. Although a small number of pickets gathered outside the school in protest, there was no serious trouble.

The following day, the crowd outside the school was a bit bigger and, at noon, Kasper – who had been acquitted that morning due to insufficient evidence – confronted the principal on the school grounds, demanding that he 'get the niggers out' or resign.[15] Over the next few weeks, Brittain – a 'gentle, scholarly' man, popular with his students – was subjected to a harrowing ordeal: 'the continuous midnight ringing of his telephone, the ugly voices out of the night snarling foul insults and threats whenever he lifted the receiver; the fiery crosses burned in front of his house; the boycott by active segregationists of any tradesman courageous enough to continue dealing with [him]'.[16] It was to Brittain's great credit that, despite these pressures, he held firm.[17]

That Tuesday evening, Kasper addressed a crowd of several hundred in the courthouse square. Accusing the local authorities of lacking 'guts', he argued that 'the people' constituted a higher authority than the Supreme Court, and pledged to fight to preserve segregation 'however long it takes'. Over the next few days, Kasper exploited growing resentment of the town's established leadership class (in the words of one resident, they had 'ruled the roost too long'), and some of his most ardent followers were to be found in the 'dingy' mining villages and 'little hard-scrabble farms' that surrounded Clinton. With little else going for them, these dirt-poor whites proved determined to hold on to the advantages (whether real or imagined) that their skin colour conferred on them. Meanwhile, recent migrants from the Deep South, who had been lured to the area by the Oak Ridge atomic facility and had brought with them a visceral loathing of African Americans, could also be found cheering on Kasper as he preached his gospel of hate.[18]

On Wednesday morning, a crowd of 125 greeted the black students with shouts of 'coon', 'nigger' and 'black ape', as they arrived on the school grounds; later that afternoon, a number of black students were chased through the streets. As darkness began to fall, some eight hundred whites gathered once more at the large, ugly brick courthouse, where they witnessed Kasper defiantly tear up a temporary injunction restraining him from interfering with school desegregation. Urging the people to continue their efforts, Kasper declared that 'no amount of injunctions, not even ten thousand of them, can stop something the people do not want and never will have'.[19] Meanwhile, in Foley Hill, African American men stood guard to ward off attack, while their families took refuge in cellars. On Thursday, there was further trouble: some black students were pelted with tomatoes, while sixteen-year-old Bobby Cain was attacked as he walked to a drive-in custard stand to buy his lunch. One woman 'clubbed him with an umbrella', while others punched him and threatened him with knives. When Cain drew his pocketknife in self-defence he was taken into protective custody by the police.[20] On the Friday, fears of further violence led to a sharp drop in school attendance (only 446 students, including ten African Americans, turned up for classes) and that evening, as news swirled around that Kasper had been found guilty of contempt and sentenced to a year in jail, the crowds that had gathered outside the courthouse were fired up by an incendiary speech from the Alabama segregationist and former radio announcer Asa Carter. After denouncing the Supreme Court and the NAACP, Carter told his audience that it was their 'duty' as 'Christian, Anglo-Saxon citizens' to protect their racial heritage, and he praised the Ku Klux Klan as 'the reason we don't have banana colored skin, kinky hair and think lips'. Marching through the streets, throwing firecrackers and chanting 'We want Kasper!' the mob attacked the cars of passing African American motorists, while a delegation headed for the mayor's house, which they threatened to dynamite.[21]

The following morning, Clinton's Board of Aldermen declared an official state of emergency and, warning of 'bloodshed before the night is over', requested urgent state assistance. With the overstretched police force at breaking point, they also organised an improvised auxiliary force under the leadership of Leo Grant, a former paratrooper who had seen action in Korea. No cheerleaders for integration, Clinton's white moderates were nevertheless determined to uphold the rule of law. As one of Grant's volunteer policemen put it: 'Hell, it ain't a matter of wanting or not wanting niggers in the school, it's a matter of who's going to run the town, the Government or that mob out there.'[22]

By 8 p.m., a crowd of two thousand whites that had gathered once more on the town square was facing down Leo Grant's men, who had formed a 'skirmish line on the lawn'. With their shotguns at the ready, the improvised police force began to move on the 'jeering, taunting mob', which, having ignored repeated orders to disperse, was now threatening to storm the courthouse. As lightning crackled overhead, Grant's men fired two volleys of tear gas, scattering most of the crowd. Within minutes a group of 150 diehards had re-formed and were striding 'menacingly toward the police', yelling, 'Let's get the nigger lovers, let's get their guns and kill them.' At this moment, thirty-nine patrol cars, carrying a hundred state troopers, roared into town, 'sirens shrieking and searchlights blazing'. With the help of moderate segregationists, who urged the crowds to be 'lawful and orderly', they were able to establish an uneasy peace.[23]

The following day, the Sunday morning calm was shattered as a hundred jeeps, seven M41 tanks and three armoured personnel carriers (with .50-calibre machine guns) rumbled along Clinton's narrow roads, bringing with them more than six hundred troops of the Tennessee National Guard.[24] They were there on the orders of Governor Frank G. Clement, a racial moderate and opponent of 'massive resistance', who justified his actions on the grounds that he could not 'sit back and allow a lawless element to take over. If they can take over Tennessee because of one issue, they can take it over on others. It may be your home that they take over next.'[25] Ironically, given this massive show of force, three thousand people – the largest crowd of the entire crisis – turned out at the courthouse that evening to denounce integration. Firecrackers were thrown at passing cars, threats were made against African Americans, a cross was burned on the school grounds, and National Guardsmen, many wearing gas masks and holding fixed bayonets, were heckled.[26] Just after eight o'clock, the mob spotted a young African American sailor, James Chandler, in town to visit his girlfriend, as he walked to the bus station. Two hundred men and teenage boys, screaming, 'Get out of town, nigger,' set off in pursuit and quickly cornered the nineteen-year-old at a gas station. As they closed in, twelve Guardsmen arrived on the scene and, forming a protective cordon around the terrified Chandler, ushered him to safety.[27]

Within twenty-four hours, order had been restored: gatherings at the courthouse were banned, the use of public address systems and outdoor speaking were prohibited, an evening curfew was imposed on the courthouse square, and roadblocks and regular street patrols were organised. Trouble did not disappear overnight (indeed, it briefly spread to nearby Oliver Springs, amid false reports that the school there was about to integrate), but it did become more isolated and sporadic. Importantly, African Americans continued to attend classes at Clinton High.[28] An undercurrent of tension, though, remained: black pupils were subjected to petty harassment from some of their classmates (ink was deliberately knocked over their books, for instance, and they were jostled in the corridors), and a slate of segregationist candidates appeared well placed to win the municipal elections, scheduled for 4 December.[29] On the Sunday before the vote, the Rev. Paul W. Turner, the minister at the town's First Baptist Church, preached a message of conciliation, telling his fellow whites that black students were legally and morally entitled to attend Clinton High 'without heckling or obstruction'. Two days later, the thirty-three-year-old minister escorted six 'nervously smiling' black children from Foley Hill to the school, braving segregationist bystanders who accused him of being a 'nigger-lovin' son of a bitch'. As he left the school, Turner was accosted by a mob and subjected to a vicious beating that left his blood smeared all over the side of a parked car. News of the disgraceful attack travelled fast and prompted widespread revulsion. Over the next few hours, hundreds of citizens turned out to cast their vote for the moderate candidates – who ended up outpolling the hardline segregationists by three to one.[30] As one citizen explained, Turner was 'a symbol. What happened, happened to us all – and it waked us up.'[31]

On 17 May 1957 – three years to the day after the Supreme Court had issued its historic *Brown* ruling, and almost nine months after he had lain awake at night, trembling with fear at the prospect of attending classes at the school down the hill – Bobby Cain became the first African American to graduate from an integrated public high school anywhere in the South.[32]

For the gutsy Gordon family of Wheatcroft, in western Kentucky, the school desegregation crisis would play out rather differently. In early September, after a mob had sought to prevent James, aged ten, and Theresa, aged eight, from attending classes in nearby Clay, Governor Albert Chandler had despatched National Guard units to the little mining town – as well as to Sturgis, ten miles away, where crowds of whites, armed with pitchforks and shovels, had blocked the school entrance – to enforce desegregation. Louise Gordon – a 'thin, wonderfully sassy' twenty-eight-year-old with a 'ready smile, and a happy twinkle in her eyes' – had been quietly determined that her children attend the formerly all-white school, no matter what the risk: 'if you got the guts to go', she explained to her young son, 'I've got the guts to take ye.' The Gordons would, though, pay a high price for their defiance: the man who supplied bottled water to their house (which had no mains supply) abruptly cancelled his deliveries; Louise's husband was dismissed from his job at a local garage and employers within a forty-mile radius refused to take him on; dynamite was exploded in their neighbourhood; local shopkeepers refused to serve Louise, who had to travel thirty miles to purchase food and other provisions. Faced with an unrelenting campaign of intimidation, Louise made the painful decision to abandon the town of her birth and build a new life for her family outside the Bluegrass State.[33]

At 10:30 a.m. on Wednesday 5 September, Dwight D. Eisenhower appeared before 191 journalists who had gathered in the Executive Office Building, a block north of the White House, for one of his regular news conferences. The school crises in the South had been headline news not just in the United States but all over the world (the Soviets, naturally, had a 'field day' over it), so it was not surprising that questions soon turned to school desegregation.[34]

Eisenhower had, to the great disappointment of civil rights supporters, repeatedly refused to endorse the *Brown* decision, arguing that it was his job to enforce the Constitution, not to interpret it. The president had instructed the federal commissioners who ran the District of Columbia to make the nation's capital a model of peaceful school desegregation, and pressed for an end to Jim Crow in the capital's hotels, restaurants and other public accommodations.[35] But there is little doubt that 'Ike' had profound reservations about the *Brown* ruling; in private he claimed that the court had 'set back badly' the 'whole issue' of civil rights.[36] As well as expressing concerns that the court was 'trying to reach out and control so many parts of the Federal government', the president also had a good deal of sympathy for white southerners. As he told his cabinet, 'these people' had not been breaking the law during the previous sixty years (the Supreme Court had, after all, previously held segregation to be constitutional) and so it was entirely understandable that they now felt shocked and angry. 'We cannot', he explained, 'erase the emotions of three generations just overnight.'[37] But while the president had no difficulty in empathising with southern whites, he seemed emotionally and intellectually incapable of empathising with blacks. Indeed, Eisenhower never fully grasped the strength of African Americans' determination to enjoy first-class citizenship under the law, nor understood their mounting frustration at the painfully slow pace of change.[38] During the crisis at the University of Alabama back in February, the president had been content to leave the matter in the hands of the local authorities. It was a formula that he had no intention of abandoning.

Asked about the racist violence that had erupted over recent days, Eisenhower simply noted that 'local governments have moved promptly to stop the violence', before reminding the reporters – and the wider public – that, under America's federal system, Washington only had the authority to intervene if a particular state was 'not able to handle the matter'. Turning to Mansfield, the president explained that 'the Texas authorities had moved in and order was restored, so the question became unimportant'. When pressed on whether Allan Shivers's decision to send Texas Rangers to prevent school desegregation constituted 'a surrender to mob rule', Eisenhower argued that it was not yet clear whether the black students had been transferred out permanently 'or until the situation was under control'. He then returned to the question of federal authority, stressing that the United States would be 'in a bad way' if the government in Washington exercised police powers 'habitually'.[39] The president also made a characteristic appeal to 'people of good will' to help the South reach an amicable solution. Tellingly, though, Eisenhower referred to 'extremists on both sides':

> The South is full of people of good will, but they are not the ones we now hear. We hear the people that are adamant and are so filled with prejudice that they even resort to violence; and the same way on the other side of the thing, the people who want to have the whole matter settled today.[40]

In NAACP headquarters in New York, the president's remarks were met with despair. Writing to the White House the next day,

Thurgood Marshall – the Association's top lawyer, and a man who had done more than anyone to help overturn the pernicious 'separate but equal' ruling of 1896 – accused the president of apportioning responsibility for the recent violence 'between lawless mobs and other Americans who seek only their lawful rights in a lawful manner, often after unbelievably long periods of waiting'. This moral equivalence between segregationist 'hate-mongers' and 'those of us who are trying under the most difficult conditions to obtain the rights which have been enjoyed by other Americans for . . . many years' was, to say the least, 'unfortunate'. Marshall and his colleagues urged Eisenhower to 'speak out in forthright terms against anyone who openly and violently interferes with the orderly and judicial processes of the federal government'.[41]

The following year, Eisenhower did sign into law a landmark, if heavily emasculated, Civil Rights Act, the first such legislation since the 1870s. The president also ordered the 101st Airborne Division to Little Rock, Arkansas, when opposition to school desegregation there erupted into a carnival of lawlessness in which the governor, Orval Faubus, was clearly complicit. But he made it very clear that these were exceptional circumstances, and seemed to go out of his way to mollify white southerners. When it came to providing a clear moral stance on desegregation, there was only silence. Indeed, when Faubus subsequently closed down Little Rock's public schools rather than see them integrated, Eisenhower claimed that he was powerless to act.[42]

Five years after the *Brown* decision, a mere 6.4 per cent of black students in the South were attending integrated schools; in the Deep South, that figure was 0.2 per cent. Eisenhower was, of course, not solely (or even, perhaps, largely) to blame for this, and his successor – John F. Kennedy – was hardly an enthusiastic interventionist.[43] But Ike's reluctance to use his enormous personal authority to press for compliance with the Constitution was striking. Twenty years later, when Roy Wilkins sat down to write his memoirs, his disappointment in Eisenhower still ran deep. The president was 'a fine general and a good, decent man', Wilkins acknowledged, 'but if he had fought World War II the way he fought for civil rights, we would all be speaking German now'.[44]

IV AUTUMN

REVOLUTION AND REACTION

15

COLLUSION AT SÈVRES

Her Majesty's Government have been informed of the course
of the conversations held at Sèvres . . . and confirm that
in the situation there envisaged they will take the action
described.
SIR ANTHONY EDEN to GUY MOLLET, 25 October 1956

On the morning of Monday 22 October 1956 Selwyn Lloyd, the
British foreign secretary, cancelled his public engagements, citing
a heavy cold. Having donned a battered raincoat to conceal his
identity, he was then bundled into a waiting car and driven to
RAF Hendon by his private secretary, Donald Logan. There, the
two men boarded an aircraft and flew to the Villacoublay military
airfield, eight miles south-west of Paris. On landing, they were
met by a French officer who drove them to a modest villa, partially
concealed by trees, on rue Emanuel Girot in the Parisian suburb of
Sèvres. Lloyd arrived at about four o'clock in the afternoon. Waiting at the house, which had served as a Resistance headquarters
during the war, were Guy Mollet, Christian Pineau and Maurice
Bourgès-Manoury, the French defence minister, together with the
Israeli prime minister, David Ben-Gurion, Moshe Dayan, the chief
of staff of the Israeli Defence Forces, and Shimon Peres, director of
the ministry of defence.[1]

The plenary discussions, which began at 7 p.m., were tense
and the personal chemistry poor. The Israelis were, Lloyd noted,
'utterly exhausted' – they had endured a gruelling seventeen-hour
flight the day before – and Ben-Gurion was 'in a rather aggressive
mood . . . implying that the Israelis had no reason to believe in
anything that a British minister might say'.[2] They also took an

instant dislike to Lloyd, whom they viewed as patronising and aloof.[3] Mordechai Bar-On, Dayan's twenty-seven-year-old personal assistant, noted in his diary that Lloyd was 'a typical English diplomat' with a 'shrill voice' and a face that 'looked as if something stinking hangs permanently under his nose'.[4] Nevertheless, as the talks progressed (there was a brief adjournment while the guests consumed an 'enormous fish'), the outlines of a plot were sketched out.[5] Ben-Gurion explained that Israel was prepared to launch a 'reprisal raid on Egypt on D-Day in the morning, reaching the canal by that evening. That night, Britain and France can meet and issue a demand to Egypt to clear all its forces from the canal zone and send a simultaneous demand to Israel to refrain from approaching the canal.' Because Israel had no interest in capturing the canal this ultimatum would 'have no real meaning to us'. However, if the Egyptians refused to comply, Britain and France would 'start to bomb Egyptian air-bases the next morning'. A non-committal Lloyd departed after midnight, with a promise to consult his colleagues back in London.[6] Just two days later, the British, French and Israeli governments signed a top-secret agreement to launch a war to overthrow Gamal Abdel Nasser.

Throughout August and September the United Kingdom and France had engaged in what one historian has described as a 'dance of diplomacy'.[7] London, in fact, hosted two international conferences. In mid-August, twenty-two maritime powers – including Australia, the USA, the USSR, the Netherlands and India – gathered to discuss Nasser's seizure of the Suez Canal. Of those invited, only the governments of Egypt and Greece declined (Greek public opinion was broadly sympathetic to Nasser and, given the increasingly bitter dispute over Cyprus, Athens judged it prudent not to attend).[8] After several days of talks, eighteen nations endorsed a resolution that called for a 'definite system destined to guarantee at all times, and for all Powers, the free use of the Canal', to be established with 'due regard to the sovereign rights of Egypt'. At the start of September the Australian prime minister, Robert Menzies, flew to Cairo to present the London proposals. On the first day of talks, he took the Egyptian leader to one side to warn that if a deal was not reached, an Anglo-French military strike was still very much alive. (Nasser promptly complained to the Americans about the 'Australian mule' who had been sent 'to threaten me'.) The mission came to nought. In private, Menzies blamed President Eisenhower for undermining the talks; during a press conference on 5 September, Eisenhower had emphasised that the US was committed to a peaceful resolution of the crisis.[9] As he prepared to leave Cairo, the Australian premier informed Eden that Egypt had 'all the markings of a Police state' and Nasser, though 'in some ways a likeable fellow', was 'rather gauche, with some irritating mannerisms, such as rolling his eyes up to the ceiling when he is talking to you and producing a quick, quite evanescent grin when he can think of nothing else to do'. The Egyptians, meanwhile, were not exactly enamoured with Menzies. Egypt's foreign minister – who described the Australian as having 'gruff eyebrows, glaring eyes and a sharp voice' – believed that he was totally insensitive to the Afro-Asian sensibility, and appeared to see nothing wrong in asking Nasser to accept that his fellow Egyptians were incapable of operating the waterway successfully without outside help.[10]

A subsequent effort, spearheaded by John Foster Dulles, to set up a Suez Canal Users' Association also ran into the sand when Nasser made it clear that Egypt would 'stand firm in safeguarding its sovereignty'. Finally, towards the end of September, the British and French governments referred the Suez dispute to the United Nations Security Council.[11]

It is difficult to avoid the suspicion that a good deal of this diplomatic activity was simply for show. Christian Pineau was dismissive about the UN, telling the British ambassador in Paris that the referral to the Security Council was 'largely immaterial, except for window dressing purposes'.[12] Throughout the summer and on into the autumn, as conferences were convened, communiqués issued and diplomatic notes exchanged, London and Paris were busy refining their war plans, moving ships, aircraft and other military assets into position, and waiting for a *casus belli* that would enable them to strike. In an insightful editorial published at the start of September the *Manchester Guardian* noted that, while all of the diplomatic hustle and bustle 'point to a settlement by conciliation', the continued government talk about the 'possible use of force', together with a heavy (and heavily censored) military build-up in the Mediterranean, 'seem to cover a less happy state of affairs'. This, the paper noted, enabled the government 'to be, if it pleases, hypocritical, two-faced: it can look wholly peace-loving while actually it prepares for an attack. We may trust that this is not so . . . but . . . it is an explosive possibility to be kept in mind.'[13]

On the evening of 8 August, Sir Anthony Eden had addressed the British people about the Suez crisis for the first time. Speaking from a hot and cramped BBC studio, he declared that Nasser's 'act of plunder' could not be allowed to stand. 'Our quarrel', he explained, 'is not with Egypt, and still less with the Arab world; it is with Colonel Nasser' – a man who could not 'be trusted to keep an agreement'. Eden then invoked the lessons of the 1930s: 'The pattern is familiar to many of us, my friends. We all know this is how fascist governments behave and we all remember, only too well, what the cost can be in giving in to fascism.' 'With dictators', he explained, 'you always have to pay a higher price later on, for the appetite grows with feeding.'[14] Coming from Eden, who had made his name as an opponent of appeasement, these words were hugely powerful. Although keen to stress that he did not 'seek a solution by force', Eden justified the recent military movements 'by land, sea, and air' as a sensible precaution. Behind the scenes, though, the prime minister was working hard to foster public support for military action. His administration waged an extraordinarily intensive propaganda campaign, exploiting relationships with newspaper proprietors and editors, making liberal use of anonymous briefings to lobby journalists and deploying its powers of censorship. The purpose was to deflect attention away from any meaningful discussion of the legality of Egypt's decision to nationalise the canal, stoke hostility towards Nasser through a relentless campaign of vilification and 'whip up public opinion'. These efforts were highly effective.[15] In its 'A Hinge of History' editorial of 1 August, for instance, *The Times* warned that if Nasser was allowed to 'get away with this *coup* all the British and other western interests in the Middle East will crumble'. Nasser's 'seizure' of the canal was a turning point – a 'hinge of history', akin to 'Hitler's march into the Rhineland'. 'Quibbling' over the legal technicalities of Nasser's move was beside the point. Not only did Nasser's actions threaten the economic security of the West, but they set a dangerous precedent: there would be 'no stability and confidence in the world so long as [international] agreements can be scrapped with impunity'. It was, then, vital that Britain took the lead in confronting Nasser, even if that meant resorting to force. After all, if a nation did not 'stand up' for its rights, it would be destined to forfeit them.[16] Sir Anthony could hardly have put the case better himself.[17]

Behind closed doors – at meetings of the cabinet and the Egypt Committee (the de facto War Cabinet) – Eden and his senior ministers were explicit about their desire not simply to secure international oversight over the canal but to 'bring about the downfall of the present Egyptian government'.[18] They were equally clear that this intention should remain hidden. As Selwyn Lloyd noted, it was 'important, from the point of view of public opinion, especially in the United States and in Asia, that the purpose of our action should appear to be confined to establishing the security of the international waterway'. Were any official document to leak that appeared to 'define our objective in wider terms' then the consequences, he warned, might very well be 'disastrous'.[19]

By the end of July the service chiefs had the outlines of a workable plan, Operation Musketeer, which envisaged an attack on Port Said involving an amphibious landing by Royal Marines and an airborne assault by the Parachute Brigade Group. Soon, though, both military and civilian leaders were expressing doubts. Port Said was far from ideal terrain, with only very limited space in which troops could be deployed, and there was a real risk that the Canal itself would be damaged, or blockaded, during the fighting. Perhaps most significant, though, was the realisation that such a localised strike was unlikely to topple Nasser's government.[20] As Harold Macmillan pointed out, if Britain satisfied itself with merely reoccupying the Canal Zone, it would be in the same highly unsatisfactory position as in 1954, though this time with far fewer forces at its disposal to deal with hostile locals and a likely campaign of sabotage and guerrilla warfare. The Chancellor of the Exchequer, who was one of the government's most vociferous hawks, argued that the military objectives should be expanded to include the destruction of Nasser's armies, the overthrow of his government and its replacement with an administration that 'will work satisfactorily with ourselves and other powers'.[21]

During the second week of August the cabinet approved a new plan. After a bombing campaign of two or three days to wipe out the Egyptian air force, troops would be landed at Alexandria and a force of eighty thousand would march to the Suez Canal, via Cairo. But in early September the plan was changed yet again – this time because of concerns about the devastating effects that a naval bombardment of Alexandria would have on the city's civilian population and on international opinion. The landings would take place at Port Said after all, though they would be preceded by a major air offensive designed to neutralise Egypt's air force, cripple its economy and shatter both military and civilian morale – thereby, it was hoped, destroying Nasser's hold on power.[22]

On the evening of 10 August the Egypt Committee had concluded that 'any military operation against Egypt should be launched in retaliation against some aggressive or provocative act by the Egyptians', and that the government 'might be compelled to take advantage of any provocative act by Egypt, even though it came at a time when the preparations for military operations were less well advanced than might have been desired'.[23] The difficulty for the British, though, was that no such provocation was forthcoming. Much to the frustration (and surprise) of Downing Street, the Egyptians seemed to be doing rather a good job of running the canal. Back on 1 August, the British Embassy had reported, 'All quiet and canal functioning normally.' By and large, that was how things remained. The Egyptian government repeatedly made clear its determination to 'honour' all of its 'international obligations' with respect to the Canal, and to ensure freedom of navigation.[24] Even when more than two hundred foreign employees of the Suez Canal Company, including ninety pilots, quit their posts in mid-September, the waterway continued to operate smoothly – despite a concerted British effort to pile up maritime traffic in the hopes of causing chaos.[25]

On 16 October the minister of defence, Sir Walter Monckton, noted that 'It now seems probable that military operations against Egypt will not be required in the immediate future, but that there will be further negotiations which may well be protracted.'[26] As one of the few cabinet members who had consistently opposed the military option (the use of force, he believed, threatened to 'precipitate disorder throughout the Middle East and to alienate a substantial body of public opinion in this country and elsewhere throughout the world'), Monckton must have been a very relieved man.[27] For all the talk of war, a negotiated settlement now seemed at hand.

Selwyn Lloyd had departed for New York on the evening of 1 October for high-level talks at the United Nations, brokered by Secretary General Dag Hammarskjöld. By the morning of 12

October, it appeared that a decisive breakthrough had been made when Mahmoud Fawzi, Egypt's foreign minister, accepted the 'six principles' that the British had been pushing – including a commitment to 'free and open transit through the Canal without discrimination' and an acknowledgement 'that the operation of the Canal should be insulated from the politics of any country'.[28] Although major issues remained unresolved, not least how these principles might actually be enforced, and despite persistent doubts about Nasser's personal commitment to an agreement, there were grounds for optimism. Lloyd certainly felt that a deal could be done which, as he told his cabinet colleagues, would 'give us the substance of our demands for effective international supervision of the Canal'. Eden, too, seemed keen. At 1.30 p.m. on Sunday 14 October, the prime minister sent a telegram to Lloyd, urging that further, substantive negotiations be undertaken to hammer out the details and suggesting Geneva as a suitable location for such a summit. Diplomacy, it seemed, would be given every chance to succeed. Within hours, everything had changed.[29]

Chequers Court, a grand sixteenth-century house in the foothills of the Chilterns, has served as the official country retreat for British prime ministers since 1921.[30] On the afternoon of 14 October Albert Gazier, France's minister for social affairs, and Major-General Maurice Challe, deputy to the chief of the French General Staff, arrived there in conditions of the utmost secrecy. The two men had come with a plan that would resolve the Suez Crisis once and for all: an Israeli strike against Egypt would be used as a justification for France and Britain to occupy the Suez Canal, under the pretext of safeguarding free maritime passage.[31]

Both Tel Aviv and Paris had reason to want Nasser gone. Egypt, along with several other Arab states, had launched a war against Israel in May 1948 in an effort to destroy the new Jewish state. Despite the 1949 armistice agreement, relations between the two countries were poor. Cairo denied Israeli ships and shipping the right to use the Suez Canal, tightened the blockade of the Straits of Tiran (cutting off Eilat, the port city on Israel's southernmost tip, from the Gulf of Aqaba and preventing access to East Africa and the Far East) and encouraged attacks by Palestinian *fedayeen* from the Egyptian-controlled Gaza strip, as well as from Lebanon and Jordan. This was all justified by a series of increasingly vitriolic attacks on the 'Zionist enemy'.[32] On 31 August 1955, for example, Nasser had declared that Egypt would 'despatch her heroes' to 'cleanse the land of Palestine . . . There will be no peace on Israel's border because we demand vengeance, and vengeance is Israel's death.'[33] All this, together with the massive build-up of modern military hardware that followed the controversial arms deal with Czechoslovakia, caused considerable alarm in Tel Aviv.[34] According to Moshe Dayan, there 'was no doubt in our minds that Egypt's purpose was to wipe us out, or at least win a decisive military victory which would leave us in helpless subjugation'. In fact, in the same speech in which he had announced the nationalisation of the Suez Canal Nasser had declared that 'the gangs which were converted into a State in 1948 are now being converted back into gangs and it is a good omen that they should go back to what they were in 1948 . . . Victory Day is coming near.' He had also pledged to support *fedayeen* attacks until the 'Arab motherland extend[s] from the Atlantic Ocean to the Persian Gulf'.[35]

Meanwhile, French convictions that Nasser posed an existential threat to their position in North Africa were strengthened after the *Athos* – a four-hundred-tonne former Canadian minesweeper flying under the Sudanese flag – was intercepted by the French navy. French submarines and aircraft had been tracking the ship for several days as she zigzagged her way across the Mediterranean. Then, on 16 October, as she headed for the Algerian coast, the *Athos* was approached by a destroyer escort and boarded. It turned out that the rusting vessel was a 'floating arsenal' with some seventy tonnes of military equipment in the hold, including seventy-two mortars, forty machine guns, seventy-four automatic rifles, 240 sub-machine guns, 2,300 rifles, two thousand mortar shells and six hundred thousand cartridges – enough, declared the French, to arm three thousand FLN fighters (and at a time when the Algerian rebels could boast fewer than twenty mortars and ten machine guns between them). Moreover, Nasser's fingerprints were all over the contraband: the ship had set sail from Alexandria, the weapons had been purchased with Egyptian money, and, after interrogating the captain and the crew, the French authorities announced that the arms had been loaded onto the *Athos* by uniformed Egyptian soldiers.[36]

The possibility of Franco-Israeli military action against Egypt, first mooted during the summer, was pursued more seriously at the end of September, when senior military and civilian officials from both countries held top-secret talks in Paris. The Israelis – afraid that their major cities would be devastated by Egyptian air raids, and reluctant to appear before the world as the sole aggressor – insisted that the two nations (or all three if Britain agreed to take part) would have to attack simultaneously. The French continued to push for an initial military strike by Israel that could be used to justify French (or Franco-British) involvement.[37] Nevertheless, the talks were encouraging, and the mood was further improved by France's willingness to provide Israel with a major shipment of arms, including one hundred Super-Sherman tanks and two hundred armoured personnel carriers. Soon the Israelis were drawing up contingency plans for a major military offensive in the Sinai Peninsula.[38]

The French, who were reluctant to proceed without British support, now sought to sell the plan to London.[39] The wider diplomatic context in which they did so was complicated. In the Tripartite Declaration of 1950, Britain, France and the United States had jointly stated their 'unalterable opposition to the use of force or the threat of force' between Israel and her Arab neighbours and had pledged to intervene to prevent any violation of national frontiers or armistice lines.[40] Britain relied heavily on strategic partnerships with Jordan and Iraq – implacable opponents of Israel – to promote her interests in the region, and had treaty obligations to assist Jordan in the event of an attack by Israel. Given escalating tensions along the Israel–Jordan border (fuelled by *fedayeen* attacks on Israel) and ominous talk from Tel Aviv about seizing parts of the Jordanian-controlled West Bank, Whitehall viewed a war against Israel as a very real possibility.[41]

Concerns that Britain might become embroiled in an Arab–Israeli war were, in fact, uppermost in Eden's mind when he entertained Gazier and Challe at Chequers on 14 October. Just a few days before, the Israel Defence Forces (IDF) had launched a major reprisal raid on Qalqilya in the West Bank, killing seventy Jordanians.[42] According to Anthony Nutting, the foreign office minister, who was present during the discussions, the prime minister could 'scarcely contain his glee' when the French reminded him that Nasser had recently repudiated the protections offered by the Tripartite Declaration: '"So that lets us off the hook," Eden said excitedly. "We have no obligation, it seems, to stop the Israelis attacking the Egyptians."'[43] The French now sought to capitalise on British fears that Israel might launch a full-scale attack on Jordan.[44] As the historian Scott Lucas has explained, they effectively 'blackmailed' the British by warning that if she declined to support the Franco-Israeli plan, the Israelis would attack Jordan instead of Egypt. This would leave London with an impossible choice: abandon their obligations to Amman, and so undermine their entire position in the Middle East, or come to Jordan's aid in a war against Israel, which, given her close military and economic ties with France, would pit the British against their French allies.[45] Eden, who remained eager to strike against Nasser, was in. Lloyd was summoned back from New York and on 16 October, during a private lunch in Downing Street, won round. Lloyd initially wanted nothing to do with the French plan, but gradually allowed himself to be persuaded that the proposed UN deal would not hold and that, with the window for military action narrowing as winter approached, it was time to act. From now on, Lloyd put all private doubts to one side, and offered full support to his prime minister.[46]

The complex and highly secret negotiations between Britain, France and Israel were finally concluded on Sunday 24 October. It was, noted Mordechai Bar-On, 'one of those wonderful days which Paris gracefully bestows upon its inhabitants and visitors. The sky was clear, but the streets and trees were still wet from the autumn shower which had briefly washed them in the morning. Red leaves were dancing in the chilly breeze. Everything was glittering and full of colour.' As the young Israeli officer approached the Sèvres villa for what would be the final time, he could 'smell the roasted chestnuts someone was selling on the corner'.[47] During several hours of discussions – first with the French and then, later that afternoon, with the British (this time Patrick Dean, deputy under-secretary at the Foreign Office, accompanied Logan) – France agreed to station a squadron of Mystères IV A jets and a squadron of fighter bombers, carrying Israeli air force markings, in Israel, to strengthen the country's air defences; Israel agreed not to attack Jordan; and Britain confirmed that in the event of Jordan attacking Israel, the mutual defence pact between London and Amman would not be activated.[48] At Ben-Gurion's suggestion, a formal protocol was drawn up. Drafted in the villa's kitchen and typed up on a portable typewriter, it summarised the undertakings that had been given by the three governments. Israel agreed that on the evening of 29 October it would launch a 'large scale attack on the Egyptian forces with the aim of reaching the Canal Zone the following day'. In response, the British and French would issue their ultimatum – requesting a ceasefire, insisting on a withdrawal of all Israeli and Egyptian troops from the Canal Zone, and demanding that Cairo accept a temporary Anglo-French occupation to safeguard the waterway. If these terms were rejected, Britain and France would commence military action against Egypt on the morning of 31 October. At 7 p.m., Ben-Gurion, Pineau and Dean signed the agreement. The Israeli prime minister, struggling to conceal his excitement, picked up his copy and 'as if holding a fragile treasure, folded it, and stuck it in his waistcoat pocket'. A bottle of champagne was produced and the operation's success was toasted – although the atmosphere was one of quiet satisfaction, rather than jubilation. Moshe Dayan, who had already sent the order to mobilise the Israeli forces, recalled that the British were 'the first to leave, mumbling as they went words of politeness tinged with humour and not quite comprehensible'. D-Day was less than a hundred hours away.[49]

16

POLISH OCTOBER

Now a person has zest for life.
    ANONYMOUS POLISH WOMAN, remarks at a mass meeting,
    22 October 1956

Sydney Gruson, the thirty-nine-year-old foreign correspondent of the *New York Times*, could practically smell trouble in the air. Writing from the Polish capital on 18 October, he told his readers that 'the bright sun, the autumn gold of the trees and the inviting snap of October weather' had 'cloaked Warsaw in a false display of serenity'. In reality, the 'mood of the city' was 'revolutionary' and the country's vexed relationship with the Soviet Union at breaking point.[1]

At the centre of this unfolding drama was Władysław Gomułka: a tough, humourless and rather austere fifty-one-year-old who had dedicated his entire adult life to the Communist cause.[2] Born in 1905 in Krosno, a provincial southern town, into a solidly proletarian family of labourers and weavers, Gomułka had trained as a locksmith after leaving school, before finding work in the oil refinery industry. Gomułka came of age during some of the most turbulent years in Poland's history. Although the country had regained her independence in 1918, after more than a century of foreign occupation, the young republic proved highly unstable and, on 12 May 1926, Marshal Józef Piłsudski seized power in a *coup d'état* and established an authoritarian government. But as the government swung to the right, Gomułka was busy carving out a political career on the revolutionary left. Indeed, his lifelong affinity with the proletarian cause had begun while still at school, when he had signed up to a workers' youth organisation. Aged seventeen, he joined a militant trade union, and in 1926 was appointed a regional official. At the end of that year, he joined the Polish Communist Party (KPP). A talented organiser and effective agitator, Gomułka was soon targeted by the state and in 1932, after leading a textile strike in Łódź, he was arrested and sentenced to four years in prison. Paroled after two years, he spent several months in the Soviet Union before returning to his homeland – and, in short order, another spell in one of the regime's jails. During the Second World War, Gomułka fought with a 'workers' battalion' in the doomed defence of Warsaw, then fled to the Soviet-occupied east and, after the onset of Operation Barbarossa, returned to Krosno, where he played a major role in establishing the underground Polish Workers' Party (the successor organisation to the KPP), was elected party secretary and helped to co-ordinate armed resistance to the Nazis.

Following the country's liberation by the Red Army, Gomułka and his comrades seized the opportunity, furnished by Soviet support, to build a 'people's democracy' in Poland. Gomułka, though, was no slavish disciple of Stalin. While maintaining fidelity to the Soviet Union in international affairs, he argued for full domestic sovereignty and became the leading proponent of what was known as the 'Polish road to socialism'. Gomułka was open to working with other political parties, saw a role for small-scale private businesses operating alongside state-controlled banks, industry and transport, and opposed the forced collectivisation of agriculture. In addition, Gomułka's Communism was to be distinctively 'Polish': he spoke of a 'party of the nation' that, respecting Polish history and culture, would 'unite with the nation and live for that nation'. At the end of August 1948, though, his fortunes took a turn for the worse as his rivals, seizing on his support for Tito and rejection of orthodox Stalinism, engineered his dismissal as secretary general. Three years later, he was expelled from the Party and imprisoned. It was only Stalin's death, in May 1953, which saved Gomułka from execution.[3]

Calls for Gomułka's return to power had first surfaced during the spring of 1956; by the autumn they had become irresistible. The months following the Poznań uprising had seen protest and public discontent erupt across Poland. Flyers, posters and slogans praising the 'heroes' of Poznań appeared on the walls of factories, public buildings, schools, railway stations and Party offices in numerous cities, while at local Party meetings activists expressed support for the Poznań workers and condemned the state's violent crackdown. During the summer, amid widespread discontent over low wages and high prices, there was a significant upsurge in work stoppages, strikes and slowdowns. Poles also voiced their grievances through mass meetings, rallies and petitions, and were increasingly directing their ire at the Polish United Workers' Party (PZPR) leadership.[4] In a telegram to London on 24 July, the British ambassador, Sir Alan Noble, explained how 'the people of Poland have demonstrated that they have no sort of confidence in the present political leadership and that they are not prepared any longer to put up with their present standard of living'.[5] Meanwhile, a wave of dissent engulfed the countryside: many farmers refused to work or failed to meet their delivery quotas; some made formal requests to leave their co-operative farms; others simply abandoned them without permission.[6]

On 26 August, in a powerful display of religious nationalism, one million pilgrims gathered at Jasna Góra (the Bright Mountain) to pay homage at the shrine of the Black Madonna – one of the holiest sites in Poland – and commemorate three hundred years since the Polish King, Jan Kazimierez, had formally dedicated the nation to the Virgin Mary. With Poland's Primate, Cardinal Wyszyński, under house arrest, the Bishop of Łódź conducted the service; a simple bouquet of red and white roses, placed on an empty throne next to the altar, symbolised the Primate's absence. When the bishop had renewed the royal proclamation and offered unto the Virgin 'every Polish heart and home', the response from the mass of kneeling pilgrims came back 'like a mighty wave': 'Queen of Poland, we promise.'[7]

During these months the Polish press was operating with widespread freedom – even fearlessness – publishing biting criticisms of the status quo and proposals for reform. At the beginning of September, for instance, *Nowa Kultura* ('New Culture') carried an article by the economist Edward Lipinski, castigating the PZPR's entire economic approach. Lipinski denounced central planning for leading to 'the omnipotence of bureaucracy and to political autocracy' and singled out Poland's state-run farms as a 'crying example of the inferiority of pseudo-Socialist economy, when compared with capitalism'.[8] There was also criticism of the Sejm (the Polish parliament) and a growing clamour for it to reassert its authority and forge a genuine connection with 'the people' (although technically the 'highest organ of state authority', it had been marginalised by the PZPR and served as little more than a rubber-stamp assembly).[9]

Students, too, were growing restless. On 4 October, five hundred students at the University of Wrocław responded to a dormitory power cut by marching through the city shouting 'We want light!' and threatening to beat up those responsible for the blackout; a few days later, a thousand students at the University of Warsaw, together with delegates from almost two dozen factories, staged a rally to call for 'complete openness in public life', worker self-government and an end to censorship. They also took up the cry of Poznań's workers, demanding 'No bread without freedom, no freedom without bread!'[10]

The Poznań trials, which commenced at the end of September, proved a lightning rod for dissent. Anxious to underline that all the recent talk of 'legality' and 'democracy' was genuine, the authorities sought to ensure that, as the Polish prime minister put it, the proceedings were conducted 'in accordance with the most scrupulous demands of the rule of law'.[11] The trials were remarkably open – foreign reporters, diplomats and a number of Western lawyers were invited to observe the hearings, and the accused were permitted to mount a robust defence.[12] Extraordinarily, it often seemed as if it was the Communist system that was on trial in the city's 'rambling cement courthouse', rather than the alleged 'hooligans' and 'looters'. On 28 September, for example, one young man explained how he had been subjected to a brutal interrogation: 'I was beaten with rods on my face and knocked over from behind. An officer dragged me by the hair down to the second floor and beat and kicked me. I was stood up with my face against the wall while he pummelled the back of my head, knocking my face into the wall.'[13] Defendants were soon lining up to expose police brutality, and several made explosive comparisons between the Polish secret police and the German SS.[14] At one point, proceedings had to be adjourned after the sister of one of the defendants shouted out: 'Our father died for Poland in 1939. My mother was killed in 1942. And now we are more oppressed than ever!'[15]

By seeking repeatedly to contextualise the actions of their clients, the defence counsel ensured that the workers' original grievances were given a fresh airing. The court heard, for example, how the strikers had demanded 'Bread and freedom!' and 'Out with the Russians!' and how some Polish soldiers had handed over their weapons to the 'mob', or even joined them. The Poznań uprising was not merely being revisited but legitimised. One of the defence lawyers, Stanisław Hejmowski, referred to Eugène Delacroix's *Liberty Guiding the People*: a famous painting of the Revolution of 1830 in which France's Charles X was overthrown. It depicts a young woman – a French flag in one hand, a bayonet in the other – leading the people (including a student, a worker and a peasant) over the bodies of the fallen, brandishing pistols and rifles.[16] 'If', Hejmowski explained, 'the king's police had won the battle, the prosecutor of that time would have dragged these young people into court and called them hooligans and criminal elements.'

But 'Since the revolution was won, they are national heroes, and their picture has become a symbol of revolution.' His message was clear.[17]

The government eventually abandoned most of the cases: of the 154 people charged, only thirty-seven ever appeared in court; those who were convicted received lenient sentences.[18]

Observing developments from the embassy in Warsaw back in July, the British ambassador had noted that 'in some degree the Party have lost control; they can no longer just give orders and assume that the people can in one way or another be brought to obey them. The Party must now take account of popular opinion, and popular opinion has some awkward demands.'[19] Among those 'awkward demands' were greater 'democracy' (including giving workers a bigger say in factory management, opening up the Communist Party structures and relaxing censorship laws), an end to Soviet control of the Polish military and the return to power of Władysław Gomułka.[20]

On 5 August the Politburo announced that it had readmitted Gomułka to the Communist Party.[21] Ten weeks later, on the eve of a full plenary session of the Party's Central Committee, came official confirmation that Gomułka had attended a meeting of the Politburo. His restoration to the leadership was imminent.[22]

In Moscow there was real alarm – not least because Gomułka had become associated with what Khrushchev called 'a banner of anti-Sovietism'. As the Soviet leader put it, 'We regarded any decision [to return him to power] as an action directed against us.' Moscow certainly had good reason to be worried.[23] Throughout the summer and early autumn graffiti, posters and flyers bearing anti-Russian slogans – including 'Death to the Russki invaders!' and 'Off with the Soviet occupation!' – had appeared in towns and cities across the country.[24] Festering anti-Russian sentiment had begun to bubble to the surface, as Poles discussed openly the Katyń massacre of 1940, in which the Red Army had shot down thousands of Polish army officers, as well as the post-war deportation of thousands of former resistance fighters to Siberia. They also complained about the forced sale of coal to the USSR, at heavily discounted prices, as well as Soviet influence over the Polish military – which was widely viewed as an affront to national pride. Indeed, the minister of defence, Marshal Konstantin Rokossovsky, though Polish-born, was a Soviet citizen – as were the chief of the General Staff, more than seventy other senior Polish army officers and numerous 'military advisers'.[25] Tellingly, when the traditional 'Polish–Soviet Friendship Month' opened on 9 September, it lacked the 'usual fanfare', while the Party newspaper, *Trybuna Ludu*, was at pains to emphasise 'the independence of countries in the Socialist camp' and the 'Polish nation's own efforts' in building socialism.[26]

PZPR reformers understood that unless Polish–Soviet relations were placed on a more equal footing, the Party had no hope of winning the support of the masses and ending the political crisis that had gripped the country since the spring. However, when Moscow learned that Rokossovsky was to be removed from the Politburo, and that Gomułka also wanted all Soviet officers to be withdrawn, they took it as a personal affront. Concerned that Poland – which was of enormous strategic and symbolic importance to the USSR – might be about to break from the Warsaw Pact, Khrushchev decided to act.[27]

On the evening of 18 October, the Soviet ambassador in Warsaw informed Edward Ochab, the PZPR's first secretary, that Moscow intended to send a delegation to Poland to assess the situation. This was a none-too-subtle attempt to force the postponement of the Eighth Plenum, the meeting of the Party's Central Committee which was scheduled to begin the following morning. The Polish response – that it would be preferable if the Soviets delayed the trip by a day or two – only heightened Moscow's anxieties, and Khrushchev testily informed Ochab that he would be leaving for Warsaw immediately.[28]

At seven o'clock the next morning, the first of two Soviet planes touched down at the Boernerowo military airfield on the outskirts of the Polish capital. The Soviet delegation that assembled in Warsaw that morning could scarcely have been more high-powered. Accompanying Nikita Khrushchev were fellow Presidium members Lazar Kaganovich, Anastas Mikoyan and Vyacheslav Molotov, the foreign minister, together with Marshal Ivan Konev, the commander-in-chief of the Warsaw Pact, and eleven other generals, including the chief of the General Staff, all in full dress uniform. Khrushchev, clearly in an agitated and highly emotional state, swept past Ochab, Cyrankiewicz and Gomułka, who were waiting for him on the tarmac, to offer a warm greeting to Marshal Rokossovsky and the other Soviet generals in attendance, exclaiming loudly that 'these are the people on whom I rely'. Then, shaking his fist, he turned to the Polish leaders, shouting, 'We know who's the enemy of the Soviet Union!' Gomułka noted that 'the entire discussion was carried out in this loud tone, such that everyone at the airport, even the chauffeurs, heard it'.[29]

Even as Khrushchev was speaking, three columns of Soviet troops – including armoured tank units – were advancing on Warsaw from bases in the north and west of the country. More than two dozen warships from the Baltic Fleet appeared in the waters off Gdańsk, and Soviet planes began to patrol the coast.[30]

It was, then, in an atmosphere of high tension that the Soviet and Polish leaders met for formal talks at the Belvedere Palace, the summer residence of the last king of Poland, in Warsaw's beautiful Łazienki Park. While the Soviets were freshening up, the Polish leaders gathered at the Council of State building nearby, where Ochab formally opened the Eighth Plenum.[31] He announced that the Politburo had decided to appoint Gomułka and a number of his allies to the Central Committee, outlined plans to reduce the size of the Politburo and proposed that Gomułka be elected first secretary. After just thirty minutes of debate, Gomułka's return to

the Central Committee was rubber-stamped and he was authorised to lead the negotiations with the Soviets.[32]

At 11 a.m., the Polish and Soviet leaders gathered for talks in
the magnificent Blue Hall, a long French gallery adorned with
tapestries.[33] The exchanges were frosty. According to Gomułka,
'we told each other the truth, face to face: what they think of us
and what we think about their moves'; Khrushchev, meanwhile,
acknowledged that the discussions were 'very stormy' and that 'we
made comments, which did nothing to reduce the tension, but
instead poured more fuel on the fire'. The Soviet leader threatened to 'intervene brutally', objected in the strongest terms to
Rokossovsky's removal from the Politburo and accused his hosts
of encouraging anti-Soviet propaganda. At noon, when the Poles
began to receive word of the Soviet troop movements, the atmosphere deteriorated further. Years later, Khrushchev even claimed
that Gomułka had 'appeared to foam at the mouth' as he took to
his feet to demand an end to the military manoeuvres.[34]

Despite the pressure, the Poles remained firm that they alone
had the right to choose their own leadership: as Edward Ochab
remarked to Khrushchev, 'Do you consult us about the make-up
of your Politburo or Central Committee?' They also pressed home
their objections to 'excessive' Soviet influence within the Polish
military and security services. But they also sought to reassure
Khrushchev that Poland was committed to the Warsaw Pact and
to a strong and friendly alliance with the Soviet Union.[35] A key
moment came after lunch. Khrushchev described how Gomułka
took to the floor and spoke with sincerity and passion: 'Do you
think you are the only ones who need friendship? As a Pole and a
Communist, I swear that Poland needs friendship with the Russians more than the Russians need friendship with the Poles . . .
without you we could never continue our existence as an independent state.' Gomułka assured Khrushchev that 'Everything's
going to be all right in our country, but you must not allow Soviet

troops to enter Warsaw, because then it will be extremely difficult to control events.' During a brief adjournment the Soviet leader, his confidence in Gomułka apparently restored, ordered Konev to halt the advance.[36]

Once the Soviet delegation had departed (they flew out of Warsaw at dawn the next day), the Eighth Plenum reconvened to hear from their new leader.[37] In a long speech, extracts of which were broadcast later that evening on Warsaw radio, Gomułka reflected on the 'evil' that had been done over the past eight years, when a system corrupted by the cult of personality had broken the 'characters and consciences of men' and deformed and distorted the very idea of socialism. He was severely critical of the PZPR's 'incompetent' and 'inefficient' economic policy, denounced the rush to collectivise agriculture and argued that attempts to blame 'imperialist agents and provocateurs' for the uprising in Poznań had been 'clumsy' and 'naïve'. The truth was that responsibility was 'to be found in ourselves, in the leadership of the Party, in the Government'. To remedy the nation's ills, Gomułka proposed a greater role for workers' self-government and private enterprise, insisted that co-operative farming had to be voluntary and called for greater democracy and openness, including a stronger role for the Sejm. And, while Gomułka had no time for those who wished to 'kindle' the anti-Soviet flame in Poland, he was clear that the people's democracies should enjoy 'full independence', with their sovereignty 'fully and mutually respected'.[38]

Gomułka's return to power caused huge excitement. In the poetic words of one Warsaw radio presenter, Poland was experiencing 'spring in October'.[39] Boisterous street demonstrations, rallies and emotional mass meetings – in which Poles pledged their support for Gomułka and the liberal reforms for which he stood – swept the country. Many Poles also demanded greater religious freedom (including the release of Cardinal Wyszyński) and a complete end to press censorship, and vented their anger with unpopular Party officials.[40] Workers' councils were organised spontaneously in large factories and shipyards in Warsaw, Gdańsk, Wrocław and other cities, with the aim of ameliorating working conditions and improving efficiency.[41] Unpopular bosses found themselves dismissed by their own employees, and a number were unceremoniously removed from their factories in wheelbarrows.[42] Some intellectuals and activists even hoped that workers' self-government would transform the wider society by building a truly democratic socialism from the bottom up.[43]

Anti-Soviet sentiment continued to build, though – not helped by persistent rumours of Soviet troop movements (early on the morning of 20 October, a Red Army battalion was even spotted in a Warsaw suburb). Across the country, portraits of Rokossovsky were smashed or defaced, red stars were pulled down and Russian street signs removed.[44] On hearing news of the 'great changes in Warsaw', railroad workers in the southern city of Katowice, which had been known officially as Stalinogród since 1953, spontaneously tore down the signs at the main station and, as the 'masses shouted with joy', put up blackboards with the former name chalked proudly on them.[45] In the south-western city of Legnica, where a crowd of six thousand stoned the headquarters of the security police, demonstrators also assaulted the leader of the Municipal People's Council. Others attacked the homes of Soviet officers, and an attempt was made to pull down the city's Monument of Gratitude to the Red Army. In Wrocław, ten thousand rallied at the university to demand the withdrawal of Soviet troops, tore down Soviet flags, ransacked the offices of the Polish–Soviet Friendship Society and chanted 'Rokossovsky go home!'[46]

These were heady days. One woman, speaking before a mass meeting in the socialist new town of Nowa Huta, declared that for the first time in her life she felt like singing the 'Internationale': 'Now', she said, 'a person has zest for life.'[47] Poles took to the streets in extraordinary numbers: thirty thousand attended a rally in Gdańsk, a mass meeting in Lublin attracted seventy thousand, and it was reported that in Poznań as many as two hundred thousand had turned out to denounce the Soviets and the secret police, and to demand freedom of speech and religion.[48] But the biggest demonstration of all took place in Warsaw.

On the afternoon of Wednesday 24 October, four hundred thousand people gathered in Parade Square, in the heart of the Polish capital, to hear from their new leader. Janina Bauman, a local Party official, attended the rally with her husband, Zygmunt, then a young philosophy lecturer at the city's university. The couple were struck by the vastness of the crowd and the overwhelming sense of solidarity. Janina explained how 'it seemed that – for once – the nation was united; communists, non-communists, and anti-communists alike; workers, farmers, intellectuals, and all'.[49] Gomułka addressed the 'sea of faces' from the balcony of the Palace of Culture and Science – a colossal, forty-two-storey socialist realist skyscraper, which Stalin had presented as a gift to the Polish nation. The tightly packed crowd chanted 'Wieslaw! Wieslaw!' (Gomułka's wartime pseudonym), sang 'Sto Lat' ('May you live for a hundred years'), waved banners and Polish flags and roared for their hero.[50] The first secretary struck some observers as rather 'professorial' and 'aloof', but he was a clear and forceful speaker, and his twenty-five-minute speech (a condensed version of his address to the Eighth Plenum), which was also broadcast live on the radio, went down well.[51] While talk of desiring a 'wholehearted friendship' with the USSR was greeted with silence, Gomułka's commitment to 'democratisation' and his emphasis on Polish sovereignty drew cheers and applause. Meanwhile the announcement that Khrushchev had agreed to order Soviet troops back to barracks within forty-eight hours, and Gomułka's insistence that it was for the Poles alone to decide 'whether we need Soviet specialist and military advisers', received a thunderous response. Gomułka ended by calling for 'provocateurs and reactionary loudmouths' to be driven away, and demanding an end to the protests that had convulsed the nation: 'Today we turn to the working people of Warsaw and of the entire country with an appeal: enough meetings and demonstrations!'[52]

For now, at least, that particular plea fell on deaf ears. Several thousand stayed on after the rally had concluded, shouting 'Down with Rokossovsky!' and 'Katyn! Katyn!' An attempt to march on the Soviet Embassy was turned back by troops but, amid news that the Red Army had entered Budapest, some two thousand protesters, waving Polish and Hungarian flags and carrying torchlights, headed for the Hungarian Embassy instead, where they shouted support for the Hungarians and expressed their hatred of the Russians.[53]

Over the following weeks Gomułka was able to defuse the situation with important concessions. Thousands of secret police were dismissed and the security services were restructured; workers' councils were encouraged, wages increased for miners and railway workers, and a greater role for private enterprise promised; the 'yellow curtain' shops which served the Party elite were closed down, and Communist Party villas were turned into nurseries and orphanages; agricultural taxes were cut, prices raised and delivery quotas reduced; the jamming of foreign radio broadcasts was ended; institutional autonomy and a measure of academic freedom were restored to the universities.[54] When it came to relations with the USSR, Gomułka negotiated the cancellation of Poland's debt (an estimated $500,000,000) and the extension of trade credits, dismissed Rokossovsky from the defence ministry and secured the withdrawal of all Soviet advisers from the Polish army and the Ministry of Internal Security.[55] One of his boldest moves, though, was to reset church–state relations. Following secret negotiations in which the government agreed to rescind a decree governing church appointments, reinstate priests whom they had forced out of their posts and grant freedom to the Catholic press, Cardinal Wyszyński was released from house arrest. He returned to Warsaw on 28 October and, the following day, blessed the joyous crowds from the balcony of his Miodowa Street Palace.[56]

Back in the United States, President Eisenhower – who was in the midst of a gruelling re-election campaign against Adlai Stevenson, the former governor of Illinois – struggled to formulate an appropriate response. During a campaign stop in Denver, Colorado, on 20 October, Ike issued a terse statement explaining that 'all friends of the Polish people recognize and sympathize with their traditional yearning for liberty and independence'.[57] Three days later, at a dinner for the Brotherhood of Carpenters and Joiners at Washington's Sheraton-Park Hotel, the president reprised this theme. He told his audience of blue-collar union members that 'the love of freedom was and is the strongest mark of Polish character'. Saluting the Poles for resisting the tyranny of 'communistic imperialism', Eisenhower declared that 'the memory of freedom is not erased by the fear of guns and the love of freedom is more enduring than the power of tyrants'. The job of the United States, he explained, was to serve as 'the champion of human freedom'. By upholding the principle of self-determination, providing aid or trade where appropriate, and through her own domestic example, America would help to 'expand the areas in which free men, free governments can flourish'.[58] Behind the scenes there was plenty of talk about providing the Poles with economic assistance, but one thing was perfectly clear: there was never any question of the West offering the Poles military support. In a televised interview, John Foster Dulles explained that such a move would risk triggering an all-out war.[59]

Moscow, too, decided against the use of force. Having toyed with the military option for several days, Khrushchev finally ordered Soviet troops back to their bases on 24 October.[60] While Khrushchev seems to have been genuinely impressed by Gomułka, whom he judged a dependable ally, the Soviets were also deterred by intelligence reports that significant numbers of Polish troops would defend the new government, and unnerved by rumours of weapons being handed out in Warsaw's factories in preparation for a possible Soviet attack. As Khrushchev noted, 'finding a reason for armed conflict' with the Poles would be easy, but 'finding a way to put an end to such a conflict later would be very hard'. Moreover, Khrushchev was increasingly preoccupied with a far more serious and fast-moving crisis that was unfolding on the streets of Budapest.[61]

CAPTION:

Revolutionaries on the streets of Budapest, 27 October 1956.
The Hungarian flag, shorn of its Communist coat of arms, flies from
surrounding buildings.

Credit: Ullstein Bild

17

UPRISING

Stand up, Hungarians, the homeland is calling!
The time is here, now or never!
Shall we be free men or slaves?
This is the question, choose your answer!
        SÁNDOR PETŐFI, '*Nemzeti Dal*' ('National Song'), 1848

Kerepesi Cemetery is Hungary's most famous burial ground; the equivalent of Père Lachaise in Paris or London's Highgate. Located near Budapest's Keleti railway station, the enchanting 140-acre site – which is ordered geometrically in the style of a French formal garden – houses the remains of the nation's most revered poets, writers and statesmen. Among the ornate tombs, the beautiful Italian-style arcades and the trees stands the mausoleum of Lajos Kossuth – Hungary's most famous son, and hero of the failed revolution of 1848. Two panthers, carved from marble, guard its entrance and above the doors, seated on an eagle throne, is the crowned figure of Hungária – a shield, bearing the national coat of arms, resting at her side. The magnificent structure is topped with a bronze statue of the Winged Genius of Freedom, holding aloft a torch and pulling on the chains of a roaring lion.[1] In the autumn of 1956, this iconic memorial provided the backdrop for a macabre ritual that helped push the nation to the brink of revolution.

On Saturday 6 October, the former foreign minister László Rajk and three of his comrades – who seven years earlier had been hanged as traitors, dumped in an unmarked grave and covered with lime – were reburied in a lavish state ceremony.[2] Across the city black flags hung from public buildings, and shops and factories closed. The four iron coffins were placed on biers at the entrance to the Kossuth Mausoleum, lighted torches were set above them and the caskets were surrounded with flagpoles carrying, alternately, the Hungarian tricolour (red, white and green) and black flags of mourning.[3] Given his complicity in Rajk's downfall, it was perhaps just as well that the funeral took place while Ernő Gerő, first secretary of the Hungarian Workers Party, was holidaying in the Crimea. But the rest of the Communist leadership, including the country's president, István Dobi, and the prime minister, András Hegedüs, were there. The families of the victims, together with old friends and comrades, gathered around the coffins in the biting wind. Rajk's widow, Júlia, dressed in black and wearing a plastic cape, was accompanied by her seven-year-old son, Laci. The funeral also drew most of the leading figures from the country's burgeoning reform movement, including the former prime minister Imre Nagy – who, placing a kiss on Júlia's cheek, assured her that 'soon' it would be Stalinism that would 'finally be buried'.[4]

The ceremony, which lasted for more than five hours, was full of bitter ironies. Rajk, a leading architect of the country's vicious police state, was lauded as a hero and martyr, while those who had signed his death warrant – now full of sorrow and regret – gushed over their erstwhile comrade. The Stalinist old guard did not, though, escape public censure. In his eulogy Ferenc Münnich, who had fought alongside Rajk in the Spanish Civil War, declared that his friend had not been permitted to 'die a great death, a death worthy of heroes'; instead he had been killed by 'sadistic criminals who had crawled into the sun from the stinking swamp of a "cult of personality"'.[5]

Once the speeches were over, the coffins were taken to the graveside as drums, draped in black, beat out the funeral march. With family members and Party leaders standing in attendance, the coffins were lowered amidst a volley of rifle fire, before the rousing strains of the 'Internationale' rang out. Once the family and leading functionaries had laid their wreaths, there was a final march past by the battalion of honour in full dress uniform, and further wreaths, sent by factories, artists' organisations and local Party associations, were piled up at the graveside.[6]

Two hundred thousand Hungarians, including labourers, office workers and even schoolchildren, reportedly braved the cold and the rain to file past the coffins in 'quiet, orderly, endless columns'. But, as the British ambassador, Sir Leslie Fry, noted, they did not display any great reverence. In truth, they were not really there to mourn at all but, in the words of the writer Béla Szász, to 'bury a whole era'.[7] It was anger, not grief, that provided the day's animating force, and Júlia Rajk recalled seeing 'hatred in the people's eyes' on that grim October day. 'All of us who attended the funeral', she explained, 'knew that it meant a turning point in the political life of our country.'[8]

Hungary's new leader, Ernő Gerő, had been persuaded by his more optimistic advisers that allowing the state funeral would draw a line under the Stalinist era. It did nothing of the sort. Just hours after the formalities at Kerepesi had drawn to a close, several hundred students converged on the Batthyány Memorial (which commemorated Hungary's first constitutional prime minister), near to the national parliament building, where they shouted anti-Communist slogans. On this occasion the police dispersed the demonstrators peacefully, but it was a sign of further trouble ahead. Six days later, during a conversation with the Soviet ambassador, Yuri Andropov, Gerő noted ruefully that the 'burial of Rajk's mortal remains caused serious harm to the party leadership, whose esteem had been rather tarnished anyway'.[9]

After assuming power on 18 July, Gerő had made some attempts to mollify the critics: rehabilitating and releasing from prison fifty leaders of the Social Democratic Party, moving towards a rapprochement with Tito's Yugoslavia, securing substantial trade credits from the USSR, ordering the removal of Rákosi's name from numerous street signs and public buildings, and ending formal disciplinary proceedings against a number of high-profile writers. Then, on 13

October, Imre Nagy was finally readmitted to the MDP.[10] It was all in vain. A poor harvest and chronic shortages of coal, oil and other raw materials, together with serious disruptions to the country's passenger rail service, caused significant economic hardships and exacerbated popular discontent. More worryingly, there was also a noticeable rise in anti-Soviet sentiment, fuelled by resentment at the presence of Soviet troops in the country and a widespread feeling that Hungary was being exploited economically by Moscow (allegations that she was being forced to sell uranium to the USSR at a heavily discounted rate proved particularly toxic).[11] One senior Red Army officer stationed outside Budapest described the atmosphere as 'increasingly acrimonious'.[12] Then, to top it all, came the dramatic news from Poland. Władysław Gomułka's return to power, promising a 'Polish path' to socialism and greater independence from the Soviet Union, stiffened the resolve – and raised the hopes – of Hungary's reformers.

On the morning of 23 October, Budapest was bathed in gorgeous autumnal sunshine. Arriving at Keleti station from Belgrade, following a successful meeting with Josep Tito and a swimming holiday on the Adriatic, Gerő was in excellent spirits. But, as he was driven to Party headquarters in his sleek ZIS limousine, the first secretary's mood darkened. The political situation had, his officials informed him, deteriorated precipitously. Everywhere one looked, there was open dissent with the government, and the capital itself was a 'tinderbox'.[13]

A week earlier, in the western city of Győr, a thousand people had flocked to hear the writer Gyula Hay deliver a lecture on political reform. The question and answer session which followed Hay's remarks had sparked a remarkably outspoken debate, as audience members denounced Stalinism, demanded the closing of Soviet military bases and called for the release of Cardinal József Mindszenty, the leader of Hungary's Catholics, who was languishing under house arrest.[14] That same day, sixteen hundred students in Szeged, a southern city of some 170,000 located on the banks of the Tisza River, gathered in the university's auditorium, where amidst shouts and loud cheers they voted overwhelmingly to leave the official Communist youth organisation, DISz, and form a new, independent group. Their purpose was to secure 'freedom of thought' and to 'brush off the burden forced on us by Stalin and Rákosi'. As well as reforms to the curriculum and improvements to student welfare, the new Association of Hungarian University and College Students (MEFESz) called for an end to press censorship and demanded free elections and the withdrawal of Soviet troops. Students in Sopron, Debrecen and other cities quickly followed suit, but it was the debate held at Budapest's Technical University on 22 October that proved momentous.[15]

The chaotic meeting began at 3 p.m. in the university's main hall – a massive, high-ceilinged auditorium with grand columns and square arches – which was crammed with five thousand students, as well as a number of faculty members and university officials. Convened by the DISz leadership in an attempt to contain dissent, the meeting fell into the hands of the rebels after a student leader from Szeged took to the floor to implore the Budapest students to 'join with us'. The decision to split from DISz, which passed by acclamation, drew sustained, deafening applause. Inspired by events in Poland, they then drew up a list of demands – known as the Sixteen Points – which would become the manifesto of the Hungarian revolution. It called for major economic reforms, freedom of speech and the press, the democratisation of the MDP, and for Imre Nagy's return to power. Proclaiming that they stood at 'the dawn of a new Hungarian history', the students also demanded the restoration of Hungary's traditional public holidays and national symbols (which had been outlawed by the regime), free and fair multi-party elections to the national parliament, and for the country's relations with the USSR to be based on 'total political and economic equality'. Most striking of all, though, was the call for the 'immediate withdrawal of all Soviet troops'.[16]

With the press and radio refusing to publicise the manifesto, the students took matters into their own hands; mimeographed copies of the document were handed out on trams, circulated among factory workers and posted up on walls, lamp posts and trees across the city. The students also mobilised support for a demonstration in support of the Poles which would be held on the afternoon of 23 October: following a march to Bem Square, wreaths would be laid at the memorial to József Bem, the Polish general who had fought alongside the Hungarians in 1848.[17]

At Communist Party headquarters – an imposing stone building on Akadémia Street, overlooking the parliament building – Ernő Gerő and other hardliners, who gathered for a Politburo meeting at ten o'clock on the morning of 23 October, were determined to prevent the demonstration from taking place. Under pressure from his furious colleagues, László Piros, a former butcher's assistant who had risen to the post of interior minister, accepted that he had erred in issuing an official permit for the march. When Márton Horváth, the reformist editor of *Szabad Nép*, asked what would happen if the students simply ignored any ban, one leading Stalinist bellowed: 'We would fire! We would open fire!' At 12.53 p.m., Radio Kossuth announced that 'to assure public order', the Ministry of the Interior had banned all public meetings and demonstrations 'until further notice'. But when the Budapest police chief explained that his poorly equipped force would struggle to contain the students – thousands of whom were already gathering outside the Technical University – Piros had second thoughts. Soon he was on the telephone to Gerő, arguing that, with the police unable to enforce the ban, the government risked looking weak. At 14.23, Radio Kossuth again interrupted its regular programming, this time to announce that the prohibition on public meetings and demonstrations had been withdrawn.[18]

At about 3 p.m., ten thousand students set off from the court-yard of the Technical University and headed north along the Buda Embankment towards the Bem monument. Wearing armbands and rosettes in the Hungarian national colours, and carrying placards proclaiming 'Democratise the Party!' and 'We want Imre Nagy!', they were cheered from office blocks and apartment buildings. Meanwhile on the Pest side of the river, in a demonstration organ-ised by Faculty of Arts students at the Karl Marx University of Eco-nomic Sciences, twelve thousand gathered at the statue of Sándor Petőfi, where, after a stirring rendition of '*Nemzeti Dal*', his paean to Hungarian nationalism, they too headed for Bem Square.[19] As the two processions inched their way along the banks of the Dan-ube, singing the 'Marseillaise', the 'Internationale' and the Hungar-ian national anthem, the ranks of the demonstrators were swelled by schoolchildren, tramcar conductors, office clerks and spectators, as well as several hundred army cadets.[20] The temper of the protests became bolder. Early on, the marchers had largely contented them-selves with proclamations about Hungarian–Polish friendship, but now chants of 'Gerő into the Danube!' and calls for Stalinism to be 'swept away' rang out. Hungarian flags also started to appear with the Communist coat of arms cut out from the middle.*[21] At Bem Square, which was overflowing with tens of thousands of protest-ers, a wreath was laid and speeches were made. Then, at about 5 p.m., a cry of 'To the parliament!' went up.

Thousands of demonstrators, marching forty abreast, streamed over Margaret Bridge, heading south to Kossuth Square, a huge public space adjacent to the country's magnificent neo-Gothic parliament building. Joined by thousands of workers from the industrial suburbs of Csepel Island and Újpest, the demonstra-tors now numbered as many as two hundred thousand, and their mood had a distinctly harder edge to it, as they roared again and

* This coat of arms, also referred to as the 'Rákosi badge', had been introduced in 1949.

again, '*Ruszkik haza!*' (Russkies go home!)²² Large crowds also convened outside the radio station on Sándor Bródy Street, close to the National Museum, as well as in Heroes' Square, the ceremonial heart of the capital. The excitement on the streets was palpable. In a despatch telephoned in from Budapest, with the 'roar of the delirious crowds' still ringing in his ears, the *Daily Express*'s Sefton Delmer declared that he had witnessed 'one of the great events of history. I have seen the people of Budapest catch the fire lit in Poznań and Warsaw and come out into the streets in open rebellion against their Soviet overlords.'²³

Nor was the tumult restricted to Budapest. In Szeged, thousands of students marched from Cathedral Square to the City Hall, where, joined by factory workers, they rallied outside the main theatre and sang the national anthem. In Debrecen, two thousand students, marching behind a Hungarian flag, protested outside Party headquarters. The protesters, soon joined by workers from local factories, distributed a manifesto, chanted 'Long live the free press!' and '*Ruszkik haza!*', and tore down the red flags that were flying to mark the city's liberation by the Red Army twelve years earlier and the stars that adorned the trolley cars and public buildings. The mood of the protest was joyful: 'windows were open everywhere; people shouted happily', and Hungarian flags (many with holes in the middle) 'flew from almost every house'. But when the crowds arrived at the police headquarters to demand the release of political prisoners, a few hotheads began to throw stones at the windows. The ÁVH opened fire, killing four people, including an elderly shoemaker.²⁴ The revolution had its first martyrs.

Back at the parliament, the protesters had begun to call for Imre Nagy. Just before 9 p.m., the former prime minister stepped forward nervously to address the enormous, expectant crowd from a window of the parliament building.²⁵ He was a most unlikely hero. With his walrus moustache and round spectacles he looked more like 'the family grocer or village schoolmaster', and while

the students in Budapest had been drawing up their revolutionary demands, Nagy had been relaxing at a wine festival in Badac-
sony, on the north shore of Lake Balaton.[26] Nagy had joined the
Communist Party aged twenty-two and fought for the Red Army
during the Russian Civil War. After working as an underground
Party organiser in the early 1920s and serving a two-year prison
sentence, Nagy was expelled from Hungary in 1929. He moved
first to Vienna and then, in 1930, to Moscow, where he remained
for fifteen years (in 1933 he was recruited as a secret police informer
and passed details about his fellow émigrés to the NKVD). Nagy
finally returned to his homeland as minister of agriculture in Hungary's first post-war government. Before long he had fallen out of
favour with Rákosi's ruling clique and might have met the same
fate as Lászlo Rajk; his contacts in Moscow quite possibly saved
him. Following Stalin's death, Nagy returned to high office, leading a reforming administration before again being outmanoeuvred
by Party hardliners.[27]

By the spring of 1956, Nagy's star was back in the ascendant.
As he took his regular walks along Budapest's fashionable shopping streets or stopped at Gerbeaud's, one of Europe's most famous
coffeehouses, to treat his two young grandchildren to an ice cream,
admirers would ask: 'Mr Prime Minister, when are you coming
back?' By the autumn, he had become a rallying figure for reformers. Nagy, though, remained a loyal Communist and believed that
leadership had to come from the Party. Indeed, he viewed the protests as a dangerous distraction, and had only agreed to address the
crowds at Kossuth Square after much persuasion. Nagy continued
to assume that he would be afforded the opportunity, and the time,
to develop a programme of political reform that could command
popular support. Now he risked being overwhelmed by events.[28]

The very first word that he uttered to the crowds on Kossuth
Square – 'Comrades!' – elicited a chorus of boos and whistles
and shouts of 'No more comrades!' that left him visibly shaken.

Recovering his composure, he offered an 'affectionate salute' to the demonstrators: 'all my esteem goes out to you young, democratic Hungarians who, by your enthusiasm, would help to remove the obstacles that stand in the way of democratic socialism'. But his emphasis on the need for 'negotiations in the bosom of the Party' left the audience disappointed. When Nagy urged the crowds to go home, they heckled him: 'We'll stay, YOU go home!' He had misjudged the mood badly, playing the role of a 'functionary' when what was needed was an impassioned display of leadership. Even one of Nagy's greatest admirers conceded that it was a 'miserable performance'.[29]

While Nagy's speech that evening was a letdown, Ernő Gerő's public remarks proved so disastrous that some have wondered whether they were a deliberate provocation. At 8 p.m., the first secretary took to the airwaves to defend the MDP and its relationship with the 'glorious Communist Party' of the USSR. The Soviets, he declared, had not only 'liberated our country from the yoke of . . . fascism and German imperialism' but had then worked, 'on the basis of full equality', to help build Hungary's socialist democracy. Condemning 'bourgeois reactionaries' for spreading 'poison . . . among our youth', Gerő warned that the 'working class' would defend the achievements of the people's democracy 'under any circumstances and from whatever quarter they may be threatened'.[30]

Gerő's bellicose words and defiant tone infuriated the protesters. Throughout the day there had been the occasional angry outburst: spotted on the streets, the limousine of Yuri Andropov, the Soviet ambassador, had been booed by the crowds; the headquarters of the Hungarian–Soviet Friendship Society had been torched; the red stars that adorned many public buildings had been destroyed. But now the mood grew angrier. The clearest symbol of Hungary's subjugation to the USSR was a giant bronze statue of Stalin that towered over Heroes' Square. Unveiled to great fanfare in 1951, Sándor Mikus's socialist realist monument was dedicated to 'the great Stalin, from the grateful Hungarian people'. Late on the evening of 23 October, with thousands of protesters surging into the square, scores of people clambered onto the statue's limestone base. Initial attempts to topple the monument proved futile, but a group of workers soon appeared, carrying ladders, metal cables and welding torches, and began cutting through the statue at the knees. Finally, at 9.37 p.m., it fell. Within seconds the crowds were swarming all over it, smashing away with hammers and pipes and prising off chunks as souvenirs. As demonstrators 'howled with joy', the dictator's head was dragged along the streets and dumped outside the National Theatre. By the end of the night only Stalin's bronze boots, 'each the size of a man', remained on the pedestal.[31]

Meanwhile at the radio station, where protesters had been attempting to convince the authorities to broadcast the Sixteen Points, the situation turned ugly. Amid rumours that a delegation, sent inside to negotiate, had been seized by the secret police (ÁVH), the protesters tried to force their way in, hurling stones at the windows and repeatedly ramming the doors with a truck. They were met first with tear gas and water hoses, then bayonet charges and warning shots. Soon, though, the ÁVH resorted to lethal force, cutting down three young students and precipitating a full-scale siege. Over the next few hours the revolutionaries – armed with weapons seized from munitions factories or handed over by army personnel, and joined by defecting soldiers – battled the ÁVH. Just before dawn, the charred and badly damaged radio building fell to the insurgents. The battle had claimed the lives of sixteen revolutionaries and five ÁVH officers.[32]

The next morning, Hungary awoke to dramatic news. An urgent announcement, broadcast over Radio Kossuth, explained that 'dastardly' attacks by 'counter-revolutionary gangs' and 'bandits' had occurred overnight. As a consequence, the government had requested the assistance of Soviet troops, who were at that very moment on the streets of the capital, helping to 'restore order'. The authorities appealed for calm and for support. The 'liquidation of the counter-revolutionary gangs' was, the government proclaimed, 'the most sacred cause of every honest Hungarian worker, of the people, and of the fatherland'.[33]

Soviet troops had arrived in Budapest at 4.30 a.m., entering the city from the south-west. Thousands of soldiers, serving with two mechanised divisions already stationed in Hungary, together with hundreds of tanks, armoured personnel carriers and artillery, took up positions across the capital. Armoured units were also deployed in major provincial centres and along the Austrian border, reinforcements were sent from Romania and Ukraine, and two fighter divisions (totalling 159 planes) provided close air support.[34]

Ernő Gerő had actually requested military support the previous afternoon, during a series of conversations with the Soviet military attaché and the ambassador, Yuri Andropov. When the commander of the Soviet forces in Hungary explained that he could not take action without clear authorisation from Moscow, Andropov and Gerő took up the matter with Nikita Khrushchev.[35] At 11 p.m. (Moscow time) members of the Presidium gathered in the Kremlin, where they were given a series of alarming updates: one hundred thousand people were reported to be on the streets of Budapest, and the radio station was in flames. They also heard rumours that in Debrecen the headquarters of both the Communist Party and the ÁVH had fallen to the rebels. Khrushchev immediately spoke in favour of using Soviet troops to help quell the protests and restore order. His suggestion commanded broad support (only Anastas Mikoyan urged caution), and Khrushchev authorised Marshal Zhukov, the defence minister, to order a military deployment. He also despatched Mikoyan, together with fellow Presidium member Mikhail Suslov and Ivan Serov, the KGB chief, to Budapest to find out what was going on.[36]

Crucially, the decision to seek Soviet military intervention was taken before Imre Nagy's readmission to the Hungarian government. Nagy had arrived at the Party's Akadémia Street headquarters shortly before ten o'clock, local time – so about an hour after the Presidium had gone into session in Moscow. He joined nine Politburo members in Gerő's office, where they heard the first secretary announce that Soviet troops would be used to help restore order. No one spoke against the move. Nagy later claimed that although he had disagreed with the decision, he had refrained from saying so because it was not yet clear that he was going to assume any official position within the government. His biographer, meanwhile, has suggested that Nagy might have been unnerved following the hostile reception from the crowds outside parliament, or affected by the evident sense of panic that was spreading among the MDP leadership. Nagy may also have feared that his opponents would seize on any dissent to scapegoat him as the irresponsible figure who first encouraged the 'mob' and then vetoed the effort to restore order.[37]

Throughout the night of 23–24 October the MDP's Central Committee met in emergency session. During these long hours Nagy paced the corridors and waited patiently in the lobby. Finally, just before 5 a.m., he was readmitted to the Politburo and offered the premiership. Nagy immediately suggested that forty-four-year-old János Kádár, a centrist and former interior minister, replace the wildly unpopular Gerő as first secretary. But, when his colleagues demurred, Nagy declined to force the issue, thereby missing an opportunity to break decisively with the Stalinist old guard. Worse, Nagy risked looking like little more than a liberal adornment to the status quo. Certainly the presence of Soviet troops on the streets of Budapest and Gerő's continued grip on power undercut Nagy's moral authority and eroded his popular support. When the new government declared martial law, many of Nagy's supporters were appalled; two of his closest allies refused to take up positions in the new administration.[38] Miklós Vásárhelyi, a journalist and confidant of Nagy, explained how, for the reform Communists, this was the moment when 'everything was lost':

'We had accumulated over the years a measure of moral and political capital; but now Nagy had accepted the role of Prime Minister in a government which was otherwise the same as two days earlier – the government against which we had been fighting.'[39]

Nagy's vulnerability was recognised by the British ambassador. In a cable sent late on the evening of 24 October, Sir Leslie Fry stated that Nagy could 'hardly hope to overcome the popular conviction that he shares responsibility [with Gerő] for bringing Russian forces into Budapest'. He also wondered just how long this 'ill-assorted pair can run in double harness'.[40] As it turned out, the answer to that particular question was less than twenty-four hours.

Hopes that the show of Soviet military strength would restore order were quickly dashed. Battles were soon raging across the capital, with continuous bursts of machine-gun fire heard throughout the morning of 24 October. By the end of that first day, three thousand street fighters had taken up arms; eight were killed, and hundreds more wounded. The rebels were heavily outgunned, but because Soviet forces (expecting little resistance) had been deployed without infantry support, the insurgents were able to use local knowledge to their advantage. Small groups were formed, weapons were procured from armaments factories and military depots, as well as from sympathetic policemen and soldiers, and strongholds were established across the city. One of the most famous centres of resistance was the Corvin Cinema. Situated in the heart of Pest, at one of the capital's major intersections, the Bauhaus-inspired building stood in a courtyard surrounded by five-storey apartment blocks and was accessible only through alleyways (notably the Corvin Passage) too narrow for tanks. Conveniently, a gasoline pump was sited at the cinema's rear, which enabled easy production of Molotov cocktails, and just across the street stood the imposing Kilián military barracks. Within twenty-four hours they would be transformed into a rebel fortress, held by a force of two thousand civilian fighters and soldiers under the command of the charismatic

Colonel Pál Maléter, who had defected to the revolutionaries.[41]

Taking full advantage of Budapest's narrow side streets and enclosed courtyards, small bands of revolutionaries engaged in a series of hit-and-run attacks on the Red Army. One nineteen-year-old elevator installation worker described how he had begun to fight, along with fifteen or twenty others, soon after Soviet tanks entered the city. His group included students, factory workers of all ages and two young women. At one point, desperately hungry, the group broke into a confectionery store, where they feasted on ice cream cones and grapes. Spotted by the Soviets, who blocked the entrance and began firing, the rebels managed to set fire to one tank before fleeing through the store's rear window. These guerrilla tactics could be spectacularly effective: over the course of several days, the fighters around the Corvin Passage were responsible for destroying six cannons, eight munitions trucks and several tanks. They also killed a dozen or more Soviet soldiers. In fact, during the fierce street fighting that took place during the last week of October, the Red Army lost a total of 120 men and twenty-five tanks – the equivalent of roughly an entire armoured battalion.[42]

Mikoyan, Suslov and Serov arrived in Hungary early on the morning of 24 October, landing at an airfield fifty-five miles from Budapest due to fog. On touching down, they were met by General Mikhail Malinin, first deputy chief of staff of the Soviet armed forces, and driven to the capital aboard armoured personnel carriers, with a tank escort, for briefings at the Ministry of Defence and the MDP Central Committee. Shortly after 3 p.m., Mikoyan and Suslov cabled Moscow their first impressions. Criticising Gerő for 'exaggerating the opponents' strength', they expressed confidence that 'all the hotbeds of insurgency have been crushed'.[43] Their report must have made for reassuring reading. Later that day, at a gathering of Eastern European leaders who were in Moscow for an update on the Polish crisis, Khrushchev explained that the situation was not as 'dire' as some had claimed, with the resistance in Budapest 'limited to certain rooftops and house balconies'. 'By morning', he declared, 'one can expect [that] there will be total calm.'[44] As dawn broke, the Hungarian government was similarly bullish: official announcements explained that the 'counter-revolutionary gangs have mostly been liquidated', and the citizens of Budapest were urged to return to normal life: 'start traffic, trams, trolley buses, and buses – wherever possible. Workers must resume work! Let factories produce and offices and enterprises function! . . . shops must open at the usual time . . .'[45] The optimism was spectacularly misplaced.

At about 10 a.m., a crowd of around two thousand men and women – smiling broadly and waving flags – marched past the US Chancery building on Liberty Square. Some waved their hats and others called out, 'Why don't you help us?' The group was on its way to the parliament building, where crowds were gathering to demonstrate their support for the revolution. By half past ten, perhaps as many as twenty thousand people had assembled in Kossuth Square, where they sang the national anthem and shouted, 'Down with Gerő' and 'We are not fascists!' Remarkably, several Soviet tanks and an armoured car, 'packed with young Hungarians fraternizing with the Russian soldiers', now joined them. The revolutionaries had won over the young soldiers with cigarettes, laughter and conversation, and even passed out Russian-language leaflets:

> Russian Friends! Do not shoot!
>   They have tricked you. You are fighting not against counter-revolutionaries, but against revolutionaries. We fighting Hungarians want an independent, democratic Hungary.
>   Your fight is pointless: you are shooting not at fascists but at workers, peasants and university students.

A number of revolutionaries actually climbed aboard the tanks, which they quickly plastered with Hungarian flags, and persuaded their crews to accompany them to the demonstration.[46]

The crowds in Kossuth Square were peaceful, and the atmosphere jubilant when, just after 11 a.m., the sound of gunfire crackled through the air. Writing in the *New York Times*, John MacCormac reported that, when the firing eventually subsided, the square was 'littered with dead and dying men and women'. One eyewitness described seeing a woman, her head and arms shot away, lying in a blood-soaked fur coat, surrounded by her three young children, who were weeping inconsolably. Dead bodies were reportedly heaped up in piles, and the British Embassy noted that 'twelve lorry-loads of corpses were later removed from the square'. The final death toll may have been as high as one thousand.[47]

As the terrible events of 'Bloody Thursday' were unfolding, the Central Committee of the Hungarian Workers' Party was meeting, just yards away, in Akadémia Street. The comrades were soon caught up in the drama themselves, seeking refuge in a cellar as machine-gun fire rattled the building and plaster fell from the walls.[48] Gerő's desperate hold on power was now finally loosened and, at 12.33 p.m., Radio Kossuth announced that he had been replaced as first secretary by Kádár. Later that afternoon, Nagy appealed for calm. Acknowledging that past mistakes had led to 'bitterness' among the workers, he promised an 'all-embracing and well-founded programme of reforms' that would help to build a 'better, more beautiful and socialist future'. Addressing directly those 'young people, workers, and soldiers' who had 'taken up arms', Nagy pledged that the government would 'show magnanimity in a spirit of reconciliation'. Expressing his 'deep grief over every drop of blood shed by innocent working people', Nagy indicated that, once order was restored, Soviet troops would be withdrawn from the streets.[49]

Unfortunately, Hungary's leaders continued to be outpaced by events. As news of the massacre spread, thousands took to the streets in defiance, waving the national flag and black flags of mourning. Some were bent on revenge. At one point, a 'furtive figure clad in a leather coat', suspected to be an ÁVH agent, was seized: 'Like tigers the crowd turned on him, began to beat him and hustled him into a courtyard. A few minutes later they emerged rubbing their hands with satisfaction. The leather-coated figure was seen no more.' Others channelled their anger into political struggle. University students, for example, distributed leaflets calling for a general strike, while a group calling itself 'The New Provisional Revolutionary Government' used an army printing press to produce a manifesto demanding an end to martial law, the immediate withdrawal of all Soviet troops from the country, and Hungary's exit from the Warsaw Pact. Uniformed army officers distributed copies to the 'cheering crowds', who eagerly read the 'smeared and crumpled leaflets under the headlamps of cars'.[50]

By day's end the Hungarian flag, shorn of its Communist coat of arms, was flying proudly from most of the city's major buildings, and large crowds, singing patriotic songs and demanding the withdrawal of Soviet forces, roamed the streets. Throughout the night there was heavy firing from tanks and mortar shells and, as dawn broke, large crowds used 'railway wagons, tramlines, flagstones and anything else on which they can lay hands' to build improvised barricades in an effort to prevent Soviet reinforcements from entering the city.[51]

Over the next few days, as news of the uprising in Budapest spread, the entire country was gripped by revolutionary fervour: mass demonstrations and street protests took place, manifestos were distributed, independent newspapers were printed and radio stations seized. Symbols of Soviet power – including war memorials, statues and the ubiquitous red stars – were damaged or destroyed, Party headquarters ransacked, local ÁVH offices attacked and prisoners released. Workers downed tools, unpopular or incompetent managers were ejected from their posts, and workers' councils were established in factories, mines and other industrial enterprises. Made up of elected representatives, the councils assumed responsibility for production, administration and management, sought to re-establish order and discipline, and made preparations to defend the country's industrial enterprises from enemy attack.

Meanwhile revolutionary councils (which often included delegates elected from local workers' and students' committees) were formed in all of the major provincial centres and quickly assumed responsibility for local administration and self-government, organised public transport and deliveries of food and other essential supplies, maintained order and sought to co-ordinate the revolutionary forces at the regional level. Their success, evident popularity – their leaders usually included some of the community's most respected figures – and ability to mobilise tens of thousands in support of the revolution's aims exposed the Communist Party's weakness and challenged its monopoly on power.[52]

Some observers were rather star-struck by all this. The political theorist Hannah Arendt famously argued that the councils signalled the 'true upsurge of democracy against dictatorship, of freedom against tyranny', while Peter Fryer, a correspondent for Britain's *Daily Worker*, wrote admiringly of how 'ordinary men, women and youths' whom the old system had 'kept submerged' were now empowered. The revolution, Fryer explained, had 'thrust them forward, aroused their civil pride and latent genius for organisation, set them to work to build democracy out of the ruins of bureaucracy'. This was a revolution, he declared, 'to be studied not in the pages of Marx, Engels and Lenin . . . but happening here in real life before the eyes of the world' – a revolution of 'flesh and blood'.[53] Like all revolutions, the situation on the ground was complicated, and the revolutionaries were often divided along generational, class and ideological lines. In Újpest, for instance, the revolutionary committee clashed with the workers' councils (whose leaders were often politically more moderate), not least about who should be in charge, while in the mining town of Tatabánya the 'workers' battled white-collar 'professionals'. As one miner put it, 'from where I'm standing, lawyers, doctors, and teachers want to take over the running of the city'. The 'professionals' were themselves split between moderates, committed to reform, and radicals eager to sweep aside the existing system.[54]

Nor were rural areas immune from the drama. Across the countryside, peasants gleefully torched the administrative records for the loathed system of compulsory deliveries and dissolved their hated agricultural co-operatives. Unpopular Party bosses were confronted, Soviet monuments were destroyed and impromptu protests were held. One twenty-five-year-old construction worker described how, while delivering timber south of Sopron on 26 October, he saw demonstrations in all of the villages that he passed: Hungarian flags were everywhere, and there was evident excitement as peasants huddled around the radio to catch the latest news. In the little village of Öttevény, a group of resourceful locals set off by truck, horseback and bicycle, determined to assist the revolutionaries in nearby Győr, while peasants elsewhere organised shipments of potatoes, flour, geese, chickens and other vital supplies to the fighters in Budapest.[55]

On the afternoon of Saturday 27 October, amidst news that large areas of Hungary were now under the control of revolutionaries, a group of Western journalists crossed the border from Austria and were driven to the nearby town of Mosonmagyaróvár. The ten-minute journey took them 'along [a] straight road, through a flat countryside of harvested fields lying fallow in the mellow autumn sunlight'. On arrival, the reporters were taken to Lenin Street, where they were shown a tree from which, earlier that morning, the lifeless body of an ÁVH officer had been strung up by the ankles and mutilated. The bloodstains on the kerb below were still visible. Next they were escorted to the town's cemetery, which was crowded with grief-stricken mourners. In one of the mortuaries, the bodies of men and women were lying on the floor. The blood was 'still unwashed from their wounds', and several had 'tiny bunches of flowers on their breasts'. Another dozen or more bodies – including those of a young woman and an eighteen-month-old baby – were laid out at the far end of the main chapel. Members of the local revolutionary committee, which had taken power less than twenty-four hours earlier, guided the journalists on this grim tour. The revolution itself appeared to command popular support: almost everyone in the town was wearing ribbons in the national colours or carrying a flag with the 'Rákosi badge' cut from the middle, and red stars had been pulled down from all of the main public buildings.[56]

The day before, this little border town of twenty-two thousand souls had witnessed one of the bloodiest atrocities of the revolution. At about 10 a.m. a crowd of about a thousand people – mostly students from the agricultural college and workers from local bauxite factories – had marched to the ÁVH's Levél Street barracks, on the western edge of town, where they were joined by hundreds of ordinary townsfolk, including the elderly and young mothers. Their goal was to replace the giant red star adorning the secret police headquarters with the Hungarian flag. On reaching the barracks – a squat structure set between two factories – a delegation approached a waiting ÁVH officer. The officer – a local resident – chatted and shook hands with a few of the men. Then, without warning, he fired his pistol into the air. Within seconds, ÁVH soldiers, who were lying in shallow trenches in front of the building, opened fire, cutting down dozens of unarmed, peaceful protesters: 'Cries of terror and horror rose to the skies . . . the blood ran from victims' torn flesh. The roar of powerful grenades thrown by the security police joined the rattle of machine guns. Bits of human flesh were strewn all around.' When, four minutes later, the guns fell silent, more than fifty lay dead. Scores more were injured.[57]

Bent on revenge, the survivors headed for the local army base, where the soldiers, though reluctant to join the rebellion, willingly handed over weapons. An appeal was also sent to the revolutionary committee in nearby Győr, which promptly despatched a small number of armed men. Soon the ÁVH barracks were under siege. When the building finally fell, shortly after dusk, many of the secret police had already fled; others surrendered quickly. One officer threw himself from a third-floor window, apparently in a desperate attempt to escape. One journalist reported that, on hitting the pavement, 'parts of his brains . . . squirted out of his open skull', and furious protesters stamped on his body. Two other officers were seized by the mob, and 'beaten until their bodies were mere sanguinary objects. Then they were split into pieces as if this had been the work of wild animals.'[58]

The Communist leadership would subsequently characterise the uprising as a fascist counter-revolution – an attempt by the bourgeoisie, imperialists and criminals to overthrow the 'people's democracy' and restore the pre-war capitalist order. Although this charge was politically motivated and based on fabricated or distorted evidence, it is worth remembering that, just a decade earlier, Hungary's government had briefly been in the hands of the fascist Arrow Cross Party. Moreover, for almost the entire interwar period the country had been subjected to the reactionary and authoritarian rule of Admiral Miklós Horthy, who had led the nation into a fateful alliance with Hitler.[59] Although the revolutionaries drew their strength predominantly from reform Communists who backed Nagy and national democrats who wanted a socialist system combined with a multi-party democracy, there is no doubt that latent forces on the right, both conservative nationalists and far-right extremists, attempted to take advantage of the turmoil in the autumn of 1956.[60]

The revolution, though, won the support of vast swathes of the population – industrial workers, miners, students, writers, intellectuals, peasants, public officials and even members of the army and the police. Those who took up arms, provided practical help or cheered along did so for many reasons, including a hatred of Rákosi and the Stalinist dictatorship that he had created, approval of the students' Sixteen Points and a desire for improved living standards. They also had very different visions of the kind of Hungary that they wanted to create. For the time being, though, the revolutionaries united around the rather nebulous demand for 'freedom' – freedom for the press, freedom of speech, freedom of political association, but, above all else, freedom from the Soviet Union. Freedom, in this context, meant an end to Hungary's political and economic dependence on Moscow, and the withdrawal of Soviet troops from the country.[61]

Given the scale and intensity of the uprising, Nagy recognised the need for decisive action. On 28 October, shortly before half past five in the evening, Hungarian radio broadcast an official statement in which Nagy acknowledged the legitimacy of the revolutionaries' grievances and pledged to implement the 'just demands of the people'. Calling for a ceasefire and offering an amnesty to those who had taken up arms, he announced wage increases and promised to dissolve the ÁVH and other state security organs. Nagy also declared that the USSR had agreed to withdraw its troops from Budapest immediately and that the government was initiating negotiations for a full withdrawal of Soviet military forces from Hungarian territory.[62]

Nagy had hoped that these concessions would bring the crisis to an end, but the revolutionaries showed no intention of laying down their arms (in any case, a series of Soviet attacks in Budapest the following day called the vaunted 'truce' into question). Instead they continued to insist on the removal of all Soviet troops from Hungary and the restoration of a pluralist political system.[63] Faced with an increasingly perilous situation, Nagy took drastic measures. On 30 October, at 2.28 p.m., he addressed the nation once again, this time to announce the abolition of the one-party state and the appointment to his cabinet of representatives of the

Social Democratic Party, the Smallholders Party and the National Peasant Party. He also recognised the legitimacy of the revolutionary councils and asked for their support, called for the immediate withdrawal of Soviet troops from Budapest and restated his commitment to begin negotiations for a full withdrawal of Soviet forces from Hungary. He ended with a dramatic appeal to his 'Hungarian brethren' to 'safeguard the achievements of the revolution' and 'stand beside the national government in the hour of this fateful decision. Long live free, democratic, and independent Hungary!'[64] That same day, Cardinal Jósef Mindszenty was freed from house arrest and the MDP was dissolved (it reformed on 31 October as the Hungarian Socialist Workers' Party, or MSzMP).[65]

Remarkably, the Soviets appeared willing to accept all this. At a Presidium meeting held on 30 October, the comrades were unanimous in the view that the 'military path of occupation' should be rejected in favour of 'the withdrawal of troops, [and] negotiations'. Zhukov, for instance, argued that 'we should withdraw troops from Budapest, and if necessary withdraw from Hungary as a whole'.[66] The Soviet government released a statement, published the next morning in *Pravda*, affirming its commitment to 'peaceful co-existence, friendship, and co-operation' and pledging to strengthen the bonds of friendship with the people's democracies 'on the firm foundation of observance of the full sovereignty of each socialist state'. Turning directly to events in Hungary, the Soviet leadership announced that they had 'given [their] military command instructions to withdraw the Soviet military units from the city of Budapest as soon as this is considered necessary by the Hungarian government'. They also expressed a willingness to 'enter into the appropriate negotiations with the government of the Hungarian People's Republic . . . on the question of the presence of Soviet troops on the territory of Hungary'.[67]

The Hungarian revolution, it seemed, had triumphed.

18

SUEZ

Those who began this operation should be left . . . to boil in
their own oil.

DWIGHT D. EISENHOWER

Early on the morning of Monday 5 November 1956, 668 men serving with 3 Parachute Battalion began landing at the El Gamil airfield, four miles west of Port Said.[1] Corporal John Morrison, who
made the jump from a Hastings aircraft at about seven thirty, 'hit
the deck with a hell of a bang' and was immediately in action:
'There was', he explained, 'a fair to-do on the ground with mor-
taring and machine gunning and a bit of an assault.'[2] Morrison
and his fellow Paras – weighed down by heavy equipment and
struggling with obsolete or inadequate kit – came under sustained
machine-gun and mortar fire from the Egyptians, and it took them
an hour to establish control of the airfield.[3]

The path to Port Said consisted of a narrow strip of ground,
just five hundred yards wide, hemmed in by the Mediterranean
Sea to the north and Lake Manzala to the south. The terrain was
challenging: the flat sand and dunes of the immediate drop zone
gave way to thick reed beds and ditches, the mosquito-infested
marshes of a sewage works, a walled cemetery, a coastguard barracks and, finally, a cluster of wooden shanty houses that bordered
Arab Town – Port Said's 'native quarter'.[4] As they began their
advance, the Paras came under fire from anti-tank guns and sni-
pers, and even (mistakenly) from French fighter jets. The battle for
El Gamil was fierce, and at 12.30 p.m. the British called in targeted
air strikes before opening up with mortars and machine guns on
the heavily defended walled cemetery, killing thirty Egyptians. By

17.30, in the face of 'stubborn resistance' and with ammunition running low, the British decided to dig in and resume the advance the following day.[5] They had lost three men (another would die later from his injuries), with twenty-nine injured.[6]

While the British were fighting at El Gamil, five hundred French paratroopers had landed at Raswa, to the south of Port Said, where they captured a water plant as well as the main road and rail bridge into the city. Again the fighting was intense, and the French troops, hardened by recent service in North Africa, reportedly 'machine-gunned every living thing' that lay in their path. A further French drop at Port Faud proved particularly successful, with the town secured within hours.[7]

That evening, reports began to circulate that the Egyptian commander, Brigadier-General Salaheddin Moguy, had agreed to a ceasefire and was prepared to negotiate the terms of surrender. After hearing this news, Sir Anthony Eden embraced his military chiefs, exclaiming, 'It's all worked out perfectly!' In fact, Moguy was probably seeking an informal truce to protect Port Said's civilian population from further attack (though he later claimed that he was buying time to enable weapons to be distributed to local residents). In any case, the reports proved wildly optimistic and, after a brief, uneasy truce, the war was back on.[8]

The next morning, as a 'wonderful dark red streaky dawn' broke over Port Said, the Royal Navy and RAF began their assault – pounding targets along the coast and then strafing the beaches – in advance of amphibious and airborne landings by several thousand Royal Marines from 3 Commando Brigade.[9] Those serving with 40 and 42 Commando came ashore in amphibious 'Buffaloes' (tracked landing vehicles), while the men of 45 Commando took part in the world's first helicopter assault. Over the course of eighty-nine minutes a total of 425 men and twenty-three tons of equipment were taken ashore aboard Sycamore 14s and Whirlwind HAR2s from HMS *Ocean* and HMS *Theseus*, two light fleet carriers that were anchored seven miles offshore.[10] One soldier described how as he and his fellow marines 'came up onto the flight deck, loaded like beasts of burden' they saw a 'great pall of black smoke over the coast'. Soon they were aboard the helicopters and in the air: 'Sitting with my legs apart, facing the open doorway, I saw first sky and then sea. It looked extremely uninviting . . . then we were over the breakwater and being directed to our landing area by the hand of a great statue – Ferdinand de Lesseps was pointing the way.'[11] The marines were 'in great heart, very fit, well equipped and confident'. Aided by fine weather and 'the paucity of defenders near the water's edge', the landings went smoothly. With the beachhead secured and a tactical headquarters established, the troops began to move out into Port Said. Their mission was to 'seize the town, the harbour, and the area to the south'.[12]

Assisted by a squadron from 6 Royal Tank Regiment, which had come ashore soon afterwards, the marines concentrated on capturing key strategic sites (including bridges and major roads), clearing the town of enemy fighters, weapons and ammunition and securing the streets. Although the local Egyptian commanders were, apparently, in some disarray, their men fought hard, deploying automatic weapons, grenades and anti-tank rockets as well as rifles and machine guns. Fighting in the Arab Quarter left forty Egyptians dead and much of the district in flames.[13] Coming ashore that morning, reservist Les Lambert had viewed the full chaos of war:

> The RAF . . . were knocking out . . . tanks only two hundred
> yards in front of us, helicopters were busy ferrying in stores
> and the Naval fighters screamed overhead, wheeling and
> darting in and out of the smoke. The whole town echoed
> to the sound of machine-gun fire and the dull 'crump' of
> mortars. The whole of Port Said appeared to be on fire.[14]

It could have been even worse. Anxious to minimise civilian casualties, the British had ordered the Royal Navy to refrain from using its larger guns; civilian warnings were broadcast, and some troops evidently adopted a 'light touch' approach to soldiering. One marine recalled how 'some of the lads on house clearing were ringing the doorbells to flats and waiting for people to answer'.[15] Even so, many civilians were killed, wounded or forced to flee their homes during the allied assault. While some, like the group of fishermen who attempted to surrender to French paratroopers near Raswa, were cut down deliberately, others were caught up inadvertently. Indeed, with civilians taking up arms, and soldiers discarding their uniforms and taking up positions within heavily populated areas, distinctions between combatant and non-combatant soon became blurred.[16] In his war diary, Lieutenant Peter Mayo noted that shortly after he and his fellow commandos had occupied three houses near to the beachfront, 'several Wogs appeared running down the street immediately in front of us. They had rifles but no uniform and must have been Home Guard. Whatever they were, Soggers shot four of them.' A few minutes later, another Egyptian, wearing a blue suit, 'appeared from somewhere . . . and started running up the street . . . he hadn't taken more than a dozen crouching steps before five or six shots tore into him and, as he fell, he half twisted to look up'. Mayo 'felt slightly sick. We weren't supposed to be shooting at civilians but it was very difficult to tell, as most of the people we met were civilians with rifles.'[17]

By early afternoon, much of the city was under allied control. Following the capture of Brigadier-General Moguy, the commanders of the allied task force had even come ashore aboard a motor launch, wearing full dress uniform, in what proved to be a farcical effort to secure an unconditional surrender: their initial landing attempt was met with a volley of enemy gunfire and, after disembarking at a more hospitable location and arriving at the Italian Consulate for talks, they failed to engage in substantive discussions with the exhausted general (it is even possible that they negotiated with the wrong man). In any case the Egyptian commander, disoriented and cut off from his forces, was in no position to agree terms, and the battle for Port Said raged on. The men of 40 Commando faced stiff opposition from Egyptian forces occupying the customs warehouse and Navy House. That evening, with the light fading fast, an air strike was called in, finally putting an end to the resistance and reducing much of Navy House – the former symbol of British power in Egypt – to rubble.[18] Meanwhile 2 Para, along with units of 6 Royal Tank Regiment, had been heading south, under orders to move as far along the Suez Canal as possible. Fortified by shots of whisky, the troops had reached Al Cap, a Canal Station twenty-five miles south of Port Said, shortly after midnight. Then they were suddenly ordered to halt. 'The Americans', their commander explained, had 'stopped the advance'.[19]

The Suez campaign had begun on the evening of 29 October, when Israeli forces crossed into the Sinai Peninsula. An official IDF communiqué justified the operation as 'necessitated by the continuous Egyptian attacks on citizens and on Israel land and sea communications, the purpose of which was to cause destruction and to deprive the people of Israel of the possibility of a peaceful existence'.[20] Israeli infantry and mobile paratroop units attacked bases just over the frontier at Ras en-Nakeb, Kuntilla and Kusseima, meeting little resistance. In the day's most daring move, 395 paratroopers were dropped at the Mitla Pass, about forty miles east of Suez. Flying close to the ground to avoid Egyptian radar, sixteen ageing Dakota transport planes, each carrying a single paratroop company and escorted by Meteor jets, made the drop at 16.59 p.m. Although the pilots had missed the landing zone by a couple of miles, by 19.30 the paratroopers had reached the Parker Memorial (named after a British governor of Sinai) and were dug in, awaiting reinforcements.[21]

Attention now switched to Westminster, where, on the afternoon of 30 October, Sir Anthony Eden informed a 'tense and packed' House of Commons that an ultimatum had been issued by

London and Paris calling on both sides to 'stop all warlike action by land, sea and air' and to withdraw their forces ten miles from the Canal Zone within twelve hours. To loud, raucous cheers, he also explained that the two governments had demanded that Cairo accept a temporary Anglo-French occupation force that would 'separate the belligerents' and 'guarantee freedom of transit through the Canal'. Finally, Eden explained that if these undertakings were not forthcoming, British and French forces would 'intervene in whatever strength may be necessary to secure compliance'.[22] Nasser, as expected, rejected these demands as a gross violation of Egypt's sovereignty, an insult to the country's dignity and a violation of the United Nations Charter (it was, after all, being asked to withdraw troops from its own territory in the face of a foreign invasion). At dusk on 31 October, allied air operations commenced.[23] First, waves of RAF Canberra and Valiant bombers pounded Egyptian airfields, cratering the runways. Then ground attack jets launched from the carriers HMS *Eagle*, *Bulwark* and *Albion*, as well as from bases on Cyprus, set about destroying Egypt's Soviet-built IL-28 bombers and MiG-15 fighters as they sat helplessly on the ground. By noon on 2 November the Egyptian air force had been wiped out and new targets, including a major bridge to the west of Port Said, heavy armour and coastal defences, as well as several Egyptian warships off the coast of Alexandria, came under attack. Indeed, the only setback during the early phase of the operation was the failure to stop the Egyptians from towing the *Akka*, a US-built ship that was filled with concrete and pig iron, into the Suez Canal, where she was scuttled in a deliberate attempt to block the waterway (dozens more vessels would be sunk over the next few days; the canal remained closed for months).[24] But while the military campaign had been going smoothly, Operation Musketeer was rapidly turning into a diplomatic and political disaster.

President Nasser had been informed of the Israeli incursions into Sinai while attending his son's birthday party – a joyous occasion, marked with special cakes, children's games and movies. As the celebrations continued around him, the Egyptian leader struggled to make sense of the news. Speaking on the telephone several hours later to Mohamed Heikal, his friend and confidant, Nasser explained that 'something very strange is happening . . . It looks to us as if all they want to do is to start up sandstorms in the desert.' The Egyptians wondered at first whether the whole thing was a feint, designed to mask an attack on Jordan or Gaza, or if the Israelis were attempting to derail the recent progress at the UN. Having ruled out a British invasion some weeks earlier, the one possibility that Egypt's leaders did not consider was Anglo-French involvement. When London and Paris issued their ultimatum on 30 October, then, it stunned Cairo's political elite. Nasser was utterly astonished. He had simply refused to believe that Britain would be prepared to risk its reputation and interests in the region by joining Israel in a military strike against an Arab nation. But with RAF bombers in action in the skies above Egypt, the shock soon turned to panic. After climbing onto the roof of his modest villa in Heliopolis to watch the bombs falling on Cairo, Nasser travelled to military headquarters for what was an emotional meeting. At one point, a veteran of the Free Officers Movement even told Nasser to his face that he should give himself up to the British, in a 'final sacrifice' for his country.[25]

Any illusions that Nasser would soon be on his way out were, though, quickly dispelled. Indeed, the allied efforts to stir up a popular rebellion proved inept. At the last minute, air strikes against railway lines, communication systems and oil facilities, which were the precursor to a planned campaign of psychological warfare, were cancelled for fear of antagonising Arab and international opinion. Cairo radio was not put out of action until 2 November, amid confusion about the location of the main transmitter, while the 'Voice of Britain', a 'black radio' station based in Cyprus, was crippled when its Arab staff walked out in protest.

Plans to drop millions of propaganda leaflets were abandoned due to a shortage of suitable planes and fuses (some of the leaflets that were dropped had landed as confetti).[26] With the Egyptian army retreating from Sinai to defend the mainland, and the government making secret plans to evacuate the capital and co-ordinate a popular guerrilla war from the Nile Delta, Nasser recovered his poise, rallying his people in a series of defiant speeches.[27] In a message broadcast on Thursday 1 November, for instance, he explained that troops were being withdrawn from Sinai 'to be with our people', and vowed, 'We shall fight and we shall not surrender. We shall fight from village to village, from place to place.'[28] The following day, the Egyptian leader travelled in an open car to Cairo's magnificent Al-Hazar Mosque for Friday prayers. Addressing the crowds, he warned that Egypt had 'always been a graveyard for invaders':

> For everyone of us, among the armed forces and the people, our watchword will be: 'we will fight and never surrender' . . . I am in Cairo and I will fight with you against any invasion . . . We will defend our country, our history and our future . . . we will fight . . . to the last drop of blood.[29]

Over the next few days, hundreds of popular resistance groups and people's militia sprang up (some four hundred thousand rifles were issued to ordinary citizens from the backs of trucks) and many of Nasser's most bitter opponents pledged to defend the nation.[30] Meanwhile, international outrage at the Anglo-French intervention stiffened Nasser's resolve.

The Arab world, unsurprisingly, rallied to Egypt's cause. Anti-Western protests erupted in Libya, Syria and Jordan. In Baghdad, amidst fears that the pro-Western government might fall, martial law was imposed in a desperate effort to restore order; in Bahrain, thousands marched through the streets in protests that left some buildings in flames. Both Jordan and Syria were eager to contribute to Egypt's defence, but Nasser proved a model of restraint, although his attempt to prevent Syrian Special Forces from destroying pumping stations on the major oil pipeline that ran from Kirkuk to Tripoli came too late (Western oil supplies would be disrupted for six months). Saudi Arabia, meanwhile, imposed an oil embargo on France and Britain.[31] Across much of Africa and Asia, opinion was strongly against the Western intervention. In Zanzibar, flags of mourning were flown from buildings, black patches were affixed to clothes and noisy protests were staged.[32] Meanwhile in Indonesia there was an eruption of hostility at European 'colonialism', which culminated in boycotts of UK business interests (Britain's state airline, BOAC, for example, was denied refuelling rights at Jakarta airport) and a series of angry demonstrations including a mob attack on the British Embassy.[33]

The reaction of the Communist nations was predictable. From Moscow came thunderous denunciations of the 'predatory colonial war' and stirring affirmations of solidarity with the Egyptian people, while the Yugoslavs accused Britain and France of 'international banditry'.[34] In China the regime organised massive demonstrations, involving millions of people. In one, delegations of workers from local factories marched around the walls of the British Embassy compound in Beijing, chanting 'Hands off Egypt!' and 'For world peace!'[35] Chairman Mao also offered Cairo £1.6 million in aid and an army of volunteers to help with 'military, medical or construction work'.[36]

More painful for the British, though, was the reaction from the Commonwealth. Although Australia's Robert Menzies was publicly supportive, he harboured private doubts about the wisdom of Eden's policy – misgivings that were shared in Wellington, where New Zealand's Sidney Holland found himself torn between loyalty to the 'old country' and his country's deep commitment to the United Nations. Among the nations of the old (or 'white') Commonwealth, it was Canada's prime minister, Louis St Laurent, who offered the most trenchant criticism. In a confidential message to

Eden, sent on 5 November, he expressed 'regret [that] you found it necessary to follow the course you are taking'. St Laurent, who was furious with the British, was particularly exercised by the fact that, as he saw it, 'the events in the Middle East have cloaked with a smoke screen the renewed brutal international crimes of the Soviets' and undermined the authority of the UN.[37] The reaction from the 'new' Commonwealth – namely India, Pakistan and Ceylon – was even worse. In Pakistan an energetic campaign, waged in the newspapers and on the streets, demanded withdrawal from the organisation.[38] Meanwhile India's prime minister, Jawaharlal Nehru, condemned the Anglo-French action as an 'affront to the Security Council and a violation of the United Nations Charter'. Warning that such military adventurism was 'likely to lead to the gravest possible consequences all over the world', he called on the UN to take robust action to prevent a wider war.[39]

But, for all the fulmination across Africa, Asia and elsewhere, the fate of the Suez operation would turn on the reaction in Washington, DC. The British and French had deliberately kept the United States in the dark about their plans, for fear of risking an explicit veto. London and Paris gambled that, when presented with a fait accompli, Washington would acquiesce. After all, they reasoned, the Americans would prefer Nasser gone, and they had accepted that under certain circumstances force might be necessary to restore international oversight over the canal.[40] Returning from Washington in late September, Harold Macmillan – who had worked alongside Eisenhower during the Second World War – assured his cabinet colleagues, 'I know Ike. He will lie doggo!'[41] He could not have been more wrong.

Eisenhower was travelling to an election rally in Richmond, Virginia, aboard the *Columbine*, the air force VC-121E Super Constellation that served as the presidential jet, when he was informed that Israeli forces had invaded Egypt. On landing, a clearly distracted president made a few cursory remarks to the waiting crowds before heading straight to the White House and a meeting with his secretary of state.[42] From the privacy of the Oval Office, the president vented his fury with the Israelis: 'Foster, you tell 'em, God-damn it, that we're going to apply sanctions, we're going to the United Nations, we're going to do everything that there is so we can stop this thing.'[43] When it came to the British, Ike recognised 'that much is on their side in their dispute with the Egyptians', but believed that 'nothing justifies double-crossing us'.[44] The next day, as the full extent of Anglo-French duplicity began to emerge, Eisenhower seethed. During a meeting to discuss the impact of the crisis on European oil supplies, for instance, the president growled that those responsible for the difficulties 'should be left to work out their own oil problems – to boil in their own oil, so to speak'.[45]

America opposed the Anglo-French intervention on several grounds. First, Eisenhower simply did not believe that there was an 'adequate cause for war'. As he explained, the British case would have been much stronger 'if the Egyptians had not simply nation-alised the Canal, and then operated it effectively afterward'.[46] Sec-ond, under the terms of the Tripartite Agreement of 1950 the United States now faced the unpalatable prospect of having to intervene to assist Egypt, or risk Nasser seeking help from the USSR. And if the Soviets got involved then, as Eisenhower put it, 'the Mid East fat would really be in the fire'. Indeed, by inflaming the Arab and Muslim world, the Anglo-French action threatened to undermine the entire US effort to contain Soviet influence in the region.[47] Given the strength of feeling across Asia and Africa, the Americans were left in an extremely awkward position. As John Foster Dulles told the National Security Council, if the United States was seen to support the Anglo-French effort to 'reassert by force colonial control over the less developed nations', then their attempts to win the allegiance of the newly independent nations (at the expense of the USSR) would lie in ruins. But the alternative – breaking with her 'oldest and most trusted allies' – was no easy matter.[48] Finally, the timing of the operation, just days before the presidential election (in which Eisenhower was campaigning as the candidate of 'peace and prosperity') and in the midst of a major crisis in Eastern Europe, could not have been worse.[49]

There is, though, reason to believe that the Americans would have (reluctantly) accepted the Anglo-French intervention if the operation had secured its aims quickly.[50] In a letter to Eden, drafted on the evening of 30 October but never sent, Eisenhower – working from the assumption that the military strike would be quick and decisive – explained that while it was 'hard . . . to see any good final result emerging from a scheme that seems certain to antagonize the entire Moslem world . . . I think I faintly understand and I certainly deeply sympathize with you in the problem you have to solve'. 'Now', he wrote, 'we must pray that everything comes out both justly and peacefully.'[51] Interviewed in 1964, Eisenhower claimed that 'had they done it quickly, we would have accepted it . . . They could have taken over and then got out . . . There'd have been no great crisis in the world.'[52]

Eden had grasped the need for any military operation to be swift, telling his cabinet colleagues on 24 October that the inevitable reaction in the Arab world, together with 'the international pressures which would develop against our continuation of the operation', meant that military action would have to be 'quick and successful'.[53] Unfortunately, however, Operation Musketeer proved somewhat pedestrian. In order to maintain the pretence of 'peacekeeping' (which no one believed), the Mediterranean fleet – a vast armada of 130 warships, as well as supply vessels, merchant ships and other support craft – was only permitted to set sail from Malta after the ultimatum had been issued. It would take six days to reach the Egyptian coast. At the last minute, options for speeding up the troop landings were suggested but, amidst concerns about Egyptian resistance, they were abandoned.[54] Rather than striking a quick and decisive blow, the long-drawn-out operation enabled a full-blown diplomatic crisis to break.

The United Nations headquarters, in New York's Turtle Bay, is dominated by the Secretariat Building, a Corbusier-inspired modernist skyscraper, thirty-nine storeys high, sculpted from blue marble, aluminium and green curtain glass. Behind it, facing directly onto the East River, is the four-storey Conference Building, which houses the Security Council Chamber – a gift from the government of Norway. The long, narrow room is dominated by Peter Krogh's giant mural which hangs on the east wall, directly behind the iconic circular table around which the Council's delegates sit.[55] Featuring a phoenix rising from the ashes of war, it represented the possibility of creating a new world, based on peace, co-operation and mutual respect. On the afternoon of Tuesday 30 October, Krogh's mural provided the backdrop for one of the most dramatic meetings in the organisation's short life. Britain's representative, Sir Pierson Dixon, looking 'white and drawn' and speaking, it was said, 'almost apologetically', attempted to defend the Anglo-French position. Dixon's arguments were brushed aside by his American counterpart, Henry Cabot Lodge, Jr, who tabled a resolution calling on Israel and Egypt 'immediately to cease fire' and enjoining all UN member states to 'refrain from the use of force or threat of force in the area'. In a shameful first, Britain and France used their status as permanent members to veto the resolution, leaving Paris and London in the extraordinary position of lining up against both the United States and the Soviet Union.[56] But they were unable to prevent the Security Council from referring the issue to the UN General Assembly, which convened in emergency session – for the first time in its history – on 1 November.[57]

That evening, John Foster Dulles rose to introduce a cease-fire resolution. 'I doubt that any delegate', he explained, 'ever spoke from this forum with as heavy a heart as I have brought here tonight. We speak on a matter of vital importance, where the United States finds itself unable to agree with three nations

with whom it has ties, deep friendships, admiration and respect.'
Indeed, two of those nations were 'our oldest, most trusted and
reliable allies'. Nevertheless, Dulles continued, the Anglo-French
intervention was completely unacceptable: 'If, whenever a nation
feels that it has been subjected to injustice, it should have the right
to resort to force . . . then I fear we should be tearing the [UN]
Charter to shreds.'[58] Sixty-four nations voted in favour of the resolution (only Australia and New Zealand joined the UK, France
and Israel in opposing the measure), leaving the European powers
isolated.[59]

Back in London, Sir Anthony Eden was also facing serious
domestic difficulties. During an acrimonious debate in the House
of Commons on 31 October, for instance, the Labour leader
Hugh Gaitskell had accused Eden of endangering the unity of
the Commonwealth, undermining the Anglo-American alliance
and disregarding the UN Charter. He also raised the possibility
of 'collusion between the British and French Governments and
the Government of Israel'. There was certainly no chance of cross-
party support: 'I must now tell the Government and the country
that we cannot support the action that they have taken and that
we shall feel bound, by every constitutional means at our disposal,
to oppose it.'

The following day, as the Commons debated a motion of censure (which the government won by 324 votes to 255), the atmosphere became so charged – with members 'howling with anger'
and 'shaking their fists' – that the Speaker was forced to suspend
the sitting for thirty minutes, to allow tempers to cool.[60] In the
Lords, meanwhile, the Archbishop of Canterbury, Dr Geoffrey
Fisher, asked repeatedly whether the nation was doing the 'right
thing'. 'The point to which the Christian conscience must acutely
address itself', he said, 'is whether or not we are standing to the
spirit of the United Nations Charter.'[61] Eden, though, remained
firm. In a message to the nation broadcast on the evening of 3

November, he claimed that it would soon become 'apparent to everybody that we acted rightly and wisely'. Eden continued:

> All my life I have been a man of peace, working for peace, striving for peace. I have been a League of Nations man and a United Nations man, and I am still the same man, with the same convictions, the same devotion to peace. I could not be other, even if I wished, but I am utterly convinced that the action we have taken is right.

'We have', he explained, 'stepped in because the United Nations could not do so in time. If the United Nations will take over the police action we shall welcome it.'[62]

Although the *Daily Mail, Express* and *Telegraph* all lined up behind Eden, *The Times*, earlier so bullish, was now more circumspect, quoting Winston Churchill to the effect that you must 'never . . . mislead your ally'.[63] The *Economist, Spectator, Mirror* and *Daily Herald* opposed the action, while the *Observer*, under the editorship of David Astor, offered the most wounding criticism of all.[64] In an infamous editorial, published on 4 November, the paper claimed the British and French were acting like 'gangsters', accused the Conservative government of 'folly and crookedness' and called on Eden to resign.[65]

In truth, the country was bitterly divided, and the conflict cut across class, party and generational lines. An opinion poll at the start of November showed 37 per cent supporting military action, with 44 per cent against and 19 per cent undecided (though once the troops were in action, the public rallied around).[66] Many Britons argued it out on the streets. At the University of Edinburgh, for example, pro- and anti-war students exchanged arguments, and occasional blows, in a series of heated altercations on the university quadrangle. In Leeds, two hundred students – led by members of the university's Arab Society – staged a lunchtime march from the university to the city centre, demanding 'Hands off Egypt!' and

'Stop aggression!' In Manchester, hundreds converged on the city's Free Trade Hall for an anti-war rally – braving insults, burning sacks of paper, buckets of cold water and even the odd firework thrown by angry counter-demonstrators.[67] Twelve hundred factory workers in Crawley, the West Sussex new town, downed tools, while in Liverpool a torchlight procession of a thousand celebrated the council's adoption of an anti-war resolution. The National Union of Mineworkers, the Fire Brigades Union, the Amalgamated Engineering Union, the Transport and General Workers Union and the British Council of Churches all came out against the government's actions.[68] The most famous anti-war demonstration took place in Trafalgar Square on Sunday 4 November, where a vast crowd, shouting 'Eden must go!' and 'Law not war!' heard Labour's Aneurin Bevan ask whether Britain was 'prepared to accept for ourselves the logic we are applying to Egypt? If nations more powerful than ourselves accept this anachronistic attitude, and launch bombs on London, what answer have we got?' During clashes with police, twenty-seven people were arrested and eight officers injured.[69]

Selwyn Lloyd recalled that as the cabinet convened in Downing Street that evening, they could hear the noise of the demonstration in the background: 'there was a steady hum of noise and then every few minutes a crescendo and an outburst of howling or booing'. Eden brought disquieting news that, earlier that day, the UN General Assembly had passed two further resolutions. The first, sponsored by Canada, called on the secretary general, Dag Hammarskjöld, to submit a plan for a United Nations Emergency Force that would 'secure and supervise the cessation of hostilities'. The second, put forward by India, reaffirmed the ceasefire demand of 2 November and called for compliance within twelve hours.[70] The Canadian resolution caused considerable difficulties for Eden since, having offered public support for a UN force just twenty-four hours earlier (on the assumption that it would take weeks to prepare), he could hardly now reject it out of hand.[71] Faced with the momentous decision of whether or not to continue with military action, the prime minister and other senior colleagues now argued that the presence of Anglo-French troops on the ground was a necessary precondition for any viable UN force.[72] Nevertheless, the strains were starting to show.[73] While twelve ministers (including Eden, Macmillan and Lloyd) were all for going ahead with the parachute landings scheduled for the following day, four favoured a twenty-four-hour postponement in the hope that the UN would accept the Anglo-French force as the 'advance guard' of the UNEF; two supported abandoning military action altogether.[74] With a majority in favour, the landings went ahead. In his message to Eisenhower, justifying the decision to press on, Eden reiterated that:

> If we had allowed things to drift, everything would have gone from bad to worse. Nasser would have become a kind of Moslem Mussolini and our friends in Iraq, Jordan, Saudi Arabia and even Iran would gradually have been brought down. His efforts would have spread westwards, and Libya and all North Africa would have been brought under his control.

'I am sure', Eden declared, 'that this is the moment to curb Nasser's ambitions. If we let it pass, all of us will bitterly regret it.'[75]

Eisenhower was unmoved. Indeed, his determination to secure a peaceful resolution to the crisis was stiffened by alarming news that the Soviet Union was contemplating a dramatic intervention of her own. In a letter sent to Ben-Gurion, Eden and Mollet on 5 November, Nikolai Bulganin accused Britain and France of using Suez as a pretext to re-establish 'colonial slavery' across the Arab world, and warned that Moscow was 'fully determined to crush the aggressors by the use of force'.[76] In a separate note to Eisenhower, the Soviet premier made the extraordinary suggestion that the two superpowers embark on co-ordinated military action in order to 'terminate further bloodshed' and 'restore peace and tranquillity'.[77]

In the White House, the Soviet antics went down very badly. The last thing that Eisenhower wanted was for the Red Army to establish a foothold in the Middle East, and he worried that if Moscow did intervene, the Suez crisis could spiral out of control. According to one aide, the president even declared that 'if those fellows start something, we may have to hit them – and, if necessary with everything in the bucket'. In the Mediterranean, the Sixth Fleet – which was capable of launching nuclear weapons – was placed on full alert, and the entire American navy was readied to implement emergency war plans. Meanwhile, the White House released a carefully crafted statement dismissing the Soviet suggestion of a joint military operation in Egypt as 'unthinkable', and making it clear that if Soviet forces entered the Middle East without a UN mandate it would 'be the duty of all United Nations members', including the US, to oppose them.[78]

Within twenty-four hours Eisenhower had his ceasefire. Britain's diplomatic isolation, and severe economic pressures, had left her in an impossible position. According to Selwyn Lloyd, on hearing news that diplomats at the UN were discussing possible oil sanctions on Britain, Harold Macmillan 'threw his arms in the air and said, "Oil sanctions! That finishes it"'. On 6 November, just before the cabinet met, Macmillan declared that, given the considerable financial and economic pressures, they had no choice but to stop. During the first week of November, Britain had lost 5 per cent of its gold and foreign currency reserves in a desperate attempt to shore up the value of the pound (then a reserve currency) against international speculators. Macmillan also told his colleagues that the American treasury secretary was blocking access to a vital bridging loan from the International Monetary Fund until the British agreed to a ceasefire.[79] To continue fighting risked economic ruin. Having been forced into a humiliating climbdown, Britain suffered further indignity when her attempts to participate in the UNEF were vetoed by Eisenhower, who insisted on an unconditional withdrawal.[80] The attempt to restore international control to the Suez Canal and to topple Nasser – or, at least, clip his wings – had ended in disaster. Even worse, it had left the Western alliance bitterly divided, and had distracted international and diplomatic attention, at what turned out to be a critical moment in the Hungarian crisis.

19

OPERATION WHIRLWIND

Budapest was like a nail being driven into my head.
NIKITA KHRUSHCHEV

At nine o'clock on the morning of Thursday 1 November 1956, members of President Eisenhower's National Security Council gathered in the Cabinet Room, in the West Wing of the White House, to discuss the fast-moving international situation. Just twenty minutes earlier, Secretary of State John Foster Dulles had confidently assured the president that the Hungarian crisis had 'largely resolved itself' and recommended switching attention to the Middle East.[1] The decision seemed sensible enough: over the past few days, the US government had received a flurry of encouraging updates on Hungary. The previous morning Spencer Barnes, the chargé d'affaires in Budapest, had reported that 'personal observations' together with 'newspaper stories and radio content tend to confirm complete Soviet troop withdrawals'. It was, he declared, 'virtually certain' that the Hungarian revolution was 'now a fact of history'.[2] As the meeting began, the CIA's Allen Dulles could not contain his excitement, exclaiming that what had happened in Hungary was little short of 'a miracle'.[3]

Dulles's elation was more than matched on the streets of Budapest, where many Hungarians were jubilant at news that Soviet troops would be withdrawing from the country. The faces of the country's 'freedom fighters' were, *Time* magazine explained, 'lit with a kind of ecstasy'.[4] On the afternoon of 31 October, Imre Nagy had told the crowds outside parliament that 'the revolution of which you were the heroes has been won! . . . We are living in the first days of our sovereignty and independence.'[5] Over the next

few days Hungarians embraced their newfound freedoms enthusiastically. Political parties, representing all shades of opinion,
'sprang up in a ferment of discussion and organization'. Dozens
of new newspapers appeared on the streets – run by independent
editors, and featuring 'clashes of opinion, full-blooded polemics,
[and] hard-hitting commentaries', they were a world away from
the drab and dreary news-sheets that had characterised the Stalinist era.[6] But, amidst the elation, more circumspect voices could be
heard. Many workers' councils and revolutionary committees, for
instance, refused to call off their strikes or lay down their arms until
Soviet troops had completed their withdrawal; others declared that
they would judge the government on its 'deeds' rather than its
words, and wait 'to see what happens'. According to Sir Leslie Fry,
the British ambassador, 'the spirit of Budapest' was one of 'cautious expectancy, with no (repeat no) dropping of guard'.[7] Such
caution proved well judged.

On the morning of 31 October, members of the Presidium
gathered in their meeting room on the second floor of the Senate building – a neoclassical structure famed for its green dome,
oval hallways and magnificent internal courtyards, which stands in
the northern part of the Kremlin, adjacent to Red Square. Nikita
Khrushchev was, as usual, seated in a leather chair at the head of
a long, rectangular table topped with baize. The Soviet leader had
barely slept for days – Budapest was, he said, 'like a nail being
driven into my head'. Now he told his colleagues that they should
're-examine' their earlier assessment and 'not withdraw our troops
from Hungary'. Instead, the Soviet Union should 'take the initiative in restoring order'. The comrades agreed, and Marshal Zhukov, the defence minister, was immediately authorised to 'prepare
a plan of measures'.[8]

What lay behind this dramatic U-turn? For one thing, the Soviet
leadership had become convinced that the situation was careering
out of control. On 30 October, Anastas Mikoyan and Mikhail

Suslov had warned their Presidium colleagues that the 'political situation in the country and in Budapest is not getting better; it is getting worse'. The MDP was in a state of collapse, 'hooligan elements' had become 'more insolent', factories and public transportation lay idle, and 'students and other resistance elements' had begun to seize control of vital institutions, including radio stations and newspaper printing plants.[9] These fears were exacerbated that evening when Khrushchev and his colleagues learned of the appalling violence that had taken place outside the headquarters of the Budapest Communist Party: twenty-three ÁVH officers had been lynched, and Imre Mező, the well-respected Budapest Party secretary (and supporter of Nagy's government) fatally wounded.[10] *Life* magazine's John Sadovy, who witnessed the dreadful scenes, described how half a dozen young officers – one of whom struck him as 'very good looking' – emerged from the building. The men begged for mercy as their shoulder boards were unceremoniously ripped from their uniforms. Suddenly, one of the officers slumped, shot at point-blank range. Within moments, the entire party 'went down like corn that had been cut . . . When they were on the ground the rebels were still loading lead into them.' Sadovy explained how 'tears started to come down my cheeks. I had spent three years in the war, but nothing I saw then could compare with the horror of this.' The horror, though, was not quite finished: finally, the bleeding corpse of a high-ranking ÁVH officer was strung up from a tree by its feet and spat upon. As Sadovy made his way back through the park, he 'saw women looking for their men among the bodies on the ground. I sat down on a tree trunk. My knees were beginning to give in, as if I was carrying a weight I couldn't carry any more.'[11]

For Moscow, this atrocity was evidence that things had gone 'too far'. With their faith in Nagy's ability to restore order shaken, they concluded that socialism in Hungary was in danger of being 'strangled'.[12] (The violence also had a transformative effect on

Mao: having previously counselled that 'the working class of Hungary' should be allowed to 'regain control of the situation', he now urged the Soviets to crack down hard.[13])

The Kremlin also feared that the instability in Hungary was threatening to spill over into the rest of its Eastern European empire.[14] In the GDR, for instance, the authorities worried over 'anti-government protests' among students, intellectuals and workers; there were reports of unrest in Czechoslovakia, and the Bulgarian security services warned that journalists, intellectuals and even many Party members admired the 'bravery of the Hungarian . . . people' and looked forward 'with great happiness for such events to occur in our country'.[15] Romania, whose Communist regime was repressive even by the standards of the Soviet bloc, had particular reason to be fearful, given the country's significant ethnic Hungarian minority. There were small demonstrations in the capital, Bucharest, as well as in the provincial centres of Iași and Cluj, but the most significant protests took place in the western city of Timișoara, whose population of 140,000 included thirty thousand ethnic Hungarians.[16] On the afternoon of Tuesday 30 October, two thousand students gathered in the dining hall of the Polytechnic Institute for a mass meeting. Soon they were shouting 'Hands off Hungary!' and 'What are the Russians doing with our uranium and oil?' and calling for the withdrawal of the Red Army from Romania. During the debate, troops from the feared Securitate sealed off the campus and, when the meeting ended at 8 p.m., arrested the most prominent student leaders. The next day eight hundred students, marching seven abreast and shouting 'We want our colleagues!' set off towards the cathedral. As they crossed over the Bega canal, they were ambushed by bayonet-wielding troops, who arrested the demonstrators *en masse* and loaded them into waiting trucks. More than two dozen students would serve jail sentences of between three and eight years for 'sedition against the popular regime', and a further eighty were expelled. The crackdown in Timişoara, along with a tightening of security and the granting of minor concessions across the country, forestalled a nationwide revolution.[17]

Finally, Moscow was concerned about the international ramifications of the Hungarian revolution. Amid signs that Hungary might seek to withdraw from the Warsaw Pact, Khrushchev fretted about 'capitalists on the frontier of the Soviet Union'. Such a setback would only be magnified by what Moscow believed to be an imminent victory for the 'imperialists' in Egypt, where early reports indicated major military successes for the British and the French. As Khrushchev explained during the Presidium meeting of 31 October, 'if we depart from Hungary, it will give a great boost to the Americans, English, and French – the imperialists. They will perceive it as a weakness on our part and will go on the offensive . . . To Egypt they will then add Hungary.' The Suez crisis was not, in the final analysis, the decisive factor in Soviet policy-making. But the diversion of the world's attention to the Middle East, and the divisions in the Western alliance, certainly presented the Soviet leadership with an opportune moment to strike.[18]

When Anastas Mikoyan returned to Moscow on the evening of 31 October and learned of the decision to invade, he was beside himself. He begged Khrushchev to reconsider, warning that the intervention would be a 'terrible mistake' that would 'undermine the reputation of our state and our party'. Early the next morning, as Khrushchev walked from his Lenin Hills dacha to the enormous black ZIS-110 limousine that was waiting for him, Mikoyan (who lived next door) accosted the first secretary once again, warning that 'if blood is shed, I don't know what I'll do with myself'. (Khrushchev believed he was hinting at suicide, Mikoyan later insisted he was simply threatening to resign.) But the decision stood: 'We have to act', explained Khrushchev. 'We have no other course.'[19]

Word of Soviet troop movements reached Budapest as early as 31 October. Indeed, Imre Nagy later claimed that, just hours before addressing the crowds on Kossuth Square, he had received reports of pontoon bridges being installed on the Upper Tisza River and motorised units, tanks and artillery 'streaming into the interior'.[20] That same day, Radio Free Miskolc broadcast claims that Soviet anti-aircraft units, tanks and troops were entering the country. By 1 November, with talk of troops massing along the Hungarian frontier and widespread rumours that Soviet forces were digging in on the outskirts of Budapest, the jubilation of earlier days gave way to anxiety. Everyone was now asking if the Red Army was poised to return.[21]

Nagy and his allies pressed Yuri Andropov repeatedly about the reported troop movements, but the Soviet ambassador's evasions only deepened their suspicions. Nagy had, on 31 October, formally requested negotiations for the withdrawal of Soviet forces from 'the entire territory of Hungary'.[22] Now, faced with an ever more desperate situation, he decided on a final roll of the dice. At 7.50 p.m., Hungarian radio broadcast a message in which Nagy declared Hungary's neutrality and expressed the country's desire to 'live in true friendship with its neighbours, the Soviet Union, and all the peoples of the world', outside of any 'power bloc'.[23] He also appealed to the United Nations secretary general for help in 'defending the country's neutrality'.[24]

The UN gambit was never likely to yield meaningful results. The USSR, like the other permanent members, possessed a Security Council veto and although resolutions could be passed by a simple majority vote in the General Assembly, they were non-binding. Divisions among the Western powers further stymied Hungarian hopes. When Britain and France attempted to refer the Hungarian question to the General Assembly, for example, they did so – in part – to deflect criticism over their own military intervention in Egypt. John Foster Dulles, who actually blocked this move, was contemptuous: 'they want the limelight off them. I think it's a mockery for them to come in, with bombs falling over Egypt, and denounce the Soviet Union . . . I want no part of it.' The Americans relented only after the Soviet invasion had begun. But while the resolutions passed by the General Assembly on 4 and 9 November condemned the Soviet Union and called for it to withdraw its troops, it amounted to little more than whistling in the wind.[25]

Even as it was moving thousands of troops, tanks and artillery into Hungary, Moscow kept up the pretence that a negotiated solution was possible. On the afternoon of 3 November, senior Red Army officers even arrived at the parliament to discuss troop withdrawals. The talks appeared to go well, and it was decided to reconvene later that evening at Soviet army headquarters in Tököl, on the outskirts of Budapest. The Hungarians, though, had walked into a trap. Just before midnight a dozen Soviet police, under the personal command of the KGB's Ivan Serov, burst into the room armed with sub-machine guns and placed the Hungarian military delegation, including the recently appointed defence minister, Pál Maléter, under arrest.[26]

At 4 a.m. on Sunday 4 November, Marshal Ivan Konev, the supreme commander of Soviet forces in Hungary, issued the code-word, 'Thunder-444', that unleashed Operation Whirlwind. The Soviet Union deployed sixty thousand troops, thousands of tanks and armoured units and two air force divisions in a decisive display of force, much of it concentrated on Budapest.[27] At 5.20 a.m., with Soviet tanks rumbling through the capital, Radio Free Kossuth broadcast a final, desperate message from Imre Nagy. Speaking live from the Parliament building, with the sound of gunfire crackling in the background, the prime minister explained: 'In the early hours of this morning, Soviet troops launched an attack against our capital city with the obvious intention of overthrowing the legal democratic Hungarian Government. Our troops are fighting. The Government is in its place. I inform the people of the country and the world . . . of this.'[28] There followed repeated appeals to Soviet troops to refrain from firing on civilians. At 8.10

a.m., the station went off air, to the sound of a woman exclaiming, 'Help Hungary. . . Help, help, help.' A Vienna monitoring station picked up the final appeal made from the last rebel-held radio station that afternoon: 'Civilised people of the world. On the watchtower of 1,000-year-old Hungary the last flames begin to go out. Soviet tanks and guns are roaring over Hungarian soil . . . Save Our Souls.'[29]

At day's end the Soviet defence minister, Marshal Zhukov, updated the Central Committee. Red Army units had, he said, 'mastered the most stubborn points of the reaction in the provinces' – including Győr, Miskolc and Debrecen – while radio stations, military facilities and other key sites had been occupied. In Budapest, strategic positions including bridges and major buildings had been secured and, with the exception of 'one large hotbed of resistance' around the Corvin Cinema, the 'resistance of the insurgents' had been broken.[30] Zhukov's report was slightly optimistic – fierce fighting continued in Kispest and Csepel Island for several days, while the factory workers of Dunapentele, an industrial town forty miles south of the capital, held out until 11 November. But, seventy-two hours after the Soviet assault had begun, the revolution had, to all intents and purposes, been crushed.[31]

Imre Nagy knew that there was no hope of repelling the invasion. To minimise loss of life and to protect the country's infrastructure and resources, he declined to order Hungarian troops into combat. The result was that as Operation Whirlwind unfolded, the bulk of Hungary's armed forces remained in their barracks, where they were quickly overpowered and disarmed by Soviet troops. Some soldiers did take up arms – most famously the Budapest unit led by General Béla Király, the army's commander-in-chief – but the majority of the resistance came from some fifteen thousand rebels, mainly students and young factory workers.[32]

The fighting was brutal. Writing in the French daily *France-soir*,

Michel Gordey described how, in the early hours of 4 November, the horizon was lit up with 'sinister flames' and for three hours the 'ground shook' as 'one explosion followed upon the other'.[33] The streets of Budapest were filled with Soviet tanks, artillery fire rained down from the hills above Buda and jet fighters, swooping low over the city, strafed rebel positions. The Kilián Barracks, Corvin Cinema and other rebel strongholds were subjected to savage assaults, but everywhere resistance was met with massive force.[34] Gordey described how:

> The tanks, in a roar of thunder, bore down upon the houses from which shots were being fired, pointing their guns first at the ground floor, then at the first floor, the second, and the third. Six, eight, ten cannon shots . . . The houses were blown apart and crumbled; the inhabitants were either killed, or lay wounded on the ground.[35]

The *Daily Worker*'s Peter Fryer, one of a number of journalists holed up in the British Embassy, explained how 'for four days and nights Budapest was under continuous bombardment. I saw a once lovely city battered, bludgeoned, smashed and bled into submission.'[36] Some of the city's most beautiful buildings suffered major damage, while others were looted.[37] In some areas of the capital, the streets were littered with bodies.[38] Many of the dead and injured were civilians who had been caught up in the violence, and some of the Soviet firing was indiscriminate – trained 'on lighted windows by night, at any gathering of persons in the street, and even on bread queues'. A number of churches and hospitals, including a children's clinic, were destroyed.[39]

In all, an area of about two square miles in Pest was utterly devastated by the fighting, as were many of Buda's neighbourhoods. The streets, which had been ploughed up by Soviet tanks, were 'strewn with the detritus of a bloody war: rubble, glass and bricks, spent cartridges and shell-cases'. Virtually every house along some of the city's main thoroughfares had been destroyed, many apartment blocks had been reduced to 'complete ruins', and 'in building after building' there were 'gaping shell holes like eye sockets'.[40] There was a heavy price, too, in terms of blood: an estimated 2,700 Hungarians lost their lives (1,500 of them civilians) during the fighting, with a further 20,000 injured; Soviet casualties were reported as 720 killed and 1,540 wounded.[41]

With the armed resistance crushed, the Kremlin installed a 'Revolutionary Worker and Peasant Government' headed by János Kádár and Ferenc Münnich. The two men, who had served in Nagy's short-lived administration, had been spirited out of Hungary on the evening of 1 November aboard a military aircraft and flown to Moscow for discussions with Soviet leaders. During these talks, Kádár agreed that it would be unconscionable to 'surrender a socialist country to counter-revolution' and claimed that 'hour by hour' the situation in Hungary was 'moving rightward', but he also warned that the use of military force would be 'destructive'. It would, he said, 'erode the morale' of Hungarian Communists to 'zero' and undermine Communist authority throughout the Eastern Bloc. In the end, he put his doubts to one side, justifying the invasion as a fight against fascism. Once the uprising was crushed, he led efforts to pacify the country and re-establish the one-party state.[42]

Although the fight against the Red Army was soon lost, Hungarians were reluctant to abandon their revolution. Posters ridiculing the country's new leader soon appeared all over Budapest. One read:

Wanted: Premier for Hungary. Qualifications: no sincere conviction, no backbone; ability to read and write not required, but must be able to sign documents drawn up by others. Applications should be addressed to Messrs Khrushchev and Bulganin.[43]

There was, though, nothing satirical about the waves of strikes and worker unrest that now hit the country, organised by the workers' councils. These bodies, which had not been cowed by the Soviet invasion, continued to press for the withdrawal of foreign troops and the establishment of a free press, and now demanded an amnesty for all those involved in the uprising. Many ordinary Hungarians also made their feelings clear. On 23 November, between two and three in the afternoon, Budapest's citizens marked the one-month anniversary of the revolution by abandoning the city's streets. In the view of Sir Leslie Fry, 'no manifestation of a people's solidarity could have been more complete or more impressive: the city was seemingly deserted and traffic (apart from strong Russian military patrols) was at a standstill. At the end of the hour's silence, many people came back into the streets with their tricolours and sang their national anthem at the Russian soldiers.'[44] Two weeks later, in defiance of an official ban on protests, several thousand 'black-clad women' – many carrying little shopping bundles of bread, cabbages and onions, others shouting, 'We shall never be slaves' – converged on Heroes' Square to mourn the dead. A few of the women were permitted to place flowers on the tomb of the Unknown Soldier but 'when others pressed forward' Soviet troops fired into the air, dispersing the crowd.[45]

Initially, Kádár adopted a conciliatory approach. Arriving back in Budapest on 7 November, he announced substantial wage increases, the abolition of an unpopular tax and the restoration of 15 March as a national holiday honouring the revolution of 1848. He also recognised the workers' councils as 'organs of worker self-governance in the factories' (while denying them any broader political role) and engaged in negotiations with the recently formed Central Workers' Council of Greater Budapest (KMT).[46] This was, though, an attempt to buy time. By the end of November the Kádár regime was bearing down on 'troublemakers'. After learning that a number of miners had been killed while protesting in

Salgótarján, the KMT called a nationwide forty-eight-hour strike, which drew broad support. The government now struck a decisive blow: the KMT's leaders and other workers' council officials were arrested, restrictive new measures were imposed, a wave of reprisals was launched and in some factories Soviet troops were deployed to maintain order.[47]

As Kádár tightened his grip – setting up new security organs and 'people's courts', banning organisations and shutting down newspapers – prominent revolutionaries, student leaders and intellectuals were rounded up and thrown into prison.[48] Imre Nagy, granted asylum in the Yugoslav Embassy, was persuaded to leave after being promised amnesty. He was arrested immediately and later deported to Romania. Following a secret trial, Nagy, General Pál Maléter and the revolutionary journalist Miklós Gimes were hanged on 16 June 1958 and buried, face down and wrapped in tar paper, in an unmarked grave.[49] In all, twenty-two thousand people were jailed, hundreds executed and scores deported to prison camps inside the Soviet Union for their role in the revolution. Tens of thousands more were dismissed from their jobs, struggled to find work or faced harassment and police surveillance.[50] Meanwhile more than 150,000 Hungarians – many of them young, intelligent and ambitious – fled the country during the final, desperate weeks of 1956 (sparking an unprecedented international effort to assist them: the United States and Canada took sixty-eight thousand, the UK twenty-one thousand, and France, Germany and Australia more than ten thousand each).[51]

The events in Hungary transfixed the world. From the Vatican, Pope Pius XII issued an encyclical expressing the 'most bitter sorrow' at news of the Soviet attack on Hungary, whose citizens had, he claimed, 'yearned for a just freedom with all their hearts'.[52] From New York, the editors of *Time* chose the 'Hungarian Freedom Fighter' as the magazine's 'Man of the Year'. Lauding the revolutionaries for having 'fought for their country's freedom' against what they characterised as 'the most brutal tyranny on earth', they declared that 'history's greatest despotism' had been 'shaken' to its foundations, and history made to 'leap forward in 1956'.[53]

The Soviet invasion of 4 November also precipitated an outpouring of public sympathy across the globe. There were protests as far afield as Australia, Angola and Argentina.[54] In New York, ten thousand walked up Fifth Avenue on 4 November in a 'Death March' replete with pallbearers and a symbolic coffin, to honour Hungary's fallen. Three days later, a similar number rallied at Madison Square Garden, chanting 'We want action!'[55] In Europe, hundreds of thousands took to the streets of Paris, Rome, Brussels, West Berlin and other cities to condemn the Soviets and proclaim solidarity with Hungary.[56] In Copenhagen, a crowd of three thousand turned their backs on the Soviet Embassy; in Salzburg, thousands of high-school and college students marched silently through the city.[57] In Berne protesters hurled stones and burned a Soviet flag and demonstrators in Reykjavik pelted the Soviet Embassy with mud and vegetables.[58] In Luxembourg, on the evening of 6 November, a crowd of two thousand, carrying torches and placards that read 'Long live Hungary!' and 'Down with the Butchers of Budapest', marched to the Soviet Embassy. Around 7 p.m., a small group broke into the embassy grounds, tore down the Soviet flag and cut the electricity supply, whereupon angry crowds swarmed into the building, smashing windows, furniture, chandeliers and official cars, before order was restored. Although the government issued a formal apology, public opinion appeared 'basically unrepentant'.[59]

In Britain, Anglo-Soviet cultural events were cancelled or postponed; a flurry of resolutions emanated from local Labour Party branches, trade unions, universities and churches; Liverpool's dock workers refused to load rubber and other cargoes bound for the Soviet Union.[60] In Leeds, several hundred undergraduates marched through the city wearing black armbands. Some Britons were apparently eager to take on the Red Army. The 'British Universities Volunteer Force' even made plans to parachute students into Hungary, and a young woman working at a travel agency in York explained that she was 'a crack shot' and 'prepared to pay her own fare'. Most, though, adopted a more mundane approach – raising money for the humanitarian aid effort, donating food, blankets and clothes, and providing bedding, crockery, furniture and hospitality for Hungarian refugees. Alderman John Gilles Shield offered up Donnington Hall in Leicestershire for 150 Hungarian children, while a building firm in Wolverhampton provided a new semi-detached house rent-free.[61] 'Not since the Spanish [Civil] War', thundered Kingsley Martin from the pages of the *New Statesman*, 'has England seen so popular a revulsion of feeling as over the Hungarian tragedy.'[62] However, much of this anger – certainly at the official level – proved transitory: by the following spring, the diplomatic breach between Moscow and London had been restored, and an extensive programme of cultural, academic and professional exchanges had been resumed.[63]

The bitter conflict between Hungary and the USSR also spilled over into the Melbourne Olympics, which became one of the most controversial Games of the modern era. In what was the first politically motivated boycott of an Olympic Games, the Netherlands, Switzerland and Spain all withdrew in protest at Soviet actions (Egypt, Lebanon and Iraq also withdrew in protest at Suez, while China refused to participate after Taiwan was permitted to compete). For their part, the Hungarians, who had left for Australia before the Soviet invasion, insisted that a flag featuring the national coat of arms, rather than the Communist one, be flown at the athletes' village. Then, on 6 December, they took on the USSR in an ill-tempered water polo semi-final, played before a partisan crowd whose strong Hungarian contingent erupted in loud chants of '*Hajrá Magyarok!*' ('Go Hungarians!') Towards the end of the

match, with the Hungarians winning 4–0, Valentin Prokopov
struck Ervin Zádo in the face, leaving him dazed and with a nasty
gash above the eye. As he exited the pool with blood dripping from
the wound, the crowd appeared ready to riot: the police quickly
intervened and the match was abandoned. The Hungarians, who
were awarded the victory, went on to win gold the following day.
When the games were over, almost half of the country's Olympi-
ans decided not to return home.[64]

The Hungarian people may have won much of the world's admiration, but what they desperately wanted was military support.
Although President Eisenhower praised the courage and commitment of the revolutionaries, there was never any prospect of him
despatching American troops.[65] Indeed, he was so concerned that
the Soviets would be 'tempted to resort to very extreme measures
and even to precipitate global war' that he authorised John Foster
Dulles to make it clear that the United States did not view the
satellite countries as 'potential military allies' – a signal to Moscow
that the US had no intention of intervening.[66] In his memoirs, Ike
explained that, given the geopolitical realities, 'we could do nothing. Sending United States troops alone into Hungary through
hostile or neutral territory would have involved us in general war.'
Meanwhile, if the UN had somehow managed to circumvent a
Soviet veto to authorise the use of force, then the result might have
been nuclear war. America then, did 'the only thing it could: We
readied ourselves in every possible way to help the refugees fleeing
from the criminal actions of the Soviets, and did everything possible to condemn the aggression.'[67]

Millions of Hungarians, though, felt betrayed. After all, the
Eisenhower administration had talked publicly about 'liberating'
the 'captive peoples' of Eastern Europe, and during the uprising
Radio Free Europe had actively encouraged the Hungarians, providing advice on anti-tank warfare and lauding the 'freedom fighters'. Some broadcasts had even hinted at Western support – if only

the Hungarians could hold out for a few more days.[68] It was little wonder that those listening, or who heard about the broadcasts second-hand, believed that help from America and her allies was imminent. When it never arrived, many felt badly let down, while others chided themselves for their naïveté.[69]

On the evening of 24 October, as the first stages of the Hungarian revolution were unfolding, John Foster Dulles had worried 'that it will be said that here are the great moments and when they came and these fellows were ready to stand up and die, we were caught napping and doing nothing'.[70] His fears were well placed. The Hungarian uprising cruelly exposed the flaws in the Eisenhower administration's goal of ending Soviet domination of Eastern Europe. As the political scientist Charles Gati has pointed out, despite all the talk about 'liberating' the satellites and 'rolling back' Soviet influence, when the 'moment of truth' arrived 'there were no plans whatever on the shelves, no diplomatic initiatives had been prepared, and of course no consideration was given to any form of military assistance . . . In the end, the White House had little to say and nothing to offer.'[71] All the Americans could do was seek solace in the fact that, by intervening so brutally, the Soviets had damaged Communism's international appeal.[72] As a *New York Times* editorial put it, 'The Hungarians have put a brand upon communism as a philosophy of life and government from which it can never recover.'[73]

In the event, Communism's romantic, revolutionary appeal would receive an unexpected boost from a rebellion that broke out just a few dozen miles off the Florida coast.

Fidel Castro (*top centre*) and his compañeros in the Sierra Maestra, Cuba.

Credit: Gilberto Ante

20

SIERRA MAESTRA

In 1956 we will be free or we will be martyrs.

FIDEL CASTRO

In the early hours of Sunday 25 November 1956 a creaking twin-engined leisure yacht set sail from Tuxpan, on Mexico's eastern shore, headed for Cuba. At fifty-eight feet long and with limited deck space, a modest lounge area and just four small cabins, the *Granma* was designed to accommodate fewer than two dozen people. Packed aboard the boat that night, however, were eighty-two men, all members of the 26th of July Movement (M-26-7), a vanguard organisation committed to ending the rule of President Fulgencio Batista, Cuba's American-backed strongman. Their leader was Fidel Castro, an enigmatic thirty-year-old lawyer and professional revolutionary, who had paid $15,000 for the vessel. The *compañeros* counted Fidel's younger brother, Raúl, and a young Argentine doctor, Ernesto 'Che' Guevara, among their number. Squeezed in among them was a substantial arsenal (two anti-tank guns, three Thompson machine guns, ninety rifles, more than three dozen pistols and ammunition), a small quantity of food and medical supplies, and some two thousand gallons of fuel stored in metal cans on deck.[1]

Just a few days earlier Mexican police had seized a cache of weapons and arrested several of the movement's activists during a raid on a rebel safe house in a well-heeled neighbourhood of the capital. Meanwhile severe storm warnings had led the local authorities to issue an order prohibiting all sea travel. With the police closing in and local officials on high alert, the *Granma*'s crew were keen to depart as quietly as possible. As she slipped away from her moorings, all the lights on board were turned out and the yacht was powered by just one engine, running at low speed. The young revolutionaries – 'crouched so closely together' that they were 'almost on top of each other' – held their breath as the boat made its way down the river and then across the harbour before reaching the Gulf of Mexico. Once they entered the open water, though, they permitted themselves a moment of emotional release. 'As one' they stood to sing first the Cuban national anthem and then the rousing 26 July hymn; its lines 'May Cuba reward our heroism, for we are soldiers who are going to free the Motherland' must have seemed especially poignant.[2]

The optimism was soon dampened as a combination of rough seas, strong winds and the poor state of the *Granma* threatened disaster. Almost the entire crew was afflicted by dreadful seasickness. As Che later explained, the 'whole boat assumed a ridiculous, tragic appearance' as, after a desperate and ultimately futile search for antihistamines, men clutched their stomachs or placed their heads in buckets, with others lying 'immobile' and 'in strange positions' on the deck, their 'clothes covered in vomit'.[3]

The boat also came perilously close to sinking. One comrade described how, as 'mountainous waves toyed with the small yacht', she began to ship water at an alarming rate. With the bilge pumps seemingly ineffective, the *compañeros* were forced to bail out the stricken craft. Moreover, the inclement weather and the wretched state of the boat's badly worn gears meant that the journey itself was painfully slow.[4] The original plan had been to land at Niquero, in the south-east of the island, on 30 November to coincide with a planned uprising in the nearby city of Santiago de Cuba. But they were hopelessly behind schedule and, with the ship's radio only able to receive messages, Castro's band of rebels could only sit and listen helplessly as a bulletin brought news that the revolution had begun without them. Cuba's second city had, in fact, awoken that morning 'under heavy fire' as up to three hundred activists launched their attack with 'weapons of every calibre . . . spitting fire and lead'. Under the direction of the youthful Frank País, and wearing their trademark drab olive-green fatigues and distinctive red-and-black armbands, they chanted, 'Down with Batista!' and 'Long live the revolution!' as they launched a series of attacks. The police station, the customs house and other public buildings came under fire, and, for a while, amidst widespread panic, the rebels were able to roam the city streets freely. It took several days and the arrival of 280 elite troops, airlifted in under the command of a senior military hardliner, to restore order. By then, the *Granma* had finally arrived on the island – although, in the words of one *compañero*, 'It wasn't a landing, it was a shipwreck.'[5]

The *Granma* eventually hit the Cuban coast as the first glimmers of dawn began to break on 2 December. With supplies of water, food and – critically – fuel almost exhausted, the situation aboard had become increasingly desperate. The rebels' predicament was not helped when, just hours before landing, Roberto Roque, a former naval lieutenant and the *Granma*'s second in command, lost his footing and plunged into the murky ocean. He was only saved when Fidel Castro ordered that the ship's searchlight be switched on – a risky act that might well have alerted the Cuban military to their presence. Rather than landing at Niquero, where allies were waiting with supplies and trucks, the *Granma* ran aground about a hundred yards from Playa de los Colorados, more than ten miles south of the agreed rendezvous. They could hardly have picked a worse spot. Forced to abandon most of their equipment, the *compañeros* – proudly wearing their new uniforms and boots and carrying rifles, knapsacks, cartridge belts and flasks – waded ashore through muddy salt water, only to find themselves faced with seemingly endless mangrove swamps where the 'thick, jumbled net' proved 'hard to penetrate'. It was, confessed Raúl Castro, 'Hell'. They struggled on for several hours before finally reaching dry land, exhausted, hungry and caked in mud. 'Everything', explained Fidel's confidant Faustino Pérez, 'had gone awry.'⁶

The rebels' only hope now was to reach the Sierra Maestra mountain range to the east, whose high peaks offered relative sanctuary and a chance to regroup. And so the ragged band of revolutionaries pushed on – often marching at night to avoid the attention of spotter planes, sucking on sugar cane for sustenance and, occasionally, receiving help from local peasant families. But, as Che put it, these were truly 'terrible days'. Malnourished, desperately thirsty and suffering from fungal infections and painful, open blisters, they were 'an army of shadows, ghosts'. By the morning of 5 December the party was on the verge of total collapse – some men were fainting, while others begged desperately for rest. There was no choice but to stop. They had reached a placed called Alegría de Pío ('Joy of the Pious'), nothing more than a 'small grove of trees, bordering a sugarcane field on one side and open to some valleys on the other, with dense woods starting farther back'.⁷ Most of the men stretched out and slept.

Later that afternoon Che was leaning against a tree, chatting to a comrade and munching on a couple of crackers and half a sausage, when the first shot rang out. Betrayed by a guide who had left the camp earlier in the day, the *compañeros* found themselves under attack from Batista's troops. As fighter jets swooped low over the woods, strafing the rebel position, an infantry unit opened fire. In the confusion, several revolutionaries were killed and others scrabbled desperately for cover. Wounded in the neck, Che returned fire with his rifle before dragging himself into the relative safety of an adjoining field. Just ten days after leaving Mexico, Castro's 'army' had been routed. His movement's boast that it would launch a revolution to overthrow the 'corrupt and criminal dictatorship' seemed utterly fantastical.⁸

Cuba, the biggest island in the Antilles, is an enchanting place of exceptional beauty but also, some say, one that labours under a curse. Although it had achieved nominal independence in 1898 after American forces 'liberated' the country from Spanish rule, the island had been run as a virtual colony of the United States for much of the subsequent half-century. Up until 1934 the US government reserved the legal right to interfere in Cuba's domestic affairs in the event of a breakdown in law and order or a threat to property rights. The United States also restricted Cuba's ability to make foreign policy and insisted on the right to maintain military bases on the island, including a major naval facility at Guantánamo Bay.[9] Even after relinquishing some of these formal powers, Uncle Sam continued to exercise a profound – some would say profoundly distorting – influence over the island's economy and political culture.[10]

On the surface, Cuba in the mid-1950s was actually doing rather well, thanks in large part to the post-war American economic boom. The price of sugar, Cuba's main export, had remained stable (it would rise significantly after the Suez Crisis) and crop yields had begun to increase, while a substantial growth in tourism from the United States had seen the construction of numerous hotels, casinos and clubs. Meanwhile Cuba's per capita income, literacy rates and life expectancy ranked among the highest in Latin America. But beneath this veneer of success lay some deep-seated problems. Cuba's economy was heavily over-reliant on sugar. It constituted 50 per cent of the island's agricultural production and 80 per cent of its exports (half its sugar was sold to the USA), employed almost a quarter of the workforce and accounted for about 30 per cent of GDP. US economic interests, worth some $1 billion (mostly in banking, utilities, mining, tourism and agriculture), also meant that much of the island's wealth was in the hands of foreign investors. Cuba's society, with its population of six million, was massively unequal. At the top were some nine hundred thousand who controlled 43 per cent of the nation's income, lived a life of luxury in their magnificent air-conditioned villas and could enjoy regular shopping excursions to Miami. Life for those at the bottom, though, could not have been more different. One and a half million Cubans either were unemployed, worked as landless labourers or eked out a living as subsistence farmers. With just 2 per cent of the nation's wealth between them, they often survived on a meagre diet of rice, beans and sugar-water.[11]

The island republic also faced some seemingly intractable political problems. Ever since independence her political institutions had been weak and there was a pervasive culture of gangsterism and corruption.[12] Aside from a brief period of democratic, constitutional rule from 1940 to 1952, Cuba's political culture was characterised by instability, intrigue and violence. The Cuban military and the interests of the United States often proved decisive when it came to the question of who was (or was not) permitted to govern. From 1934, when a self-styled 'revolutionary' government was overthrown by a group of Cuban army officers, through to the end of the 1950s, one man dominated Cuban politics – Fulgencio Batista.

Born in 1902, of mixed-race peasant stock, Batista joined the army as a private in 1921, following a stint as a labourer. A decade later he was appointed as a military court stenographer with the rank of sergeant and, in 1934, this ambitious opportunist rose to the very top by leading a military takeover of the government. Batista introduced a new constitution in 1940 and, four years later, stepped down from office in the aftermath of free elections in which the opposition Auténtico Party prevailed. But the ensuing eight years were extraordinarily corrupt, even when measured by the island's own appallingly low standards. The verdict of Louis Pérez, one of Cuba's leading historians, is unsparing: 'Embezzlement, graft, corruption, and malfeasance of public office permeated every branch of national, provincial, and municipal government.' In March 1952 Batista led a second coup, cancelled the scheduled elections and appointed himself president. During his first period in office he had embarked on progressive reforms, shown a willingness to co-operate with the Cuban Communist Party (the Partido Communista de Cuba, or PCC) and enjoyed a measure of public support. His second term, though, was quite different. Structural problems were ignored, corruption continued and, in the face of rising discontent, Batista turned to repression and brutality to maintain his position: the PCC was outlawed, the labour movement and civil organisations were co-opted and dissent was crushed.[13] In September 1955, the *New York Times* lamented that Batista, drunk on the 'heady wine of power', had sold his political soul to the 'devil of dictatorship'.[14] In the months leading up to the *Granma*'s expedition Cuba had been rocked by student protests, outbreaks of violence – including an armed assault on an army barracks and the assassination of the chief of military intelligence – and the uncovering of several anti-Batista plots. But this only brought fresh waves of repression and violence from the regime. The island was, it seemed, primed for revolution.[15]

One of the earliest challenges to Batista's second power-grab had actually come from none other than Fidel Castro. Born in 1926, Castro enjoyed a relatively privileged upbringing thanks to his father, Angel, a Galician immigrant, who had managed to pull himself up by his bootstraps to become a wealthy landowner. The young Fidel attended an elite high school in Havana before enrolling at the city's university in 1945 to study law. But Castro displayed a rebellious streak from an early age – refusing to take regular baths, clashing repeatedly with his parents and teachers; aged thirteen, he had even tried to organise a strike by his father's sugar workers. He also had a famously short temper. The university, whose magnificent buildings dominate Aróstegui Hill in the northern suburb of Vedado, provided an ideal environment for fashioning a revolutionary. According to Castro himself, he 'never attended lectures, never opened a book except just before examinations'; instead, he immersed himself in the cut and thrust of student radicalism. At a time when factional disputes – and even elections – were often settled violently, Castro became adept in the dark arts of street politics, participating in raucous protests, a pistol seldom far from his side. In the spring of 1948 he was arrested during an investigation into the murder of a local politician, but was released without charge. Castro, a prize-winning debater, also displayed an early penchant for the long, fiery speeches for which he would later become famous – although, in these days, he sported a pencil-thin moustache rather than a beard and donned fashionable, dark-coloured suits rather than olive-green fatigues.[16]

Castro, who had married Mirta Díaz Balart in October 1948, joined one of Havana's many law firms after graduating in 1950. But his first love was politics. Although he had shown some superficial interest in the ideas of Marx and Lenin, Castro was no Communist (or not yet, at least). Instead, he threw in his lot with the Ortodoxos, one of a number of left-wing parties that had sprung up in opposition to Batista. Inspired by Cuba's long struggle for independence, Castro railed against US imperialism in Latin America, attacked corruption and demanded 'justice for the workers and Cuban peasantry'. He was preparing to run for a seat in the lower house of Congress when Batista launched his coup and abruptly cancelled the elections. A few days later, the mercurial young lawyer distributed a manifesto denouncing this usurpation of power and calling for the restoration of the constitution. 'To live in chains', he declared, 'is to live in shame!' Sixteen months later, Castro's reputation for impetuosity, risk-taking and action would be on full display.[17]

Just after dawn on 26 July 1953, Castro led a daring assault on the Moncada Army Barracks in Santiago, whose crenellated walls housed the country's second largest military garrison. His plan was simple enough: use the element of surprise to seize the barracks, and its mighty arsenal, while most of the soldiers were still in their bunks; simultaneously, use smaller groups of fighters to occupy the

Palace of Justice next door, as well as the city's hospital and radio station; then demand a return to constitutional government while arousing 'the people' to join the rebellion. The plan may have been straightforward and daring, but it was also extremely foolhardy. Castro's band of 150 or so rebels – idealistic young men who had cut their teeth in student politics, as well as labourers, farm workers and a smattering of white-collar professionals, armed mainly with rifles – were never likely to overpower a heavily armed fortress and a thousand troops. In the event, Castro's plan unravelled almost immediately: his forces (all dressed as sergeants, in a nice send-up of Batista's own route to the top) were spotted by an army patrol car shortly after they arrived at the barracks. Within minutes, the rebels were pinned down by gunfire. Castro recalled that 'more than the shooting, I remember the deafening, bitter sounds of the alarm sirens that thwarted our plan'. Although he managed to escape, many of his companions were not so fortunate. More than sixty lost their lives – most of them after having been captured and then tortured. The treatment meted out by the army and security personnel was sickening: many prisoners were beaten with rifle butts, and at least three were dragged to their deaths behind a jeep. According to one widely believed story, Haydée Santamaría, one of two young women involved in the attempted putsch, was presented with an eye belonging to her brother, Abel, during her own interrogation (certainly Abel did not survive being taken prisoner). Her boyfriend, Boris de la Coloma, was also tortured to death. In the aftermath of the assault a number of civilians, wrongly suspected of involvement, were also rounded up; some were killed. Castro himself was finally caught on 1 August, while sleeping in a small hut on the outskirts of a farm; his life was spared only because the officer who captured him was, in contrast to many of his colleagues, a fundamentally decent man.[18]

Put on trial in the autumn, charged with organising an armed uprising against the 'Constitutional Powers of the State', Castro mounted his own defence. In a brilliant courtroom performance, he sought to expose the 'horrible, repulsive crimes' that the Batista regime had inflicted on the prisoners and to 'show the nation and the world the infinite misfortune of the Cuban people', who were, he said, 'suffering the cruelest, the most inhuman oppression of their history'. Presenting his fellow rebels as brave, patriotic heroes dedicated to the cause of freedom and justice, he condemned the president as a 'criminal and a thief'. He concluded his lengthy speech with a defiant cry: 'I do not fear prison, as I do not fear the fury of the miserable tyrant who took the lives of seventy of my comrades. Condemn me. It does not matter. History will absolve me.'[19] It would become one of the most famous political speeches in modern history and would transform Castro into a popular revolutionary icon.

Found guilty and sentenced to fifteen years, Castro was, along with a number of his fellow rebels, incarcerated in a prison on the Isle of Pines, fifty miles south of the mainland. Here he put his time to good use: reading widely, writing numerous letters and working to shore up his nascent opposition movement (which, it was quickly decided, would be named the 26th July Movement, or M-26-7, in honour of the attack on Moncada). A number of the M-26-7 leaders tutored their comrades, holding classes in the prison library. Castro taught seminars in philosophy, world history and public speaking. In his letters, he wrote warmly of his comrades, praising their discipline and spirit and explaining proudly how, having 'learned to handle weapons', they were now 'learning to wield books for the important battles of the future'. Apart from a brief period that saw their privileges suspended and Castro cast into solitary confinement, the Moncadistas were permitted to receive regular visitors and had plenty of opportunity for exercise, and even to enhance their culinary skills (steak with guava jelly, spaghetti and omelettes were some of Castro's specialities). With a regular supply of books, food and, crucially, cigars – the floor of his cell was, Castro confessed, 'strewn with butts' – life could certainly have been a lot worse. In the spring of 1955 it got a great deal better. That April, in what would prove to be a catastrophic error of judgement, General Batista – basking in the glow of economic growth and American support, and increasingly complacent about his hold on power – granted an amnesty; on 15 May Fidel and Raúl Castro and eighteen other members of the 26th July Movement walked free. Within weeks, Fidel headed into exile. Insisting that the 'hour has come to take one's rights, not to ask for them; to seize them, not to beg for them', he left for Mexico, declaring that 'from such voyages, either one does not return, or one returns with the beheaded tyranny at one's feet'.[20]

In mid-December 1956, nobody – except perhaps for Fidel Castro – thought that the little band of *Granma* rebels would prove victorious. Indeed, Castro's attempt to launch a revolution was widely dismissed by journalists as 'quixotic', 'pathetic' and even 'suicidal'.[21] Rumours abounded that he had been killed, and the respected news bureau United Press International even reported his death as 'fact'.[22] Having noted Castro's arrival in Cuba in its leader column on 4 December, the London *Times* confidently swatted aside its significance. Pointing out that Batista was a 'veteran of many revolutions', it predicted that 'it is unlikely that the latest will shake his position'.[23]

With many of the *Granma*'s landing party either killed or captured and the remainder scattered, the 26 July Movement's prospects in early December certainly looked pretty bleak. For several days, Castro himself commanded the grand total of two men. Between them they could muster just a couple of rifles and 120 rounds of ammunition, and much of their time was spent hiding in sugar cane fields. Castro recounted how they 'threw ourselves under the leaves and straw' as low-flying jets strafed the area with .50-calibre machine guns, causing the very 'earth to shake' beneath them. Determined that he would not be taken alive, Castro took to sleeping with the barrel of his rifle resting against his chin.[24] Slowly, though, the twenty or so survivors of the *Granma* began to regroup in the foothills of the Sierra Maestra, nearing Mount Caracas, whose summit lay more than four thousand feet above sea level, by year's end. It was from here that Castro launched a remarkable military campaign, which was to culminate in his triumphant march into Havana on 8 January 1959, following Batista's flight nine days earlier, on New Year's Eve.[25]

A hundred miles long and thirty miles across at its widest point, the Sierra Maestra, with its towering peaks, steep slopes and dense forests, made an ideal base for Castro's rebel army. The Sierra Maestra had enjoyed a long association with 'outlaws, squatters, and rebels', and the writ of the government in Havana ran particularly thin in this remote region. Moreover, Castro and his forces stood an excellent chance of winning substantial support from the region's dispossessed, marginalised and impoverished peasantry. By using guerrilla warfare – ambushing Batista's forces in a series of hit-and-run attacks – Castro hoped to negate the huge advantages in manpower and material that the Cuban military enjoyed (at least on paper), and to inspire a mass uprising.[26]

Official mythology notwithstanding, the success of the Cuban revolution was not due solely to the pluck and heroism of Castro's mountain guerrillas. In recent years, historians have emphasised the significant role played by members of the urban-based opposition movement (not all of them supporters of Castro) who engaged in sabotage and terrorism, organised strikes and provided Castro's forces with a steady supply of arms and ammunition, medicine, food, money and other vital resources. They also distributed tens of thousands of copies of Castro's *History Will Absolve Me* (the transcript of his famous four-hour trial speech) and other M-26-7 propaganda.[27] Tactical alliances forged with other opposition groups, which drew in support from the churches, the labour movement, middle-class professionals and (eventually) the PCC, also proved critical.[28]

Castro benefited, too, from the misjudgements or misfortune of his rivals (the charismatic student leader José Antonio Echevarría, for instance, lost his life during an ill-fated attempt to seize the presidential palace in March 1957), as well as from the flaws of his enemy. While the Cuban armed forces were well armed, they were poorly trained and increasingly reluctant to fight.[29] Castro's revolutionaries also drew strength from the repressive measures unleashed by Batista's government, which imposed press censorship, suspended constitutional guarantees (including the freedom of assembly) and engaged in abduction, torture and murder. In the immediate aftermath of the Santiago uprising, for instance, hundreds of people were thrown into prison and more than twenty young men – all opponents of the regime – disappeared. Most of these alleged 'terrorists' were shot through the head, but two were strung up from trees alongside a major highway, just in time for Christmas. Such savagery caused widespread outrage – the Ortodoxo Party even accused Batista of attempting to turn Cuba into 'a Hungary of the Antilles'.[30] Ultimately, such harsh measures helped to shift public support decisively behind Castro. In March 1958 the Americans, despairing at the regime's authoritarianism, finally withdrew their own backing for Batista.[31]

In early December 1956, however, Castro's apparent defeat seemed destined to serve as a minor episode in a sobering tale of how, right across the globe, the 'old order' was able to successfully defend its interests, outmanoeuvre its rivals and put those fighting for freedom onto the back foot. Indeed, eight thousand miles from the Sierra Maestra, in the Union of South Africa, the defenders of apartheid were preparing what they hoped would prove a decisive blow against the forces ranged against them.

TREASON TRIAL

The ACCUSED

DECEMBER 1956

21

FREEDOM ON TRIAL

We didn't know what would happen. But the feeling was,
'They can never kill 156 people.'
BLANCHE LA GUMA, South African Communist

In his autobiography, *Long Walk to Freedom*, Nelson Mandela
recalled how 'just after dawn on the morning of 5 December 1956,
I was woken by a loud knocking at my door. No neighbour or
friend ever knocks in such a peremptory way, and I knew immediately that it was the security police.' Three officers had come to
search Mandela's house. As his worried children looked on, they
rifled through drawers and cabinets, combing the entire dwelling
in an attempt to find incriminating material. After about forty-five
minutes, the officer in charge of the search turned to Mandela and
told him that 'we have a warrant for your arrest. Come with me.'
The charge on the warrant read 'HOOGVERRAAD', or high treason
– a capital offence.[1] Escorted from his home, Mandela was driven
along a stretch of 'desolate highway' before heading into downtown
Johannesburg and the offices of his law practice, where a second
search was undertaken. Eventually, several hours after the police
had made their early morning call, Mandela was taken to Marshall
Square, the 'rambling red-brick' police station in the city centre.[2]

As the thirty-eight-year-old lawyer and influential ANC leader
soon discovered, he was not the only one arrested that morning.
In fact, a series of nationwide raids had seen 140 anti-apartheid
activists rounded up (sixteen more were seized a week later). All
were charged with treason. The scale of the operation was impressive, with those arrested hundreds of miles away in Port Elizabeth
and Cape Town flown into Johannesburg's military airfield aboard

[373]

Dakota transport planes.³ Within days, virtually the entire leadership of the freedom movement had been corralled inside Johannesburg's main prison – a 'bleak, castle-like structure located on a hill in the heart of the city', known as the Fort. Mandela described how, upon arrival, he, along with the other non-white men, was 'taken to an outdoor quadrangle and ordered to strip completely and line up against the wall. We were forced to stand there for more than an hour, shivering in the breeze and feeling awkward . . .' Despite the humiliating circumstances, Mandela was unable to 'suppress a laugh' as he looked at his naked comrades: 'For the first time the truth of the aphorism "clothes make the man" came home to me.' 'If fine bodies and impressive physiques were essential to being a leader', he wrote, 'I saw that few among us would have qualified.'⁴

Among those confined behind the prison's imposing walls were Albert Luthuli – a Zulu chief, Methodist lay preacher, future Nobel Peace Prize winner, and the ANC's widely respected president; two founders of the organisation's Youth League, Walter Sisulu and Oliver Tambo (who was also Mandela's law partner); Yusuf Dadoo and Ahmed Kathrada of the Indian Congress; the Communist leader Joe Slovo and his wife, the campaigning journalist Ruth First; E. S. 'Solly' Sachs, a Lithuanian immigrant and legendary trade union organiser; Lilian Ngoyi, president of the Federation of South African Women, and Helen Joseph, the group's national secretary. One of a handful of white women to be arrested, Joseph – born in Sussex in 1905 and educated at King's College, London – had worked as a governess in India before settling in South Africa during the 1930s. A long-time supporter of racial equality and human rights, she had, in October 1953, helped to found the Congress of Democrats, which provided a home for white opponents of apartheid.⁵

Life inside the Fort was grim. Washing facilities were limited and basic, prisoners had to leap over the puddles of urine that flowed from the perennially blocked drain as they made their way to the food hall, and the bland, unappetising meals were eaten squatting in the yard – a paved cement enclosure with a net of barbed wire overhead. The prison itself was, of course, arranged on racial lines as well as segregated by gender. Whereas the white male detainees were placed two to a cell (measuring nine feet by nine feet) and provided with blankets, a pillow and a mattress, their non-white comrades were herded into cramped, dormitory-style cells and issued with lice-ridden blankets and thin straw mats that were rolled out on the cold, hard floor. Meanwhile the six white women – all from comfortable, middle-class homes – endured several sleepless nights thanks to an infestation of mice.[6]

The treason trial detainees were subjected to the regular prison routine: lights were switched on at five thirty in the morning, and cell doors unlocked at six fifteen, at which point the prisoners joined the long queues for the lavatory and washing facilities. After breakfast and the ritual cell inspection, the inmates were permitted to exercise in the prison yard until lunch at eleven thirty, before being confined once more until another yard break, at two thirty. The prisoners were required to return to their cells after supper, which was served at four, with lights out at eight. Although they were allowed to receive visitors, most of the treason trial inmates found the experience far from pleasant. In their celebrated account of the trial, Lionel Forman and Solly Sachs explained how 'five or six prisoners' would be lined up in a row 'behind a wire mesh, like monkeys in a cage'. In front of the mesh was a small passageway and a metal grille, behind which stood the visitors. 'Each man talks to his visitor. Each visitor talks to his man. Nobody can hear what anyone is saying. So each man shouts to his visitor and each visitor shouts to his man.' Soon all six prisoners would be screaming at the visitors, and the visitors screaming back.[7] It proved to be a humiliating and nerve-shredding experience.

The dramatic arrests of 5 December were, as Albert Luthuli later wrote, 'deliberately calculated to strike terror into hesitant minds and impress upon the entire nation the determination of the governing clique to stifle all opposition'.[8] But if the authorities in Pretoria hoped that the leaders of the anti-apartheid movement would be cowed, or that dissent would quickly dissipate, they were to be disappointed. Indeed, by bringing the country's leading freedom fighters together, the apartheid regime – entirely unintentionally – actually helped to reinforce a sense of solidarity. As Mandela explained, 'Many of us had been living under severe restrictions, making it illegal for us to meet and talk. Now, our enemy had gathered us all under one roof for what became the largest and longest unbanned meeting of the [movement] in years . . .' Now, 'We revelled in the opportunity to exchange ideas and experiences for two weeks while we awaited trial.'[9]

The detainees, in fact, quickly improvised a programme of activities that drew on their collective knowledge, experience and interests. There were games, debates, talks on black history and discussions of African music and culture, all interspersed with the regular singing of freedom songs.[10] On one occasion, Chief Luthuli's electrifying performance as Shaka, the legendary Zulu warrior, prompted mass participation in the traditional *indlamu* war dance. Mandela recalled (perhaps rather idealistically) how 'some moved gracefully, others resembled frozen mountaineers trying to shake off the cold, but all danced with enthusiasm and emotion' and, as they did so, racial, ethnic, class and political distinctions seemed to temporarily dissolve. In that moment, Mandela explained, 'We were all . . . bound together by a love of our common history, our culture, our country and our people . . . something stirred deep inside us, something strong and intimate, that bound us to one another . . . the power of the great cause that linked us all together.'[11]

The treason trial detainees were also buoyed by demonstrations of support from the outside. A National Defence Fund – sponsored by such notables as the Archbishop of Cape Town, the Chancellor of Witwatersrand University, Liberal and Labour members of the South African parliament, a former High Commissioner and a retired Supreme Court judge – was established immediately, as was a 'Stand By Our Leaders Committee'. During the weekend of 8–9 December a number of activists, holding placards, took up positions at bus stops and other public places to demonstrate their support.[12] Taking advantage of the fact that remand prisoners were permitted to receive food and other gifts, supporters rallied to provide newspapers, books, clothes and food – including fruit, vegetables and meat. From the suburb of Fordsburg, a group of Indian women prepared regular shipments of curried eggs, meat and fish, while others sent sandwiches, fresh coffee and even wrapped parcels of fish and chips.[13]

Public support was also on show on Wednesday 19 December when the accused were taken to the Army Drill Hall – a 'large cheerless barn with a galvanised iron roof' – for the first day of the 'preparatory examination', a series of hearings presided over by a magistrate who would decide whether there was a case to answer. The prisoners were driven to the improvised court in police vans, sirens blaring, accompanied by an armed military escort. As they approached the Union Grounds, a 'dreary patch of baked red earth enclosed by utilitarian iron railings' opposite the Drill Hall, they were greeted by enormous crowds of cheering, singing supporters. Their presence transformed the grim military convoy into a triumphal cavalcade and the festive spirit spilled over into the Drill Hall itself: as they entered, the accused exchanged freedom salutes with hundreds of supporters in the public gallery and, just as the proceedings began, the room shook to the roar of '*Mayibuye I Afrika*' from the crowds outside.[14]

Almost immediately, the legal proceedings themselves descended into farce, with adjournments first to install loudspeakers (the prosecuting counsel was inaudible) and then to locate interpreters for those defendants who were not proficient in English. On day two, though, events took a more sombre turn. As the hearings began, the defendants were forced into a specially constructed cage (one of the accused quickly scribbled a sign, 'Dangerous. Please Do Not Feed', and attached it to the outside). The defence counsel was apoplectic, and Maurice Franks QC insisted that the structure be removed, otherwise the entire defence team would walk out in protest.[16] Meanwhile, outside the Drill Hall, another large crowd had gathered, and many were pressed up against the metal gates, hoping to gain admission to the court. As the police attempted to push the crowd back, one officer suddenly ordered a baton charge. As the police raised their truncheons and began swinging – clubbing elderly protesters, women and watching journalists – a number of young men retaliated by throwing stones. This prompted the police to draw their weapons and begin firing indiscriminately into the crowds. They continued shooting even as the stragglers attempted to flee. No one was safe from the violence; one journalist noted that among those running for cover was 'a pregnant African woman who, stumbling . . . fell on her hands and knees. The policeman caught up with her, stopped and kicked her three times in the side.' Fortuitously, no one was killed, although twenty people were injured.[17]

The heart of the prosecution case – which drew on speeches, documents and published writings, including the Freedom Charter and the anti-pass petitions that had been left in Prime Minister Strijdom's office back in August – was that the accused, working in concert with the agents of international Communism, had sought to overthrow the South African state and install in its place a so-called 'people's democracy'. As the chief prosecutor, J. C. van Niekerk, put it at the end of his lengthy opening address, the accused 'not only advocated that the revolutionary change-over is desirable, inevitable or imminent, but also actively created unrest among the people of the Union of South Africa, encouraging hostility between the European and non-European races, and inciting members to revolt against the existing authority by way of insurrection and rebellion, by force and violence . . .'[18]

On 20 December all of the defendants were finally granted bail, set at £250 for Europeans, £100 for Indians and £25 for Africans and Coloreds, but they were subjected to severe restrictions that limited their movement and prohibited political activism. They also remained embroiled in a complex legal fight that would continue for four long years.[19] While charges against sixty-five of the accused were dropped, without explanation, in January 1958, ninety-one of the original defendants were brought before a special court in Pretoria that August. Two months later, the state summarily withdrew its original indictment and drew up fresh charges against thirty of the defendants. Following further legal wrangling, the trial proper finally began in August 1959. It ended on 29 March 1961 with a unanimous verdict of 'not guilty' against all of the defendants.[20]

While the leaders of the freedom struggle in South Africa were facing a possible death sentence, black activists in the United States were savouring the fruits of a hard-won victory. On 17 December 1956, the US Supreme Court dismissed a final appeal by the Montgomery city authorities, thereby consigning segregated seating on the city's buses to the history books.[21] African Americans, who had endured many months of hardship, were understandably elated. Georgia Gilmore, who had been in her kitchen listening to gospel music on the radio when the news of the ruling came through, was 'just so excited, I just didn't believe it . . . and I ran outside, and there's my neighbor, and she said yes, and we were so happy. We felt that we had accomplished something that no one ever thought would happen.' Jo Ann Robinson, who had done so much to make the victory possible, recalled that she and many of the city's activists 'just rejoiced together. We had won self-respect . . . we felt that we were somebody . . . we had forced the white man to give what we knew was a part of our own citizenship.'[22]

Martin Luther King and the MIA had been preparing for this moment for weeks, and a series of nonviolent training workshops had been held to ready activists for integration.[23] King took an important lead by preaching a message of reconciliation, emphasising that the purpose of the boycott was to achieve the 'creation of the beloved community' in which all people – black and white – would be treated with dignity and equality. At two MIA mass meetings, held the night before the integration order was due to come into force on 21 December, the crowds were reminded to greet bus desegregation calmly and with dignity. Specific instructions issued to African Americans included: 'Do not deliberately sit by a white person unless there is no other seat' and 'If cursed, do not curse back. If pushed, do not push back. If struck, do not strike back, but evidence love and goodwill at all times.' They were also reminded that the victory was 'not for Negroes alone, but for all Montgomery and the South'.[24]

At a quarter to six the next morning, the white pacifist Glenn Smiley joined E. D. Nixon, Rosa Parks, Ralph Abernathy and the MIA president at the King family home. A few minutes later, the group boarded the first bus of the day at a nearby corner. As news photographers snapped away, King paid his fare and took a seat towards the front, in a section previously reserved for whites. Smiley took the seat next to him. After 382 days of extraordinary sacrifice and discipline, Montgomery's African American citizens had won a famous victory.[25]

AFTERMATH

Tomorrow's midnight . . . will remorselessly arrive, and
so will the pain, the hope, the fear, the ecstasy that years
bring. But whether what comes . . . after . . . is a new dawn
or a polar darkness we cannot yet know: all we can do is to
summon up our courage and our wisdom and go forward.
  New York Times, 30 December 1956

The *New Yorker* that hit the news-stands in the last week of December informed its readers that, among other things, '1956 was the year in which . . . the rental of top hats was authorized in East Germany for the first time since the war.'[1] Such trivia doubtless provided some welcome relief at the end of a tumultuous twelve months that had seen global tensions smouldering from the satellite states of Eastern Europe to the Sierra Maestra, and from the Suez Canal Zone to the American South.[2] It had, by any reckoning, been a quite remarkable year.

1956 marked a fateful moment in the history of international Communism. In the words of the Marxist historian and lifelong Communist Eric Hobsbawm, 'The October Revolution created a world communist movement, the Twentieth Congress destroyed it.'[3] Nikita Khrushchev's denunciation of Stalin triggered a lasting rift with Beijing and plunged the Communist Parties of the West into an existential crisis. Amidst bitter feuding between Stalinists and reformers, thousands of members, typically the younger and more educated ones, deserted the Party.[4] While many abandoned political organising altogether, others, working with left-wing intellectuals and activists, attempted to build a 'New Left' free from the stain of Stalinism. As they did so, they took their inspiration from a new generation of thinkers, such as the American sociologist C. Wright Mills, whose searing attack on the 'Power Elite' (an interlocking set of military, corporate and political interests) had itself been published in 1956. Rather than lionising the traditional working class, this New Left would place its hopes for revolutionary change in an alliance of students and intellectuals.[5]

Although shaken by the outpouring of dissent that had followed the Twentieth Party Congress, Khrushchev would press on with his attempts to liberalise the USSR (the effort would end only after he was ousted in 1964). Over the next few years the Party's internal structures were opened up, writers and artists were permitted to operate a little more freely, a new criminal code strengthening the rights of Soviet citizens was introduced, educational reforms were enacted, significant progress was made in meeting the chronic housing shortage and living standards rose. The new freedoms were somewhat precarious and the reforms did not always suc-ceed – Khrushchev's agricultural policies, for instance, proved disastrous – but his attempt to relaunch the Soviet project was a qualified success. (As Mikhail Gorbachev and his fellow 'children of the Twentieth Congress' discovered in the 1980s, implementing major reforms without bringing the entire USSR crashing down was an exceptionally difficult task.) When, in the summer of 1959, a chortling Khrushchev boasted to Richard Nixon that the USSR would soon catch up with the Americans and then 'wave bye-bye', more than one Western commentator wondered if he might turn out to be right.[6]

In the People's Republic of China, in contrast, the promise of reform quickly soured. To begin with, the so-called Hundred Flowers campaign, which ran through to 1957, had been viewed, both inside and outside China, as a genuine attempt at liberalisa-tion. During the Hungarian uprising, for instance, there had been excited talk on the streets of Budapest that 'the Chinese are with us' (in fact, behind the scenes Mao, after some initial hesitation, had urged the Soviets to crack down hard).[7] Within China, few were initially prepared to speak up, but after repeated encouragement and exhortation, intellectuals, artists, scientists, government employees, students and workers began to voice their ideas – and their criticisms of the Party – with growing confidence. Then, in the summer of 1957, Mao abruptly changed course, denouncing 'Rightists' and 'reactionaries' and initiating a series of purges.[8] While his original intent is hard to discern, it does seem that, alarmed by the outbreak of serious dissent in the Eastern Bloc, Mao came to regard the Hundred Flowers campaign primarily as a useful tool for exposing his own internal 'enemies'. As he put it to his inner circle, 'How can we catch the snakes if we don't let them out of their lairs? We wanted those sons of turtles [i.e. bastards] to wriggle out and sing and fart . . . that way we can catch them.'[9] According to some estimates, up to 750,000 Party members were sent for 're-education' in remote labour camps, with some languishing in the Chinese gulag for twenty years. With the benefit of hindsight, it is clear that the miserable dénouement to the Hundred Flowers campaign was an indicator of the brutal repression that lay at the heart of Maoism; it also augured the much greater and more terrible disasters to come.[10]

In neighbouring North Vietnam, the Communist leader Ho Chi Minh had initially followed Mao's lead in easing restrictions on political and artistic expression and encouraging dissent. However, at the end of 1956, following months of fierce criticisms, the policy of liberalisation was thrown into reverse: journals were shut down, some prominent intellectuals 'disappeared' and others were sent off to brutal labour camps. An uprising that gripped the coastal province of Nghe An (150 miles south of Hanoi) that November had caused particular alarm. At the start of the month, several thousand of the region's predominantly Catholic peasants had marched on the district capital, Quynh Luu, armed with farm implements and basic weapons, to voice their anger at a botched land reform programme, which had been characterised by violent and indiscriminate reprisals. In clashes with Communist forces, a number of protesters were killed. A full army division was quickly despatched to crush the insurgency: its ringleaders were hunted down and killed, and thousands more were forcibly deported.[11] As Ho was cracking down on internal dissent, Ngo Dinh Diem, his South Vietnamese counterpart, embarked on a vicious anti-Communist campaign to root out his enemies: banning labour unions, sending suspected 'subversives' to 're-education centres' or ordering their execution, and launching a major propaganda offensive. Having summarily cancelled the national elections that, under the terms of the 1954 Geneva Accords, were supposed to lead to Vietnamese reunification, Diem's grip on power was further fortified by military support from the United States. In April 1956 the US had assumed complete responsibility for the training of the South Vietnamese army, and President Eisenhower quickly doubled the number of US military advisers on the ground, taking the total to just under seven hundred.[12] It was an early step on a journey that would lead the United States to disaster.

As we have seen, Khrushchev's 'secret speech' also fuelled a series of rebellions across the 'people's democracies' of Eastern Europe. Indeed, for a few extraordinary days, the Hungarian revolutionaries had appeared to be on the brink of a historic triumph. Although the Red Army crushed the uprising, for millions of ordinary Hungarians the years that followed were actually a good deal better than many had feared. The harsh repression that accompanied the restoration of Communist rule proved temporary, and János Kádár's government offered a number of reforms, unprecedented in the Soviet bloc, to try and win over the population (or, at least, gain their grudging acceptance). Access to higher education was opened up, the Party's monopoly on technical and administrative posts was eased, a greater degree of religious and cultural freedom was permitted and Hungarians were allowed to travel to the West (in 1954, fewer than one hundred private citizens had done so; by 1962, the figure was 120,000). There were changes, too, in agricultural and economic policy that made space for private enterprise and rewarded individual talent and effort. The economy also did well: in the decade that followed the revolution, real wages increased by 47 per cent, and Hungarians enjoyed greater access to consumer goods and a higher standard of living than their contemporaries in East Germany, Poland and Romania. Moreover, Hungarians were no longer expected to attend compulsory political meetings, enthusiastically applaud the Party line or make public demonstrations of allegiance to Communism: in Kádár's famously cynical phrase, 'He who is not against us is with us.'

This 'goulash Communism', though, came at a price: there could be no questioning of one-party rule or the country's alliance with the Soviet Union, nor was it permitted to challenge the official line that the 1956 uprising was the work of fascist counter-revolutionaries. Kádár's Hungary may have been the 'happiest barracks in Eastern Europe', but the ideals for which the revolution had been fought – national independence, a free press and a more democratic politics – remained out of reach until the summer of 1989, when demands for 'freedom' and the withdrawal of Soviet troops once again echoed around Heroes' Square.[13]

Crude military force enabled the USSR to maintain its Eastern European empire (a stark reality that was underlined again in 1968 when Leonid Brezhnev, Khrushchev's reactionary successor, sent tanks to crush the Prague Spring).[14] But the price was a heavy one: the brutal suppression of the Hungarian revolution destroyed Moscow's claims to represent an idealistic, global revolutionary movement that both sought to meet the needs of the people and commanded genuine popular support. During the 1960s, left-wing idealists would look not to Moscow but to the Cuba of Fidel Castro and Che Guevara for inspiration.

Indeed, the Cuban revolution reverberated far beyond the Caribbean – and not just because for thirteen days in October 1962 the world teetered on the brink of nuclear annihilation during the tense standoff over the presence of Soviet missiles on the island. Revolutionary Cuba, under Castro's leadership, helped to inspire (and sometimes actively exported) socialism throughout Latin America, and also played a major role in the global struggles against imperialism, racism and capitalism. Castro provided military support to leftist revolutionaries in Algeria and Angola, for example, and launched a massive civil aid programme – training (for free) more than forty thousand health professionals from the third world and sending tens of thousands of Cuban health workers and physicians overseas.[15] In the late 1950s and early 1960s many African Americans, attracted by its unequivocal stance on behalf of racial equality, glimpsed in Castro's revolution the possibilities for a new world. As the journalist Ralph Matthews wrote in the *Baltimore Afro-American* in 1959: 'Every white man who cuffs, deprives, and abuses even the lowest colored person, simply because he is white and the other colored, should have seared upon his consciousness the fact that it is possible for the tables to be turned. Castro has proved it in our time.' During a visit to New York in September 1960 to address the UN General Assembly, Castro, enraged by demands that his delegation pay their bill up front and in cash, famously stormed out of the Shelburne Hotel in Manhattan's Midtown and took up residence at the Hotel Theresa, in the heart of Harlem, where he was afforded a rapturous reception. And when, a year later, the US government launched an abortive attempt to topple him, numerous black leaders, activists and intellectuals spoke out in opposition. A bitter critic of South African apartheid, Castro's revolutionary government also proved a vital source of support and inspiration to Nelson Mandela's ANC.[16]

Although its lustre would eventually fade (not least because of Castro's own terrible human rights record), the Cuban revolution's apparent success also re-energised leftist movements across Europe and in the United States, many of which had struggled to find their moorings in the aftermath of the Twentieth Party Congress and the Soviet invasion of Hungary. Interestingly, given Castro's later loyalty to Moscow, Cuban revolutionaries and their allies had sought to exploit Western sympathy for the doomed freedom fighters of Budapest by drawing a direct parallel between the two struggles. Cuban-American supporters of the 26 July Movement, for instance, marched with placards denouncing Batista's Cuba as 'the Hungary of the Americas', while Castro himself asked, 'Why be afraid of freeing the people, whether Hungarians or Cubans?' In the spring of 1957, sensational news broke that three young Americans – all the sons of US navy personnel at Guantánamo Bay – had actually taken up arms for Castro. One of the recruits explained how revelations about Batista's 'cruel . . . dictatorship' and the inspiring example of Hungary's 'freedom fighters' had motivated them to 'do our part for the freedom of the world'. It was a taste of what was to come: Fidel and his *compañeros* (above all, Che Guevara) would be revolutionary icons for a generation of Sixties radicals.[17] As Arthur Schlesinger, Jr, a historian and former adviser to President Kennedy, put it, the students saw Castro as 'the hipster who in the era of the Organization Man had joyfully defied the system, summoned a dozen good friends and overturned a government of wicked old men'. Certainly the 26 July Movement's use of revolutionary violence and guerrilla warfare proved influential, not least on white leftists' own drift toward armed struggle at the end of the 1960s, while Che's ruminations about the need to create a 'new man' and to fight not just economic exploitation but the forces of 'alienation' chimed strongly with a generation of students who fretted about the consequences of automation and uniformity, and who sought, almost above all else, a politics of 'authenticity'.[18]

*

Writing in the South African anti-apartheid monthly *Fighting Talk* at the start of the year, the campaigning journalist Ruth First declared that 'this is the year 1956. The colonial people have learnt the science of the struggle for liberty. And the weapons of the past are proving ineffective against the movements of the present.'[19] While colonialism still had some life left in it, 1956 was a watershed in the erosion of the old European empires. Sudan, Tunisia and Morocco took their place among the family of independent nations; in Trinidad, the People's National Movement swept to power under the leadership of Eric Williams, who became the island's first black chief minister (he would lead the country to full independence in 1962), and a final agreement was reached for an end to colonial rule in what would become Ghana.[20]

The reality of independence in Kwame Nkrumah's Ghana would, like elsewhere in the post-colonial world, prove somewhat sobering. Socialist economic planning was ruinous, living standards fell and senior government officials amassed fortunes through bribes and kickbacks.[21] In February 1966 an increasingly autocratic Nkrumah was swept from power in a military coup, and genuine multi-party democracy would not return until the century's end.[22] Nevertheless, Ghanaian independence – the first surrender of European colonial power in sub-Saharan Africa – was a genuinely transformative moment that energised anti-colonial nationalists and their supporters across Africa and the Caribbean.[23] In the East African territory of Tanganyika, for instance, the nationalist leader Julius Nyerere was fired up by Kwame Nkrumah's historic triumph. Nyerere, hitherto regarded as a gradualist, now pressed London to set a firm date for independence, appealed for international support, threatened a campaign of mass civil disobedience and intimated that if substantive concessions were not forthcoming, he – like Nkrumah – might demand 'Self-government Now!'[24] In Nigeria, meanwhile, Ghanaian independence precipitated a rare outburst of ethnic and regional unity: on 26

March 1957, the Federal House of Representatives unanimously endorsed a motion, submitted by the nationalist politician Samuel Akintola, demanding self-government by 1959. In the event, Nigeria would win her independence in 1960, Tanganyika a year later.[25] As Indonesia's President Sukarno put it, Ghanaian independence had 'opened the gate'; within a decade, most of Britain's formal empire was consigned to history.[26]

In his seminal 1961 book *The Wretched of the Earth*, the Martinique-born psychiatrist, intellectual and FLN medical officer Frantz Fanon wrote that 'the violence of the colonial regime and the counter-violence of the native balance each other out and respond to each other in an extraordinary reciprocal homogeneity'.[27] By late 1956, as the French fought fiercely to maintain their position in Algeria, this pattern seemed set firm. On the morning of 28 December, for example, the seventy-four-year-old president of the Federation of Algerian Mayors was gunned down in broad daylight on the rue Michelet, in the commercial heart of French Algiers. The next day, thousands of *pieds noirs* lined the streets to pay their respects as the funeral cortège passed by. When a bomb, designed to explode while the mourners were at the graveside, detonated early, it sparked an outpouring of anger. A mob, ten thousand strong, ran wild through the streets, smashing windows and 'yanking Moslems from their cars and lynching them'. Some 'young thugs' used iron bars to 'smash in the heads of veiled women'. The riot left eight Muslims dead and forty-eight injured.[28]

The terrible acts of violence that engulfed the Algerian capital during the second half of 1956 were the opening skirmishes in the Battle of Algiers. This military encounter – the subject of Gillo Pontecorvo's iconic film and the defining moment of the war – saw the FLN routed. But France's victory was pyrrhic. The routine torture of FLN suspects, together with the use of mass detention and harsh, repressive measures, had destroyed France's moral claim to remain in Algeria.[29] With the French public, shocked by revelations of torture and other war crimes, abandoning support for the war, and with the treasury in Paris running dry, it became increasingly clear that continued French rule was untenable. Moreover, the growing alliance between *pied noir* ultras and sympathetic elements of the military came to threaten French democracy itself. Amidst a major political crisis, precipitated by an attempted military coup, Charles de Gaulle returned to power in the summer of 1958 and quickly inaugurated a new constitution to replace the weak and ineffective Fourth Republic. Convinced that the war in Algeria was placing an intolerable strain on France – sapping its military, political, economic and diplomatic strength, undermining its efforts to act as a counterweight to the Anglo-Saxon powers and distracting it from playing a major role in shaping a new Europe – he sought a negotiated settlement. His determination to end the war was only strengthened by further challenges to civilian rule by settlers and dissident army officers. Following protracted negotiations, France reached an agreement with the FLN on 18 March 1962, and Algeria became an independent, sovereign state on 1 July. The bitter conflict had cost the lives of an estimated eighteen thousand French troops, several thousand European civilians and at least three hundred thousand Algerian Muslims.[30] It also marked the decisive end of 'European' Algeria, as almost the entire settler population abandoned the country: seven hundred thousand fled to mainland France between April and August 1962 alone.[31]

1956 had also seen Britain get sucked into a bloody colonial conflict, as she sought to defend her strategic interests in Cyprus in the face of EOKA's campaign to secure *enosis* – political union – with Greece. In fact, 1956 would prove to be the most intense year of the war, with 2,500 separate acts of violence that left 210 people dead.[32] Moreover, in a portent of the island's divided future, worsening relations between the Greek and Turkish communities erupted into serious intercommunal violence.[33] In March 1957 a truce, announced by Colonel Grivas, effectively signalled the end

of EOKA's campaign of terror and, following painstaking negotiations that took place against a backdrop of intensifying sectarian
conflict, the outlines of a final settlement were finally reached in
February 1959: Britain lifted the state of emergency, granted most
EOKA fighters an amnesty and, with the exception of two military bases that covered ninety-nine square miles of territory, agreed
to relinquish sovereignty over the island. Cypriot independence
was to be guaranteed by Britain, Greece and Turkey. Both *enosis*
and the partition of the island were expressly prohibited, although
this did not prevent the de facto partition of the country in 1974
when, in response to a Greek-sponsored coup, Turkish military
forces occupied the north-eastern part of the island. A new constitution established a presidential system consisting of a Greek
president and a Turkish vice-president, with the Turkish minority
also allocated 30 per cent of seats in the Council of Ministers and
the House of Representatives.[34] On 16 August 1960 the Republic of
Cyprus, led by Makarios III, its newly elected president, was born.

During 1956, however, the declining fortunes and diminished
status of the major European powers were best captured by Suez –
a crisis which would have profound consequences for all the major
protagonists.

For Israel, the short conflict brought an end to the blockade of
the Straits of Tiran and a decade of peace, thanks to the several
thousand UN troops who, under the ceasefire agreement, were
stationed along its frontier with Egypt. Over the medium term,
though, the regional perception that Israel had acted aggressively
only exacerbated the wider Arab–Israeli conflict, which erupted
in another war, pitting the Jewish state against Egypt, Jordan and
Syria, in June 1967. As in 1956, the IDF demonstrated its overwhelming military superiority, but this time Israel also secured
substantial territorial gains – notably Gaza, East Jerusalem and the
West Bank of the River Jordan – with fateful consequences for the
region and the world.[35]

The French had been livid with the British for calling off Operation Musketeer at the very moment when, they believed, a decisive victory was within reach (Mollet had begged Eden to hold out for two or three more days), and the abandonment convinced French commanders that it was imperative to obtain the amphibious vessels and long-range aircraft that would give them the capability to act unilaterally in the future, potentially outside NATO's integrated command structure (which they would leave a decade later). Mistrustful of Britain, France also moved to make West Germany her major international partner, thereby laying the foundations for the powerful Franco-German axis that would continue to define the political and economic landscape of western Europe well into the twenty-first century.[36]

For the two central figures in the drama, the Suez Crisis had very different results. In Egypt, Nasser was unassailable (his colleagues now referred to him as *al-ra'īs* – 'the boss'), and he emerged from the crisis as a genuine hero of the Arab world and an icon of anti-colonial resistance. For the next decade Nasser would be at the heart of efforts to promote anti-imperialism, socialism and Arab unity across the Middle East and North Africa (his most striking, if ultimately short-lived, success was the 1958 merger between Egypt and Syria that created the United Arab Republic).[37] For Sir Anthony Eden, however, Suez proved ruinous. On 23 November 1956, an exhausted Eden and his wife, Clarissa, left for a vacation at Ian Fleming's Jamaican estate, Goldeneye. Although the prime minister returned to London on 14 December looking tanned and relaxed, his doctors advised that his health was no longer strong enough to enable him to 'sustain the heavy burdens' of high office. On 9 January 1957, after informing the cabinet of his intentions, Eden was driven to Buckingham Palace, where he handed his letter of resignation to the Queen.[38] A long and distinguished career of public service had ended in failure.

As for the wider significance for Britain, historians are – sixty years on – still arguing the odds. One certainly should not over-state the case. Suez did not lead to the collapse of British influ-ence in the Middle East, nor did it prevent London from using its military muscle to defend what it believed to be vital national interests in the region (between 1957 and 1961, for instance, the British intervened in Oman, Jordan, Kuwait and Aden). It is also worth noting that British imperial power had been in decline long before the Suez debacle: the end of colonial rule in the Indian subcontinent, independence for the Sudan and advanced planning for an end to colonialism in the Gold Coast and Malaya – as well as the original decision to evacuate the Suez Canal Zone – had all testified to that. As Eden noted, somewhat ruefully, the crisis had 'not so much changed our fortunes as revealed realities'.[39]

But Suez was a watershed nonetheless. Above all, it symbolised the striking contrast between the country's old imperial mindset and the harsh geopolitical truths of the post-war world. Britain had attempted to act independently of the United States and the United Nations to protect what it believed were its vital interests, and it had failed. Worse, the limits on British power had been exposed before the entire world, damaging both its international prestige and reputation. Britain's evident weakness may well have emboldened the forces of anti-colonial nationalism and, perhaps, hastened the end of empire. When it came to relations with the United States, meanwhile, the transatlantic alliance was quickly restored, thanks to the assiduous efforts of Eden's successor, Harold Macmillan. But the price was, effectively, subservience to Wash-ington. Certainly in Whitehall it became an article of faith that no significant gap could ever be allowed to open up between the British and the Americans on a major foreign policy question.[40]

Suez was a domestic turning point too, helping to undermine the authority of the British establishment and its stifling culture of deference. As the historian Ronald Hyam has argued, Suez 'com-pletely shattered the automatic trust and confidence of younger generations – and some older ones as well – in the good faith and honesty of their governments'. It thus, wholly unintentionally, helped to usher in the irreverent, liberal and anti-authoritarian spirit that characterised 'the Sixties'.[41]

Finally, faced with the apparent decline of Britain's position in the Middle East, the United States moved quickly to fill the vacuum. In a major speech to a joint session of Congress on 5 January 1957, President Eisenhower (who had been re-elected in a landslide two months earlier) declared that the United States would, if necessary, act unilaterally to assist any nation in the Middle East against the 'menace of International Communism'.[42] The 'Eisenhower doctrine' marked a major shift in American foreign policy that, for better or worse, committed the United States to the goal of ensuring security and stability in this most volatile region. It is a mission that continues to pose the stiffest of tests.[43]

1956 also marked a major turning point in the global struggle against white supremacy. Opponents of segregation, for instance, were quick to declare the Montgomery bus boycott a historic triumph, with the NAACP's Roy Wilkins proclaiming that it had demonstrated before the whole world that black people possessed the 'capacity for sustained collective action' and that 'non-violent resistance to racial tyranny' could succeed. He even described Montgomery as the 'peace capital of a new liberation movement'.[44] But, as the segregationist mobs that had taken to the streets of Tuscaloosa, Mansfield and Clinton had shown, the path to racial equality would not be a smooth one. Even the victory in Montgomery would have a nasty sting in the tail, as the turn of the year witnessed a spate of shootings and bombings, an ugly campaign of intimidation that silenced white moderates and a tightening of the city's other segregation laws.[45] In March 1957, for instance, the City Commission declared it 'unlawful for white and colored persons to play together, or, in company with each other . . . in any game of cards, dice, dominoes, checkers, pool, billiards, softball, basketball, baseball, football, golf, track, and at swimming pools, beaches, lakes or ponds or any other game or games or athletic contests, either indoors or outdoors'. When the MIA filed suit to desegregate the municipal parks the following year, the city commission promptly closed them all; they would not reopen until February 1965.[46] In August 1957, eight months after the boycott that she had inspired had ended, Rosa Parks – unable to find regular work, worn down by constant death threats and in poor health – abandoned Montgomery (though not her commitment to political activism) for Detroit.[47] But the bus boycott was a defining moment in the African American freedom struggle nonetheless. Although there would be a few false steps on the way (the 'Crusade for Citizenship' and a 'Prayer Pilgrimage for Freedom', both launched by King in 1957, proved underwhelming), the boycott contained the key ingredients of the movement's later success: strong local leadership, mass direct action, a clear commitment to nonviolence (at least in public), the framing of desegregation as a patriotic Cold War weapon, and, of course, the charismatic leadership of Martin Luther King himself. King and his organisation, the Southern Christian Leadership Conference (which was founded in the immediate aftermath of the boycott), would be at the heart of the civil rights movement's iconic campaigns in Birmingham in 1963 and Selma in 1965, which saw African Americans and their allies mobilise on a massive scale to bring segregation crashing down.[48]

The success of the bus boycott also raised the spirits of Z. K. Matthews, the distinguished black South African anthropologist, activist and treason trial defendant, who had spent several years studying and working in the United States. Writing in New York's *Liberation* magazine, Matthews declared that 'all the world over lovers of freedom have been thrilled by the magnificent way in which the people of Montgomery . . . have stood up and fought for [their] rights'. Their example had, he said, 'been an inspiration to others faced with similar problems in other parts of the world.'[49] But, when it came to his beloved South Africa, Matthews's own hopes for nonviolent change would go unrealised.

The treason trial did not bring an immediate end to nonviolent resistance to apartheid. During the early months of 1957, for instance, there was a visible and highly effective bus boycott in Alexandria, on the Eastern Cape. Sparked by a one-penny fare increase, the boycott – which was supported by tens of thousands of local residents – tapped into long-standing resentments over overcrowded buses, rude drivers, inadequate or inconvenient routes and schedules, and the dangers that black women faced at unsheltered or unlit terminals.[50] Black women, both in townships and in the countryside, continued to resist the pass laws, and between June 1958 and June 1959 some twenty thousand women across Natal protested against forced removals, pass regulations, low wages and the loss of farmlands.[51] Nor did the trial crush the movement's leaders. Indeed, by bringing them together for such an extended period of time, it served to solidify and deepen individual relationships and provided a forum in which strategy could be hammered out collectively. As the architect and Communist Rusty Bernstein recalled, the Johannesburg Drill Hall fostered a 'collegiate spirit' that transformed a 'company of strangers into something more like an extended family'. The result was a leadership, previously 'a loose assemblage of people from different places and different organizations . . . separated by differences of race, culture, class and ideology', that was now 'more united and effective' than ever.[52] Indeed, according to one historian, the treason trial was the moment when the 'struggle became genuinely national'.[53]

The dramatic trial also helped to mobilise international opposition to apartheid. In London, for example, Canon John Collins of St Paul's Cathedral founded British Defence and Aid to raise money for the treason trial defendants; over the following decades, as International Defence and Aid, it would furnish the families of jailed activists with vital legal and material support and would campaign tirelessly against the evils of the apartheid regime.[54] Meanwhile in the United States, the American Committee on Africa, which had been founded in 1953 by a small number of pacifists and civil rights pioneers, raised $75,000 for the treason trial defendants.[55]

Despite these positives, the treason trial dealt the movement a grievous blow, sucking up time, energy and resources that could otherwise have been deployed in the fight against apartheid, placing strains on family relationships and finances, and immobilising many of the movement's most talented and effective leaders, strategists and organisers.[56] The trial was an unmistakable signal of the South African government's determination to crush all dissent, a stance that was underlined further on 21 March 1960, when sixty-nine people were shot dead in the black township of Sharpeville during a protest against the pass laws. By the time that the treason trial itself had concluded, the ANC had been banned and the limitations of using mass direct action and nonviolent civil disobedience to try and topple apartheid had been exposed. With key figures within the freedom struggle now preparing to adopt armed resistance, a new, and more violent era in South Africa's troubled history was about to begin.[57]

During 1956, many of those who took to the streets or called for change, as well as those who defended the status quo, were aware of the global context in which they were acting; indeed, some sensed that they were part of a larger, interconnected story.[58] In August, for example, fearing that the federal government might use troops to enforce the *Brown* decision, segregationists conjured up a dystopian vision of the South as a Soviet-style police state. 'What would the troops do?' demanded the Citizens' Council; 'Send tanks and shoot into the crowds as the Russians did in Poznań?'[59] Meanwhile both the French government in Paris and the *pied noir* leadership in Algiers argued that Soviet repression in Hungary and FLN terrorism in Algeria were two faces of the same Communistic monster.[60]

Elsewhere, international parallels were drawn and foreign struggles invoked to challenge the existing order. Some Poles, for instance, wondered whether the uprising in Poznań was really any different from the liberation struggles being waged against the British in Cyprus or the French in North Africa (struggles that, as good Communists, they were expected to support), while the revolutionaries who had taken to the streets of Budapest in October had done so at first with loud proclamations of Polish–Hungarian friendship.[61] In South Africa the ANC, which viewed its own struggle against apartheid as part of the wider revolt against European colonialism, cheered on the progress of nationalists in the Gold Coast, Nigeria and Algeria, and sided with Nasser in his struggle against Britain and France.[62] Anti-apartheid campaigners were also increasingly interested in the burgeoning freedom struggle in the United States. In May, for instance, the ANC's Alfred Hutchinson had written to Autherine Lucy, expressing admiration for her courage and urging 'the youth of the United States to take up the fight for equality with redoubled efforts'. Claiming that the 'brave wind of freedom' was 'blowing', Hutchinson pledged solidarity with his American 'comrades-in-arms', declaring that 'We are with you every inch of the road – thorny though it be.'[63]

But it was Martin Luther King who best captured the notion of 1956 as a year of global revolution. Looking back on the remarkable events of the previous twelve months, he saw that 'all over the world men are in revolt . . . Africa's present ferment for independence, Hungary's death struggle against Communism, and the determined drive of Negro Americans to become first class citizens are inextricably bound together.'[64] King was perceptive. During 1956, people all across the globe – from Montgomery to Budapest,

Johannesburg to Warsaw, and Havana to Cairo – had taken to the streets, spoken out and risen up to demand their freedom. Their exhilarating triumphs and shattering defeats transformed their world – and ours.

ACKNOWLEDGEMENTS

It is a great pleasure to be able to place on record my sincere thanks to the many people who have helped in various ways during the writing of this book.

The School of History, University of Leeds, has been my academic home for the whole time that I have been working on *1956*, and I could not wish for a more generous or supportive group of colleagues. Financial assistance from both my department and the Faculty of Arts funded archival visits and a year of sabbatical leave. I also benefited from the largesse of the Eisenhower Foundation and the Roosevelt Study Center. Peter Anderson, Kester Aspden, Simon Ball, Malcolm Chase, Martin Evans, Dan Exeter, Moritz Föllmer, Matthew Frank, Oscar Jose Martin Garcia, Jim House, Will Jackson, Christoph Laucht, George Lewis, Paweł Machcewicz, Anita Prazmowska, Dan Stone, Brian Ward and Hugh Wilford responded to queries both large and small, and offered numerous helpful suggestions; Emilia Jamroziak, Vincent Hiribarren and János Szuhánszki translated various documents; and Rozalia Kollar, Nicholas Pronay, János Szuhánszki (Sr) and Maria Szuhánsky were kind enough to share their stories of 1956 with me. For taking the trouble to read parts of the manuscript and offering characteristically insightful and trenchant criticisms, I am more than happy to salute Shane Doyle, Nick Grant, Andrew Preston, Joe Street and, especially, Mark B. Smith – who interrogated me on everything from the structural problems of US foreign policy to the length of a Polish sausage!

A book of this kind inevitably relies heavily on the work of other scholars, and – as the detailed notes and bibliography show – I owe an enormous amount to those who have written previously on particular aspects of 1956. I would also like to acknowledge the sterling work of Valoise Armstrong (Dwight D. Eisenhower Presidential Library), Hans Krabbendam (assistant director, Roosevelt Study Center, Middelburg), and the staff of the National Archives, Kew; the Manuscript, Archives and Rare Book Library and the Robert R. Woodruff Library at Emory University, Atlanta; and the Brotherton Library, University of Leeds.

This project would never have got off the ground in the first place but for the support of my literary agent, Sally Holloway, and Felicity Bryan Associates. Sally not only had faith in this book – and in me – from the start, she also urged me to broaden my horizons and provided wise editorial advice. I am also indebted to Faber, where Neil Belton offered crucial early encouragement, Alex Russell fielded innumerable queries, Eleanor Rees copyedited the manuscript with admirable thoroughness, Kate Ward guided the book through to production and Julian Loose wielded his editorial pen to great effect (even if, tragically, the first ever Eurovision Song Contest failed to make the final cut).

Writing a book can be a pretty solitary business, and I am immensely grateful to all my friends and family for raising my spirits and cheering me on. My sister, Emma, is an inspiration, and my parents, Brian and Marilyn, have offered nothing less than unconditional love and support. For János, who has lived with this book (and put up with its occasionally grumpy author) these past years, words simply will not do.

SELECT BIBLIOGRAPHY

Full details of all manuscript sources and scholarly works cited in the text (including journal articles) can be found in the endnotes.

GENERAL

Max Boot, *Invisible Armies: An Epic History of Guerrilla Warfare from Ancient Times to the Present* (New York, Liveright, 2013)

Carole Fink, Frank Hadler and Tomasz Schramm, eds, *1956: European and Global Perspectives* (Leipzig: Leipziger Universitätsverlag, 2006)

Keith Flett, ed., *1956 and All That* (Newcastle: Cambridge Scholars Publishing, 2007)

Eric Hobsbawm, *Interesting Times: A Twentieth-Century Life* (London: Abacus, 2010)

Gerd-Rainer Horn, *The Spirit of '68: Rebellion in Western Europe and North America, 1956–1976* (Oxford: Oxford University Press, 2007)

Tony Judt, *Postwar: A History of Europe Since 1945* (New London: Vintage, 2010)

Dominic Sandbrook, *Never Had It So Good: A History of Britain from Suez to the Beatles* (London: Little, Brown, 2005)

EISENHOWER'S AMERICA

Dale Carter, ed., *Cracking the Ike Age: Aspects of Fifties America* (Aarhus: Aarhus University Press, 1992)

William Chafe, *The Unfinished Journey: America Since World War II* (New York: Oxford University Press, 1991, second edition)

John Patrick Diggins, *The Proud Decades: America in War and Peace, 1941–1960* (New York: W. W. Norton, 1989)

Dwight D. Eisenhower, *Waging Peace: The White House Years, A Personal Account, 1956–1961* (New York: Doubleday, 1965)

Stephen Kinzer, *The Brothers: John Foster Dulles, Allen Dulles, and Their Secret World War* (New York: Henry Holt, 2013)

David A. Nichols, *A Matter of Justice: Eisenhower and the Beginning of the Civil Rights Revolution* (New York: Simon & Schuster, 2007)

David A. Nichols, *Eisenhower 1956* (New York: Simon & Schuster, 2011)

Chester J. Pach, Jr and Elmo Richardson, *The Presidency of Dwight D. Eisenhower* (Lawrence: University Press of Kansas, 1991)

THE CIVIL RIGHTS MOVEMENT

Taylor Branch, *Parting the Waters: America in the King Years, 1954–1963* (New York: Simon and Schuster, 1988)

Douglas Brinkley, *Mine Eyes Have Seen the Glory: The Life of Rosa Parks* (London: Phoenix, 2001)

Stewart Burns, ed., *Daybreak of Freedom: The Montgomery Bus Boycott* (Chapel Hill: University of North Carolina Press, 1997)

Clayborne Carson et al., eds, *The Eyes on the Prize Civil Rights Reader* (New York: Penguin Books, 1991)

Clayborne Carson, ed., *The Papers of Martin Luther King, Jr., Volume III: Birth of a New Age, December 1955–December 1956* (Berkeley: University of California Press, 1997)

Clayborne Carson, ed., *The Papers of Martin Luther King, Jr., Volume VI: Advocate of the Social Gospel, September 1948–March 1963* (Berkeley: University of California Press, 2007)

Clayborne Carson et al., *Reporting Civil Rights, Part One: American Journalism 1941–1963* (New York: Library of America, 2003)

Mary Dudziak, *Cold War Civil Rights: Race and the Image of American Democracy* (Princeton: Princeton University Press, 2000)

Uriah J. Fields, *Inside the Montgomery Bus Boycott: My Personal Story* (Baltimore: America House, 2002)

David Garrow, *Bearing the Cross: Martin Luther King, Jr., and the Southern Christian Leadership Conference* (London: Vintage, 1986)

Henry Hampton and Steve Fayer, eds, *Voices of Freedom: An Oral History of the Civil Rights Movement from the 1950s through the 1980s* (New York: Bantam Books, 1990)

Troy Jackson, *Becoming King: Martin Luther King Jr. and the Making of a National Leader* (Lexington: The University Press of Kentucky, 2008)

Coretta Scott King, *My Life With Martin Luther King, Jr.* (New York: Holt, Rinehart and Winston, 1969)

Martin Luther King, Jr, *Stride Toward Freedom: The Montgomery Story* (Boston: Beacon Press, 1958)

Azza Salama Layton, *International Politics and Civil Rights Policies in the United States, 1941–1960* (Cambridge: Cambridge University Press, 2000)

Peter J. Ling, *Martin Luther King, Jr.* (London: Routledge, 2002)

Danielle L. McGuire, *At the Dark End of the Street: Black Women, Rape, and Resistance – a New History of the Civil Rights Movement from Rosa Parks to the Rise of Black Power* (New York: Vintage Books, 2010)

James H. Meriwether, *Proudly We Can Be Africans: Black Americans and Africa, 1935–1961* (Chapel Hill: The University of North Carolina Press, 2002)

Brenda Gayle Plummer, ed., *Window on Freedom: Race, Civil Rights, and Foreign Affairs, 1945–1988* (Chapel Hill: The University of North Carolina Press, 2003)

Jo Ann Gibson Robinson, *The Montgomery Bus Boycott and the Women Who Started It* (Knoxville: University of Tennessee Press, 1987)

Belinda Robnett, *How Long, How Long?: African American Women in the Struggle for Civil Rights* (New York: Oxford University Press, 2000)

Jeanne Theoharis, *The Rebellious Life of Mrs. Rosa Parks* (Boston: Beacon Press, 2013)

J. Mills Thornton, *Dividing Lines: Municipal Politics and the Struggle for Civil Rights in Montgomery, Birmingham, and Selma* (Tuscaloosa: University of Alabama Press, 2002)

Penny M. Von Eschen, *Race Against Empire: Black Americans and Anticolonialism, 1937–1957* (Ithaca: Cornell University Press, 1997)

Donnie Williams with Wayne Greenhaw, *Thunder of Angels: The Montgomery Bus Boycott and the People Who Broke the Back of Jim Crow* (Chicago: Lawrence Hill Books, 2006)

MASSIVE RESISTANCE

Chris Myers Asch, *The Senator and the Sharecropper: The Freedom Struggles of James O. Eastland and Fannie Lou Hamer* (Chapel Hill: University of North Carolina Press, 2008)

E. Culpepper Clark, *The Schoolhouse Door: Segregation's Last Stand at the University of Alabama* (New York: Oxford University Press, 1993)

Gene L. Howard, *Patterson for Alabama: The Life and Career of John Patterson* (Tuscaloosa: University of Alabama Press, 2008)

Robyn Duff Ladino, *Desegregating Texas Schools: Eisenhower, Shivers, and the Crisis at Mansfield High* (Austin: University of Texas Press, 1996)

George Lewis, *The White South and the Red Menace: Segregationists, Anticommunism, and Massive Resistance, 1945–1965* (Gainesville: University Press of Florida, 2004)

George Lewis, *Massive Resistance: The White Response to the Civil Rights Movement* (London: Hodder Arnold, 2006)

Neil R. McMillen, *The Citizens' Council: Organized Resistance to the Second Reconstruction, 1954–1964* (Urbana: University of Illinois Press, 1994 edition)

Clive Webb, ed., *Massive Resistance: Southern Opposition to the Second Reconstruction* (Oxford: Oxford University Press, 2005)

Clive Webb, *Rabble Rousers: The American Far Right in the Civil Rights Era* (Athens: University of Georgia Press, 2010)

THE ANTI-APARTHEID MOVEMENT

Frances Baard and Barbie Schreiner, *My Spirit Is Not Banned* (Harare: Zimbabwe Publishing House, 1986)

Rusty Bernstein, *Memory Against Forgetting: Memoirs from a Life in South African Politics, 1938–1964* (London: Viking, 1999)

Pamela E. Brooks, *Boycotts, Buses, and Passes: Black Women's Resistance in the US South and South Africa* (Amherst: University of Massachusetts Press, 2008)

Nancy J. Clark and William H. Worger, *South Africa: The Rise and Fall of Apartheid* (Harlow: Pearson Education, 2011)

Basil Davidson, Joe Slovo, Anthony R. Wilkinson, *Southern Africa: The New Politics of Revolution* (Harmondsworth: Penguin Books, 1976)

Saul Dubow, *Apartheid, 1948–1994* (Oxford: Oxford University Press, 2014)

Lionel Forman and E. S. [Solly] Sachs, *The South African Treason Trial* (London, John Calder, 1957)

George M. Fredrickson, *Black Liberation: A Comparative History of Black Ideologies in the United States and South Africa* (Oxford: Oxford University Press, 1995)

Nomboniso Gasa, ed., *Women in South Africa* (Cape Town: HSRC Press, 2007)

Shireen Hassim, *Women's Organizations and Democracy in South Africa: Contesting Authority* (Madison: University of Wisconsin Press, 2006)

Helen Joseph, *If This Be Treason* (London: Andre Deutsch, 1963)

Helen Joseph, *Side By Side: The Autobiography of Helen Joseph* (New York: William Morrow and Company, Inc., 1986)

Thomas Karis and Gwendolen M. Carter, eds, *From Protest to Challenge: A Documentary History of African Politics in South Africa, 1882–1964, Volume 3, Challenge and Violence, 1953–1964* (Stanford: Hoover Institution Press, 1977)

Blanche La Guma with Martin Klammer, *In the Dark With My Dress on Fire: My Life in Cape Town, London, Havana and Home Again* (Aukland Park: Jacana, 2010)

Tom Lodge, *Black Politics in South Africa Since 1945* (London: Longman, 1983)

Nelson Mandela, *Long Walk to Freedom: The Autobiography of Nelson Mandela* (London: Abacus, 1995)

Elinor Batezat Sisulu, *Walter and Albertina Sisulu: In Our Lifetime* (London: Abacus, 2002)

Rob Skinner, *The Foundations of Anti-Apartheid: Liberal Humanitarianism and Transnational Activists in Britain and the United States, c.1919–1964* (Basingstoke: Palgrave Macmillan, 2010)

Cherryl Walker, *Women and Resistance in South Africa* (London: Onyx Press, 1982)

FRENCH NORTH AFRICA

Raymond F. Betts, *France and Decolonization 1900–1960* (Basingstoke: Palgrave Macmillan, 1991)

Habib Bourguiba, *My Life, My Ideas, My Struggle* (Tunis: Ministry of Information, 1979)

Albert Camus, *The Algerian Chronicles* (Cambridge, MA: Belknap, 2013), edited by Alice Kaplan, translated by Arthur Goldhammer

Anthony Clayton, *The Wars of French Decolonization* (London: Longman, 1994)

Alice L. Conklin, Sarah Fishman and Robert Zaretsky, *France and Its Empire Since 1870* (New York: Oxford University Press, 2011)

Matthew Connelly, *A Diplomatic Revolution: Algeria's Fight for Independence and the Origins of the Post-Cold War Era* (Oxford: Oxford University Press, 2003)

Martin Evans, *Algeria: France's Undeclared War* (Oxford: Oxford University Press, 2012)

Frantz Fanon, *The Wretched of the Earth* (London: Penguin Classics, 2001)

Derek Hopwood, *Habib Bourguiba of Tunisia: The Tragedy of Longevity* (Basingstoke: Macmillan, 1992)

Alistair Horne, *A Savage War of Peace: Algeria 1954–1962* (New York: New York Review of Books, 2006)

James F. McMillan, *Twentieth Century France: Politics and Society, 1898–1991* (London: Arnold, 1992)

Robert Merle, *Ben Bella* (London: Michael Joseph, 1967)

Gil Merom, *How Democracies Lose Small Wars* (Cambridge: Cambridge University Press, 2003)

Norma Salem, *Habib Bourguiba, Islam and the Creation of Tunisia* (London: Croom Helm, 1984)

Todd Shepard, *The Invention of Decolonization: The Algerian War and the Remaking of France* (Ithaca: Cornell University Press, 2006)

Martin Thomas, *The French North African Crisis: Colonial Breakdown and Anglo-French Relations, 1945–1962* (Basingstoke: Macmillan, 2000)

Martin Thomas, *Fight or Flight: Britain, France, and Their Roads from Empire* (Oxford: Oxford University Press, 2014)

Irwin M. Wall, *France, the United States, and the Algerian War* (Berkeley: University of California Press, 2001)

Irwin Wall, *A Diplomatic Revolution: Algeria's Fight for Independence and the Origins of the Post-Cold War Era* (New York: Oxford University Press, 2002)

BRITAIN AND THE END OF EMPIRE

Jean Marie Allman, *The Quills of the Porcupine: Asante Nationalism in an Emergent Ghana* (Madison: University of Wisconsin Press, 1993)

David Anderson, *Histories of the Hanged: Britain's Dirty War in Kenya and the End of Empire* (London: Weidenfeld & Nicolson, 2005)

Dennis Austin, *Politics in Ghana, 1946–1960* (London: Oxford University Press, 1964)

Glen Balfour-Paul, *The End of Empire in the Middle East: Britain's Relinquishment of Power in Her Last Three Arab Dependencies* (Cambridge: Cambridge University Press, 1991)

David Birmingham, *Kwame Nkrumah: The Father of African Nationalism* (Athens: Ohio University Press, 1998)

Piers Brendon, *The Decline and Fall of the British Empire, 1781–1997* (New York: Alfred A. Knopf, 2008)

W. Byford-Jones, *Grivas and the Story of EOKA* (London: Robert Hale Limited, 1959)

Nancy Crawshaw, *The Cyprus Revolt: An Account of the Struggle for Union with Greece* (London: George Allen & Unwin, 1978)

John Darwin, *The End of the British Empire: The Historical Debate* (Oxford: Basil Blackwell, 1991)

Caroline Elkins, *Britain's Gulag: The Brutal End of Empire in Kenya* (London: Pimlico, 2005)

Charles Foley, ed., *The Memoirs of General Grivas* (London: Longmans, 1964)

John Bagot Glubb, *A Soldier With the Arabs* (London: Hodder and Stoughton, 1957)

Robert Holland, *Britain and the Revolt in Cyprus, 1954–1959* (Oxford: Clarendon Press, 1998)

Ronald Hyam, *Britain's Declining Empire: The Road to Decolonisation, 1918–1968* (Cambridge: Cambridge University Press, 2006)

Douglas H. Johnson, *The Root Causes of Sudan's Civil Wars* (Oxford: James Currey, 2003)

Wm. Roger Louis, *Ends of British Imperialism: The Scramble for Empire, Suez and Decolonization* (London: I. B. Tauris, 2006)

Martin Lynn, ed., *The British Empire in the 1950s: Retreat or Revival?* (Basingstoke: Palgrave Macmillan, 2006)

Philip Murphy, *Alan Lennox-Boyd: A Biography* (London: I. B. Tauris, 1999)

Robin Neillands, *A Fighting Retreat: The British Empire 1947–97* (London: Hodder and Stoughton, 1996)

Kwame Nkrumah, *The Autobiography of Kwame Nkrumah* (London: Panaf Books, 2002)

Paul Nugent, *Africa Since Independence* (Basingstoke: Palgrave Macmillan, 2004)

Julius K. Nyerere, *Freedom and Unity/Uhuru na Umoja: A Selection from Writings and Speeches, 1952–65* (London: Oxford University Press, 1967)

Richard Rathbone, *Nkrumah and the Chiefs: The Politics of Chieftaincy in Ghana, 1951–1960* (Oxford: James Currey, 2000).

Robin W. Winks, ed., *The Oxford History of the British Empire, Volume V: Historiography* (Oxford: Oxford University Press, 1999)

SUEZ

Anne Alexander, *Nasser* (London: Haus Publishing, 2005)

Peter Catterall, ed., *The Macmillan Diaries: The Cabinet Years, 1950–1957* (London: Macmillan, 2003)

Moshe Dayan, *Diary of the Sinai Campaign* (New York: Schocken Books, 1967)

Moshe Dayan, *Story of My Life* (London: Weidenfeld and Nicolson, 1976)

Joel Gordon, *Nasser: Hero of the Arab Nation* (Oxford: Oneworld Publications, 2009)

Anthony Gorst and Lewis Johnman, *The Suez Crisis* (London: Routledge, 1997)

Mohamed Heikal, *The Cairo Documents: The Inside Story of Nasser and His Relationship with World Leaders, Rebels, and Statesmen* (New York: Doubleday, 1973)

Mohamed H. Heikal, *Cutting The Lion's Tail: Suez Through Egyptian Eyes* (London: André Deutsch, 1986)

Laura M. James, *Nasser at War: Arab Images of the Enemy* (Basingstoke: Palgrave Macmillan, 2006)

James Jankowski, *Nasser's Egypt, Arab Nationalism, and the United Arab Republic* (London: Lynn Rienner Publishers, 2002)

Keith Kyle, *Suez: Britain's End of Empire in the Middle East* (London: I. B. Tauris, 2011)

Selwyn Lloyd, *Suez 1956: A Personal Account* (London: Book Club Associates, 1978)

W. Scott Lucas, *Divided We Stand: Britain, the US and the Suez Crisis* (London: Hodder & Stoughton, 1991)

Scott Lucas, ed., *Britain and Suez: The Lion's Last Roar* (Manchester: Manchester University Press, 1996)

Tony Shaw, *Eden, Suez and the Mass Media: Propaganda and Persuasion During the Suez Crisis* (London: I. B. Tauris, 1996)

Simon C. Smith, ed., *Reassessing Suez 1956: New Perspectives on the Crisis and its Aftermath* (Aldershot: Ashgate, 2008)

D. R. Thorpe, *Selwyn Lloyd* (London: Jonathan Cape, 1989)

D. R. Thorpe, *Eden: The Life and Times of Anthony Eden, First Earl of Avon, 1897–1977* (London: Pimlico, 2004)

THE SECRET SPEECH AND DE-STALINISATION

Balázs Apor et al., eds, *The Leader Cult in Communist Dictatorships: Stalin and the Eastern Bloc* (New York: Palgrave Macmillan, 2004)

Anne Applebaum, *Iron Curtain: The Crushing of Eastern Europe 1944–1956* (London: Allen Lane, 2012)

Jung Chang and Jon Halliday, *Mao: The Unknown Story* (London: Jonathan Cape, 2005)

John Connelly and Michael Grüttner, eds, *Universities Under Dictatorship* (University Park, PA: Pennsylvania State University Press, 2005)

Miriam Dobson, *Khrushchev's Cold Summer: Gulag Returnees, Crime, and the Fate of Reform After Stalin* (Ithaca: Cornell University Press, 2009)

Lee Feigon, *Mao: A Reinterpretation* (Chicago: Ivan R. Dee, 2002)

Robert Hornsby, *Protest, Reform and Repression in Khrushchev's Soviet Union* (Cambridge: Cambridge University Press, 2013)

Geoffrey Hosking, *A History of the Soviet Union* (London: Fontana, 1985)

Polly Jones, ed., *The Dilemmas of De-Stalinization. Negotiating Social and Political Change in the Khrushchev Era* (London: Routledge, 2006)

Jakub Karpiński, *Countdown: The Polish Upheavals of 1956, 1968, 1970, 1980 . . .* (New York: Karz-Cohl Publishers, 1982)

A. Kemp-Welch, *Stalinism in Poland, 1955–1956* (New York: St. Martin's Press, 1999)

A. Kemp-Welch, *Poland under Communism: A Cold War History* (Cambridge: Cambridge University Press, 2008)

Nikita Khrushchev, *Khrushchev Remembers: The Glasnost Tapes* (Boston: Little, Brown and Company, 1990)

Sergei Khrushchev, ed., *Memoirs of Nikita Khrushchev: Volume 3, Statesman [1953–1964]* (University Park, PA: Pennsylvania State University, 2007)

Vladimir A. Kozlov, *Mass Uprisings in the USSR: Protest and Rebellion in the Post-Stalin Years* (London: M. E. Sharpe, 2002)

Erik Kulavig, *Dissent in the Years of Khrushchev: Nine Stories about Disobedient Russians* (Basingstoke: Palgrave Macmillan, 2002)

Vladimir V. Kusin, *The Intellectual Origins of the Prague Spring: The Development of Reformist Ideas in Czechoslovakia 1956–1967* (Cambridge: Cambridge University Press, 1971)

Katherine Lebow, *Unfinished Utopia: Nowa Huta, Stalinism, and Polish Society, 1949–1956* (Ithaca: Cornell University Press, 2013)

Michael Lynch, *Mao* (London: Routledge, 2004)

Kevin McDermott and Matthew Stibbe, eds, *Revolution and Resistance in Eastern Europe: Challenges to Communist Rule* (Oxford: Berg, 2006)

Roderick MacFarquhar, *The Hundred Flowers* (London: Stevens & Sons, 1960)

Paweł Machcewicz, *Rebellious Satellite: Poland 1956* (Stanford: Stanford University Press, 2009)

Martin Malia, *The Soviet Tragedy: A History of Socialism in Russia* (New York: Free Press, 1995)

John P. C. Matthews, *Tinderbox: East-Central Europe in the Spring, Summer, and Early Fall of 1956* (Tucson, Arizona: Fenestra Books, 2003)

Zhores A. Medvedev and Roy A. Medvedev, *The Unknown Stalin* (London: I. B. Tauris, 2005)

Anita Prazmowska, *Wladyslaw Gomulka: A Biography* (London: I. B. Tauris, 2015)

Robert Service, *The Penguin History of Modern Russia: From Tsarism to the Twenty-First Century* (London: Penguin Books, 2009)

Robert Service, *Comrades: Communism: A World History* (London: Pan Books, 2008)

Konrad Syrop, *Spring in October: The Polish Revolution of 1956* (London: Weidenfeld and Nicolson, 1957)

William Taubman, Sergei Khrushchev and Abbott Gleason, eds, *Nikita Khrushchev* (New Haven: Yale University Press, 2000)

William Taubman, *Khrushchev: The Man, His Era* (London: The Free Press, 2005)

William J. Tompson, *Khrushchev: A Political Life* (London: St Martin's Press, 1997)

Teresa Toranska, *Oni: Stalin's Polish Puppets* (London: William Collins, 1987)

Vittorio Vidali, *Diary of the Twentieth Congress of the Communist Party of the Soviet Union* (London: Journeyman Press, 1974)

Paul E. Zinner, ed., *National Communism and Popular Revolt in Eastern Europe: A Selection of Documents on Events in Poland and Hungary, February–November, 1956* (New York: Columbia University Press, 1956)

THE HUNGARIAN REVOLUTION

Tamás Aczél and Tibor Méray, *The Revolt of the Mind: A Case History of Intellectual Resistance Behind the Iron Curtain* (New York: Frederick A. Praeger, 1959)

Leslie B. Bain, *The Reluctant Satellites: An Eyewitness Report on East Europe and the Hungarian Revolution* (New York: The Macmillan Company, 1960)

Csaba Békés et al., *The 1956 Hungarian Revolution: A History in Documents* (Budapest: Central European University Press, 2002)

Karl P. Benziger, *Imre Nagy: Martyr of the Nation* (New York: Lexington Books, 2010)

Bryan Cartledge, *The Will to Survive: A History of Hungary* (London: Hurst & Company, 2011)

Lee Congdon et al., *1956: The Hungarian revolution and War for Independence* (Boulder, Colorado: Social Science monographs, 2006)

Terry Cox, ed., *Hungary 1956 – Forty Years On* (London: Frank Cass, 1997)

Peter Fryer, *Hungarian Tragedy* (London: Index Books, 1997)

Charles Gati, *Failed Illusions: Moscow, Washington, Budapest, and the 1956 Hungarian Revolt* (Stanford: Stanford University Press, 2006)

Roger Gough, *A Good Comrade: Janos Kadar, Communism, and Hungary* (London: I. B. Tauris, 2006)

Johanna Granville, *The First Domino: International Decision Making During the Hungarian Crisis of 1956* (College Station: Texas A&M University Press, 2004)

Béla K. Király and Paul Jónás, eds, *The Hungarian Revolution of 1956 in Retrospect* (East European Quarterly, Boulder, Distributed by Columbia University Press, 1978)

Bennett Kovrig, *Communism in Hungary: From Kun to Kádár* (Stanford: Hoover Institution Press, 1979)

Melvin J. Lasky, ed., *The Hungarian Revolution: The Story of the October Uprising as Recorded in Documents, Dispatches, Eye-Witness Accounts, and World-wide Reactions* (London: Martin Secker & Warburg Ltd, 1957)

Paul Lendvai, *One Day That Shook the Communist World: The 1956 Hungarian Uprising and its Legacy* (Princeton: Princeton University Press, 2008)

György Litván, ed., *The Hungarian Revolution of 1956: Reform, Revolt and Repression, 1953–1963* (Harlow: Longman, 1996)

John P. C. Matthews, *Explosion: The Hungarian Revolution of 1956* (New York: Hippocrene Books, 2007)

Miklós Molnár, *Budapest 1956: A History of the Hungarian Revolution* (London: George Allen & Unwin, 1971)

Mark Pittaway, *The Workers' State: Industrial Labor and the Making of Socialist Hungary, 1944–1958* (Pittsburgh: University of Pittsburgh Press, 2012)

János M. Rainer, *Imre Nagy: A Biography* (London: I. B. Tauris, 2009)

Victor Sebestyen, *Twelve Days: Revolution 1956* (London: Phoenix, 2007)

Paul E. Zinner, *Revolution in Hungary* (New York: Columbia University Press, 1962)

THE CUBAN REVOLUTION

Jorge Castañeda, *Compañero: The Life and Death of Che Guevara* (London: Bloomsbury, 1997)

Fidel Castro and Ignacio Ramonet, *Fidel Castro: My Life. A Spoken Autobiography* (New York: Scribner, 2009)

Aviva Chomsky, *A History of the Cuban Revolution* (Chichester: Wiley-Blackwell, 2011)

Leycester Coltman, *The Real Fidel Castro* (New Haven: Yale University Press, 2003)

Carlos Franqui, *Diary of the Cuban Revolution* (New York: Viking Press, 1976)

Piero Gleijeses, *Visions of Freedom: Havana, Washington, Pretoria, and the Struggle for Southern Africa, 1976–1991* (Chapel Hill: University of North Carolina Press, 2013)

Van Gosse, *Where the Boys Are: Cuba, Cold War America and the Making of a New Left* (London: Verso, 1993)

Ernesto Che Guevara, *Reminiscences of the Cuban Revolutionary War* (London: Harper Perennial, 2009)

Julio García Luis, *Cuban Revolution Reader: A Documentary History of 40 Key Moments of the Cuban Revolution* (New York: Ocean Press, 2001)

Herbert L. Matthews, *Revolution in Cuba: An Essay in Understanding* (New York: Charles Scribner's Sons, 1975)

James O'Connor, *The Origins of Socialism in Cuba* (Ithaca: Cornell University Press, 1970)

Julia E. Sweig, *Inside the Cuban Revolution: Fidel Castro and the Urban Underground* (Cambridge, MA: Harvard University Press, 2002)

Hugh Thomas, *Cuba: or The Pursuit of Freedom* (New York: DaCapo Press, 1998)

POPULAR CULTURE

Glenn C. Altschuler, *All Shook Up: How Rock 'n' Roll Changed America* (Oxford: Oxford University Press, 2003)

Michael T. Bertrand, *Race, Rock, and Elvis* (Urbana: University of Illinois Press, 2005)

Ann Charters, ed., *The Portable Beat Reader* (New York: Penguin, 1992)

Rick Coleman, *Blue Monday: Fats Domino and the Lost Dawn of Rock 'n' Roll* (New York: DaCapo Press, 2007)

Anthony DeCurtis, ed., *Present Tense: Rock & Roll and Culture* (Durham, NC: Duke University Press, 1992)

Peter Guralnick, *Last Train to Memphis: The Rise of Elvis Presley* (London: Little, Brown, 1994)

Robert Hewison, *In Anger: Culture in the First Cold War* (London: Weidenfeld and Nicolson, 1981)

Michael Kenny, *First New Left: British Intellectuals After Stalin* (London: Lawrence & Wishart, 1995)

Gertrud Pickhan and Rüdiger Ritter, eds, *Jazz Behind the Iron Curtain* (Frankfurt am Main: Peter Lang, 2011)

Murray Pomerance, ed., *American Cinema of the 1950s: Themes and Variations* (New Brunswick, NJ: University Press, 2005)

S. Frederick Starr, *Red and Hot: The Fate of Jazz in the Soviet Union* (New York: Proscenium Publishers, 1994)

Edmund Stillman, ed., *Bitter Harvest: The Intellectual Revolt behind the Iron Curtain* (London: Thames and Hudson, 1959)

Brian Ward, *Just My Soul Responding: Rhythm and Blues, Black Consciousness, and Race Relations* (Berkeley: University of California Press, 1998)

Stuart Ward, ed., *British Culture and the End of Empire* (Manchester: Manchester University Press, 2001)

Colin Wilson, *The Angry Years: The Rise and Fall of the Angry Young Men* (London: Robson Books, 2007)

NOTES

ADM, CAB, CO, FO, HO, LAB, PREM and WO refer to materials held at the National Archives, Kew.

PROLOGUE

1 'Flagpole Lights in Times Sq. Fail', *New York Times*, 1 January 1956, 43.
2 '112 Japanese Die in Panic at Shrine', *NYT*, 1 January 1956, 1, 3; 'Japanese Shrine Disaster', *The Times* (London), 2 January 1956, 8.
3 'Franco's New Year Message of 1956' quoted in Sebastian Balfour, *Dictatorship, Workers, and the City: Labour in Greater Barcelona Since 1939* (Oxford: Clarendon Press, 1989), 41.
4 'A Time for Courage', *The Times*, 2 January 1956, 9; 'The Premier's Message for 1956', available at http://www.britishpathe.com/video/premiers-message-for-1956-aka-edens-new-year-speec; Thomas J. Hamilton, 'Difficult Year Ahead in U.S. Foreign Policy', *NYT*, 1 January 1956, E3.
5 'The Premier's Message for 1956'.
6 Martin Luther King, Jr, 'Our God Is Able', 1 January 1956, Dexter Avenue Baptist Church, Montgomery, Alabama, in Clayborne Carson, ed., *The Papers of Martin Luther King, Jr., Volume VI: Advocate of the Social Gospel, September 1948–March 1963* (Berkeley: University of California Press, 2007), 243–6.
7 'The Sudan as a Republic', *The Times*, 2 January 1956, 7.
8 'Regional Powers in Gold Coast', *The Times*, 2 January 1956, 8; '58 Moroccan Rebels Killed', *The Times*, 2 January 1956, 8; 'French Kill 56 Rebels in Riff Mountains', *Observer*, 1 January 1956, 1A; Albert Camus, 'Call for a Civilian Truce in Algeria', 22 January 1956, in *The Algerian Chronicles* (Cambridge, MA: Belknap, 2013), edited by Alice Kaplan, translated by Arthur Goldhammer, 153.
9 Jack Raymond, 'Tito is Optimistic on Peace Outlook', *NYT*, 1 January 1956; 'Tito's Attack on Colonial Powers', *The Observer*, 1 January 1956, 1.
10 'New Summit Talks Could Be Fruitful – Bulganin', *Observer*, 1 January 1956, 1, 5; see also 'Marshal Bulganin on Peace Hopes', *The Times*, 2 January 1956, 7.
11 'Russians Interrupt New Year's Supper to See What Latest Pravda Has to Say', *NYT*, 1 January 1956, 5; 'Marshal Bulganin on Peace Hopes'.
12 W. H. Lawrence, 'Mrs. Eisenhower Flies to Key West', *NYT*, 1 January 1956, 36; W. H. Lawrence, 'Two Presidents: A Key West View', *NYT*, 1 January 1956, F4.

13 Antonio Gramsci, 'I Hate New Year's Day', *Viewpoint Magazine*, 1 January 2015 (originally published in *Avanti!*, 1 January 1916), at https://viewpoint-mag.com/2015/01/01/i-hate-new-years-day/.

14 On the trend for books about years see, for instance, 'Books of year(s)', *Times Literary Supplement*, 9 July 2014, and Louis Menand, 'Thinking Sideways: The one-dot theory of history', *The New Yorker*, 30 March 2015. Recent books about specific years include (in chronological order, by year studied): Felipe Fernandez-Armesto, *1492: The Year Our World Began* (Bloomsbury, 2011); Suzannah Lipscomb, *1536: The Year That Changed Henry VIII* (Lion Books, 2006); David Andress, *1789: The Revolutions that Shook the World* (Abacus, 2010); Malcolm Chase, *1820: Disorder and Stability in the United Kingdom* (Manchester University Press, 2015); Mike Rapport, *1848: A Year of Revolution* (Abacus, 2009); Charles Emmerson, *1913: The Year Before the Great War* (Vintage, 2014); Florian Illies, *1913: The Year Before the Storm* (Clerkenwell Press, 2013); Victor Sebestyen, *1946: The Making of the Modern World* (Macmillan, 2014); Fred Kaplan, *1959: The Year Everything Changed* (John Wiley and Sons, 2010); Robin Morgan and Ariel Leve, *1963: The Year of the Revolution: How Youth Changed the World With Music, Art, and Fashion* (Dey Street Books, 2014); Christopher Bray, *1965: The Year Modern Britain Was Born* (Simon and Schuster, 2015); Mark Kurlansky, *1968: The Year that Rocked the World* (New York: Ballantine Books, 2004); Christian Caryl, *Strange Rebels: 1979 and the Birth of the 21st Century* (Basic Books, 2014); Michael Meyer, *1989: The Year That Changed the World* (Simon and Schuster, 2009); and W. Joseph Campbell, *1995: The Year the Future Began* (University of California Press, 2014).

15 William Chafe, *The Unfinished Journey: America Since World War II* (New York: Oxford University Press, 1991, second edition), 111–5; Mark Kurlansky, *1968: The Year that Rocked the World* (New York: Ballantine Books, 2004); John Patrick Diggins, *The Proud Decades: America in War and Peace, 1941–1960* (New York: W. W. Norton, 1989), 178.

16 'Atlantic Charter', 14 August 1941, available at http://avalon.law.yale.edu/wwii/atlantic.asp. See also http://www.atlanticcharter.ca/backgroundinfo.php.

I. MONTGOMERY

1 Joe Azbell, 'Blast Rocks Residence of Bus Boycott Leader', *Montgomery Advertiser*, 31 January 1956; David Garrow, *Bearing the Cross: Martin Luther King, Jr., and the Southern Christian Leadership Conference* (London: Vintage, 1986), 59. For a brief history of the house see http://www.dexterkingmemorial.org/tours/parsonage-museum/.

2 Coretta Scott King, *My Life with Martin Luther King, Jr.* (New York: Holt, Rinehart and Winston, 1969), 126–7.

3 Azbell, 'Blast Rocks Residence'.

4 King, *My Life with Martin Luther King, Jr.*, 127.

5 Taylor Branch, *Parting the Waters: America in the King Years, 1954–1963* (New York: Simon and Schuster, 1988), 163–4; Garrow, *Bearing the Cross*, 60.

6 Martin Luther King, Jr., *Stride Toward Freedom: The Montgomery Story* (Boston: Beacon Press, 1958), 126.

7 King, *My Life with Martin Luther King, Jr.*, 125–6; Garrow, *Bearing the Cross*, 55–6; Peter J. Ling, *Martin Luther King, Jr.* (London: Routledge, 2002), 45–56; King, *Stride Toward Freedom*, 118.

8 Garrow, *Bearing the Cross*, 56–8.

9 King, *Stride Toward Freedom*, 124–5.

10 Garrow, *Bearing the Cross*, 60; King, *Stride Toward Freedom*, 126.

11 Jo Ann Gibson Robinson, *The Montgomery Bus Boycott and the Women Who Started It* (University of Tennessee Press, 1987), 131.

12 King, *Stride Toward Freedom*, 126–7; Branch, *Parting the Waters*, 165; Garrow, *Bearing the Cross*, 60; Azbell, 'Blast Rocks Residence'; King, *My Life With Martin Luther King, Jr.*, 129.

13 Azbell, 'Blast Rocks Residence'; Branch, *Parting the Waters*, 166; King, *Stride Toward Freedom*, 128-129; King, *My Life with Martin Luther King, Jr.*, 130.

14 Robinson, *The Montgomery Bus Boycott*, 133; King, *My Life with Martin Luther King, Jr.*, 130.

15 'Table Ca74-90 – Gross domestic product, by major component: 1929–2002' in Richard Sutch and Susan B. Carter, eds, *Historical Statistics of the United States: Millennial Edition Online* (Cambridge University Press); Chafe, *The Unfinished Journey*, 112–19.

16 Callum MacDonald, 'The Paradox of Power: Eisenhower and the "New Look"', in Dale Carter, ed., *Cracking the Ike Age: Aspects of Fifties America* (Aarhus: Aarhus University Press, 1992), 15.

17 Troy Jackson, *Becoming King: Martin Luther King Jr. and the Making of a National Leader* (University Press of Kentucky, 2008), 10; Robert Cook, *Sweet Land of Liberty? The African-American Struggle for Civil Rights in the Twentieth Century* (Longman, 1998), 99; Stewart Burns, ed., *Daybreak of Freedom: The Montgomery Bus Boycott* (University of North Carolina Press, 1997), 1; http://www.exploresouthernhistory.com/montgomerycapitol2.

18 Cook, *Sweet Land of Liberty?*, 99; Branch, *Parting the Waters*, 13; Burns, *Daybreak of Freedom*, 2.

19 Cook, *Sweet Land of Liberty?*, 99; J. Mills Thornton, *Dividing Lines: Municipal Politics and the Struggle for Civil Rights in Montgomery, Birmingham, and Selma* (University of Alabama Press, 2002), 27–9.

20 Burns, *Daybreak of Freedom*, 2.

21 Henry Hampton and Steve Fayer, eds, *Voices of Freedom: An Oral History of the Civil Rights Movement from the 1950s through the 1980s* (Bantam Books, 1990), 19.

22 Jackson, *Becoming King*, 12.

23 Ling, *Martin Luther King, Jr.*, 35.

24 Robinson, *The Montgomery Bus Boycott*, 34–5.

25 SER-DNA. Transcript of Record and Proceedings, *Browder* v. *Gayle*, May 11, 1956, in Burns, *Daybreak of Freedom*, 70.

26 Thornton, *Dividing Lines*, 20–9, 33–9; Danielle L. McGuire, *At the Dark End of the Street: Black Women, Rape, and Resistance – a New History of the Civil Rights Movement from Rosa Parks to the Rise of Black Power* (New York: Vintage Books, 2010), 62–9, 71.

27 Thornton, *Dividing Lines*, 45, 46.

28 Ibid., 41.

29 Ibid., 46–7; Garrow, *Bearing the Cross*, 14–15; Robinson, *The Montgomery Bus Boycott*, 32.

30 Jo Ann Robinson, 'Letter from the Women's Political Council to the Mayor of Montgomery, Alabama', in Clayborne Carson et al., eds, *The Eyes on the Prize Civil Rights Reader* (Penguin Books, 1991), 44–5.

31 Thornton, *Dividing Lines*, 47–50.

32 Ibid., 50; Campaign Advertisement by Clyde C. Sellers, *Montgomery Advertiser*, 20 March 1955, in Burns, *Daybreak of Freedom*, 78–80.

33 Thornton, *Dividing Lines*, 50.

34 Garrow, *Bearing the Cross*, 15.

35 SER-DNA. Transcript of Record and Proceedings, *Browder* v. *Gayle*, May 11, 1956 in Burns, *Daybreak of Freedom*, 75.

36 Thornton, *Dividing Lines*, 53; 'Segregation Case Reset for March 18', *Montgomery Advertiser*, 10 March 1955.

37 Garrow, *Bearing the Cross*, 15–16.

38 Robinson, *The Montgomery Bus Boycott*, 42; Thornton, *Dividing Lines*, 55–6.

39 Garrow, *Bearing the Cross*, 11–12; *Voices of Freedom*, 19–20; 'Interview with Rosa Parks', in *Eyes on the Prize*, 45–7; Douglas Brinkley, *Mine Eyes Have Seen the Glory: The Life of Rosa Parks* (London: Phoenix, 2001), 104–9.

40 McGuire, *At the Dark End of the Street*, 14–17; Jeanne Theoharis, *The Rebellious Life of Mrs. Rosa Parks* (Boston: Beacon Press, 2013), 23–4.

41 Thornton, *Dividing Lines*, 58–61; Cook, *Sweet Land of Liberty?*, 100–1; Garrow, *Bearing the Cross*, 13.

42 Burns, *Daybreak of Freedom*, 82.

43 Hampton and Fayer, *Voices of Freedom*, 19.

44 'Rosa Parks Radio Interview, by Sidney Rogers', April 1956, Pacifica Radio Archive, Los Angeles, in Burns, *Daybreak of Freedom*, 85; Thornton, *Dividing Lines*, 60–1.

45 Garrow, *Bearing the Cross*, 11–12; 'Rosa Parks Radio Interview, by Sidney Rogers', in Burns, *Daybreak of Freedom*, 83.

46 Garrow, *Bearing the Cross*, 13–14; Ling, *Martin Luther King, Jr.*, 38–9; Thornton, *Dividing Lines*, 61.

47 Garrow, *Bearing the Cross*, 16; Thornton, *Dividing Lines*, 61; Robinson, *The Montgomery Bus Boycott*, 44–5.

48 Robinson, *The Montgomery Bus Boycott*, 45–6.

49 Ibid., 46–7.

50 Garrow, *Bearing the Cross*, 17–19; Thornton, *Dividing Lines*, 61–2; King, *Stride Toward Freedom*, 34.

51 Clayborne Carson, ed., *The Papers of Martin Luther King, Jr., Volume III: Birth of a New Age, December 1955–December 1956* (Berkeley: University of California Press, 1997), 67.

52 Garrow, *Bearing the Cross*, 19; King, *Stride Toward Freedom*, 36.

53 Garrow, *Bearing the Cross*, 19.

54 Donnie Williams with Wayne Greenhaw, *Thunder of Angels: The Montgomery Bus Boycott and the People Who Broke the Back of Jim Crow* (Lawrence Hill Books, 2006), 68–71; http://reportingcivilrights.loa.org/authors/bio.jsp?authorId=2.

55 Williams, *Thunder of Angels*, 74–5.

56 Joe Azbell, 'Negro Groups Ready Boycott of City Lines', *Montgomery Advertiser*, 4 December 1955.

57 Garrow, *Bearing the Cross*, 19–20; Robinson, *The Montgomery Bus Boycott*, 55.

58 King, *Stride Toward Freedom*, 40.

59 Ibid., 41–2.

60 Robinson, *The Montgomery Bus Boycott*, 58; Bunny Honicker, 'Negress Draws Fine in Segregation Case Involving Bus Ride', *Montgomery Advertiser*, 5 December 1955.

61 Garrow, *Bearing the Cross*, 21; Williams, *Thunder of Angels*, 79; Honicker, 'Negress Draws Fine'.

62 Garrow, *Bearing the Cross*, 17–18, 22–3, 49; Ling, *Martin Luther King, Jr.*, 42; Thornton, *Dividing Lines*, 62–3; King, *Stride Toward Freedom*, 44–7; McGuire, *At the Dark End of the Street*, 69.

63 King, *Stride Toward Freedom*, 48–9.

64 Ibid., 49.

65 Joe Azbell, 'At Holt Street Baptist Church', *Montgomery Advertiser*, 7 December 1955, reprinted in Carson, *Reporting Civil Rights, Part One: American Journalism 1941–1963* (Library of America, 2003), 228.

66 Robinson, *The Montgomery Bus Boycott*, 61–2; Azbell, 'At Holt Street Baptist Church', 228–9; Garrow, *Bearing the Cross*, 23.

67 King, *Stride Toward Freedom*, 49.

68 'Agenda' in Carson, ed., *The Papers of Martin Luther King, Jr., Volume III*, 70; Azbell, 'At Holt Street Baptist Church', 229; King, *Stride Toward Freedom*, 50.

69 Azbell, 'At Holt Street Baptist Church', 229–30; King, *Stride Toward Freedom*, 50.

70 Ralph D. Abernathy, 'The Natural History of a Social Movement' (MA Thesis, Atlanta University, 1958) in Burns, *Daybreak of Freedom*, 94; Carson, *The Papers of Martin Luther King, Jr., Volume III*, 71–4.

71 Hampton and Fayer, *Voices of Freedom*, 24.

72 French remarks in Carson, *The Papers of Martin Luther King, Jr., Volume III*, 74–5; Garrow, *Bearing the Cross*, 24; King, *Stride Toward Freedom*, 52; Abernathy in Carson, *The Papers of Martin Luther King, Jr., Volume III*, 76–8; Azbell, 'At Holt Street Baptist Church', 231.

73 Garrow, *Bearing the Cross*, 24; 'To the National City Lines, Inc', in Carson, *The Papers of Martin Luther King, Jr., Volume III*, 81.

74 Garrow, *Bearing the Cross*, 26; King, *Stride Toward Freedom*, 101.

75 Garrow, *Bearing the Cross*, 25–6; Tom Johnson, '4-Hour Huddle: Bus Boycott Conference Fails to Find Solution', *Montgomery Advertiser*, 9 December 1955, in Burns, *Daybreak of Freedom*, 98–9.

76 Thornton, *Dividing Lines*, 65; King, *Stride Toward Freedom*, 99–101.

77 Emory O. Jackson quoted in Garrow, *Bearing the Cross*, 31.

78 'To the Montgomery Public' in Burns, *Daybreak of Freedom*, 105–9.

79 Ibid., 108.

80 Roy Wilkins, letter to W. C. Patton, 27 December 1955, in Burns, *Daybreak of Freedom*, 110.

81 U. J. Fields, 'Negroes Cannot Compromise', in Burns, *Daybreak of Freedom*, 114. For Fields' account of this see Uriah J. Fields, *Inside the Montgomery Bus Boycott: My Personal Story* (America House, 2002), 71–2; Robinson, *The Montgomery Bus Boycott*, 78.

2. MOLLET'S SURRENDER

1 Tony Judt, *Postwar: A History of Europe Since 1945* (New London: Vintage, 2010), 282, 285, 286; Martin Evans, *Algeria: France's Undeclared War* (Oxford: Oxford University Press, 2012), xiv, 77–8, 85, 111–12.

2 Evans, *Algeria*, 113–17, 145.

3 Ibid., 144–5, 147.

4 Ibid., 147; 'M. Mollet Restates His Aim in Visit to Algeria', *The Times*, 6 February 1956, 7.

5 Alistair Horne, *A Savage War of Peace: Algeria 1954–1962* (New York: New York Review of Books, 2006), 147–9; 'The World: Plan for Algeria', *NYT*, 5 February 1956, 182; Evans, *Algeria*, 146–7; Anthony Clayton, *The Wars of French Decolonization* (London: Longman, 1994), 29; 'France: The Algeria Hurdle', *Time*, 13 February 1967; 'General Catroux', *The Times*, 22 December 1969, 8.

6 Horne, *Savage War*, 148–9; Evans, *Algeria*, 148–9.

7 Evans, *Algeria*, 149; Horne, *Savage War*, 147, 149.

8 JF 1019/38, Confidential Cypher; JF1019/40, D. J. Mill Irving, 'Report on Departure of M. Jacques Soustelle, the Retiring Governor General of Algeria', 2 February 1956, 1-4, FO 371/119357.

9 Horne, *Savage War*, 147–8; Evans, *Algeria*, 148; Despatch from HM Consul-General, JF1019/39, 6 February 1956, FO 371/119357.

10 http://www.paul-landowski.com/en/?p=252 and http://alger-roi.fr/Alger/cdha/textes/40_monument_aux_morts_cdha_54.htm; Evans, *Algeria*, 149.

11 Evans, *Algeria*, 149–50; Horne, *Savage War*, 149–50; Thomas F. Brady, 'Mollet Menaced by Mob in Algeria; Catroux Resigns', *NYT*, 7 February 1956, 1, 5; 'France: Algiers Speaking', *Time*, 20 February 1956; 'Troops in Algiers Will Guard Mollet', *NYT*, 6 February 1956, 2.

12 Horne, *Savage War*, 150; Brady, 'Mollet Menaced', 5; 'France: Algiers Speaking'.

13 Clayton, *Wars of French Decolonization*, 3–6, 12; Alice L. Conklin, Sarah Fishman and Robert Zaretsky, *France and Its Empire Since 1870* (New York: Oxford University Press, 2011), 265–6.

14 Conklin, *France and Its Empire*, 244, 250–1; Raymond F. Betts, *France and Decolonization 1900–1960* (Basingstoke: Palgrave Macmillan, 1991), 70–2.

15 Clayton, *Wars of French Decolonization*, 8–11; James F. McMillan, *Twentieth Century France: Politics and Society, 1898–1991* (London: Arnold, 1992), 154–62.

16 Clayton, *Wars of French Decolonization*, 2–3.

17 Conklin, *France and Its Empire*, 265–6.

18 Ibid., 265–9.

19 Ibid., 16, 67; Clayton, *Wars of French Decolonization*, 13; Todd Shepard, *The Invention of Decolonization: The Algerian War and the Remaking of France* (Ithaca: Cornell University Press, 2006), 19–21.

20 Conklin, *France and Its Empire*, 270–1; Clayton, *Wars of French Decolonization*, 13.

21 Shepard, *The Invention of Decolonization*, 8.

22 Betts, *France and Decolonization*, 102; Clayton, *Wars of French Decolonization*, 108–9; Conklin, *France and Its Empire*, 281–2.

23 Clayton, *Wars of French Decolonization*, 108–9.

24 Conklin, *France and Its Empire*, 24, 67.

25 Shepard, *The Invention of Decolonization*, 40–3.

26 Betts, *France and Decolonization*, 7, 98–9; Evans, *Algeria*, 77–8; Henry Giniger, 'Problems for France Intensified in Africa', *NYT*, 7 November 1954, E9; 'Troubled Arc', *NYT*, 28 August 1955, E1.

27 Clayton, *Wars of French Decolonization*, 97–9.

28 'Troubled Arc'; Betts, *France and Decolonization*, 99–100; Clayton, *Wars of French Decolonization*, 100.

29 'Rebel Forces Merge', *NYT*, 5 October 1955, 8; Clayton, *Wars of French Decolonization*, 101–2.

30 Clayton, *Wars of French Decolonization*, 102; Betts, *France and Decolonization*, 100.

31 Betts, *France and Decolonization*, 7; Derek Hopwood, *Habib Bourguiba of Tunisia: The Tragedy of Longevity* (Basingstoke: Macmillan, 1992), 3, 6; Norma Salem, *Habib Bourguiba, Islam and the Creation of Tunisia* (London: Croom Helm, 1984), 29, 31–4.

32 Hopwood, *Habib Bourguiba*, 12.

33 Ibid., 12, 13–20, 30.

34 Clayton, *Wars of French Decolonization*, 22–3; Betts, *France and Decolonization*, 7, 35, 97, 100; 'Habib Bourguiba: Father of Tunisia' at http://news.bbc.co.uk/1/hi/obituaries/703907.stm; Simon Kavanaugh, 'Habib Bourguiba, the Moses of Tunisia', *Contact*, 28 June 1958, 13, available at http://www.bourguiba.com/pages/pressreleases.aspx.

35 Betts, *France and Decolonization*, 35; Kavanaugh, 'Habib Bourguiba, the Moses of Tunisia'; Hopwood, *Habib Bourguiba*, 68–9.

36 Hopwood, *Habib Bourguiba*, 68–9, 71; Betts, *France and Decolonization*, 100.

37 Betts, *France and Decolonization*, 100.

38 Hopwood, *Habib Bourguiba*, 31.

39 Ibid., 40.

40 Kavanaugh, 'Habib Bourguiba, the Moses of Tunisia'.

41 Hopwood, *Habib Bourguiba*, 39–40.

42 Clayton, *Wars of French Decolonization*, 88; Hopwood, *Habib Bourguiba*, 67, 70.

43 Hopwood, *Habib Bourguiba*, 71; Betts, *France and Decolonization*, 100–1; Clayton, *Wars of French Decolonization*, 88–9; Habib Bourguiba, *My Life, My Ideas, My Struggle* (Tunis: Ministry of Information, 1979), 245–6, 252–4.

44 Clayton, *Wars of French Decolonization*, 89–90. See also Robert C. Doty, 'Tunisia Outbursts Checked By French', *NYT*, 21 January 1952, 5; Doty, 'Tunisia Rioting at New Peak', *NYT*, 24 January 1952, 1; Doty, 'Now Tunisia is Shaken by Rising of Arabs', *NYT*, 27 January 1952, E3.

45 Hopwood, *Habib Bourguiba*, 73–4; Bourguiba, *My Life*, 246, 253; 'Ultimatum to Terrorists', *Manchester Guardian*, 23 November 1954, 1.

46 Betts, *France and Decolonization*, 101; Hopwood, *Habib Bourguiba*, 73–6; Clayton, *Wars of French Decolonization*, 89–90.

47 Clayton, *Wars of French Decolonization*, 91; Hopwood, *Habib Bourguiba*, 76; 'Premier Broadcasts Plea', *NYT*, 1 August 1954, 4.

48 Hopwood, *Habib Bourguiba*, 76–7; Bourguiba, *My Life*, 293, 295–306; Clayton, *Wars of French Decolonization*, 91–2; Betts, *France and Decolonization*, 101–2.

49 'Exile's Triumphant Return', *Manchester Guardian*, 2 June 1955, 1; Hopwood, *Habib Bourguiba*, 77.

50 'Exiled Tunisian Leader Receives Tumultuous Welcome on Return', *NYT*, 2 June 1955, 8. See also Bourguiba, *My Life*, 308.

51 Clayton, *Wars of French Decolonization*, 93; Henry Giniger, 'France Accepts Tunisia's Status of Independence', *NYT*, 18 March 1956, 1; Henry Giniger, 'French Sign Pact on a Free Tunisia', *NYT*, 21 March 1956, 4.

52 Thomas F. Brady, 'Tunisian Urging Algeria Liberty', *NYT*, 23 March 1956, 10; Hopwood, *Habib Bourguiba*, 81; 'Tunis Goes to the Polls', *Manchester Guardian*, 26 March 1956, 7.

53 Horne, *Savage War*, 90–4; Evans, *Algeria*, 113–14; Conklin, *France and Its Empire*, 271–2; 'France: Suitcase or Coffin?', *Time*, 15 November 1954; 'Terrorist Bands Kill 7 in Algeria', *NYT*, 2 November 1954, 1; 'Influences Behind the Algerian Murders', *Manchester Guardian*, 3 November 1954, 5.
54 Evans, *Algeria*, 114.
55 Ibid., 115–16.
56 Clayton, *Wars of French Decolonization*, 109–12; Betts, *France and Decolonization*, 103–4; Evans, *Algeria*, 139–40.
57 Clayton, *Wars of French Decolonization*, 113, 119; Evans, *Algeria*, 116, 139–40.
58 Evans, *Algeria*, 120.
59 Ibid., 123; Clayton, *Wars of French Decolonization*, 113.
60 Conklin, *France and Its Empire*, 271.
61 Evans, *Algeria*, 125, 127; Horne, *Savage War*, 112.
62 Horne, *Savage War*, 119.
63 Ibid., 120.
64 Ibid., 120–1. See also Evans, *Algeria*, 140–1; Clayton, *Wars of French Decolonization*, 118–19; 'Fresh Violence in North Africa', *Manchester Guardian*, 22 August 1955, 1.
65 Evans, *Algeria*, 141.
66 Horne, *Savage War*, 121.
67 Ibid., 122; Evans, *Algeria*, 141; Clayton, *Wars of French Decolonization*, 119.
68 Clayton, *Wars of French Decolonization*, 117, 119; Horne, *Savage War*, 107–10, 115–17, 122–4; Evans, *Algeria*, 131–3, 141–2.
69 Horne, *Savage War*, 122.
70 Ibid., 150.
71 Ibid., 151; Evans, *Algeria*, 126, 154–5; Martin Thomas, *The French North African Crisis: Colonial Breakdown and Anglo-French Relations, 1945–1962* (Basingstoke: Macmillan, 2000), 103. Martin Evans, in particular, has emphasised 1956 as a critical turning point in the history of the French–Algerian War.
72 Evans, *Algeria*, 172
73 Ibid., 172–3.

3. THE SECRET SPEECH

1 William Taubman, *Khrushchev: The Man, His Era* (London: The Free Press, 2005), 270–1.
2 Ibid., 270; Vittorio Vidali, *Diary of the Twentieth Congress of the Communist Party of the Soviet Union* (London: Journeyman Press, 1974), vii–xiii, 14–15.
3 Vidali, *Diary*, 14–15; Taubman, *Khrushchev*, 270; William J. Tompson, *Khrushchev: A Political Life* (London: St Martin's Press, 1997), 153.
4 Tompson, *Khrushchev*, 153–4, 156; Taubman, *Khrushchev*, 271. For Stalin's February 1946 speech see 'Speech Delivered by J. V. Stalin at a Meeting of

Voters of the Stalin Electoral District, Moscow, 9 February 1946' in Stalin, *Speeches Delivered at Meetings of Voters at the Stalin Electoral District, Moscow, December 11, 1937 and February 9, 1946* (Moscow: Foreign Languages Publishing House, 1954), 19–43, at http://collections.mun.ca/PDFs/radical/JStalinSpeechesDeliveredAtMeetingsOfVoters.pdf.

5 John Rettie, 'How Khrushchev Leaked his Secret Speech to the World', *History Workshop Journal*, 62 (2006), 187, and Richard Gott, 'John Rettie (obituary)', *Guardian*, 20 January 2009 at http://www.guardian.co.uk/media/2009/jan/20/obituary-john-rettie.

6 Taubman, *Khrushchev*, 271; Tompson, *Khrushchev*, 156.

7 Nikita Khrushchev, 'The Cult of the Individual', 25 February 1956, available at http://www.theguardian.com/theguardian/2007/apr/26/greatspeeches2 (see also the link to the full version).

8 Taubman, *Khrushchev*, 273.

9 Khrushchev, 'The Cult of the Individual'.

10 Ibid.

11 Roy Medvedev, 'The Twentieth Party Congress: Before and After' in Zhores A. Medvedev and Roy A. Medvedev, *The Unknown Stalin* (London: I. B. Tauris, 2005), 95.

12 John Gray, '50 years later: How Khrushchev's "act of repentance" changed the world', CBC News Online, 22 February 2006 at http://www.cbc.ca/news2/background/russia/khrushchev.html; Taubman, *Khrushchev*, 273.

13 A. N. Yakovlev quoted at http://www.prlib.ru/en-us/history/pages/item.aspx?itemid=425.

14 Taubman, *Khrushchev*, 273–4.

15 Ibid., xi, xix.

16 Ibid., 231–2.

17 'Khrushchev Reaches Top After Long, Steady Rise', 17 February 1955, Intelligence Report Prepared by the Office of Intelligence Research, in *Foreign Relations of the United States, 1955–1957*, Volume XIV, Soviet Union; Eastern Mediterranean, 29.

18 Peter Catterall, ed., *The Macmillan Diaries: The Cabinet Years, 1950–1957* (London: Macmillan, 2003), 452 (entry for 19 July 1955), 456 (entry for 22 July 1955). For Geneva Summit see Taubman, *Khrushchev*, 240–1, 349–53.

19 Taubman, *Khrushchev*, 18, 21, 26, 30, 35, 36–7, 40–3, 47–52, 55–7, 61–9.

20 Tompson, *Khrushchev*, 13, 15–16; Taubman, *Khrushchev*, 58.

21 Taubman, *Khrushchev*, 29, 43, 46, 55, 62, 72–3, 105.

22 Ibid., 95, 96, 97–100.

23 Ibid., 114–17, 119–20, 125–7, 133–4, 137, 147, 151, 181, 183, 193–7, 201–2, 205–7.

24 Ibid., 231–2, 236–41.

25 Ibid., 274.

26 'Memorandum: Discussion at the 280th Meeting of the National Security Council, Thursday, March 22, 1956', 5, 6, in Ann Whitman File, NSC

Series, Box 7, 280th Meeting of NSC, March 22, 1956, Dwight David Eisenhower Presidential Library (Eisenhower Library). On word of the speech reaching the US see *Foreign Relations of the United States, 1955–1957*, Volume XIV, Soviet Union; Eastern Mediterranean, 72.

27 Miriam Dobson, *Khrushchev's Cold Summer: Gulag Returnees, Crime, and the Fate of Reform After Stalin* (Ithaca: Cornell University Press, 2009), 2, 7; Taubman, *Khrushchev*, 241–2, 246; Geoffrey Hosking, *A History of the Soviet Union* (London: Fontana, 1985), 326–32; Robert Hornsby, *Protest, Reform and Repression in Khrushchev's Soviet Union* (Cambridge: Cambridge University Press, 2013), 27. On camp uprisings see also Erik Kulavig, 'Uprisings in the Camps' in Erik Kulavig, *Dissent in the Years of Krushchev: Nine Stories about Disobedient Russians* (Basingstoke: Palgrave Macmillan, 2002), 106–22.

28 Taubman, *Khrushchev*, 241–4. For a comprehensive history of housing see Mark B. Smith, *Property of Communists: The Urban Housing Program from Stalin to Khrushchev* (Northern Illinois University Press, 2010).

29 Taubman, *Khrushchev*, 241–4; Mark Kramer, 'The Early Post-Stalin Succession Struggle and Upheavals in East-Central Europe: Internal-External Linkages in Soviet Policy Making (Part 1)', *Journal of Cold War Studies* 1.1 (1999), 3–55.

30 Dobson, *Khrushchev's Cold Summer*, 37; Taubman, *Khrushchev*, 246.

31 Taubman, *Khrushchev*, 246–8; Kramer, 'The Early Post-Stalin Succession Struggle', esp. 4, 10–12, 15–22. See also Anne Applebaum, *Iron Curtain: The Crushing of Eastern Europe 1944–1956* (London: Allen Lane, 2012), 238–62.

32 Robert Service, *The Penguin History of Modern Russia: From Tsarism to the Twenty-First Century* (Penguin Books, 2009), 332–3; Tompson, *Khrushchev*, 118–19; Taubman, *Khrushchev*, 245–8.

33 Tompson, *Khrushchev*, 124–9; Taubman, *Khrushchev*, 260–9 – for Beria's arrest and execution see 253–6; on Tito see 267–8, 276. For a comprehensive account of the move against Beria see Kramer, 'The Early Post-Stalin Succession Struggle and Upheavals in East-Central Europe: Internal-External Linkages in Soviet Policy Making (Part 2)', *Journal of Cold War Studies* 1.2 (1999), 9–38. Modest reforms were enacted in Eastern Europe, though they were opposed – increasingly effectively – by the Stalinists who were in power. See Mark Kramer, 'The Early Post-Stalin Succession Struggle and Upheavals in East-Central Europe: Internal-External Linkages in Soviet Policy Making (Part 3)', *Journal of Cold War Studies* 1.3 (1999), 28–35, 54.

34 Taubman, *Khrushchev*, 275–6; Tompson, *Khrushchev*, 154; Martin Malia, *The Soviet Tragedy: A History of Socialism in Russia* (New York: Free Press, 1995), 319; Medvedev, 'The Twentieth Party Congress: Before and After', 101–3.

35 Nikita Khrushchev, *Khrushchev Remembers: The Glasnost Tapes* (Boston: Little, Brown and Company, 1990), 43.

36 Thompson 154–5, *Khrushchev*; Malia, *Soviet Tragedy*, 319.
37 Taubman, *Khrushchev*, 276; Malia, *Soviet Tragedy*, 319. See also Dobson, *Khrushchev's Cold Summer*, 79–81.
38 Taubman, *Khrushchev*, 276; Malia, *Soviet Tragedy*, 319–20.
39 Thompson, *Khrushchev*, 155.
40 Ibid., 155; Taubman, *Khrushchev*, 280.
41 Taubman, *Khrushchev*, 278–82; Dobson, *Khrushchev's Cold Summer*, 81–2.
42 Service, *Penguin History of Modern Russia*, 340; Taubman, *Khrushchev*, 272.
43 Khrushchev, 'The Cult of the Individual'; Karl E. Loewenstein, 'Re-emergence of Public Opinion in the Soviet Union: Khrushchev and Responses to the Secret Speech', *Europe-Asia Studies* 58, no. 8 (December 2006), 1,334.
44 Hornsby, *Protest, Reform and Repression*, 31.
45 Phillip Deery and Rachael Calkin, '"We All Make Mistakes": the Communist Party of Australia and Khrushchev's Secret Speech, 1956', *Australian Journal of Politics and History* 54, no. 1 (2008), 73–4; Medvedev, 96–7; Taubman, *Khrushchev*, 283–4; Service, *The Penguin History of Modern Russia*, 341; Rettie, 'How Khrushchev Leaked his Secret Speech to the World'; Paul Flewers, 'Major Changes or Minor Tinkering? Responses in Britain to the Twentieth Congress of the CPSU' in Keith Flett, ed., *1956 and All That* (Newcastle: Cambridge Scholars Publishing, 2007), 211–12.
46 Taubman, *Khrushchev*, 283; Medvedev, 'The Twentieth Party Congress', 96–7.
47 Hornsby, *Protest, Reform and Repression*, 31–2; Taubman, *Khrushchev*, 283.
48 Medvedev, 'The Twentieth Party Congress', 97.
49 Hornsby, *Protest, Reform and Repression*, 34; Dobson, *Khrushchev's Cold Summer*, 83, 87, 88–93.
50 Hornsby, *Protest, Reform and Repression*, 36; Cynthia Hooper, 'What Can and Cannot Be Said: Between the Stalinist Past and New Soviet Future', *The Slavonic and East European Review*, vol. 86, no. 2 (April, 2008), 314–15.
51 Hornsby, *Protest, Reform and Repression*, 35–7.
52 Taubman, *Khrushchev*, 286.
53 Iurii Akisiutin, 'Popular Responses to Khrushchev' in William Taubman, Sergei Khrushchev and Abbott Gleason, eds, *Nikita Khrushchev* (New Haven: Yale University Press, 2000), 187.
54 Hornsby, *Protest, Reform and Repression*, 38–9; Akisiutin, 'Popular Responses', 187.
55 Hornsby, *Protest, Reform and Repression*, 33–4.
56 Ibid., 44–5.
57 Taubman, *Khrushchev*, 286.
58 Akisiutin, 'Popular Responses', 185.
59 Taubman, *Khrushchev*, 286.
60 Vladimir A. Kozlov, 'Political Disturbances in Georgia After the CPSU Twentieth Party Congress', in Kozlov, *Mass Uprisings in the USSR: Protest and Rebellion in the Post-Stalin Years* (London: M. E. Sharpe, 2002), 112–15.

61 Medvedev, 'The Twentieth Party Congress', 97–8; Taubman, *Khrushchev*, 286–7; 'Georgians Resent Their Idol's Overthrow', *The Times*, 19 March 1956, 10. See also Kozlov, 'Political Disturbances in Georgia', 112–35.

62 Kozlov, 'Political Disturbances in Georgia'.

63 Ibid., 124–6.

64 Medvedev, 'The Twentieth Party Congress', 97–8; Taubman, *Khrushchev*, 286–7; 'Georgians Resent Their Idol's Overthrow'; Kozlov, 'Political Disturbances in Georgia', 112–35.

65 Kozlov, 'Political Disturbances in Georgia', 129–32; Hornsby, *Protest, Reform and Repression*, 34.

66 Taubman, *Khrushchev*, 278.

67 Ibid., 285, 287.

68 Erik Kulavig, 'The Closed Letter', in Kulavig, *Dissent*, 16–17.

69 Taubman, *Khrushchev*, 287. See also Hornsby, *Protest, Reform and Repression*, 54–78.

70 Hornsby, *Protest, Reform and Repression*, 108–17.

4. MASSIVE RESISTANCE

1 'Walter F. George, 79, Dies; Georgia Senator 34 Years', *NYT*, 5 August 1957, 1, 21; 'George, Walter Franklin (1878–1957)', Biographical Dictionary of the United States Congress, at http://bioguide.congress.gov/scripts/biodisplay.pl?index=g000131; Robert A. Caro, *Master of the Senate: The Years of Lyndon Johnson* (New York: Vintage Books, 2003), 786; Dominic Sandbrook, *Eugene McCarthy: The Rise and Fall of Postwar American Liberalism* (Alfred A. Knopf: New York, 2004), 89–90.

2 George Lewis, *Massive Resistance: The White Response to the Civil Rights Movement* (London: Hodder Arnold, 2006), 65.

3 http://www.pbs.org/wnet/supremecourt/rights/sources_document2.html.

4 Anthony Badger, 'The South Confronts the Court: The Southern Manifesto of 1956', *Journal of Policy History*, vol. 20, no. 1 (2008), 126, 130. Elliott quote taken from David Brown and Clive Webb, *Race in the American South: From Slavery to Civil Rights* (Edinburgh: Edinburgh University Press, 2007), 277.

5 The phrase was first used by Virginia's Harry F. Byrd in a speech delivered on 25 February: see Jack Bell (Associated Press), 'Byrd Calls for Unity, "Massive Resistance" to School Integration', *Commercial Appeal*, 26 February 1956, 1; Lewis, *Massive Resistance*, 1–3.

6 C. Vann Woodward, 'The "New Reconstruction" in the South: Desegregation in Historical Perspective', *Commentary Magazine*, June 1956, 506; Michael J. Klarman, 'How Brown Changed Race Relations: The Backlash Thesis', *Journal of American History*, vol. 81, no. 1 (June 1994), 81–118.

7 State of South Carolina, A Joint Resolution', Calendar No. S. 514, 14 February 1956, 7–8, in *Civil Rights During the Eisenhower Administration*

(UPA – LexisNexis), Part 1, Series A, Reel 10, 0580-124-A-1(2), Roosevelt Study Center, Middelburg, Netherlands (RSC). See also Letter, Thos. B. Stanley to Dwight D. Eisenhower, 3 February 1956 and 'Commonwealth of Virginia, General Assembly, Senate Joint Resolution No. 3, and 'State of Mississippi, Senate Concurrent Resolution No. 125', in *Civil Rights During the Eisenhower Administration*, Part 1, Series A, Reel 10, 0580-124-A-1(2).

8 William A. Emerson, Jr (Newsweek), 'For Nation: Part II Segregation and Politics', P. 3, in Newsweek Atlanta Bureau Records, Box 55, Folder 16, Manuscript, Archives and Rare Book Library, Emory Univeristy (MARBL). See also James Rorty, 'Virginia's Creeping Desegregation: Force of the Inevitable', *Commentary Magazine*, July 1956, 54; Lewis, *Massive Resistance*, 63.

9 Clive Webb, ed., *Massive Resistance: Southern Opposition to the Second Reconstruction* (Oxford: Oxford University Press, 2005), 6; Gene L. Howard, *Patterson for Alabama: The Life and Career of John Patterson* (University of Alabama Press, 2008), 100–3. See also Southern Education Reporting Service (Nashville, TN), 'Statistical Summary, State-by-State, of Segregation-Desegregation Activity Affecting Southern Schools from 1954 to Present, Together With Pertinent Data on Enrollment, Teacher Pay, Etc. Revised to December 12, 1956' in Ralph McGill Papers, Box 58 (Series V), Folder 7, Subject File – Integration, 1956, MARBL; Woodward, 'The "New Reconstruction" in the South', 505–6.

10 Lewis, *Massive Resistance*, 39–40; J. Edgar Hoover, 'Racial Tension and Civil Rights', 1 March 1956, 16, statement presented to Cabinet, 9 March 1956, in Ann Whitman File, Cabinet Series, Box 6, 'Cabinet Meeting of March 9, 1956', Eisenhower Library. See also Neil R. McMillen, *The Citizens' Council: Organized Resistance to the Second Reconstruction, 1954–1964* (University of Illinois Press, 1994 edition).

11 Hoover, 'Racial Tension and Civil Rights', 15–16; Webb, ed., *Massive Resistance*, 4–5; David Halberstam, 'The White Citizens Councils: Respectable Means for Unrespectable Ends', *Commentary Magazine*, October 1956, esp. 294, 298, 300; Lewis, *Massive Resistance*, 39, 42, 44.

12 Lewis, *Massive Resistance*, 42, 44.

13 Ibid., 73; Thomas Noer, 'Segregationists and the World: The Foreign Policy of the White Resistance' in Brenda Gayle Plummer, ed., *Window on Freedom: Race, Civil Rights, and Foreign Affairs, 1945–1988* (Chapel Hill: The University of North Carolina Press), 159 note 2.

14 Tony Badger, 'Brown and Backlash' in Webb, ed., *Massive Resistance*, 46.

15 Webb, ed., *Massive Resistance*, 5.

16 Ralph McGill, 'The Angry South', *Atlantic Monthly*, April 1956, 33. See also Halberstam, 'The White Citizens' Councils', 299.

17 'Wilkins: Southern Manifesto May Be Vital Election Factor', Press Release, 15 March 1956 in papers of the NAACP Part 20, White Resistance

and Reprisals, 1956–1965 (University Publications of America), Reel 7, General Office File, Reprisals, General, 1956, Mar.–July.

18 For Wilkins see Simon Hall, *Peace and Freedom: The Civil Rights and Antiwar Movements in the 1960s* (Philadephia: University of Pennsylvania Press, 2005), 81; 'NAACP History: Roy Wilkins' at http://www.naacp.org/pages/naacp-history-Roy-Wilkins and http://www.thecrisismagazine.com/history3.html.

19 E. Culpepper Clark, *The Schoolhouse Door: Segregation's Last Stand at the University of Alabama* (New York: Oxford University Press, 1993), xii–xiv; Wayne Phillips, 'Tuscaloosa: A Tense Drama Unfolds', *NYT*, 26 February 1956, SM15, 47–9; *Census of Population: 1950*, vol. II – Characteristics of the Population, Part 2, Alabama (US Government Printing Office: Washington, DC, 1952), 28; *Census of the Population: 1960*, vol. I – Characteristics of the Population, Part 2, Alabama (US Government Printing Office: Washington, DC, 1963), 24.

20 'Miss Lucy Goes to College', *NYT*, 6 February 1956, 22; Phillips, 'Tuscaloosa: A Tense Drama Unfolds', SM15.

21 'Alabama Storm Center', *NYT*, 9 February 1956, 26; Clark, *The Schoolhouse Door*, 3–8.

22 'Alabama Storm Center', 26; 'Negro Student Admitted', *NYT*, 1 February 1956, 64; 'Miss Lucy Goes to College', *NYT*, 6 February 1956, 22; Wayne Phillips, 'Alabama to Heed Courts on Taking Negro Students', *NYT*, 4 March 1956, 1, 52; Wayne Phillips, 'Miss Lucy's Education: Segregation Test Case', *NYT*, 12 February 1956, E8; Clark, *The Schoolhouse Door*, 86, 89.

23 Clark, *The Schoolhouse Door*, 56.

24 'Alabama Storm Center', 26; Clark, *The Schoolhouse Door*, 40.

25 Peter Kihss, 'Negro Co-Ed Asks End of Suspension', *NYT*, 8 February 1956, 22.

26 Account taken from *L'Unità*, 15 February 1956 in NAACP Part 20, Reel 6, General Office Files, Reprisals, Alabama, University of Alabama, Autherine Lucy, Jan.–Feb. 1956; 'Alabama Storm Center', 26.

27 'Alabama Storm Center', 26.

28 Clark, *The Schoolhouse Door*, 56, 58, 61–2.

29 'Miss Lucy Goes to College', 22.

30 'Alabama U. Rally Protests a Negro', *NYT*, 5 February 1956, 60.

31 Clark, *The Schoolhouse Door*, 63–4, 67.

32 *L'Unità*, 15 February 1956.

33 Clark, *The Schoolhouse Door*, 65–71.

34 *L'Unità*, 15 February 1956; 'Alabama Negro Co-Ed Spirited to Safety', *News & Observer*, 7 February 1956; Peter Kihss, 'Negro Co-Ed Is Suspended to Curb Alabama Clashes', *NYT*, 7 February 1956, 1, 25; Clark, *The Schoolhouse Door*, 71–80.

35 Kihss, 'Negro Co-Ed Is Suspended', 1, 25.

36 'Alabama U. Replies', *NYT*, 11 December 1956, 44; Wayne Phillips, 'Ala-

bama to Heed Courts on Taking Negro Students', *NYT*, 4 March 1956, 1; 'Troubled Educator', *NYT*, 8 February 1956, 22; Clark, *The Schoolhouse Door*, 23–6, 30–6, 80–2, 88, 94–8.

37 'Statement by Roy Wilkins to United Press', 13 February 1956 in NAACP Part 20, Reel 6, General Office Files, Reprisals, Alabama, University of Alabama, Autherine Lucy, Jan.–Feb. 1956; and Letter, Roy Wilkins to Owen Tudor, 14 March 1956, in NAACP Part 20, Reel 6, General Office Files, Reprisals, Alabama, University of Alabama, Autherine Lucy, Mar. 1956.

38 Press Release, St Louis Branch, NAACP, 7 February 1956 in NAACP Part 20, Reel 6, General Office Files, Reprisals, Alabama, University of Alabama, Autherine Lucy, Jan.–Feb. 1956; 'Wilkins: Southern Manifesto May Be Vital Election Factor', Press Release, 15 March 1956 in NAACP Part 20, Reel 7, General Office File, Reprisals, General, 1956, Mar.–July.

39 Letter, Roy Wilkins to H. Claude Hudson, 14 February 1956 in NAACP Part 20, Reel 4, General Office Files, Reprisals, Alabama, General, 1956–59.

40 See the collection of letters and telegrams in NAACP Part 20, Reel 6, General Office Files, Reprisals, Alabama, University of Alabama, Autherine Lucy, Jan.–Feb. 1956 and 'Lucy, Autherine', folders 1–5 in Central Files, Alphabetical File, Boxes 1894 and 1895, Eisenhower Library.

41 Letter, Ben Atkins to President Eisenhower, 7 February 1956, 1, in 'Lucy, Autherine (1)', Central Files, Alphabetical File, Box 1894, Eisenhower Library.

42 'What a Price for Peace', *Tuscaloosa News*, 7 February 1956, 1; 'Students Denounce Violence' and Peter Kihss, 'Negro Co-Ed Asks End of Suspension', *NYT*, 8 February 1956, 22; Wayne Phillips, '500 Sign Petition to Readmit Co-Ed', *NYT*, 21 February 1956, 23; Murray Kempton, 'When the Riots Came' (February 1956), in Carson, *Reporting Civil Rights*, Part One, 241–8.

43 Chris Myers Asch, *The Senator and the Sharecropper: The Freedom Struggles of James O. Eastland and Fannie Lou Hamer* (Chapel Hill: University of North Carolina Press, 2008), 113–17; George Lewis, *The White South and the Red Menace: Segregationists, Anticommunism, and Massive Resistance, 1945–1965* (Gainesville: University Press of Florida, 2004), esp. chapters 1 and 2; 'The NAACP and Communism', *Tuscaloosa News*, 14 March 1956, 4; Lewis, *Massive Resistance*, 79; George Lewis, 'White South, Red Nation: Massive Resistance and the Cold War' in Webb, *Massive Resistance*, 121. See also Noer, 'Segregationists and the World'.

44 Lewis, *Massive Resistance*, 79; the *Tuscaloosa News* argued that the Association's leaders had been 'fondling the ideological rattlesnake far too much for their own, and their country's, good'. See 'The NAACP and Communism'.

45 Mary Dudziak, *Cold War Civil Rights: Race and the Image of American Democracy* (Princeton: Princeton University Press, 2000), 141; *Ohio Sentinel*, 11 February 1956, 1; 'Harriman Assails "Mob Rule" in South', *NYT*, 16 February 1956, 20. For the international dimension of the Lucy incident see also 'Moscow Notes Dispute', *NYT*, 9 February 1956, 26; Michael L. Hoffman, 'Lucy Case Draws Soviet Criticism', *NYT*, 17 March 1956, 10; and The American Jewish Committee, memorandum from Paris Office to Edwin J. Lukas, re: European Reactions to Racial Discrimination in the United States, 5 March 1956 in NAACP Part 20, Reel 6, General Office Files, Reprisals, Alabama, University of Alabama, Autherine Lucy, Apr. 1956–1958; Azza Salama Layton, *International Politics and Civil Rights Policies in the United States, 1941–1960* (Cambridge: Cambridge University Press, 2000), 101–2, 118–22.

46 J. E. Holloway, 'J. E. Holloway (Ambassador) to Secretary for External Affairs (Pretoria) Re. Racial Conflict in the United States', March 23, 1956. National Archives Pretoria – SAB – BTS, 1/33/13, vol. 2, Negro Problem in USA, 1953–1958. I am grateful to Nick Grant for bringing this source to my attention.

47 Alfred Hutchinson, 'Against the College Colour-bar: A Letter to the Negro Woman Student Who Challenged the Alabama University Colour-bar', *Fighting Talk*, May 1956, vol. 12, no. 5 edition.

48 Statement by Autherine Lucy in NAACP Part 20, Reel 6, General Office Files, Reprisals, Alabama, University of Alabama, Autherine Lucy, Apr. 1956–1958.

49 *Ohio Sentinel*, 11 February 1956, 2 in NAACP Part 20, Reel 6, General Office Files, Reprisals, Alabama, University of Alabama, Autherine Lucy, Jan.–Feb. 1956.

50 Howard, *Patterson for Alabama*, 95–7; 'US University Segregation', *The Times* (London), 8 February 1956, 8; Roy Wilkins, Telegram to Jim Folsom, 6 February 1956, in NAACP Part 20, Reel 6, General Office Files, Reprisals, Alabama, University of Alabama, Autherine Lucy, Jan.–Feb. 1956.

51 David A. Nichols, *A Matter of Justice: Eisenhower and the Beginning of the Civil Rights Revolution* (New York: Simon & Schuster, 2007), esp., 6, 99, 103–4; Chester J. Pach, Jr. and Elmo Richardson, *The Presidency of Dwight D. Eisenhower* (Lawrence: University Press of Kansas, 1991), 137, 140, 142–6, 148–9; Dwight D. Eisenhower, 'Annual Message to the Congress on the State of the Union', 5 January 1956, in *Public Papers of the Presidents of the United States: Dwight D. Eisenhower, 1956* (US Government Printing Office: Washington, DC, 1958), 25.

52 The President's News Conference, 8 February 1956, in *Public Papers of the Presidents of the United States*.

53 Form letter, Maxwell M. Rabb, Secretary to the Cabinet, in 'Lucy, Autherine' (1), Central Files, Alphabetical File, Box 1894, Eisenhower Library.

54 Rev. Thomas R. Thrasher, 'Alabama's Bus Boycott', *The Reporter*, 8 March 1956; Garrow, *Bearing the Cross*, 54–5; Thornton, *Dividing Lines*, 72–3; King, *Stride Toward Freedom*, 113–16.

55 Thornton, *Dividing Lines*, 74.

56 King, *Stride Toward Freedom*, 116–17; Garrow, *Bearing the Cross*, 55; Thornton, *Dividing Lines*, 73–4.

57 Wayne Phillips, '10,000 in Alabama Hail Segregation', *NYT*, 11 February 1956, 1, 4.

58 'A Review of the Declaration of Segregation' in NAACP Part 20, Reel 5, 'Alabama-Montgomery Bus Boycott, 1956, folder 1'.

59 Bayard Rustin, 'Montgomery Diary', *Liberation*, vol. 1, no. 2, April 1956, 9.

60 William A. Emerson, Jr., 'For Nation: Montgomery', c.5 March 1956, 7, in Newsweek Atlanta Bureau, Box 4, Folder 21, MARBL.

61 Hoover, 'Racial Tension and Civil Rights'.

62 Robinson, *The Montgomery Bus Boycott*, 125–8.

63 William A. Emerson, Jr., 'For Nation: Montgomery' (c. late February), 12 in Newsweek, Atlanta Bureau Records, Box 4, Folder 21, 'Alabama, Montgomery, Bus boycott Drafts, January 1–November 26, 1956', MARBL.

64 'Biographical Sketch of Attorney Fred D. Gray', 1–2, in NAACP Part 20, Reel 5, Alabama–Montgomery Bus Boycott, 1956, folder 2.

65 Rex Thomas, 'Negroes in Bus Boycott Undismayed Despite Mounting Legal Reprisals' (AP), *The State* (South Carolina), 26 February 1956, 14A; Donnie Williams with Wayne Greenhaw, *The Thunder of Angels: The Montgomery Bus Boycott and the People Who Broke the Back of Jim Crow* (Lawrence Hill Books, 2007), 162; Garrow, *Bearing the Cross*, 63.

66 '115 Indicted in Montgomery Bus Boycott', 23 February 1956 (Associated Press); Garrow, *Bearing the Cross*, 64.

67 'Notes of mass meeting at First Baptist Church', 30 January 1956, in Burns, ed., *Daybreak of Freedom*, 131.

68 Hampton and Fayer, *Voices of Freedom*, 28.

69 Garrow, *Bearing the Cross*, 61; Thornton, *Dividing Lines*, 77.

70 Hampton and Fayer, *Voices of Freedom*, 31.

71 Garrow, *Bearing the Cross*, 66, 69; 'Wilkins Asks for Funds for Bus Case Defense', 25 February 1956, in NAACP Part 20, Reel 5, 'Alabama-Montgomery Bus Boycott, 1956, folder 1'. See various letters, telegrams and resolutions of support in NAACP Part 20, Reel 5, 'Alabama-Montgomery Bus Boycott, 1956, folder 1'.

72 Emerson, 'For Nation: Montgomery'.

73 Garrow, *Bearing the Cross*, 65; Williams, *Thunder of Angels*, 170–4; King, *Stride Toward Freedom*, 137–8.

74 Rustin, 'Montgomery Diary', 8.

75 Ibid.; Emerson, 'For Nation: Montgomery'.

76 King, *Stride Toward Freedom*, 138.

77 Rex Thomas, '"Not Afraid", Say Indicted Ministers' (AP), *Birmingham Post-Herald*, 28 February 1956, 1.

78 'Notes on MIA Mass Meeting at Holt Street Baptist Church, by Donald Ferron', in *The Papers of MLK*, vol. III, 144.

5. THE LONG WALK

1 'Books Published Today', *NYT*, 25 April 1956, 32. On the veracity of Rawicz's account see Hugh Levinson, 'Walking the Talk?', at http://news.bbc.co.uk/1/hi/6098218.stm and 'Witold Glinski: Obituary', *Telegraph*, 3 July 2013, at http://www.telegraph.co.uk/news/obituaries/10158049/Witold-Glinski.html.

2 Slavomir Rawicz, *The Long Walk: The True Story of a Trek to Freedom* (London: Robinson, 2007), 6, 7.

3 Rawicz, *The Long Walk*; Anna Gorbagsevich, 'Escape from Bondage', *NYT*, 29 April 1956, 7, 26; 'Books – Authors', *NYT*, 6 April 1956, 23.

4 R. L. West, 'Out of Siberia', *Manchester Guardian*, 13 April 1956, 6.

5 Nash K. Burger, 'Books of the Times', *NYT*, 28 April 1956, 30. See also Harold Nicolson, 'Four Thousand Miles', *Observer*, 8 April 1956, 13; R. D. Charques, 'Enduring to the End', *Times Literary Supplement*, 27 April 1956 (Issue 2826), 249.

6 'Meeting of the 280th NSC', 7, in Ann Whitman File, NSC Series, Box 7, '280th Meeting of the National Security Council, 22 March 1956', Eisenhower Library.

7 Robert Service, *Comrades: Communism: A World History* (Pan Books, 2008), 239–50; Applebaum, *Iron Curtain*, xxvi–xxxv, 45–51; Balázs Apor, 'Leader in the Making: The Role of Biographies in Constructing the Cult of Mátyás Rákosi' in Apor et al., eds, *The Leader Cult in Communist Dictatorships: Stalin and the Eastern Bloc* (New York: Palgrave Macmillan, 2004), 73; Tamás Aczél and Tibor Méray, *The Revolt of the Mind: A Case History of Intellectual Resistance Behind the Iron Curtain* (New York: Frederick A. Praeger, 1959), 162.

8 'Destalinization Confuses Comrades of Steti Paper Mill', 28 June 1956 [Electronic Resource]. HU OSA 300-1-2-72583; Records of Radio Free Europe/Radio Liberty Research Institute: General Records: Information Items; Open Society Archives at Central European University, Budapest, http://hdl.handle.net/10891/osa:e90caf6f-a179-462a-83eb-1c17b4610400.

9 'Communist Functionary Cagey about De-Stalinization', 30 May 1956 [Electronic Resource]. HU OSA 300-1-2-71538; Records of Radio Free Europe/Radio Liberty Research Institute: General Records: Information Items; Open Society Archives at Central European University, Budapest, http://hdl.handle.net/10891/osa:e7640496-34c8-4e18-ae90-54e817c2e10b.

10 'Destalinization Relaxes Party Discipline', 29 June 1956 [Electronic Resource]. HU OSA 300-1-2-72736; Records of Radio Free Europe/ Radio Liberty Research Institute: General Records: Information Items; Open Society Archives at Central European University, Budapest, http:// hdl.handle.net/10891/osa:17547f33-3dbb-4401-bfce-124925099f64. See also 'Budapest Wits Deride Stalin', 5 April 1956 [Electronic Resource]. HU OSA 300-1-2-69567; Records of Radio Free Europe/Radio Liberty Research Institute: General Records: Information Items; Open Society Archives at Central European University, Budapest, http://hdl.handle. net/10891/osa:5e74b282-6083-472b-a2ae-3b0ed49a13d5.

11 See, for example, Department of State, 'Intelligence Brief: Current Status of the Anti-Stalin Campaign in the Soviet Bloc', 5 May 1956, 3, in White House Office, National Security Council Staff, Papers, 1948–61, OCB Central File Series, Box1, OCB 000.1 USSR (File 1) (4) [November 1953– June 1956], Eisenhower Library; Jakub Karpiński, *Countdown: The Polish Upheavals of 1956, 1968, 1970, 1980 . . .* (New York: Karz-Cohl Publishers, 1982), 43.

12 Applebaum, *Iron Curtain*, 482; Service, *Comrades*, 311; Ted Hopf, *Reconstructing the Cold War: The Early Years, 1945–1958* (New York: Oxford University Press, 2012), 212; John Gray, '50 years later: How Khrushchev's "act of repentance" changed the world', CBC News Online, 22 February 2006 at http://www.cbc.ca/news2/background/russia/khrushchev.html.

13 Teresa Toranska, *Oni: Stalin's Polish Puppets* (London: William Collins, 1987), 55.

14 Paweł Machcewicz, 'Social Protest and Political Crisis in 1956' in A. Kemp-Welch, *Stalinism in Poland, 1955–1956* (New York: St Martin's Press, 1999), 103.

15 Tony Kemp-Welch, 'Khrushchev's "Secret Speech" and Polish Politics: The Spring of 1956', *Europe-Asia Studies*, vol. 48, no. 2 (March 1996), 189; Machcewicz, 'Social Protest and Political Crisis in 1956', 103.

16 Machcewicz, 'Social Protest and Political Crisis in 1956', 103; Kemp-Welch, 'Khrushchev's "Secret Speech"', 189.

17 'Communist Propaganda Problems in the East European Bloc 1956', 3, Records of the US Information Agency, Part 1: Cold War Era Special Reports, Series A: 1953–1963 (Bethesda, MD: A UPA Collection from Lexis Nexis), Reel 9, RSC.

18 Kemp-Welch, 'Khrushchev's "Secret Speech"', 189; Machcewicz, 'Social Protest and Political Crisis in 1956', 103.

19 Kemp-Welch, 'Khrushchev's "Secret Speech"', 189, 190, 193.

20 NP 10110/13, 'Reaction to denunciation of Stalin: Comments on two articles illustrating the new spirit', 3 April 1956, 1, in FO 371/122592, National Archives, Kew, London.

21 Machcewicz, 'Social Protest and Political Crisis in 1956', 104; Tony Kemp-

Welch, 'Dethroning Stalin: Poland 1956 and Its Legacy', *Europe-Asia Studies*, 58, 8 (December 2006), 1264.

22 'Anti-Stalin Campaign Gives Poles New Hope', 24 May 1956 [Electronic Resource]. HU OSA 300-1-2-71381; Records of Radio Free Europe/Radio Liberty Research Institute: General Records: Information Items; Open Society Archives at Central European University, Budapest, http://hdl. handle.net/10891/osa:14308f35-e4c4-460f-8aa4-911716b75231.

23 NP 10110/16, 'Denunciation of Stalin: Reports various Press articles condemning the cult of the individual', FO 371/122592.

24 Aczél and Méray, *Revolt of the Mind*, 391.

25 Paweł Machcewicz, *Rebellious Satellite: Poland 1956* (Stanford University Press, 2009), 61–2.

26 Paweł Machcewicz, 'Intellectuals and Mass Movements: The Study of Political Dissent in Poland in 1956', *Contemporary European History*, vol. 6, no. 3 (1997), 370–2.

27 Machcewicz, *Rebellious Satellite*, 63.

28 Kemp-Welch, 'Dethroning Stalin', 1265.

29 Paul E. Zinner, ed., *National Communism and Popular Revolt in Eastern Europe: A Selection of Documents on Events in Poland and Hungary, February–November, 1956* (New York: Columbia University Press, 1956), 48, 49, 51. For Jan Kott see Michael Kustow, 'Jan Kott', *Guardian*, 10 January 2002, http://www.theguardian.com/news/2002/jan/10/guardianobituaries. books. On cultural freedom see also Karpiński, *Countdown*, 45.

30 Machcewicz, *Rebellious Satellite*, 60–6.

31 'Anti-Stalin Campaign Gives Poles New Hope', 24 May 1956, 1.

32 Machcewicz, *Rebellious Satellite*, 67–8, 69–73.

33 Ibid., 75–8, 78–80; Machcewicz, 'Social Protest and Political Crisis in 1956', 108.

34 Kemp-Welch, 'Dethroning Stalin', 1,266.

35 Machcewicz, *Rebellious Satellite*, 81.

36 NP 10110/19, Sir Alan Noble, 'Comments on greater freedom of expression, as instanced by an article in "Po Prostu", denouncing the privileges of senior officials', 11 April 1956, 1, in FO 371/122592.

37 Machcewicz, *Rebellious Satellite*, 15–16 (including note 17), 59–60, 76, 82–3; A. Kemp-Welch, *Poland under Communism: A Cold War History* (Cambridge: Cambridge University Press, 2008), esp. 26, 31–2; NP 10110/18, Sir Alan Noble, 'Reports on a Speech Made by Ochab at a Meeting of the Warsaw Party Committee', 10 April 1956, 3, FO 371/122592.

38 NP 10110/18, Sir Alan Noble, 'Reports on a Speech Made by Ochab at a Meeting of the Warsaw Party Committee', 10 April 1956, 3, FO 371/122592.

39 Machcewicz, *Rebellious Satellite*, 83, also 82–5.

40 See Johanna Granville, 'East Germany in 1956: Walter Ulbricht's Tenacity in the Face of Opposition', *Australian Journal of Politics and History* 52, 3

(2006), 417–38. On the East German Uprising see Robert Service, *Comrades*, 309–10; Applebaum, *Iron Curtain*, 466–71.

41 'Intelligence Brief Prepared by the Office of Intelligence Research: The Desecration of Stalin', 30 March 1956, in *Foreign Relations of the United States, 1955–1957, Volume XXIV, Soviet Union; Eastern Mediterranean* (Washington: United States Government Printing Office, 1989), 75.

42 See 'After the Cult: Embarrassed Satellites', *Manchester Guardian*, 9 April 1956, 1; 'Bulgarian Premier Quits; Victim of Anti-Stalin Drive', *NYT*, 17 April 1956, 1, 8; 'Bulgaria's Collective Puppets Submit', *Manchester Guardian*, 17 April 1956, 7; 'Bulgaria Falls Into Line', *New York Times*, 18 April 1956, 30; and 'Shift Takes Three Minutes', *New York Times*, 18 April 1956, 13.

43 John P. C. Matthews, *Explosion: The Hungarian Revolution of 1956* (New York: Hippocrene Books, 2007), 103.

44 Paul E. Zinner, *Revolution in Hungary* (New York: Columbia University Press, 1962), 212.

45 'Resolution Adopted by the Central Committee of the Hungarian Workers Party, March 12–13, 1956', in Zinner, ed. *National Communism and Popular Revolt in Eastern Europe*, 317–21; Bennett Kovrig, *Communism in Hungary: From Kun to Kádár* (Stanford: Hoover Institution Press, 1979), 290.

46 'Resolution Adopted by the Central Committee of the Hungarian Workers Party, March 12–13, 1956', 320; Applebaum, *Iron Curtain*, 464–5, 473.

47 Aczél and Méray, *Revolt of the Mind*, 390.

48 Kovrig, *Communism in Hungary*, 290.

49 Bryan Cartledge, *The Will to Survive: A History of Hungary* (London: Hurst & Company, 2011), 418, 424–5, 433, 440; Kovrig, *Communism in Hungary*, 290; Paul Kecskemeti, *The Unexpected Revolution: Social Forces in the Hungarian Uprising* (Stanford: Stanford University Press, 1961), 74–5.

50 Cartledge, *Will to Survive*, 440; Zinner, ed., *National Communism and Popular Revolt in Eastern Europe*, 323.

51 Cartledge, *Will to Survive*, 440; Aczél and Méray, *Revolt of the Mind*, 395; see also George Gomori, 'Gyorgy Litvan', *Guardian*, 30 November 2006, http://www.theguardian.com/news/2006/nov/30/guardianobituaries.mainsection.

52 Kecskemeti, *The Unexpected Revolution*, 75.

53 Zinner, *Revolution in Hungary*, 213; Zinner, ed. *National Communism and Popular Revolt in Eastern Europe*, 326–7.

54 Miklós Molnár, *Budapest 1956: A History of the Hungarian Revolution* (London: George Allen & Unwin, 1971), 83.

55 Sydney Gruson, 'Prague Festival Lampoons Regime', *NYT*, 21 May 1956, 5; John P. C. Matthews, *Tinderbox: East-Central Europe in the Spring, Summer, and Early Fall of 1956* (Tucson, Arizona: Fenestra Books, 2003), 66, 72, 78, 292 (note 2); Jane Pavitt, *Prague: The Buildings of*

Europe (Manchester: Manchester University Press, 2000), 7; http://
www.1pragueguide.com/cechuv-bridge; Dita Asiedu, 'World's biggest Stalin monument would have turned 50 on May Day', at http://www.radio.
cz/en/section/curraffrs/worlds-biggest-stalin-monument-would-have-
turned-50-on-may-day. For CSM's involvement and motivation see 'CSM
Organized Famed Majales Parade in Prague', 14 August 1956 [Electronic
Resource], 1. HU OSA 300-1-2-73996; Records of Radio Free Europe/
Radio Liberty Research Institute: General Records: Information Items;
Open Society Archives at Central European University, Budapest, http://
hdl.handle.net/10891/osa:5361b62a-6121-43c4-af51-486a925c8c43.

56 Matthews, *Tinderbox*, 292 note 2.

57 Gruson, 'Prague Festival Lampoons Regime'.

58 ' The Student Demonstrations in Prague and Bratislava, 14 June 1956, 2–3
[Electronic Resource]. HU OSA 300-1-2-72008; Records of Radio Free
Europe/Radio Liberty Research Institute: General Records: Information
Items; Open Society Archives at Central European University, Budapest.
http://hdl.handle.net/10891/osa:f14580bf-a8bc-4ca1-9568-2f3787c9e90a;
Matthews, *Tinderbox*, 80.

59 Gruson, 'Prague Festival Lampoons Regime'.

60 'CSM Organized Famed Majales Parade in Prague'.

61 'The Student Demonstrations in Prague and Bratislava, 14 June 1956, 3;
'Bratislava University Students Ridicule Regime in "Majales" Parade',
25 June 1956, 1 [Electronic Resource]. HU OSA 300-1-2-72381; Records
of Radio Free Europe/Radio Liberty Research Institute: General
Records: Information Items; Open Society Archives at Central European
University, Budapest, http://hdl.handle.net/10891/osa:e3e645b3-3651-4441-
98e9-a24080d5c9b9; John MacCormac, 'Czechs' Protests Said to be Wide',
NYT, 3 June 1956, 29.

62 Gruson, 'Prague Festival Lampoons Regime'; MacCormac, 'Czechs' Protests Said to be Wide'.

63 Faculty of Mathematics and Physics at Charles University, Prague, 'Resolution adopted by the Faculty Organization of the Czechoslovak Youth
Union', 26 April 1956, available at Wilson Center Digital Archive, http://
digitalarchive.wilsoncenter.org/document/117878. For an account of the
meeting see Matthews, *Tinderbox*, 59–62. See also Sydney Gruson, 'Czech
Youths Ask for Freedom', *NYT*, 28 May 1956, 2; John Connelly, 'Students,
Workers, and Social Change: The Limits of Czech Stalinism', *Slavic Review*
vol. 56, no. 2 (Summer 1997), 307–35.

64 Matthews, *Tinderbox*, 63–5; Richard Lowenthal, '"Democratic Outburst"
by Czech Students', *Observer*, 3 June 1956, 4; 'Czechoslovakia: Dirty
Clothes on the Line', *Time*, 25 June 1956.

65 Matthews, *Tinderbox*, 66, 68–9.

66 John McCormac, 'Red Writers Push Anti-Stalin Drive', *NYT*, 27 May

1956, 6; 'Czechoslovak Satire as Sign of Changed Conditions', *The Times* (London), 18 June 1956, 9; 'Czech Miner's Frankness', *The Times*, 13 June 1956, 10; 'Czechoslovakia: Dirty Clothes on the Line'. For the Czech response to Khrushchev's 'secret speech' see Vladimir V. Kusin, *The Intellectual Origins of the Prague Spring: The Development of Reformist Ideas in Czechoslovakia 1956–1967* (Cambridge: Cambridge University Press, 1971), esp. 19–27.

67 'Czechs Warned, Too', *Manchester Guardian*, 3 July 1956, 7.

68 Flora Lewis, 'Red Czechoslovakia Is a Drab Gray', *NYT*, 3 June 1956, 42. Matthews, *Tinderbox*, 56–7.

69 'Czechoslovakia: Dirty Clothes on the Line'; 'Resolution adopted by the Faculty Organization of the Czechoslovak Youth Union', 26 April 1956.

70 'Czechoslovakia: Dirty Clothes on the Line'; 'Czech Communists in Congress', *The Times*, 12 June 1956, 9.

71 John MacCormac, 'Czech Reds Score Misuse of New Line', *NYT*, 16 June 1956, 1, 3.

72 Sydney Gruson, 'Czech Party Line Set for Students', *NYT*, 27 June 1956, 1, 8; Jan Havránek, 'Czech Universities under Communism' in John Connelly and Michael Grüttner, eds, *Universities Under Dictatorship* (University Park, PA: Pennsylvania State University Press, 2005), 167–83.

73 '"Majales" Student Demonstrations Reported Interrogated by Police', 27 June 1956 [Electronic Source]. HU OSA 300-1-2-72481; Records of Radio Free Europe/Radio Liberty Research Institute: General Records: Information Items; Open Society Archives at Central European University, Budapest, http://hdl.handle.net/10891/osa:ac4c57fa-e05c-4743-a266-bca482bebb2f; Matthews, *Tinderbox*, 80–5.

74 Kusin, *Intellectual Origins of the Prague Spring*, 26–7; Lewis, 'Red Czechoslovakia Is a Drab Gray', 38; Cartledge, *Will to Survive*, 418. On the electoral unpopularity of Communists in Eastern Europe see Applebaum, *Iron Curtain*, 205–37.

75 Service, *Comrades*, 311–12; Judt, *Postwar*, 311, 321; Eric Hobsbawm, *Interesting Times: A Twentieth-Century Life* (London: Abacus, 2010), 202–18.

76 Taubman, *Khrushchev*, 338–9.

77 Michael Lynch, *Mao* (London: Routledge, 2004), 160–1; Lee Feigon, *Mao: A Reinterpretation* (Chicago: Ivan R. Dee, 2002), 110–13. For an overview of the 'Hundred Flowers' campaign see Roderick MacFarquhar, *The Hundred Flowers* (London: Stevens & Sons, 1960).

6. RETREAT FROM EMPIRE

1 'Renaming Gold Coast', *Manchester Guardian*, 20 April 1956, 11; 'Proposals for the Gold Coast', *The Times*, 20 April 1956, 8.

2 'Plebiscite in Togoland', *The Times*, 10 May 1956, 10; Kwame Nkrumah, *The Autobiography of Kwame Nkrumah* (London: Panaf Books, 2002), 259.

3 Nkrumah, *Autobiography*, 266.

4 CAB 129/83/4, 'The Gold Coast', 5, National Archives.

5 Wm. Roger Louis, 'The Colonial Empires in the Late Nineteenth and Early Twentieth Centuries' in Louis, *Ends of British Imperialism: The Scramble for Empire, Suez and Decolonization* (London: I. B. Tauris, 2006), 44–5; Robin Neillands, *A Fighting Retreat: The British Empire 1947–97* (London: Hodder and Stoughton, 1996), 17; Dominic Sandbrook, *Never Had It So Good: A History of Britain from Suez to the Beatles* (London: Little, Brown, 2005), 262, 66.

6 John Darwin, *The End of the British Empire: The Historical Debate* (Oxford: Basil Blackwell, 1991), 43–7, 107, 121–2. On the economic importance of the colonies to the British Exchequer see, for instance, Paul Nugent, *Africa Since Independence* (Basingstoke: Palgrave Macmillan, 2004), 26–7.

7 John Darwin, 'Decolonization and the End of Empire' in Robin W. Winks, ed., *The Oxford History of the British Empire, Volume V: Historiography* (Oxford: Oxford University Press, 1999), 548; Charter of the United Nations available at http://www.un.org/en/documents/charter/.

8 Darwin, *The End of the British Empire*, 60; Darwin, 'Decolonization and the End of Empire', 548.

9 Darwin, 'Decolonization and the End of Empire', 549–50; Darwin, *The End of the British Empire*, 85–110.

10 Dennis Austin, *Politics in Ghana, 1946–1960* (London: Oxford University Press, 1964), xi–xii, 2, 4–5, 13–15; Piers Brendon, *The Decline and Fall of the British Empire*, 513–14.

11 Ronald Hyam, *Britain's Declining Empire: The Road to Decolonisation, 1918–1968* (Cambridge: Cambridge University Press, 2006), 146. See also Richard Rathbone, 'Things Fall Apart: The Erosion of Local Government, Local Justice and Civil Rights in Ghana, 1955–1960' in Martin Lynn, ed., *The British Empire in the 1950s: Retreat or Revival?* (Basingstoke: Palgrave Macmillan, 2006), 122–43.

12 Austin, *Politics in Ghana*, xi–xii, 2, 4–5, 13–15; Brendon, *Decline and Fall*, 513–14.

13 Austin, *Politics in Ghana*, 6.

14 Hyam, *Britain's Declining Empire*, 139–41.

15 Austin, *Politics in Ghana*, 7–9, 11; Hyam, *Britain's Declining Empire*, 146–8; Brendon, *Decline and Fall*, 516–19; 'Constitution of the Convention People's Party' in Nkrumah, *Autobiography*, 291.

16 Brendon, *Decline and Fall*, 517.

17 Nkrumah, *Autobiography*, 1, 3, 4, 13–16, 35, 48–63; Brendon, *Decline and Fall*, 517.

18 Hyam, *Britain's Declining Empire*, 148, 150; Brendon, *Decline and Fall*, 517–19; Nkrumah, *Autobiography*, 66–78; Austin, *Politics in Ghana*, 12.

19 Brendon, *Decline and Fall*, 519–20; Austin, *Politics in Ghana*, 88–90, 103; Nkrumah, *Autobiography*, 110–22; David Birmingham, *Kwame Nkrumah: The Father of African Nationalism* (Athens: Ohio University Press, 1998), 34–5.

20 Hyam, *Britain's Declining Empire*, 150.

21 Nkrumah, *Autobiography*, 135, 137. On the veracity of Nkrumah's account of his release see Birmingham, *Kwame Nkrumah*, 36–7.

22 Brendon, *Decline and Fall*, 515, 520.

23 Hyam, *Britain's Declining Empire*, 183–4.

24 Jean Marie Allman, *The Quills of the Porcupine: Asante Nationalism in an Emergent Ghana* (Madison: University of Wisconsin Press, 1993), 16–19, 26.

25 Allman, *Quills*, 22, 36–40, 44, 47, 49; CO 554/1162, no. 9, Arden-Clarke to Lennox-Boyd, 22 December 1954 in Richard Rathbone, ed., *British Documents on the End of Empire, Series B, Volume 1, Ghana, Part II, 1952–1957* (London: HMSO, 1992), 107. On Nkrumah's centralising tendencies see Richard Rathbone, *Nkrumah and the Chiefs: The Politics of Chieftaincy in Ghana, 1951–1960* (Oxford: James Currey, 2000).

26 CO 554/805, no. 22, in Rathbone, *BDEE*, 112.

27 Hyam, *Britain's Declining Empire*, 184; Nkrumah, *Autobiography*, 240; Brendon, *Decline and Fall*, 523–4; CO 554/805, no. 22, in Rathbone, *BDEE*, 112; Allman, *Quills*, 143–5, 162–77.

28 Austin, *Politics in Ghana*, 332–4; Allman, *Quills*, 149–50.

29 CPP Election Manifesto, 1956, in Austin, *Politics in Ghana*, 329–30.

30 Austin, *Politics in Ghana*, 334.

31 Nkrumah, *Autobiography*, 269.

32 'Nationalist Challenge in Gold Coast Election', *The Times*, 12 July 1956, 9; 'Ballot-Boxes By Canoe', *The Times*, 13 July 1956, 9.

33 'Election Issues in Gold Coast', *The Times*, 18 July 1956, 8; 'Election Day', *Manchester Guardian*, 17 July 1956, 6; Austin, *Politics in Ghana*, 340.

34 Austin, *Politics in Ghana*, 354, 355.

35 Nkrumah, *Autobiography*, 284–6.

36 'The Sudan as a Republic', *The Times*, 2 January 1956, 7; Douglas H. Johnson, *The Root Causes of Sudan's Civil Wars* (Oxford: James Currey, 2003) esp. 21–37; Wm. Roger Louis, 'The Coming of Independence in the Sudan', in Louis, *Ends of British Imperialism*, 533, 544, 547; Glen Balfour-Paul, 'The Sudan Episode', in Balfour-Paul, *The End of Empire in the Middle East: Britain's Relinquishment of Power in Her Last Three Arab Dependencies* (Cambridge: Cambridge University Press, 1991), 16–48.

37 Brendon, *Decline and Fall*, 489–90; Wm. Roger Louis, 'A Prima Donna with Honour: Eden and Suez', in Louis, *Ends of British Imperialism*, 637; John Bagot Glubb, *A Soldier with the Arabs* (London: Hodder and Stoughton, 1957), 422–8; D. R. Thorpe, *Eden: The Life and Times of*

Anthony Eden, First Earl of Avon, 1897–1977 (London: Pimlico, 2004), 465–6.

38 Robert Holland, *Britain and the Revolt in Cyprus, 1954–1959* (Oxford: Clarendon Press, 1998), 116, 117, 118–19.

39 Nancy Crawshaw, *The Cyprus Revolt: An Account of the Struggle for Union with Greece* (London: George Allen & Unwin, 1978), 168–9.

40 Brendon, *Decline and Fall*, 611–12, 615; Hyam, *Britain's Declining Empire*, 151, 153–4; Holland, *Britain and the Revolt in Cyprus*, 21–2; Philip Murphy, *Alan Lennox-Boyd: A Biography* (London: I. B. Tauris, 1999), 114; Peter Sluglett, 'Formal and Informal Empire in the Middle East' in Winks, ed., *The Oxford History of the British Empire, Volume V: Historiography*, 433.

41 Robert Holland, 'Never, Never Land: British Colonial Policy and the Roots of Violence in Cyprus, 1950–54', *Journal of Imperial and Commonwealth History*, vol. 21, no. 3 (September 1993), 149.

42 Hyam, *Britain's Declining Empire*, 151.

43 Brendon, *Decline and Fall*, 618; Holland, *Britain and the Revolt in Cyprus*, 32, 34, 42–4. See also, Süha Bölükbaşı, 'The Cyprus Dispute and the United Nations: Peaceful Non-Settlement between 1954 and 1996', *International Journal of Middle East Studies*, vol. 30, no. 3 (August 1998), 413–14.

44 Hyam, *Britain's Declining Empire*, 152.

45 Brendon, *Decline and Fall*, 611, 612, 615; Holland, *Britain and the Revolt in Cyprus*, 6, 18–19, 24–5.

46 Brendon, *Decline and Fall*, 615; Holland, *Britain and the Revolt in Cyprus*, 24–5.

47 Holland, *Britain and the Revolt in Cyprus*, 52; 'The EOKA Oath' in Crawshaw, *The Cyprus Revolt*, Appendix 4.

48 Holland, *Britain and the Revolt in Cyprus*, 29–30; Robert Stimson, 'Grivas: Wanted Man of Cyprus', *The Listener*, 29 September 1956, 408.

49 Holland, *Britain and the Revolt in Cyprus*, 30.

50 Ibid., 54; Murphy, *Alan Lennox-Boyd*, 117; Naomi Rosenbaum, 'Success in Foreign Policy: the British in Cyprus, 1878–1960', *Canadian Journal of Political Science*, vol. 3, no. 4 (December 1970), 626.

51 Brendon, *Decline and Fall*, 620–1; Charles Foley, ed., *The Memoirs of General Grivas* (London: Longmans, 1964), 68; Holland, *Britain and the Revolt in Cyprus*, 153.

52 Murphy, *Alan Lennox-Boyd*, vii–viii, 33, 66, 102, 110.

53 Murphy, *Alan Lennox-Boyd*, 104; Holland, *Britain and the Revolt in Cyprus*, 113–14.

54 Holland, *Britain and the Revolt in Cyprus*, 29, 30; Brendon, *Decline and Fall*, 616.

55 *Terrorism in Cyprus: The Captured Documents* (London: HMSO), iii, v; Holland, *Britain and the Revolt in Cyprus*, 113.

56 Thorpe, *Eden*, 467.

57 Kennett Love, 'Britain's Primate Deplores Exiling of Cyprus Cleric', *NYT*, 16 March 1956, 1, 4.

58 'Writes about U.S. Press & Radio Comments on Cyprus', 13 March 1956, FO 371/123877/RG1081/509; Alistair Cooke, 'Makarios a "Martyr": A Tableau for New Yorkers', *NYT*, 27 March 1956, 1.

59 Cooke, 'Makarios a "Martyr"'; 'Action on Makarios Dismaying to U.S.', *NYT*, 10 March 1956, 2; 'Washington to Foreign Office', 10 April 1956, FO 371/123882/RG1081/706.

60 FO 371/123877/RG1081/510, 514 and 518; 'Writes about the Norwegian attitude on the Cyprus question & discussion of it in NATO', FO 371/123881/RG1081/668.

61 'Writes about Russian Press comments on the Cyprus Situation', FO371/123879/RG1081/593; 'Writes about articles in the Polish Press about the arrest & deportation of Archbishop Makarios', 13 March 1956, FO 371/123877/RG1081/523.

62 FO 371/123880/RG1081/652, Washington to Foreign Office, 29 March 1956; 'Greek Rioters Stone Troops', *Manchester Guardian*, 11 March 1956, 1; 'Bomb Attacks on Families', *Manchester Guardian*, 16 March 1956, 1; 'Cyprus Crippled in Protest Strike; British Use Force', *NYT*, 11 March 1956, 1, 9.

63 Foley, *Memoirs of General Grivas*, 67.

64 David M. Anderson, 'Policing and Communal Conflict: The Cyprus Emergency, 1954–60', *Journal of Imperial and Commonwealth History*, vol. 21, no. 3 (September 1993), 184, 189–90, 194–6.

65 Holland, *Britain and the Revolt in Cyprus*, 134.

66 Crawshaw, *The Cyprus Revolt*, 166.

67 Holland, *Britain and the Revolt in Cyprus*, 130, 133; Foley, *Memoirs of General Grivas*, 69–72.

68 *Terrorism in Cyprus*, 76; Crawshaw, *The Cyprus Revolt*, 188; http://www.hm-waterguard.org.uk/George%20Kaberry's%20murder.pdf.

69 Holland, *Britain and the Revolt in Cyprus*, 155.

70 Foley, *Memoirs of General Grivas*, 96.

71 Anderson, 'Policing and Communal Conflict', 200. On the use of torture by the British see David Anderson, *Histories of the Hanged: Britain's Dirty War in Kenya and the End of Empire* (London: Weidenfeld & Nicolson, 2005); Anderson, 'Mau Mau in the High Court and the "Lost" British Empire Archives: Colonial Conspiracy or Bureaucratic Bungle?', *Journal of Imperial and Commonwealth History*, vol. 39, no. 5 (2011), 699–716; Caroline Elkins, *Britain's Gulag: The Brutal End of Empire in Kenya* (London: Pimlico, 2005).

72 Neillands, *A Fighting Retreat*, 311.

73 Brendon, *Decline and Fall*, 621–2; George Clay, 'More Murders in Cyprus', *Observer*, 3 August 1958, 1; David Bonner, *Executive Measures and National*

Security: Have the Rules of the Game Changed? (Aldershot: Ashgate Publishing, 2007), 166.

74 'Casualty Tables' in Crawshaw, *The Cyprus Revolt*, Appendix 6.

7. THE PALESTRO MASSACRE

1 Michael Clark, 'French Soldiers Lost in Algeria', *NYT*, 20 May 1956, 9; Horne, *Savage War of Peace*, 152–3; Evans, *Algeria*, 166; Joshua Cole, review of Raphaëlle Branche, *L'Embuscade de Palestro: Algérie 1956* (Paris: Armand Colin, 2010), *H-France Review*, vol. 11 (July 2011), no. 161, 1.

2 Horne, *Savage War*, 153; Cole, 'review', 1–2; JF1013/6, 'Monthly Report for Algeria, May 1956', Appendix 2, 'Principal Military Events and Anti-Terrorist Measures – Algeria, May 1956', 3, FO 371/119348.

3 Cole, 'review', 1; Martin Thomas, *Fight or Flight: Britain, France, and Their Roads from Empire* (Oxford: Oxford University Press, 2014), 178.

4 JF1013/6, 'Monthly Report for Algeria, May 1956', Appendix 2, 'Principal Military Events and Anti-Terrorist Measures – Algeria, May 1956', 1, FO 371/119348.

5 Ibid., 1–2, FO 371/119348, National Archives, Kew.

6 Thomas, *Fight or Flight*, 178; Cole, 'review', 2–3; Evans, *Algeria*, 166–7; Horne, *Savage War*, 153; Gil Merom, *How Democracies Lose Small Wars* (Cambridge: Cambridge University Press, 2003), 101.

7 Merom, *How Democracies Lose*, 101–2;

8 '90 Hurt in Riots', *The Manchester Guardian*, 19 May 1956, 1; 'French Riot Delays Troops for Algeria', *NYT*, 19 May 1956, 1; Evans, *Algeria*, 164–5.

9 Evans, *Algeria*, 164–5; Merom, *How Democracies Lose*, 102–3.

10 'Algeria: Logic v. Scruples', *Time*, 16 April 1956. See also Evans, *Algeria*, 163.

11 'The Press: No Man's Land', *Time*, 11 June 1956; 'Across the Rebel Line in Algeria', *Observer*, 27 May 1956, 1, 6.

12 'Algeria: Logic v. Scruples', *Time*, 16 April 1956; 'The Press: No Man's Land', *Time*, 11 June 1956; 'Crisis for M. Mollet', *Manchester Guardian*, 30 May 1956, 1 and 'Mlle Gérard to be Tried in Paris', *Observer*, 3 June 1956, 4.

13 Evans, *Algeria*, 166–7; Irwin Wall, *A Diplomatic Revolution: Algeria's Fight for Independence and the Origins of the Post-Cold War Era* (New York: Oxford University Press, 2002), 106.

14 Horne, *Savage War of Peace*, 154; Evans, *Algeria*, 154.

15 Evans, *Algeria*, 155–9.

16 JF 1019/138, 'The Duration of the Operations in Algeria', 24 April 1956, 1–2, in FO 371/119361.

17 'Algeria: The Reform That Failed', *Time*, 6 August 1956.

18 JF 1019/138, 'The Duration of the Operations in Algeria'.

19 'Algeria: Wasting War', *Time*, 23 April 1956 and 'Algeria: Harassed on All Sides', *Time*, 21 May 1956. The 2014 figure, which represents 'purchasing power', was calculated at http://www.measuringworth.com.

20 'A General Report on the Algerian Situation, 25th June, 1956, by Brigadier A. C. F. Jackson, C.B.E., Military Attaché, British Embassy, Paris', 6–7, in FO 371/119362; 'Algeria: Wasting War'.

21 'A General Report on the Algerian Situation, 25th June, 1956', 7.

22 Evans, *Algeria*, 168–9, Horne, *Savage War*, 174.

23 Evans, *Algeria*, 169; Horne, *Savage War*, 198-200; JF1019/210, letter from Roderick Sarell, 31 August 1956, 1, in FO 371/119363.

24 Roderick Sarell obituary, *Daily Telegraph*, 25 August 2001, at http://www.telegraph.co.uk/news/obituaries/1338438/Sir-Roderick-Sarell.html; Thomas, *Fight or Flight*, 318. JF1019/210, letter from Roderick Sarell, 31 August 1956, 1–2.

25 JF1019/210, letter from Roderick Sarell, 31 August 1956, 3.

26 Horne, *Savage War*, 171–4; Evans, *Algeria*, 169–71.

27 Horne, *Savage War*, 153; JF1019/151, 30 May 1956, 6, in FO 371/119361.

28 Horne, *Savage War*, 153, 183; Thomas, *Fight or Flight*, 178; Evans, *Algeria*, 181; Michael Clark, 'Two Algerian Terrorists Executed, First Since Revolt Began in '54', *NYT*, 20 June 1956, 4; 'First Executions in Algeria', *Manchester Guardian*, 20 June 1956, 9.

29 Horne, *Savage War*, 153, 183; Evans, *Algeria*, 181, Thomas, *Fight or Flight*, 178.

30 Michael Clark, 'Algerian Rebels Warn of Revenge', *NYT*, 22 June 1956, 6; Guy Pervillé, 'Le terrorisme urbain dans le guerre d'Algérie (1954–1962)' in Jean-Charles Jauffret, ed., *Militaires et guérilla dans la guerre d'Algérie* (2001), 454. See also Horne, *Savage War*, 183. The French phrase is '*Pour chaque maquisard guillotiné, cent Français seront abattus sans distinction*'.

31 'Terrorists Strike Back', *NYT*, 21 June 1956, 6; JF1019/168, 23 June 1956, 1, in FO 371/119361; Horne, *Savage War*, 184; Evans, *Algeria*, 181.

32 Clark, 'Algerian Rebels Warn of Revenge'; Horne, *Savage War*, 184.

33 Horne, *Savage War*, 184–6; Evans, *Algeria*, 181–2; James Gannon, *Military Occupations in the Age of Self-Determination: The History Neocons Neglected* (Westport, CT: Praegar Security International, 2008), 49; '3 Killed, 63 Injured by Bombs in Algiers', *NYT*, 1 October 1956, 10; JF1019/214, 'Report on two serious explosions which took place on Sept 30 in Algiers', FO 371/119363.

34 'North Africa: Ariel Kidnap', *Time*, 5 November 1956; Evans, *Algeria*, 186; Horne, *Savage War*, 159.

35 Robert Merle, *Ben Bella* (London: Michael Joseph, 1967), 39, 42–4, 46–8; Joseph R. Gregory, 'Ahmed Ben Bella, Revolutionary Who Led Algeria After Independence, Dies at 93', *NYT*, 12 April 2012; Evans, *Algeria*, 95, 106, 119.

36 Evans, *Algeria*, 176–7, 186; Michael Clark, 'Neighbors Chart Peace in Algeria', *NYT*, 1 October 1956, 1. 3. On the negotiations and secret contacts between the French and the FLN, see also Irwin M. Wall, *France, the United States, and the Algerian War* (Berkeley: University of California Press, 2001), 50–4.

37 Thomas, *Fight or Flight*, 182.

38 'North Africa: Ariel Kidnap'.

39 Thomas F. Brady, 'Seizure of Algerian Rebels Described by Correspondent on Their Plane', *NYT*, 24 October 1956, 1, 4.

40 Merle, *Ben Bella*, 113; Brady, 'Seizure of Algerian Rebels', 4; Horne, *Savage War*, 160; Evans, *Algeria*, 186; Robert C. Doty, 'France Accuses Five of Treason', *NYT*, 30 October 1956, 1; 'France Kidnaps Five Rebels', *Manchester Guardian*, 23 October 1956, 1; Michael Clark, 'French Seize Five Rebel Chiefs; Draw Algerians' Plane into Trap', *NYT*, 23 October 1956, 1, 6.

41 Michael Clark, 'Rioting in Tunis Aimed at French', *NYT*, 24 October 1956, 3; Horne, 160.

42 'North Africa: Ariel Kidnap'.

43 'North Africa: Ariel Kidnap'; JF 1019/221, 'From Paris to Foreign Office', 25 October 1956, 1–2, and JF 1019/222, 'From Paris to Foreign Office', 1, in FO 371/119363; Thomas, *Fight or Flight*, 182.

44 Thomas, *Fight or Flight*, 183; Horne, *Savage War*, 160–1; Evans, *Algeria*, 186–7.

45 Evans, *Algeria*, 187.

46 Merle, *Ben Bella*, 109–11.

47 Horne, *Savage War*, 160; Clark, 'Rioting in Tunis Aimed at French', 3; 'Plane's Seizure Called "Piracy"', *NYT*, 24 October 1956, 5; Robert C. Doty, 'New Africa Crisis Faced by French', *NYT*, 24 October 1956, 1, 2; Wall, *France, the United States, and the Algerian War*, 52–3; see also numerous telegrams and reports – JF 1025/7–JF 1025/30 in FO 371/119372.

48 'Telegram from the Department of State to the Embassy in Libya', 26 October 1956, in *FRUS, 1955–1957, Africa, Volume XVIII*, 247–8; Wall, *France, the United States, and the Algerian War*, 50–6; Thomas, *Fight or Flight*, 182–3.

49 Wall, *France, the United States, and the Algerian War*, 57; Matthew Connelly, *A Diplomatic Revolution: Algeria's Fight for Independence and the Origins of the Post-Cold War Era* (Oxford University Press, 2003), 115–16.

8. PART OF A GREAT STRUGGLE ALL OVER THE WORLD

1 Carson, *The Papers of Martin Luther King*, vol. III, 256–8; 'Written History' at http://www.stjohndivine.org/about/history; 'Cathedral of St. John the Divine, New York City', at http://www.sacred-destinations.com/usa/new-york-city-cathedral-st-john-the-divine.

2 Martin Luther King, Jr., 'The Death of Evil upon the Seashore', Sermon Delivered at the Service of Prayer and Thanksgiving, Cathedral of St John the Divine, 17 May 1956, in Carson, *The Papers of Martin Luther King*, vol. III, 256–62.

3 Ling, *Martin Luther King, Jr.*, 47–9; Garrow, *Bearing the Cross*, 62–3, 64,

68.

4 King, *Stride Toward Freedom*, 65–6, 68–9; Garrow, *Bearing the Cross*, 71–5; Robinson, *The Montgomery Bus Boycott*, 65–75, 114; Belinda Robnett, *How Long, How Long?: African American Women in the Struggle for Civil Rights* (Oxford University Press, 2000), 63–4. For speakers' bureau see, for example, 'Recommendations of MIA Strategy Committee, March 14', in Burns, *Daybreak of Freedom*, 205. On the work of the welfare committee see 'Interview with Mrs Johnnie Carr', 25, in Southern Regional Council: Will the Circle Be Unbroken program files and sound recordings, Box 12, Folder 14 – Montgomery, Carr, Johnnie R., August 18, 1983, Interviewer Worth Long, MARBL.

5 'Interview with Mrs Johnnie Carr', 24.

6 Ling, *Martin Luther King, Jr.*, 50.

7 'Address to MIA Mass Meeting at Holt Street Baptist Church', 22 March 1956, in Carson, *Papers of Martin Luther King, Vol. III*, 200–1.

8 Garrow, *Bearing the Cross*, 71; Carson, *Papers of Martin Luther King, Vol. III*, 72–3.

9 Penny M. Von Eschen, *Race Against Empire: Black Americans and Anticolonialism, 1937–1957* (Ithaca: Cornell University Press, 1997), 167–73; Brenda Gayle Plummer, *Rising Wind: Black Americans and US Foreign Affairs, 1935–1960* (Chapel Hill: University of North Carolina Press, 1996), 247–53; 'Bandung Conference (Asian-African Conference), 1955', http://history.state.gov/milestones/1953-1960/BandungConf.

10 Garrow, *Bearing the Cross*, 90; Ling, *Martin Luther King, Jr.*, 52.

11 Garrow, *Bearing the Cross*, 71.

12 'Non-Aggression Procedures to Interracial Harmony', Address Delivered at the American Baptist Assembly and American Home Mission Agencies Conference, 23 July 1956, in Carson, *Papers of Martin Luther King, Vol. III*, 324.

13 Martin Luther King, 'The "New Negro" of the South: Behind the Montgomery Story', *The Socialist Call*, June 1956, in Carson, *Papers of Martin Luther King, Vol. III*, 285.

14 King, 'The Montgomery Story', Address Delivered at the Forty-Seventh Annual NAACP Convention, 27 June 1956, in Carson, *Papers of Martin Luther King, Vol. III*, 308.

15 Layton, *International Politics and Civil Right Policies*, 110; Dudziak, *Cold War Civil Rights*, 112–13, 118.

16 Letter from Henri Varin de la Brunelière, 11 May 1956, in Carson, *Papers of Martin Luther King, Vol. III*, 254–5.

17 King, *Stride Toward Freedom*, 68.

18 'Edward Morgan and the News', 24 February 1956, American Broadcasting Company, in Rabb, Maxwell M. Papers, 1938–1958, 1989, Box 34, Folder Mo(2), Eisenhower Library.

19 King, *Stride Toward Freedom*, 128.

20 Garrow, *Bearing the Cross*, 62; 'Notes on MIA Executive Board Meeting, by Donald T. Ferron', 2 February 1956, in Carson, *Papers of Martin Luther King, Vol. III*, 120; 'Interview by Donald T. Ferron', 4 February 1956, in Carson, *Papers of Martin Luther King, Vol. III*, 125. See also Rustin's comments in 'Montgomery Diary', *Liberation*, April 1956, reproduced in Burns, *Daybreak of Freedom*, 169.

21 Hall, *Peace and Freedom*, 82; Ling, *Martin Luther King, Jr.*, 47–8; Garrow, *Bearing the Cross*, 66–9; Carson, *Papers of Martin Luther King, Vol. III*, 17–19; http://mlk-kpp01.stanford.edu/index.php/encyclopedia/encyclo-pedia/enc_rustin_bayard_1910_1987/. Rustin drafted many of the journal articles and books that appeared under King's name, provided strategic advice, and deployed his formidable organisational skills for the benefit of both King and the wider civil rights movement.

22 http://mlk-kpp01.stanford.edu/kingweb/about_king/encyclopedia/smiley_glenn.html; Ling, *Martin Luther King, Jr.*, 47–8; Garrow, *Bearing the Cross*, 68–70; Carson, *Papers of Martin Luther King, Vol. III*, 19–20.

23 Garrow, *Bearing the Cross*, 68.

24 'Letter to John and Al from Glenn Smiley, 29 February 1956', 1, Bayard Rustin Papers (University Publications of America), reel 1, Woodruff Library.

25 Branch, *Parting the Waters*, 180. For King's intellectual evolution and embrace of nonviolence see, for example, Carson, 'Introduction', in Carson, *Papers of Martin Luther King, Vol. III*, 16–22; David J. Garrow, 'The Intellectual Development of Martin Luther King, Jr.,: Influences and Commentaries' at http://www.davidgarrow.com/File/DJG%201986%20USQRMLK.pdf; Burns, *Daybreak of Freedom*, 195.

26 King, *Stride Toward Freedom*, 89.

27 'To Lillian Eugenia Smith', 24 May 1956 in Carson, *Papers of Martin Luther King, Vol. III*, 273.

28 See, for example, 'To the Montgomery Public', 25 December 1955 in Carson, *Papers of Martin Luther King, Vol. III*, 92; 'Notes on MIA Mass Meeting at Hutchison Street Baptist Church, by Donald T. Ferron', 1 March 1956 in Carson, *Papers of Martin Luther King, Vol. III*, 151; 'Address to MIA Mass Meeting at Holt Street Baptist Church', 22 March 1956 in Carson, *Papers of Martin Luther King, Vol. III*, 200.

29 King, 'Walk for Freedom', *Fellowship*, May 1956 in Carson, *Papers of Martin Luther King, Vol. III*, 278.

30 'The Montgomery Story', 305–6.

31 'Non-Aggression Procedures to Interracial Harmony', Address Delivered at the American Baptist Assembly and Home Mission Agencies Conference, 23 July 1956 in Carson, *Papers of Martin Luther King, Vol. III*, 325–327.

32 'The Montgomery Story', 307, and 'Non-Aggression Procedures', 328. See also King's reference to Gandhi on 31 March in Carson, *Papers of Martin*

Luther King, Vol. III, 210.

33 'The Montgomery Story', 307.

34 A. Philip Randolph, 'March on Washington Movement Presents Program for the Negro' in Rayford W. Logan, ed., *What the Negro Wants* (Chapel Hill: University of North Carolina Press, 1944), 150–2; Brown & Webb, *Race in the American South*, 295.

35 Garrow, *Bearing the Cross*, 75; King, *Stride Toward Freedom*, 72.

36 Matthew 5:44, The Holy Bible, King James Version.

37 King, 'The "New Negro"', 286.

38 Julian Bond, 'Nonviolence: An Interpretation', *Freedomways*, Spring 1963, available at http://www.crmvet.org/info/nv_jbond.htm. There is a substantial body of scholarship on the role of armed self-defence in the civil rights movement. See for example Timothy B. Tyson, *Radio Free Dixie: Robert F. Williams and the Roots of Black Power* (Chapel Hill: University of North Carolina Press, 1999) and Simon Wendt, *The Spirit and the Shotgun: Armed Resistance and the Struggle for Civil Rights* (Gainesville: The University Press of Florida, 2007).

39 'Interview with E. D. Nixon', 28–30, in Southern Regional Council: Will the Circle Be Unbroken program files and sound recordings, Box 13, Folder 6 – Montgomery – Nixon, E.D., nd, Interviewer Judy Barton, MARBL.

40 'Non-Aggression Procedures', 325.

9. BREAD AND FREEDOM

1 Matthews, *Tinderbox*, 93; T. David Curp, *A Clean Sweep: The Politics of Ethnic Cleansing in Western Poland, 1945–1960* (University of Rochester Press, 2006), 25–7, 39.

2 Matthews, *Tinderbox*, 93–4.

3 Machcewicz, *Rebellious Satellite*, 87–100; Matthews, *Tinderbox*, 94, 96–8.

4 Poznań, June '56, Institute of National Remembrance, 'History' at http://www.june56.ipn.gov.pl/portal/j56/346/2215/History.html; Machcewicz, *Rebellious Satellite*, 99, 100; Matthews, *Tinderbox*, 98–101; Curp, *Clean Sweep*, 160; Kemp-Welch, *Poland under Communism*, 87.

5 'Report by Mr. Gurrey on the Poznań Riot of June 28, 1956', 1, FO 371/122595. For the Polish national anthem (Dąbrowski's Mazurka) see Maja Trochimczyk, 'National Anthems of Poland: Dąbrowski's Mazurka', at http://www.usc.edu/dept/polish_music/repertoi/dabrowski.html.

6 Machcewicz, *Rebellious Satellite*, 106; 'Black Thursday: Course of Events' at http://www.Poznań.pl/mim/main/en/black-thursday-course-of-events,p,3043,3060.html; 'A Danish Businessman Gives Eyewitness Account of the Poznań Riot', 13 September 1956, 3 [Electronic record]. HU OSA 300-1-2-74854; Records of Radio Free Europe/Radio Liberty Research Institute: General Records: Information Items; Open Society

Archives at Central European University, Budapest, http://hdl.handle.
net/10891/osa:fc0d50c3-8e28-4b11-8772-75e87968eada.

7 Machcewicz, *Rebellious Satellite*, 106, 109; Matthews, *Tinderbox*, 101–7;
Curp, *Clean Sweep*, 161–2.

8 'Poland: This Is Our Revolution', *Time*, 9 July 1956; Machcewicz, *Rebellious Satellite*, 100.

9 'Report by Mr. Gurrey', 1.

10 Machcewicz, *Rebellious Satellite*, 102; 'Poland: This Is Our Revolution'.

11 'Professor Peter Wiles' at http://www2.warwick.ac.uk/fac/soc/economics/
staff/academic/harrison/comment/wiles.pdf; Letter, British Embassy, Warsaw to Northern Department, Foreign Office, 3 July 1956; Letter, Foreign
Office to Wiles, 23 July 1956, FO 371/122594; P. J. D. Wiles, Report on
Poznań Uprising, 4, FO 371/122594.

12 'A British Business Man Gets Grandstand View of the Poznań Riot', 10
July 1956, 2 [Electronic record]. HU OSA 300-1-2-73037; Records of Radio
Free Europe/Radio Liberty Research Institute: General Records: Infor-
mation Items; Open Society Archives at Central European University,
Budapest; http://hdl.handle.net/10891/osa:6968e6fa-c592-4e59-9043-
b0c48646icc0.

13 Wiles, Report on Poznań Uprising, 1–2.

14 Ibid., 2; Machcewicz, *Rebellious Satellite*, 116.

15 Machcewicz, *Rebellious Satellite*, 99, 104; Kemp-Welch, *Poland under Communism*, 87.

16 'Report by Mr. Gurrey', 2; Machcewicz, *Rebellious Satellite*, 107–9.

17 'Report by Mr. Gurrey', 2–3; 'Poland: This Is Our Revolution'; Curp,
Clean Sweep, 162; Machcewicz, *Rebellious Satellite*, 112.

18 'Poland: This Is Our Revolution', *Time*, 9 July 1956; 'A British Business
Man Gets Grandstand View', 2; Machcewicz, *Rebellious Satellite*, 102;
'Report by Mr. Gurrey', 2; 'RFE and the Poznań Demonstrations', 6 July
1956, 2, in C. D. Jackson, Box 54, 'Free Europe Committee (5)', Eisenhower Library.

19 'A Danish Businessman Gives Eyewitness Account', 3; Machcewicz,
Rebellious Satellite, 105, 110; Despatch no. 131, 3 July 1956, 3; 'Report by
American Eyewitness on Poznań Disturbances', 1, FO 371/122595; Curp,
Clean Sweep, 163.

20 Machcewicz, *Rebellious Satellite*, 113; Curp, *Clean Sweep*, 163; Wiles, Report
on Poznań Uprising, 2.

21 Matthews, *Tinderbox*, 112, 114, 115, 116; Wiles, Report on Poznań Uprising,
3; 'Report by Mr. Gurrey', 2; 'Deaths Reported', *NYT*, 29 June 1956, 3;
http://www.june56.ipn.gov.pl/j56/calendary/2264,June-28-1956.html.

22 'Poland: This Is Our Revolution'.

23 Matthews, *Tinderbox*, 112, 114, 115, 116; Wiles, Report on Poznań Uprising,
3; 'Report by Mr. Gurrey', 2; 'Deaths Reported', 3; 'Poland: This Is Our

Revolution'.

24 'Report by Mr. Gurrey', 3; Matthews, *Tinderbox*, 117,123, Machcewicz, *Rebellious Satellite*, 113.

25 http://www.1956.pl/3,36.html; Matthews, *Tinderbox*, 119–20; Wiles, Report on Poznań Uprising, 3; '38 Killed, 270 Wounded in Poznań Riots', *The Times*, 30 June 1956, 6.

26 'Poland: This Is Our Revolution'.

27 'Report by Mr. Gurrey', 4; Machcewicz, *Rebellious Satellite*, 120.

28 Machcewicz, *Rebellious Satellite*, 114–15; Matthews, *Tinderbox*, 123–4.

29 Matthews, *Tinderbox*, 109; Toranska, *Oni*, 62.

30 Curp, *Clean Sweep*, 164; Matthews, *Tinderbox*, 124; Toranska, *Oni*, 62.

31 Telegram no. 417, 29 June 1956, 2, FO371/122593; Telegram no. 143 (Berlin to London), 29 June 1956, 2, FO371/122593; Matthews, *Tinderbox*, 122, 124–5.

32 Despatch no. 131, 3 July 1956, 3, FO 371/122595.

33 '38 Killed, 270 Wounded in Poznań Riots', 6.

34 '38 Killed in Poznań "Bread" Riots', *Manchester Guardian*, 30 June 1956, 1; Matthews, *Tinderbox*, 120, 125.

35 Matthews, *Tinderbox*, 121–2, 126; Kemp-Welch, *Poland under Communism*, 89 ; 'Report by Mr. Gurrey', 4.

36 'Tanks Called Out to Quell Poland Riot', *The Times*, 29 June 1956, 8; 'Report by Mr. Gurrey', 6.

37 Machcewicz, *Rebellious Satellite*, 103.

38 Telegram no. 143 (Berlin to London), 29 June 1956, 1–2, FO371/122593.

39 'RFE and the Poznań demonstrations', 6 July 1956, 1, in C. D. Jackson, Box 54, 'Free Europe Committee (5)', Eisenhower Library.

40 Telegram no. 143 (Berlin to London), 29 June 1956, 2, FO371/122593; Matthews, *Tinderbox*, 125, 127.

41 Telegram no. 417, 29 June 1956, 2, FO371/122593; Matthews, *Tinderbox*, 129.

42 Machcewicz, *Rebellious Satellite*, 118; Curp, *Clean Sweep*, 164; Kemp-Welch, *Poland under Communism*, 88.

43 Matthews, *Tinderbox*, 125; http://www.1956.pl/4,37.html.

44 'Confidential: From Warsaw to Foreign Office, 29 June 1956', telegram no. 414, 2, FO 371/122593.

45 Machcewicz, *Rebellious Satellite*, 87, 90; Curp, *Clean Sweep*, 158; 'Poznań Pay and Prices', 22 January 1955 [Electronic record], 1–2. HU OSA 300-1-2-54734; Records of Radio Free Europe/Radio Liberty Research Institute: General Records: Information Items; Open Society Archives at Central European University, Budapest, http://hdl.handle.net/10891/osa:142a1d92-961d-4f69-849c-6c6849bc53a2; 'A German Trader on the Poznań Fair', 17 September 1955 [Electronic record], 2. HU OSA 300-1-2-62174; Records of Radio Free Europe/Radio Liberty Research Institute: General Records: Information Items; Open Society Archives at Central European University, Budapest, http://hdl.handle.net/10891/osa:b02b347d-40cd-

4d46-af29-5d6aee1ed5a5.

46 Machcewicz, *Rebellious Satellite*, 87; Curp, *Clean Sweep*, 158.

47 Machcewicz, *Rebellious Satellite*, 91–2; Matthews, *Tinderbox*, 94.

48 Machcewicz, *Rebellious Satellite*, 92, 94; Matthews, *Tinderbox*, 94.

49 Foreign Office Note, 'Riots in Poznań', 29 June 1956, FO371/122594; Kemp-Welch, *Poland under Communism*, 76-84; 'Poland in Ferment', *The Times*, 4 July 1956, 11.

50 'Tanks Called Out to Quell Poland Riot', *The Times*, 29 June 1956, 8; Curp, *Clean Sweep*, 159; Machcewicz, *Rebellious Satellite*, 93.

51 Machcewicz, *Rebellious Satellite*, 93.

52 'Poznań', *Manchester Guardian*, 30 June 1956, 4.

53 Machcewicz, *Rebellious Satellite*, 97; Matthews, *Tinderbox*, 95.

54 'Local Discontent Held Cause', *NYT*, 30 June 1956, 2; 'U.S. Urges Soviet Free Satellites', *NYT*, 30 June 1956, 1.

55 International Confederation of Free Trade Unions, 'Draft Statement on the Oppression of the Workers of Poland', 1, in FO 371/122594. See also 'RFE and the Poznań demonstrations', 6 July 1956, Annex, in C. D. Jackson, Box 54, 'Free Europe Committee (5)', Eisenhower Library.

56 'Protest in Poland', *NYT*, 30 June 1956, 16.

57 Telegram no. 257 Saving, from Paris to London, 1, 29 June 1956, FO371/122593.

58 'Proclamation of the Chairman of the Council of Ministers, Cyrankiewicz, to the People of Poznań, June 29, 1956', in Zinner, ed. *National Communism and Popular Revolt in Eastern Europe*, 131–5.

59 'That's What We Think' (editorial), *Sztandar Młodych*, no. 155, June 29, 1956 in Despatch no. 132, 3 July 1956, 10–11, FO 371/122595. See also 'Provocation', *Trybuna Ludu*, 29 June 1956 in 'Communist Propaganda Problems in the East European Bloc 1956', 18–19, in Records of the US Information Agency, Part 1-A (UPA – LexisNexis), Reel 9, RSC.

60 Sir Andrew Noble, 'Report on the Poznań Riot' (Despatch no. 131, 3 July 1956), 5, FO371/122595; Taubman, *Khrushchev*, 290.

61 'Bulletin on the Poznań Incidents' (Polish Press Agency), *Trybuna Ludu*, 29 June 1956 in Zinner, ed. *National Communism and Popular Revolt*, 127; '"Provocation": Editorial in *Trybuna Ludu* on the Poznań Incidents, 29 June 1956 in Zinner, ed. *National Communism and Popular Revolt*, 128; 'The Events in Poznań', *Trybuna Ludu* no. 181, 30 June 1956, in Despatch no. 132, 3 July 1956, 11, FO 371/122595; Machcewicz, *Rebellious Satellite*, 119.

62 'The Events in Poznań', 9.

63 'Poznań Taxes Repayment', *The Times*, 11 July 1956, 10; 'Polish Minister Dismissed', *The Times*, 9 July 1956, 8; Matthews, *Tinderbox*, 136.

64 'Statement of Policy Proposed by the National Security Council on United States Policy Toward the Soviet Satellites in Eastern Europe', NSC 174, 11 December 1953, in *FRUS, 1952–1954*, VIII, Eastern Europe,

Soviet Union, Eastern Mediterranean, Document 51, at http://history. state.gov/historicaldocuments/frus1952-54v08/d51.

65 Memorandum of a Telephone Conversation Between the Secretary of State and the Director of Central Intelligence (Dulles), Washington, June 28, 1956, 5:55 p.m., *FRUS, 1955–1957*, vol. xxv, Eastern Europe, 181.

66 'NATO and the Poznań Riots', cable from J. F. Dulles, State Department, 20 July 1956, FO 371/122596.

67 'American Offer of Food', *The Times*, 2 July 1956, 8; 'Polish Rejection of US Food Offer', *The Times*, 5 July 1956, 8; Telephone conversations, John Foster Dulles and Allen Dulles, 29 June 1956 – documents 68 and 69, *FRUS 1955–1957*, vol III, pp. 183–4.

68 See 'RFE and the Poznań Demonstrations'; Memorandum, 'Special Interim Report on RFE's Coverage in Commentaries of Poznań Rising, June 29–July 1, 1956', 5, C. D. Jackson Papers, Box 54, Radio Free Europe Committee (5), Eisenhower Library.

69 Memorandum, 'Special Interim Report on RFE's Coverage in Commentaries of Poznań Rising, June 29–July 1, 1956', 3 and 'Special Interim Report (no. 2) on RFE's Coverage in Commentaries of Poznań Rising, July 2–4, 1956', 3, in C. D. Jackson Papers, Box 54, Radio Free Europe Committee (5).

70 Machcewicz, *Rebellious Satellite*, 125; Matthews, *Tinderbox*, 127. See also Kemp-Welch, *Poland under Communism*, 92.

71 Machcewicz, *Rebellious Satellite*, 125–38, 148–55, 157, Kemp-Welch, *Poland under Communism*, 31–2.

72 'Police Alerted following Poznań Revolt, 23 October 1956 [Electronic record]. HU OSA 300-1-2-76039; Records of Radio Free Europe/Radio Liberty Research Institute: General Records: Information Items; Open Society Archives at Central European University, Budapest, http://hdl. handle.net/10891/osa:bbefcc2d-b099-41b1-933d-6afabf4d3a03 accessed 19 August 2013; 'Police Alerted for Whole Week in Gyor and Csepel during Poznań Uprising', 23 July 1956 [Electronic record]. HU OSA 300-1-2-73352; Records of Radio Free Europe/Radio Liberty Research Institute: General Records: Information Items; Open Society Archives at Central European University, Budapest, http://hdl.handle.net/10891/osa:68a68d1e-6bdb-4999-a680-f084dabfd766 accessed 19 August 2013.

73 'Resolution Adopted by the Central Committee of the Hungarian Workers' Party', 30 June 1956, in Zinner, ed. *National Communism and Popular Revolt*, 328–31; 'Hungarian Workers Warned of Increased Unrest', *The Times*, 2 July 1956, 8.

10. THE PETŐFI CIRCLE

1 Taubman, *Khrushchev*, 290; 5; Applebaum, *Iron Curtain*, 483; Sergei Khrushchev, ed., *Memoirs of Nikita Khrushchev: Volume 3, Statesman [1953–*

1964] (Providence: Brown University, 2007), 648; 'Report from Anastas Mikoyan on the Situation in the Hungarian Workers' Party, July 14, 1956' in Csaba Békés et al., *The 1956 Hungarian Revolution: A History in Documents* (Budapest: Central European University Press, 2002), 143–7.

2 Matyas Rákosi, Letter to the Central Committee, Szabad Nép, 19 July 1956, reprinted in Melvin J. Lasky, ed., *The Hungarian Revolution: The Story of the October Uprising as Recorded in Documents, Dispatches, Eye-Witness Accounts, and World-wide Reactions* (London: Martin Secker & Warburg Ltd, 1957), 33.

3 Applebaum, *Iron Curtain*, 483; Matthews, *Tinderbox*, 162; NH 10110/69, Letter from Sir Leslie Fry, 10 September 1956, 1, FO 371/122375.

4 Simon Bourgin, 'An American Writes from Budapest', 5 July 1956, in Lasky, *The Hungarian Revolution*, 32; Khrushchev, ed., *Memoirs of Nikita Khrushchev*, 648.

5 Matthews, *Explosion*, 103; Cartledge, *Will to Survive*, 440.

6 NH 10110/35, Letter, C. L. S. Cope re: review of Hungarian periodicals, 1, in FO 371/122373; Kovrig, *Communism in Hungary*, 292.

7 Tibor Tardos, 'Alone in Budapest', *Nok Lapja*, no. 23, 7 June 1956, in NH 10110/35, Review of Hungarian Periodicals, 28 June 1956, 33; Cartledge, *Will to Survive*, 426–9.

8 László Sárkány, 'The Communist Factory Leader', *Partelet*, no. 5, May 1956, in NH 10110/35, Review of Hungarian Periodicals, 28 June 1956, 24.

9 William E. Griffith, 'The Petofi Circle: Forum for Ferment in the Hungarian Thaw', *Hungarian Quarterly*, 25 January 1962, 22.

10 Applebaum, *Iron Curtain*, 478.

11 Tamás Aczél, 'Large Village N.', *Beke es Szabadsag*, no. 19, 9 May 1956, 10–11, in NH 10110/35, Review of Hungarian Periodicals, 28 June 1956, 18–22.

12 András B. Hegedűs, 'The Petőfi Circle: The Forum for Reform in 1956', *Journal of Communist Studies and Transition Politics*, 13: 2 (1997), 110–17, 131–2 (note 11); Griffith, 'The Petofi Circle', 15–16; Cartledge, *Will to Survive*, 438–40; Applebaum, *Iron Curtain*, 476–9; Charles Gati, *Failed Illusions: Moscow, Washington, Budapest, and the 1956 Hungarian Revolt* (Stanford: Stanford University Press, 2006), 10–11, 131; Aczél and Méray, *Revolt of the Mind*, 399.

13 János M. Rainer, *Imre Nagy: A Biography* (London: I. B. Tauris, 2009), 91–3; Hegedűs, 'The Petőfi Circle', 116–17, 122.

14 Hegedűs, 'The Petőfi Circle', 110–17, 131–2 note 11; Griffith, 'The Petofi Circle', 15–16; Cartledge, *Will to Survive*, 438–40; Applebaum, *Iron Curtain*, 476–9; Gati, *Failed Illusions*, 10–11, 131; 'Hungary' (11 October 1956), p. 7, in C. D. Jackson Papers, 1931–1967, Box 54, 'Free Europe Committee, 1956 (4), Eisenhower Library.

15 Hegedűs, 'The Petőfi Circle', 112, 118–19; Griffith, 'The Petofi Circle',

17–19; Matthews, *Tinderbox*, 147; Applebaum, *Iron Curtain*, 482.

16 Griffith, 'The Petofi Circle', 19–20; Bourgin, 'An American Writes from Budapest' and Leslie Bain, 'Rajk's Widow', *The Reporter* (New York), 4 October 1956 in Lasky, *The Hungarian Revolution*, 29–30; Victor Sebestyen, *Twelve Days: Revolution 1956* (London: Phoenix, 2007), 86–7; Applebaum, *Iron Curtain*, 482–3; Matthews, *Explosion*, 104–5; Matthews, *Tinderbox*, 148; NH 10110/37 – C. L. S. Cope's summary of a meeting in the Officers' Club in Budapest, 27 June 1956, esp. p. 2, in FO 371/122374.

17 Matthews, *Explosion*, 105; Griffith, 'The Petofi Circle', 20–1.

18 Bourgin, 'An American Writes from Budapest', 30; Matthews, *Tinderbox*, 149–50, 159; Griffith, 'The Petofi Circle', 23–4; Aczél and Méray, *Revolt of the Mind*, 402.

19 Matthews, *Tinderbox*, 153; http://ndbooks.com/author/tibor-dery.

20 Griffith, 'The Petofi Circle', 23–4; Gati, *Failed Illusions*, 131; Matthews, *Tinderbox*, 153–7; Hegedüs, 'The Petőfi Circle', 123; Aczél and Méray, *Revolt of the Mind*, 404.

21 István Eörsi, 'The Petőfi-circle', in Alexander van der Haven et al., eds, *Intellectuele kringen in de twintigste eeuw* (Bureau Studium Generale, 1995), 116–17 available at http://www.rev.hu/rev/images/content/kiadvanyok/petofikor/petofikor_eorsi.pdf.

22 Matthews, *Tinderbox*, 157–8, 160–1; Griffith, 'The Petofi Circle', 26–7; James Mark, 'Society, Resistance and Revolution: The Budapest Middle Class and the Hungarian Communist State 1948–56', *English Historical Review*, vol. CXX, no. 488 (September 2005), 978.

23 Matthews, *Tinderbox*, 159–60.

24 Griffith, 'The Petofi Circle', 27; Gati, *Failed Illusions*, 132; Aczél and Méray, *Revolt of the Mind*, 411; Matthews, *Tinderbox*, 161; John MacCormac, 'Hungary's Youth Reported in Revolt Against Stalinism', *NYT*, 2 July 1956, 1.

25 Bourgin, 'An American Writes from Budapest', 32.

26 Griffith, 'The Petofi Circle', 27–8; Hegedüs, 'The Petofi Circle', 123–4; Matthews, *Tinderbox*, 161; 'Resolution Adopted by the Central Committee of the Hungarian Workers' Party, June 30, 1956' in Zinner, ed. *National Communism and Popular Revolt*, 328–31.

27 'Resolution Adopted by the Central Committee of the Hungarian Workers' Party, June 30, 1956', 328–31.

28 Gati, *Failed Illusions*, 136–7; Hegedüs, 'The Petofi Circle', 124; Matthews, *Tinderbox*, 162; Rainer, *Imre Nagy*, 94–5; George Mikes, 'The Fall of Mr. Rakosi in Hungary', *The Listener*, vol. LVI, no. 1,426, 26 July 1956, 112; Aczél and Méray, *Revolt of the Mind*, 419.

29 Paul Lendvai, *One Day That Shook the Communist World: The 1956 Hungarian Uprising and its Legacy* (Princeton University Press, 2008), 42.

30 Johanna Granville, *The First Domino: International Decision Making During the Hungarian Crisis of 1956* (Texas A&M University Press, 2004), 34; 'Rakosi Gives Up Top Hungary Post, Admitting Errors', *NYT*, 19 July 1956, 10.

31 Rainer, *Imre Nagy*, 96.

32 Aczél and Méray, *Revolt of the Mind*, 425–7; 'Report from Ambassador Yurii Andropov on Deteriorating Conditions in Hungary', 29 August 1956, in Békés, *The 1956 Hungarian Revolution*, 161.

33 Aczél and Méray, *Revolt of the Mind*, 423–4; Paul Jónás, 'Economic Aspects', in Béla K. Király and Paul Jónás, eds, *The Hungarian Revolution of 1956 in Retrospect* (East European Quarterly, Boulder, Distributed by Columbia University Press, 1978), 34.

34 Aczél and Méray, *Revolt of the Mind*, 425–7; 'Report from Ambassador Yurii Andropov on Deteriorating Conditions in Hungary', 29 August 1956, 161.

35 Támas Aczél, 'Intellectual Aspects', in Király and Jónás, *The Hungarian Revolution of 1956 in Retrospect*, 31–2.

36 Zinner, *Revolution in Hungary*, 225; Griffith, 'The Petofi Circle', 30.

37 'Nepszava – Petofi Circle and Intellectuals', 5 September 1956 [Electronic Resource]. HU OSA 300-8-3-3026; Records of Radio Free Europe/ Radio Liberty Research Institute: Publications Department: Background Reports; Open Society Archives at Central European University, Budapest. http://hdl.handle.net/10891/osa:915f89fa-0831-4e66-a407-ebd9f07ee84b.

38 'Report from Ambassador Yurii Andropov on Deteriorating Conditions in Hungary', 29 August 1956, 159–61; John MacCormac, 'Hungary Slows Collective Pace', *NYT*, 12 August 1956, 7.

39 'Hungarians Protest Cuts', *NYT*, 13 July 1956 and 'AVH Intervenes to Suppress Strike', 31 July 1956 [Electronic Resource]. HU OSA 300-1-2-73569; Records of Radio Free Europe/Radio Liberty Research Institute: General Records: Information Items; Open Society Archives at Central European University, Budapest. http://hdl.handle.net/10891/osa:0256a620-4f19-4892-aee8-8e20a69a09f9; Gati, *Failed Illusions*, 134.

40 'Strikes in Csepel', 16 October 1956 [Electronic Resource]. HU OSA 300-1-2-75858; Records of Radio Free Europe/Radio Liberty Research Institute: General Records: Information Items; Open Society Archives at Central European University, Budapest. http://hdl.handle.net/10891/osa:95d7aeeb-d233-4de6-8515-760ed4b811e5; Cartledge, *Will to Survive*, 442.

41 Kovrig, *Communism in Hungary*, 295.

11. ANGRY YOUNG MEN

1 Rick Coleman, *Blue Monday: Fats Domino and the Lost Dawn of Rock 'n' Roll* (New York: DaCapo Press, 2007), 127–8; Brian Ward, *Just My Soul Responding: Rhythm and Blues, Black Consciousness, and Race Relations*

(Berkeley: University of California Press, 1998), 52; '2,500 Youths Riot at Dance on Coast', *NYT*, 9 July 1956, 13; Larry Eaglemann, 'Ain't That a Shame: Thirty Years Ago, America Experienced its First Rock 'n' Roll Riot', *Los Angeles Times*, 6 July 1986 at http://articles.latimes.com/1986-07-06/magazine/tm-23375_1_rock-n-roll.

2 Glenn C. Altschuler, *All Shook Up: How Rock 'n' Roll Changed America* (Oxford: Oxford University Press, 2003), 4; 'Gas Ends Rock 'n' Roll Riot', *NYT*, 4 November 1956, 20; 'Jersey City Orders Rock 'n' Roll Ban', *NYT*, 10 July 1956, 26; 'Music: Yeh-Heh-Heh-Hes, Baby', *Time*, 18 June 1956; 'Music: Rock 'n' Roll', *Time*, 23 July 1956.

3 For Johnnie Ray see extracts from the Brisbane *Courier-Mail* at http://www.chapelhill.homeip.net/FamilyHistory/Other/QueenslandHistory/RocknRollinBrisbaneTown.htm. See also Keith Moore, 'Bodgies, widgies and moral panic in Australia 1955–1959', 4–5, available at http://eprints.qut.edu.au/633/1/moore_keith.pdf; 'Rioters Rock 'n' Roll in Oslo', *NYT*, 24 September 1956, 3; Thomas P. Ronan, 'British Rattled by Rock 'n' Roll', *NYT*, 12 September 1956, 40; 'Great Britain: The Teds', *Time*, 24 September 1956.

4 'Rock-and-Roll Brawls Laid to Film in Britain', *NYT*, 11 September 1956, 40; Ronan, 'British Rattled by Rock 'n' Roll', 40; 'Great Britain: The Teds'; 'Rioters Rock 'n' Roll in Oslo', 3; 'This Is the Scene that "Sends" Them', *Daily Express*, 5 September 1956, 3; 'Rock 'n' Roll Gang Move In', *Daily Mirror*, 11 September 1956, 3; 'Bottles Hurled at "Rock" Riot Police', *Daily Express*, 12 September 1956, 1; 'This Crazy Summer's Weirdest Craze', *Daily Express*, 12 September 1956, 5.

5 'Rock Around the Clock: List of Situations Banned', in HO 300/5/ENT170/5/15.

6 Altschuler, *All Shook Up*, 31, 33, 132; 'Bill Haley Biography', Rock & Roll Hall of Fame, at http://www.rockhall.com/inductees/bill-haley/bio/; Ronan, 'British Rattled', 40.

7 Altschuler, *All Shook Up*, 31, 33, 132.

8 Sir Harold Barnwell to Town Clerks, 30 November 1956; Sir Austin Strutt to Sir Harold Barnwell, 10 December 1956; summary of the meeting with the CEA, 30 November 1956 and R. H. Dewes to Sir Austin Strutt, 18 January 1957 in HO 300/5/ENT170/5/15, National Archives, Kew; Sandbrook, *Never Had It So Good*, 432–3.

9 Ward, *Just My Soul Responding*, 19–55; Altschuler, *All Shook Up*, 3–34, 131–2. Brian Ward, 'Civil Rights and Rock and Roll: Revisiting the Nat King Cole Attack of 1956', *OAH Magazine of History*, April 2010, 22; Trent Hill, 'The Enemy Within: Censorship in Rock Music in the 1950s' in Anthony DeCurtis, ed., *Present Tense: Rock & Roll and Culture* (Durham, NC: Duke University Press, 1992), 46, 62.

10 'Music: Rock 'n' Roll', *Time*, 23 July 1956; Pat Long, *The History of the*

NME: High Times and Low Lives at the World's Most Famous Music Magazine (London: Portico, 2012), 20–1.

11 'Music: Yeh-Heh-Heh-Hes, Baby', *Time*, 18 June 1956.

12 Sandbrook, *Never Had It So Good*, 433.

13 Altschuler, *All Shook Up*, 6.

14 Long, *History of the NME*, 21.

15 'Rock-and-Roll Called Communicable Disease', *NYT*, 28 March 1956, 33; 'Music: Rock 'n' Roll'.

16 Hill, 'The Enemy Within', 52–3; 'Music: Yeh-Heh-Heh-Hes, Baby'; Altschuler, *All Shook Up*, 67–98.

17 Sandbrook, *Never Had It So Good*, 433.

18 Hill, 'The Enemy Within', 54.

19 Altschuler, *All Shook Up*, 24–30; Ian Penman, 'Shapeshifter', *London Review of Books*, 25 September 2014, 16; Peter Guralnick, *Last Train to Memphis: The Rise of Elvis Presley* (London: Little, Brown, 1994), 58, 63–4.

20 Hill, 'The Enemy Within', 55; 'The Rage of the Year', *Daily Mirror*, 28 December 1956, 7.

21 Guralnick, *Last Train to Memphis*, 259.

22 Ibid., 165–9, 241; Chafe, *The Unfinished Journey*, 112.

23 Guralnick, *Last Train to Memphis*, 263; Altschuler, *All Shook Up*, 87, 89.

24 Guralnick, *Last Train to Memphis*, 337–8; Altschuler, *All Shook Up*, 57–62.

25 'Rock and Roll is Banned in Santa Cruz, California', at http://www.history.com/this-day-in-history/rock-and-roll-is-banned-in-santa-cruz-california.

26 Altschuler, *All Shook Up*, 37–9, 47–9; Ward, 'Civil Rights and Rock and Roll', 22; Ward, *Just My Soul Responding*, 103–4; Michael T. Bertrand, *Race, Rock, and Elvis* (Urbana: University of Illinois Press, 2005), 158–88; 'Segregationist Wants Ban on "Rock and Roll"', *NYT*, 30 March 1956, 27.

27 Ward, 'Civil Rights and Rock and Roll', 21–4; Ward, *Just My Soul Responding*, 104–5.

28 Altschuler, *All Shook Up*, 40; Sandbrook, *Never Had It So Good*, 433.

29 Barry Keith Grant, '1956: Movies and the Crack of Doom' in Murray Pomerance, ed., *American Cinema of the 1950s: Themes and Variations* (Rutgers University Press, 2005), 171–4.

30 Applebaum, *Iron Curtain*, 159–60, 441–2; Marshall Winslow Stearns, *The Story of Jazz* (Oxford: Oxford University Press, 1956), 288; Christoph Neidhart, *Russia's Carnival: The Smells, Sights, and Sounds of Transition* (Lanham, MD: Rowman & Littlefield, 2003), 83–4; Gertrud Pickhan and Rüdiger Ritter, eds, *Jazz Behind the Iron Curtain* (Peter Lang, 2011); S. Frederick Starr, *Red and Hot: The Fate of Jazz in the Soviet Union* (New York: Proscenium Publishers, 1994).

31 Karl Brown, 'Stalinization and its Discontents: Subcultures and Opposition in Hungary, 1948–1956', esp. 157–8, available at http://www.fulbright.hu/book1/karlbrown.pdf, and Brown, 'Dance Hall Days: Jazz and Hooligan-

ism in Communist Hungary, 1948–1956' in Pickhan and Ritter, eds, *Jazz Behind the Iron Curtain*, 267–94. See also Frank Gibney, *The Frozen Revolution: Poland: A Study in Communist Decay* (New York: Farrar, Straus and Cudahy, 1959), 29.

32 Adam Ważyk, 'A Poem For Adults', in Edmund Stillman, ed., *Bitter Harvest: The Intellectual Revolt behind the Iron Curtain* (London: Thames and Hudson, 1960), 133, 134.

33 'Translator's Note' in Adam Ważyk, 'A Critique of the Poem for Adults', *The New Reasoner*, Summer 1957, 51; Zinner, *National Communism and Popular Revolt*, 40, 48.

34 'Behind the Brick Wall' by Tibor Déry, *The New Reasoner*, Summer 1957, 39–50.

35 Ann Charters, ed., *The Portable Beat Reader* (New York: Penguin, 1992), 60–1.

36 Allen Ginsberg, 'Howl', in Charters, *The Portable Beat Reader*, 62, 68; Eric Mottram, 'San Francisco: Arts in The City that Defies Fate' in Carter, *Cracking the Ike Age*, 143.

37 See 'Allen Ginsberg' and 'Howl' at Poetry Foundation, available at http://www.poetryfoundation.org/; Heidi Benson, 'Howl', *San Francisco Chronicle*, 4 October 2005 available at http://www.sfgate.com/entertainment/article/HOWL-When-Allen-Ginsberg-hurled-his-shattering-2604715.php; Richard Eberhart, 'West Coast Rhythms', *NYT*, 2 September 1956, 18; Simon Hall, *Rethinking the American Anti-War Movement* (New York: Routledge, 2012), 28–34; Gerd-Rainer Horn, *The Spirit of '68: Rebellion in Western Europe and North America, 1956–1976* (Oxford: Oxford University Press, 2007), 16, 18.

38 Sandbrook, *Never Had It So Good*, 177–8; Colin Wilson, *The Angry Years: The Rise and Fall of the Angry Young Men* (London: Robson Books, 2007), 31–6.

39 Sandbrook, *Never Had It So Good*, 179–80, 362–3; Wilson, *The Angry Years*, 36–7; Dan Rebellato, 'Look Back at Empire: British Theatre and Imperial Decline' in Stuart Ward, ed., *British Culture and the End of Empire* (Manchester: Manchester University Press, 2001), 74; http://thelondonmagazine.org/about/. See also Robert Hewison, *In Anger: Culture in the First Cold War* (London: Weidenfeld and Nicolson, 1981), 130, 136–41.

40 Hewison, *In Anger*, 133, 143, 174–5.

12. A COUP DE MAIN

1 W. Scott Lucas, *Divided We Stand: Britain, the US and the Suez Crisis* (London: Hodder & Stoughton, 1991), 135–6; David A. Nichols, *Eisenhower 1956* (New York: Simon & Schuster, 2011), 124, 126; Keith Kyle, *Suez: Britain's End of Empire in the Middle East* (London: I. B. Tauris, 2011), 129; 'Memorandum of meeting between Secretary of State Dulles and Ambassador Hussein', 19 July 1956, in Scott Lucas, ed., *Britain and*

Suez: The Lion's Last Roar (Manchester: Manchester University Press, 1996), 43–4; Dana Adams Schmidt, 'U.S. Annuls Offer of Fund to Egypt to Build High Dam', *NYT*, 20 July 1956, 1–3; Kennett Love, 'Britain Cancels Aswan Dam Offer in Line with U.S.', *NYT*, 21 July 1956, 1–3; 'World Bank Not to Finance Dam', *Manchester Guardian*, 24 July 1956, 7.

2 Brendon, *Decline and Fall*, 489; Kyle, *Suez*, 82–3;

3 U.S.-British Step a Shock to Cairo', *NYT*, 21 July 1956, 3; Sam Pope Brewer, 'Blow to Nasser Prestige', *NYT*, 21 July 1956, 3.

4 Kyle, *Suez*, 130–1; Lucas, *Divided We Stand*, 137; Nichols, *Eisenhower 1956*, 127; Brendon, *Decline and Fall*, 490; 'Text of Nile Dam Statement', *NYT*, 20 July 1956, 3.

5 Osgood Caruthers, 'Nasser Says U.S. Lied in Explaining Bar to Aswan Aid', *NYT*, 25 July 1956, 1, 2; 'President Nasser's Defiant Reply', *Manchester Guardian*, 25 July 1956, 7.

6 Brendon, *Decline and Fall*, 482–87.

7 Nichols, *Eisenhower 1956*, 152; Kyle, *Suez*, 12–14.

8 Brendon, *Decline and Fall*, 484–86.

9 Sandbrook, *Never Had It So Good*, 4.

10 Thorpe, *Eden*, 473; Kyle, *Suez*, 127; Brendon, *Decline and Fall*, 490.

11 Osgood Caruthers, 'British Quietly Give Suez Base to Egypt After 74-Year Stay', *NYT*, 14 June 1956, 1, 8.

12 Osgood Caruthers, 'Egyptians Laud Nasser over Suez', *NYT*, 19 June 1956, 4.

13 Kyle, *Suez*, 48; Lindsay Frederick Braun, 'Suez Reconsidered: Anthony Eden's Orientalism and the Suez Crisis', *The Historian*, vol. 65, no. 3 (March 2003), 547.

14 Memorandum of Discussion at the 147th Meeting of the National Security Council, Monday, June 1, 1953, in *Foreign Relations of the United States, 1952–1954*, Volume IX, Part 1, the Near and Middle East (in two parts), document 137; Brendon, *Decline and Fall*, 486–7; Kyle, *Suez*, 48–54; Lucas, *Britain and Suez*, 9; Lucas, *Divided We Stand*, 25–6.

15 'Text of Secretary Dulles' Report on Near East Trip', *NYT*, 2 June 1953, 4; 'Dulles Says U.S. Aim is to Gain Friends', *NYT*, 2 June 1953, 1.

16 'The Suez Base Agreement', 19 October 1954, in Anthony Gorst and Lewis Johnman, *The Suez Crisis* (London: Routledge, 1997), 32–3.

17 Sandbrook, *Never Had It So Good*, 4.

18 Tony Shaw, *Eden, Suez and the Mass Media: Propaganda and Persuasion During the Suez Crisis* (London: I. B. Tauris, 1996), 6–8; Brendon, *Decline and Fall*, 488–90.

19 Eden to Eisenhower, 5 March 1956, in Gorst and Johnman, *The Suez Crisis*, 44.

20 'Cabinet Discussion on Middle East Policy, 21 March 1956', in Gorst and Johnman, *The Suez Crisis*, 46–7.

21 Sandbrook, *Never Had It So Good*, 6–8.

22 'Nutting's Conversation with Eden on the Removal of Nasser', March 1956, in Gorst and Johnman, *The Suez Crisis*, 46; 'Phone call from Prime Minister Eden to Minister of State Nutting', 12 March 1956, in Lucas, *Britain and Suez*, 27; Sandbrook, *Never Had It So Good*, 9.

23 Brendon, *Decline and Fall*, 490.

24 D. R. Thorpe, 'Obituary: Sir Anthony Nutting, Bt.', *The Independent*, 3 March 1999, available at http://www.independent.co.uk/arts-entertain-ment/obituary-sir-anthony-nutting-bt-1077988.html; 'Nutting's View of Eden, 1967' in Gorst and Johnman, *The Suez Crisis*, 45; Thorpe, *Eden*, 384–7; Sandbrook, *Never Had It So Good*, 8.

25 Mohamed H. Heikal, *Cutting The Lion's Tail: Suez Through Egyptian Eyes* (London: André Deutsch, 1986), 126.

26 FO 371/119080/JE14211/108; 'Speech by President Nasser', in Lucas, *Britain and Suez*, 46; 'Egypt: Nasser's Revenge', *Time*, 6 August 1956; Lucas, *Divided We Stand*, 139.

27 'Egypt Nationalises Suez Canal Company; Will Use Revenues to Build Aswan Dam', *NYT*, 27 July 1956, 1, 2.

28 Lucas, *Britain and Suez*, 46; Lucas, *Divided We Stand*, 139; Heikal, *Cutting the Lion's Tail*, 127.

29 Laura M. James, *Nasser at War: Arab Images of the Enemy* (Basingstoke: Palgrave Macmillan, 2006), 26; Lucas, *Divided We Stand*, 139; Joel Gordon, *Nasser: Hero of the Arab Nation* (Oxford: Oneworld Publications, 2009), 45–6.

30 FO 371/119079/JE14211/37; FO 371/119079/JE14211/42.

31 FO 371/119079/JE14211/38; FO 371/119079/JE14211/39; FO 371/119080/JE14211/74; 'Egypt: Nasser's Revenge', *Time*, 6 August 1956.

32 FO 371/119078/JE14211/34; James Jankowski, *Nasser's Egypt, Arab Nationalism, and the United Arab Republic* (London: Lynn Rienner Publishers, 2002), 83.

33 FO 371/119079/JE14211/53; FO 371/119083/JE14211/495.

34 FO 371/119078/JE14211/30; Jankowski, *Nasser's Egypt*, 83–4; FO 371/119078/JE14211/31; FO 371/119800/JE14211/107; FO 371/119800/JE14211/70; FO 371/119800/JE14211/101.

35 FO 371/119116/JE14211/1077; FO 371/119095/JE14211/498.

36 FO 371/119079/JE14211/56; FO 371/119078/JE14211/30; Jankowski, *Nasser's Egypt*, 83; 'General Strike in Arab World', *Times of India*, 17 August 1956, 1.

37 FO 371/119800/JE14211/94.

38 FO 371/119079/JE14211/1081.

39 FO 371/119079/JE14211/57; Khrushchev, *Statesman*, 812–13; Kyle, *Suez*, 572.

40 Kyle, *Suez*, 137.

41 'French Press View', *Jerusalem Post*, 29 July 1956, 3.

42 Thorpe, *Eden*, 475–7, 479–80; Kyle, *Suez*, 135–7; Lucas, *Divided We Stand*, 142–3.

43 FO 371/119078/JE14211/1.

44 ' The Suez Canal Convention of April 1888' in Gorst and Johnman, *The Suez Crisis*, 3.

45 Cabinet Minutes, 27 July 1956, 11:10 a.m., 2–4, in CAB 134/4107.

46 Thorpe, *Eden*, 481–2; Kyle, *Suez*, 139, 164.

47 FO 371/119079/JE14211/63.

48 Evans, *Algeria*, 159–61, 183; Horne, *Savage War*, 85, 129, 162; Lucas, *Britain and Suez*, 50.

49 Catterall, ed., *The Macmillan Diaries*, 580.

50 Lucas, *Britain and Suez*, 50.

51 'Memorandum of Conference with the President, July 31, 1956, 9:45 AM', in *The Diaries of Dwight David Eisenhower, 1953–1961* (Frederick, MD: University Publications of America, 1986), Box 16, 'Diary Staff Memos, July 1956', Reel 9, RSC.

52 Lucas, *Divided We Stand*, 145–6; David Reynolds, 'Eden the Diplomatist, 1931–56: Suezide of a Statesman?', *History*, vol. 74, issue 240 (1989), 79–80.

53 'Memorandum of Conference with the President, July 31, 1956, 9:45 AM'; Stephen Kinzer, *The Brothers: John Foster Dulles, Allen Dulles, and Their Secret World War* (New York: Henry Holt, 2013), 124–5, 202–3, 234–5.

54 Eisenhower to Eden, 1 August 1956, FO 371/119083/JE14211/196.

55 Eden to Eisenhower, 5 August 1956, FO 371/119083/JE14211/196.

13. THE WOMEN'S MARCH

1 'Strijdom . . . you have struck a rock', Federation of South African Women, 1954–1963, AD1137, Cb2.3.4, pp. 6, 8, available at http://www.histori-calpapers.wits.ac.za/?inventory_enhanced/U/Collections&c=144635/R/AD1137-Cb2-3-4; Helen Joseph, *Side By Side: The Autobiography of Helen Joseph* (New York: William Morrow and Company, Inc., 1986), 1; 'The Presidency, Republic of South Africa: The Union Buildings' at http://www.thepresidency.gov.za/pebble.asp?relid=187; Frances Baard and Barbie Schreiner, *My Spirit Is Not Banned* (Harare: Zimbabwe Publishing House, 1986), 59.

2 http://www.sahistory.org.za/people/phyllis-altman; Phyllis Altman, 'Daughters of 1919', *Fighting Talk*, vol. 12, no. 9 (September 1956), 7.

3 Joseph, *Side by Side*, 1–2; Cherryl Walker, *Women and Resistance in South Africa* (London: Onyx Press, 1982), 195; Les Switzer, 'South Africa's Alternative Press in Perspective' in Switzer, ed., *South Africa's Alternative Press: Voices of Protest and Resistance, 1880s–1960s* (Cambridge: Cambridge University Press, 1997), 44.

4 Altman, 'Daughters of 1919', 7; Joseph, *Side by Side*, 2; Pamela E. Brooks, *Boycotts, Buses, and Passes: Black Women's Resistance in the US South and South Africa* (Amherst: University of Massachusetts Press, 2008), 204; http://overcomingapartheid.msu.edu/multimedia.php?id=65-259-C.

5 Baard, *My Spirit Is Not Banned*, 59-60.

6 'Strijdom . . . You have struck a rock', p. 8; Baard, *My Spirit Is Not Banned*, 60; Joseph, *Side by Side*, 2.

7 Altman, 'Daughters of 1919', 7; 'Baard, *My Spirit Is Not Banned*, 60; Joseph, *Side by Side*, 2. For an overview of Ngoyi's activist career see Barbara Caine, 'The Trials and Tribulations of a Black Woman Leader: Lilian Ngoyi and the South African Liberation Struggle' in Francisca de Haan et al., eds, *Women's Activism: Global Perspectives from the 1890s to the Present* (London: Routledge, 2013), 90–105. See also 'History of Lilian Masediba Ngoyi' at http://www.ru.ac.za/lilianngoyi/lilianngoyihall/history/ and Nicholas Grant, 'Lilian Masedba Ngoyi' at http://nicholasgrant.co.uk/wordpress/?p=43.

8 Altman, 'Daughters of 1919', 7.

9 Baard, *My Spirit Is Not Banned*, 60; Brooks, *Boycotts, Buses, and Passes*, 227.

10 Joseph, *Side by Side*, 2.

11 Brooks, *Boycotts, Buses, and Passes*, 227, 226.

12 Nancy J. Clark and William H. Worger, *South Africa: The Rise and Fall of Apartheid* (Harlow: Pearson Education, 2011), 3.

13 Saul Dubow, *Apartheid, 1948–1994* (Oxford: Oxford University Press, 2014), 1, 30.

14 Clark and Worger, *South Africa*, 3–4, 13, 49–57.

15 Seth Steinberg, ed., *The Statesman's Year Book: Statistical and Historical Annual of the States of the World for the Year 1956* (London: Macmillan & Co, Ltd, 1956), 252.

16 Clark and Worger, *South Africa*, 49–50; Dubow, *Apartheid*, 12, 37; 'Women in Chains', published jointly by FEDSAW and the ANC Women's League, 1956, Federation of South African Women, 1954–1963, AD1137, Cb1.8.1 available at http://www.historicalpapers.wits.ac.za/?inventory_enhanced/U/Collections&c=144625/R/AD1137-Cb1-8-1.

17 Desmond Tutu, *No Future Without Forgiveness: A Personal Overview of South Africa's Truth and Reconciliation Commission* (New Yor: Doubleday, 1999), 15–16.

18 Clark and Worger, *South Africa*, 50–1.

19 Ruth First, 'The New Slavery', *Fighting Talk*, vol. 12, no. 10 (October 1956), 3, 4; Walter Sisulu, 'The Extension of the Pass Laws', *Liberation* (Johannesburg), 1 March 1956, 12.

20 Dubow, *Apartheid*, 38, 39–41, 42–4; Clark and Worger, *South Africa*, 57–60; George M. Fredrickson, *Black Liberation: A Comparative History of Black Ideologies in the United States and South Africa* (Oxford: Oxford University Press, 1995), 241–52; James H. Meriwether, *Proudly We Can Be Africans: Black Americans and Africa, 1935–1961* (Chapel Hill: University of North Carolina Press, 2002), 111–23 and Nicholas Grant, 'Crossing the Black Atlantic: The Global Anti-Apartheid Movement and the Racial Poli-

tics of the Cold War', *Radical History Review* (Spring, 2014).

21 Dubow, *Apartheid*, 69; Clark and Worger, *South Africa*, 60–1; 'Freedom Charter', available at http://www.anc.org.za/show.php?id=72; Thomas Karis and Gwendolen M. Carter, eds, *From Protest to Challenge: A Documentary History of African Politics in South Africa, 1882–1964, Volume 3, Challenge and Violence, 1953–1964* (Stanford: Hoover Institution Press, 1977), 58–64.

22 Dubow, *Apartheid*, 45, 54, 58–9; Clark and Worger, *South Africa*, 60.

23 'Women in Chains', p. 2.

24 Walker, *Women and Resistance in South Africa*, 185, 190; 'Women in Chains', 6–9; Tom Lodge, *Black Politics in South Africa Since 1945* (London: Longman, 1983), 144. See also Helen Joseph, 'Women Against Passes', *Fighting Talk*, vol. 12, no. 1 (January 1956), 3–4.

25 Lodge, *Black Politics in South Africa Since 1945*, 144.

26 'Women in Chains', 7, 11; Walker, *Women and Resistance in South Africa*, 153–9; Lodge, *Black Politics in South Africa Since 1945*, 142; Brooks, *Boycotts, Buses, and Passes*, 209–14.

27 Walker, *Women and Resistance in South Africa*, 190–1.

28 Joseph, 'Women Against Passes', 4.

29 Helen Joseph, 'Angry Women', *Fighting Talk*, vol. 12, no. 4 (April 1956), 5–6; Walker, *Women and Resistance in South Africa*, 190–1.

30 Walker, *Women and Resistance in South Africa*, 191; 'Strijdom . . . You have struck a rock', 2.

31 'Strijdom . . . You have struck a rock', 4; Walker, *Women and Resistance in South Africa*, 192–3; Brooks, *Boycotts, Buses, and Passes*, 223.

32 Walker, *Women and Resistance in South Africa*, 193–4; Nomboniso Gasa, 'Feminisms, motherisms, patriarchies and women's voices in the 1950s' in Gasa, ed., *Women in South Africa* (Cape Town: HSRC Press, 2007), 220–1.

33 Sisulu, 'The Extension of the Pass Laws', 14.

34 Brooks, *Boycotts, Buses, and Passes*, 7; Jacqueline Castledine, '"In a Solid Bond of Unity": Anticolonial Feminism in the Cold War Era', *Journal of Women's History*, vol. 20, no. 4 (Winter 2008), esp. 61–5; Shireen Hassim, *Women's Organizations and Democracy in South Africa: Contesting Authority* (Madison: University of Wisconsin Press, 2006), 27–8; M. Bahati Kuumba, '"You've Struck a Rock": Comparing Gender, Social Movements, and Transformation in the United States and South Africa', *Gender & Society*, vol. 16, no. 4 (August 2002), 504–23.

35 Dubow, *Apartheid, 1948–1994*, 55; Caine, 'The Trials and Tribulations of a Black Woman Leader', 95–6.

36 Strijdom . . . You have struck a rock', 1.

37 Walker, *Women and Resistance in South Africa*, 193.

14. MOB RULE

1 John Howard Griffin and Theodore Freedman, *What Happened in Mansfield: A report of the crisis situation in Mansfield, Texas, resulting from efforts to desegregate its school system* (New York: Anti-Defamation League of B'Nai B'rith – Field Reports on Desegregation in the South), 1, 3 in John H. Bracey and August Meier, eds, *Papers of the NAACP, Part 3, The Campaign for Educational Equality, Series D, Central Office Records, 1956–1965* (Bethesda, MD: University Publications of America, 1995), Reel 8 – General Office File – Desegregation, Schools, Texas, 1956–57, Woodruff Library; Robyn Duff Ladino, *Desegregating Texas Schools: Eisenhower, Shivers, and the Crisis at Mansfield High* (Austin: University of Texas Press, 1996), 94–5; Luther A. Huston, 'Texas Town Asks Integration Stay', *NYT*, 2 September 1956, 40.

2 Ladino, *Desegregating Texas Schools*, 71–6.

3 Griffin and Freedman, *What Happened in Mansfield*, 2–3.

4 Ladino, *Desegregating Texas Schools*, 79–80, 81–5, 87, 89, 93.

5 Ladino, *Desegregating Texas Schools*, 80–1.

6 Griffin and Freedman, *What Happened in Mansfield*, 3, 4; Ladino, *Desegregating Texas Schools*, 91–2.

7 Griffin and Freedman, *What Happened in Mansfield*, 5-6; Ladino, *Desegregating Texas Schools*, 96–7, 99–102.

8 U. Simpson Tate to Roy Wilkins, 31 August 1956, in *Papers of the NAACP, Part 3, Series D*, Reel 8 – General Office File – Desegregation, Schools, Texas, 1956–57; Griffin and Freedman, *What Happened in Mansfield*, 7.

9 Ladino, *Desegregating Texas Schools*, 102–3, 142; Luther A Huston, 'Justice Black Bars Delay in Integration for a Texas School', *New York Times*, 5 September 1956, 1.

10 Anna Holden et al., *A Tentative Description and Analysis of the School Desegregation Crisis in Clinton, Tennessee* (Published by the Anti-Defamation League of B'nai B'rith in co-operation with The Society for the Study of Social Problems, December 1, 1956), 1, 2, 3, 4, 12 in *Civil Rights During the Eisenhower Administration*, Reel 8, RSC; Clive Webb, *Rabble Rousers: The American Far Right in the Civil Rights Era* (Athens: University of Georgia Press, 2010), 41–2.

11 Holden, *A Tentative Description*, 3–4, 8–9; 'The Principal in the Middle', *Newsweek*, 17 September 1956, 72; Webb, *Rabble Rousers*, 43.

12 Bill Emerson, 'For Nation: Regarding John Kasper', 1, in Ralph McGill Papers, Box 59 (Series V), Folder 13 – Subject File, Kasper, John, MARBL.

13 Webb, *Rabble Rousers*, 49–54, 69–70; James Rorty, 'Hate-Monger with Literary Trimmings: From Avant-Garde Poetry to Rear-Guard Politics', *Commentary* 22 (December 1956), 533–42.

14 Holden, *A Tentative Description*, 4; George McMillan, 'The Ordeal of

Bobby Cain', *Collier's*, 23 November 1956, in Carson, *Reporting Civil Rights, Part One*, 335.

15 Holden, *A Tentative Description*, 4; 'The Principal in the Middle', *Newsweek*, 17 September 1956, 72; Webb, *Rabble Rousers*, 44.

16 Rorty, 'Hate-Monger with Literary Trimmings', 541.

17 Letter, D. J. Brittain, Sr, to President Eisenhower, 19 September 1956 in *Civil Rights During the Eisenhower Administration*, Reel 8.

18 Webb, *Rabble Rousers*, 55–6; Rorty, 'Hate-Monger with Literary Trimmings', 538; Holden, *A Tentative Description*, 2, 4, 8, 9.

19 Holden, *A Tentative Description*, 5, 18; Webb, *Rabble Rousers*, 44–5; Rorty, 'Hate-Monger with Literary Trimmings', 538.

20 Rorty, 'Hate-Monger with Literary Trimmings', 539; June N. Adamson, 'Few Black Voices Heard: The Black Community and the Desegregation Crisis in Clinton, Tennessee, 1956', *Tennessee Historical Quarterly*, vol. 53, no. 1 (1994), 40; McMillan, 'The Ordeal of Bobby Cain', 340; Holden, *A Tentative Description*, 5, 18–19.

21 Holden, *A Tentative Description*, 5; Webb, *Rabble Rousers*, 45; Adamson, 'Few Black Voices Heard', 34.

22 Holden, *A Tentative Description*, 6, 12, 13; Webb, *Rabble Rousers*, 45; Adamson, 'Few Black Voices Heard', 34; 'Wounded in Korea', *New York Times*, 2 September 1956, 41; 'The Nation: Back to School', *Time*, 10 September 1956.

23 John N. Popham, 'Volunteers Rout a Tennessee Mob in Clash in Bias', *NYT*, 2 September 1956, 1, 41; 'The Nation: Back to School'; Webb, *Rabble Rousers*, 45; Holden, *A Tentative Description*, 6.

24 John N. Popham, 'Tank-Led National Guard Quiets Town in Tennessee', *NYT*, 3 September 1956, 1, 8; 'The Nation: Back to School'.

25 Webb, *Rabble Rousers*, 43; 'Cannot Sit Back', *NYT*, 2 September 1956, 41.

26 Holden, *A Tentative Description*, 6; Popham, 'Tank-Led National Guard Quiets Town', 1; Webb, *Rabble Rousers*, 46.

27 Popham, 'Tank-Led National Guard Quiets Town', 1, 8; Adamson, 'Few Black Voices Heard', 38–9.

28 'The Nation: Back to School'; Webb, *Rabble Rousers*, 46; John N. Popham, 'Clinton Resumes Customary Role', *NYT*, 8 September 1956, 9.

29 Webb, *Rabble Rousers*, 47–8.

30 'The South: The True Face of Clinton', *Time*, 17 December 1956.

31 Webb, *Rabble Rousers*, 48.

32 Ibid., 49; McMillan, 'The Ordeal of Bobby Cain'.

33 Murray Kempton, 'If You Got the Guts . . .', in Carson, *Reporting Civil Rights, Part One*, 331–4; Catherine Fosl and Tracey E. K'Meyer, *Freedom on the Border: An Oral History of the Civil Rights Movement in Kentucky* (Louisville: University Press of Kentucky, 2009), 53, 65–6; Roscoe Griffin, 'A Tentative Description and Analysis of the School Desegregation Crisis

in Sturgis, Kentucky, August 31–Sept. 19, 1956' (New York: Anti-Defamation League of B'Nai B'rith – Field Reports on Desegregation in the South) and 'What Kind of a Mother . . . ?' in *Papers of the NAACP, Part 3, Series D*, reel 5 – General Office File – Desegregation, Schools, Kentucky, 1956–62; David L. Wolfford, 'Resistance on the Border: School Desegregation in Western Kentucky, 1954–1964', *Ohio Valley History* vol. 4, no. 2 (2004), 41–63.

34 'The President's News Conference of September 5, 1956', in *Public Papers of the Presidents of the United States, Dwight D. Eisenhower, 1956: Concerning the Public Messages, Speeches, and Statements of the President, January 1 to December 31, 1956* (Washington, DC: US Government Printing Office, 1958), 200; Norman Thomas to President Eisenhower, 6 September 1956, 1, in *Civil Rights During the Eisenhower Administration*, Reel 8; Adamson, 'Few Black Voices Heard', 36.

35 Nichols, *A Matter of Justice*, 98, 108; Pach & Richardson, *The Presidency of Dwight D. Eisenhower*, 143.

36 'April 25 1956 pre-press conference briefing', 3, in Ann Whitman File, Ann Whitman Diary, Box 8, April 56 Diary ACW (1); 'Telephone Calls, August 19', in Ann Whitman File, Ann Whitman Diary, Box 8, Aug. 56 Diary ACW (1), Eisenhower Library; Pach and Richardson, *The Presidency of Dwight D. Eisenhower*, 143.

37 Maxwell M. Rabb, 'Memorandum for the Attorney General, re: the President's Views on the proposed Civil Rights Program' (CP – 56–48), 1–2, Ann Whitman File, Cabinet Series, Box 6, 'Cabinet Meeting of March 9, 1956', Eisenhower Library; Nichols, *A Matter of Justice*, 107.

38 Pach and Richardson, *The Presidency of Dwight D. Eisenhower*, 144–5.

39 'The President's News Conference of September 5, 1956', 734–5, 741.

40 Ibid., 736.

41 Thurgood Marshall to President Eisenhower, 6 September 1956, in *Civil Rights During the Eisenhower Administration*, Reel 8.

42 Pach and Richardson, *The Presidency of Dwight D. Eisenhower*, 147–8, 150–5; John A. Kirk, *Redefining the Color Line: Black Activism in Little Rock, Arkansas, 1940–1970* (Gainesville: University Press of Florida, 2002).

43 Pach and Richardson, *The Presidency of Dwight D. Eisenhower*, 157; Nick Bryant, *The Bystander: John F. Kennedy and the Struggle for Black Equality* (New York: Basic Books, 2006).

44 Roy Wilkins with Tom Matthews, *Standing Fast: The Autobiography of Roy Wilkins* (New York: DaCapo Press, 1994), 222.

15. COLLUSION AT SÈVRES

1 Thorpe, *Eden*, 516; Thorpe, *Selwyn Lloyd* (London: Jonathan Cape, 1989), 237; Selwyn Lloyd, *Suez 1956: A Personal Account* (London: Book Club Associates, 1978), 180–1; Colonel Mordechai Bar-On, 'Remembering 1956:

Three Days in Sèvres, October 1956', *History Workshop Journal* 62 (2006), 173; Avi Shlaim, 'The Protocol of Sèvres, 1956: Anatomy of a War Plot', *International Affairs*, 73, 3 (1997), 514.

2 Bar-On, 'Remembering 1956', 173, 177; Lloyd, *Suez 1956*, 181, 183.

3 Shlaim, 'The Protocol of Sèvres', 513–14.

4 Bar-On, 'Remembering 1956', 177; Shlaim, 'The Protocol of Sèvres', 516.

5 Thorpe, *Eden*, 515–16; Lloyd, *Suez 1956*, 184; Moshe Dayan, *Story of My Life* (London: Weidenfeld and Nicolson, 1976), 180.

6 Bar-On, 'Remembering 1956', 178–9; Lucas, *Divided We Stand*, 245.

7 Lucas, *Divided We Stand*, 153; Lucas, *Britain and Suez*, 49.

8 Kyle, *Suez*, 162–3, 186; on Greek reaction see FO 371/119082/JE14211/171 and 188.

9 Lucas, *Britain and Suez*, 56; Kyle, *Suez*, 193–5, 219–22; James, *Nasser at War*, 31; 'The President's News Conference of September 5, 1956' in *Public Papers of the Presidents of the United States: Dwight D. Eisenhower, 1956* (Washington: U.S. Government Printing Office, 1958), 737.

10 Lucas, *Britain and Suez*, 60; Kyle, *Suez*, 220–1.

11 Kyle, *Suez*, 251–5; Lloyd, *Suez 1956*, 143–4; James, *Nasser at War*, 31; Thorpe, *Eden*, 508, 511.

12 Gorst and Johnman, *The Suez Crisis*, 84–5.

13 'Suez', *Manchester Guardian*, 1 September 1956, 4; Shaw, *Eden, Suez and the Mass Media*, 51–2; Minutes of the Egypt Committee, 2 August 1956, 6 p.m., 2, in CAB/134/4107.

14 Gorst and Johnman, 69–70; Lucas, *Britain and Suez*, 54–5; Shaw, *Eden, Suez and the Mass Media*, 113–14; Thorpe, *Eden*, 498.

15 Shaw, *Eden, Suez and the Mass Media*, 10, 15, 43, 189–91.

16 'A Hinge of History', *The Times*, 1 August 1956, 9.

17 Shaw, *Eden, Suez and the Mass Media*, 24–8.

18 CAB 134/4107, Egypt Committee, 30 July 1956.

19 E.C. (56) 10, 7 August 1956, CAB 134/4107.

20 Kyle, *Suez*, 168–73.

21 Harold Macmillan Minute – E.C. (56) 8, 7 August 1956, CAB 134/4107. See also minutes of the Egypt Committee meeting, 7 August 1956, 3 p.m.

22 Kyle, *Suez*, 174–5, 233–7.

23 CAB 134/4107, Egypt Committee, 10 August 1956, 10 p.m.

24 JE14211/161 and 163 (Cairo to London, 1 August 1956) in FO 371/119082.

25 Kyle, *Suez*, 249.

26 CAB 134/4108, Memorandum by Minister of Defence, Egypt Committee, 16 October 1956.

27 See, for example, Monckton's comments in cabinet on 28 August and 11 September, CAB 134/4108.

28 Thorpe, *Lloyd*, 227; Lloyd, *Suez 1956*, 159–60; Kyle, *Suez*, 272–90; Lucas, *Divided We Stand*, 221–5.

29 Lloyd, *Suez 1956*, 160, 169–70; Thorpe, *Lloyd*, 229–30; Kyle, *Suez*, 286; Lucas, *Divided We Stand*, 223–4; 'Television Broadcast: "The People Ask the President"', 12 October 1956, in *Public Papers of the Presidents of the United States: Dwight D. Eisenhower, 1956*, 903; CAB 134/4108, Cabinet Meeting, 23 October 1956; Lucas, *Britain and Suez*, 73–5.

30 Phil Carradice, 'Lloyd George Takes a Hold on Chequers', 6 January 2014, http://www.bbc.co.uk/blogs/wales/posts/Lloyd-George-takes-a-hold-on-Chequers; http://www.britannica.com/EBchecked/topic/109349/Chequers#.

31 Thorpe, *Eden*, 513; Thorpe, *Lloyd*, 230, 260; Kyle, *Suez*, 296–7.

32 James, *Nasser At War*, 7–10, 12–16; Joel Gordon, *Nasser*, 41–5; Moshe Dayan, *My Life*, 146–7.

33 James Rothrock, *Live by the Sword: Israel's Struggle for Existence in the Holy Land* (Bloomington: WestBow Press, 2011), 29.

34 Moshe Dayan, *My Life*, 146–7.

35 Yossi Melman, 'Targeted Killings – a Retro Fashion Very Much in Vogue', *Haaretz*, 24 March 2004 at http://www.haaretz.com/print-edition/features/targeted-killings-a-retro-fashion-very-much-in-vogue-1.117714; FO 371/119080/JE14211/108, text of speech by President Nasser at Alexandria on 26 July.

36 Horne, *Savage War*, 158; 'Algeria: Floating Catch', *Time*, 29 October 1956.

37 Kyle, *Suez*, 266–71; Lucas, *Divided We Stand*, 159–60; Dayan, *Story of My Life*, 151; Zach Levey, 'French–Israeli Relations, 1950–1956: The Strategic Dimension' in Simon C. Smith, ed., *Reassessing Suez 1956: New Perspectives on the Crisis and its Aftermath* (Aldershot: Ashgate, 2008), 103–4.

38 Kyle, *Suez*, 268–9; Dayan, *Story of My Life*, 171; Levey, 'French-Israeli Relations', 104.

39 Kyle, *Suez*, 270–1.

40 Lucas, *Britain and Suez*, 77; 'The Tripartite Declaration of 25 May 1950', *State Department Bulletin*, 5 June 1950, available at http://content.lib.utah.edu:81/cgi-bin/showfile.exe?CISOROOT=/uu-fasc&CISOPTR=562&CISOMODE=print.

41 See Eric Grove, 'Who to Fight in 1956, Egypt or Israel? Operation Musketeer versus Operation Cordage', in Smith, ed., *Reassessing Suez 1956*, 79–85; Lucas, *Divided We Stand*, 228–32.

42 Lucas, *Divided We Stand*, 230–1, 236–7.

43 Quoted in Lucas, *Britain and Suez*, 75–6.

44 Lucas, *Divided We Stand*, 231.

45 Lucas, *Britain and Suez*, 76–7; Lucas, 'Conclusion' in Smith, ed., *Reassessing Suez 1956*, 241. For an excellent summary of the regional dimension see W. Scott Lucas, 'Redefining the Suez "Collusion"', *Middle Eastern Studies*, 26:1 (1990), 88–112.

46 Thorpe, *Lloyd*, 230–2; Lloyd, *Suez 1956*, 166, 167–70; Thorpe, *Eden*, 513–14.

47 Bar-On, 'Remembering 1956', 183.

48 Thorpe, *Eden*, 517; Bar-On, 'Remembering 1956', 183–4; Shlaim, 'The Protocol of Sèvres', 520–2.

49 Bar-On, 'Remembering 1956', 184–5; Shlaim, 'The Protocol of Sèvres', 522, 530; Kyle, *Suez*, 590–1; Dayan, *Story of My Life*, 193.

16. POLISH OCTOBER

1 Eric Pace, 'Sydney Gruson, 81, Correspondent, Editor and Executive for New York Times, Dies', *NYT*, 9 March 1998; Sydney Gruson New York Death Record available at http://www.death-record.com/d/n/Sydney-Gruson/New-York; Sydney Gruson, 'Warsaw Is in "Peaceful" Revolutionary Mood to Ease Regime', *NYT*, 19 October 1956, 1, 4.

2 Andrzej Werblan, 'Wladyslaw Gomulka and the Dilemma of Polish Communism', *International Political Science Review*, vol. 9, no. 2 (April 1988), 143–58; Johanna Granville, '1956 Reconsidered: Why Hungary and Not Poland?', *The Slavonic and East European Review*, vol. 80, no. 4 (October 2002), 669–70; 'Profile – Gomulka', *Observer*, 28 October 1956, 3; 'Poland: The Return of Little Stalin', *Time*, 20 August 1956; 'Poland: Rebellious Compromiser', *Time*, 10 December 1956; Anita Prazmowska, *Wladyslaw Gomulka: A Biography* (London: I. B. Tauris, 2015).

3 Werblan, 'Wladyslaw Gomulka'; 'Profile – Gomulka'.

4 Machcewicz, *Rebellious Satellite*, 125–7, 135–6, 150–5, 163.

5 NP 10110/100, 'Reports on the VIIth Plenum of the Central Committee of the United Workers Party', 6, in FO 371/122596.

6 Machcewicz, *Rebellious Satellite*, 159–61.

7 Konrad Syrop, *Spring in October: The Polish Revolution of 1956* (London: Weidenfeld and Nicolson, 1957), 67–9; Machcewicz, *Rebellious Satellite*, 159. For the shrine see http://www.jasnagora.pl/en; Cathelijne de Busser and Anna Niedźwiedź, 'Mary in Poland: A Polish Master Symbol' in Anna-Karina Hermkens et al., *Moved by Mary: The Power of Pilgrimage in the Modern World* (Farnham: Ashgate Publishing, 2009), 87–100; 'Voice in "Silent Church"', *New York Times*, 29 October 1956, 7.

8 Syrop, *Spring in October*, 70.

9 David M. Olson and Maurice D. Simon, 'The Institutional Development of a Minimal Parliament: the Case of the Polish Sejm' in Daniel Nelson and Stephen White, eds, *Communist Legislatures in Comparative Perspectives* (Albany: State University of New York Press, 1982), 47–9; NP 10110/135, 'Comments on articles in various newspapers discussing the Sejm', FO 371/122598; Sydney Gruson, 'Parliament Role Debated by Poles', *NYT*, 9 September 1956, 29.

10 Machcewicz, *Rebellious Satellite*, 164; Kemp-Welch, *Poland under Communism*, 94–5; Kemp-Welch, 'Dethroning Stalin', 1,271–2; Matthews, *Tinderbox*, 243.

11 Sydney Gruson, 'Poland Rules Out Trial Observers', *NYT*, 7 September 1956, 5; Syrop, *Spring in October*, 72–3; Machcewicz, *Rebellious Satellite*, 163.

12 Sydney Gruson, 'Trials in Poznan Start Thursday', *NYT*, 23 September 1956, 35; Gruson, 'Poznan Bolsters Police', *NYT*, 27 September 1956, 3.

13 Sydney Gruson, 'Poznan Court Lets Accused Testify Freely on Uprising', *NYT*, 29 September 1956, 1, 4.

14 Sydney Gruson, 'Third Riot Trial Begun in Poznan', *NYT*, 6 October 1956, 4; 'Poland: Beating the King's Police', *Time*, 15 October 1956; Gruson, 'Reds Upbraided at Poznan Trial', *NYT*, 30 September 1956, 1, 34.

15 'Poland: Beating the King's Police'.

16 July 28: Liberty Leading the People at http://www.louvre.fr/en/oeuvre-notices/july-28-liberty-leading-people.

17 'Poland: Beating the King's Police'; *Spring in October*, 75–6; Sydney Gruson, 'Poznan Judge Rejects Plea for Mass Trial of All Arrested in Riots', *NYT*, 2 October 1956, 1, 8; Gruson, 'Poznan Counsel Push Wider Trial', *NYT*, 3 October 1956, 3; Gruson, 'Poznan Court Lets Accused Testify', 1.

18 Syrop, *Spring in October*, 76; Gruson, 'Poland is Reported Ready to Abandon Poznan Trials', *NYT*, 7 October 1956, 1, 30; Gruson, 'Poznan Trial End Now Seems Sure', *NYT*, 11 October 1956, 3.

19 NP 10110/100, 'Reports on the VIIth Plenum of the Central Committee of the United Workers Party', 6, in FO 371/122596.

20 Machcewicz, *Rebellious Satellite*, 159, 161; Kemp-Welch, ed. *Poland under Communism*, 95; Zinner, ed. *National Communism and Popular Revolt*, 191.

21 NP 10110/122, 'Farewell despatch reflecting the present state of Poland', 10 August 1956, 6 in FO 371/122598; 'Communiqué on the Reinstatement of Władysław Gomułka as a Member of the PUWP, August 4, 1956', *Trybuna Ludu*, 5 August 1956, in Zinner, ed., *National Communism and Popular Revolt in Eastern Europe*, 187.

22 'Communiqué of the Politburo of the Central Committee of the Polish United Workers Party on Calling a New Plenary Session, October 15, 1956', *Trybuna Ludu*, 16 October 1956, in Zinner, ed., *National Communism and Popular Revolt in Eastern Europe*, 195.

23 *Memoirs of Nikita Khrushchev. Volume 3*, 625.

24 Machcewicz, *Rebellious Satellite*, 128–9, 163–4; Zinner, ed. *National Communism and Popular Revolt*, 257–8.

25 Krzysztof Persak, 'The Polish–Soviet Confrontation and the Attempted Soviet Military Intervention in Poland', *Europe-Asia Studies*, vol. 58, no. 8 (December 2006), 1,288; Applebaum, *Iron Curtain*, 485; 'Symbol of Soviet Rule', *NYT*, 22 October 1956, 7.

26 Gruson, 'Fete Underlines Shift in Poland', *NYT*, 10 September 1956, 11.

27 Persak, 'The Polish–Soviet Confrontation', 1,290-91; Taubman, *Khrushchev*, 293; Mark Kramer, 'The Soviet Union and the 1956 Crises in Hungary

and Poland: Reassessments and New Findings', *Journal of Contemporary History*, vol. 33, no. 2 (April 1998); Gruson, 'Poles Would Rid Army of Russians', *NYT*, 17 October 1956, 1, 14.

28 L. W. Gluchowski, 'Poland, 1956: Khrushchev, Gomulka, and the "Polish October"', *Cold War International History Project Bulletin*, Issue 5 (Spring 1995), 39; Persak, 'The Polish–Soviet Confrontation', 1,290; Kemp-Welch, *Poland under Communism*, 97; *Memoirs of Nikita Khrushchev, Volume 3*, 626.

29 Gluchowski, 'Poland, 1956', 39–40; Kemp-Welch, *Poland under Communism*, 97–8; Taubman, *Khrushchev*, 293; Toranska, *Oni*, 75–6; Persak, 'The Polish–Soviet Confrontation', 1,290; Kemp-Welch, 'Dethroning Stalin', 1,272–4.

30 Persak, 'The Polish–Soviet Confrontation', 1,294–5; Kemp-Welch, *Poland under Communism*, 96.

31 Matthews, *Tinderbox*, 248; http://www.president.pl/en/presidential-residences/belweder/.

32 Gluchowski, 'Poland, 1956', 39–41.

33 Matthews, *Tinderbox*, 248; http://www.president.pl/en/presidential-residences/belweder/; Persak, 'The Polish–Soviet Confrontation', 1,292–8; Gluchowski, 'Poland, 1956', 41–5.

34 Persak, 'The Polish–Soviet Confrontation', 1,293; Kemp-Welch, *Poland under Communism*, 98; Kramer, 'The Soviet Union and the 1956 Crises in Hungary and Poland', 170; *Memoirs of Nikita Khrushchev, Volume 3*, 627–9.

35 *Memoirs of Nikita Khrushchev, Volume 3*, 627, 629; Toranska, *Oni*, 76; Persak, 'The Polish–Soviet Confrontation', 1,293; Kemp-Welch, *Poland under Communism*, 98.

36 *Memoirs of Nikita Khrushchev*, Volume 3, 629–30; Matthews, Tinderbox, 255–6; Kramer, 'The Soviet Union and the 1956 Crises', 171; Persak, 'The Polish–Soviet Confrontation', 1,299–1,300; Gluchowski, 'Poland, 1956', 41.

37 Matthews, *Tinderbox*, 256.

38 'Address by Władysław Gomułka Before the Central Committee of the Polish United Workers Party, October 20, 1956' in Zinner, ed. *National Communism and Popular Revolt in Eastern Europe*, 197–238; 'Mr Gomulka on Different Roads to Socialism', *Manchester Guardian*, 22 October 1956, 7. On the disbanding of collective farms see Kemp-Welch, *Poland under Communism*, 101.

39 Syrop, *Spring in October*, 136.

40 Machcewicz, *Rebellious Satellite*, 170–4, 182–5, 189–96; Kemp-Welch, *Poland under Communism*, 101; Katherine Lebow, *Unfinished Utopia: Nowa Huta, Stalinism, and Polish Society, 1949–1956* (Ithaca: Cornell University Press, 2013), 155; Paweł Machcewicz, 'Social Protest and Political Crisis in 1956', in A. Kemp-Welch, ed., *Stalinism in Poland, 1944–1956*

(Basingstoke: Macmillan Press, 1999), 113–18 and Machcewicz, 'Intellectuals and Mass Movements: The Study of Political Dissent in Poland in 1956', *Contemporary European History*, vol. 6, no. 3 (1997), 365–7.

41 Machcewicz, 'Intellectuals and Mass Movements', 374–6.

42 Lebow, *Unfinished Utopia*, 155; S. A. Smith, *Red Petrograd: Revolution in the Factories, 1917–1918* (Cambridge: Cambridge University Press, 1983), 56–7.

43 Machcewicz, 'Intellectuals and Mass Movements', 374–6.

44 Machcewicz, *Rebellious Satellite*, 170–4, 182–5, 189–96; Kemp-Welch, *Poland under Communism*, 101; Persak, 'The Polish–Soviet Confrontation', 1,295.

45 'October Days in Poland', 14 December 1956, 1 [Electronic resource]. HU OSA 300-1-2-77343; Records of Radio Free Europe/Radio Liberty Research Institute: General Records: Information Items; Open Society Archives at Central European University, Budapest. http://hdl.handle. net/10891/osa:224c60aa-91d0-4af8-a003-935162646ac1.

46 Machcewicz, *Rebellious Satellite*, 171–2; Syrop, *Spring in October*, 139; 'Poland: Genie from the Bottle', *Time*, 5 November 1956.

47 Lebow, *Unfinished Utopia*, 156–7.

48 Machcewicz, *Rebellious Satellite*, 177, 179; Syrop, *Spring in October*, 142.

49 John H. Summers, 'The Cultural Break: C. Wright Mills and the Polish October', *Intellectual History Review*, vol. 18, no. 2 (2008), 262, 266.

50 http://www.warsawtour.pl/en/tourist-attractions/palace-of-cul-ture-and-science-pa-ac-kultury-i-nauki-2036.html; http://www. nobelforpeace-summits.org/warsaw-around-the-city/the-palace-of-culture-and-science-warsaws-most-famous-building/; Peter Wiles, 'In a Land of Unwashed Brains', *Encounter* (October 1956), 14–15; Toranska, *Oni*, 180; Machcewicz, *Rebellious Satellite*, 176; Syrop, *Spring in October*, 144; Matthews, *Tinderbox*, 266; Jakub Karpiński, *Countdown*, 63–4.

51 John Gunther, *Inside Europe Today* (Harper & Brothers, 1961), 332; Matthews, *Tinderbox*, 266; 'Poland: Genie from the Bottle', *Time*, 5 November 1956; 'Attempted March on Soviet Embassy in Warsaw', *Manchester Guardian*, 25 October 1956, 1; Kemp-Welch, 'Dethroning Stalin', 1,275–6; Jakub Karpiński, *Countdown*, 63–4. I am grateful to Anita Prazmowska for sharing her impressions of Gomulka's oratorical style with me.

52 'Poland: Genie from the Bottle', *Time*, 5 November 1956; 'Attempted March on Soviet Embassy in Warsaw', 1; 'Address by the First Secretary of the Polish United Workers Party, Gomulka, Before a Citizens' Rally at Warsaw, October 24, 1956' in Zinner, ed. *National Communism and Popular Revolt*, 270–6.

53 Gruson, 'March by Poles', *NYT*, 25 October 1956, 1, 14; 'Attempted March on Soviet Embassy in Warsaw', 1; 'Poland: Genie from the Bottle'; Syrop, *Spring in October*, 146.

54 Machcewicz, *Rebellious Satellite*, 208–9; John Connelly, 'Polish Universities and State Socialism, 1944–1968' in Connelly and Grüttner, *Universities*

under Dictatorship, 200; Guy Hadley, 'The Changing Picture in Poland', *The Listener*, 22 November 1956, 827.

55 Kemp-Welch, *Poland under Communism*, 117; Machcewicz, *Rebellious Satellite*, 210–11; Gruson, 'Poles to Demand Moscow Redress', *NYT*, 31 October 1956, 1, 22; Gruson, 'Soviet Assenting to 3 Polish Bids in Moscow Talks', *NYT*, 18 November 1956, 1, 30; Gruson, 'Huge Polish Debt Settled in Soviet', *NYT*, 20 November 1956, 12; 'Poland: Rebellious Compromiser', *Time*, 10 December 1956.

56 Kemp-Welch, *Poland under Communism*, 118–19; Machcewicz, *Rebellious Satellite*, 209–10; 'Polish Primate Reinstated', *Manchester Guardian*, 29 October 1956, 1; 'Crowds Cheer the Cardinal', *Manchester Guardian*, 30 October 1956, 7; Poland: Concordat of Coexistence', *Time*, 17 December 1956.

57 No. 260: 'Statement by the President on Reports from Poland', 20 October 1956, in *Public Papers of the Presidents of the United States, Dwight D. Eisenhower, 1956* (US Government Printing Office, 1958), 981.

58 'No. 265: 'Address at the Anniversary Dinner of the Brotherhood of Carpenters and Joiners', 23 October 1956, in ibid., 994–5, 997.

59 'Discussion at the 301st Meeting of the National Security Council, Friday, October 26, 1956', 1–5, in Ann Whitman File, NSC Series, Box 8, 301st Meeting of NSC, 26 October 1956, Eisenhower Library; 'Memorandum From the Deputy Assistant Secretary of State for European Affairs (Elbrick) to the Secretary of State, re: Approach to the Polish Government Concerning U.S. Economic Aid', 24 October 1956, in *Foreign Relations of the United States, 1955–1957, Volume XXV: Eastern Europe* (Washington: US Government Printing Office, 1990), 268–70; Gati, *Failed Illusions*, 163–5; Memorandum from the Chief of the News Policy Staff of the Office of Policy and Programs of the United States Information Agency (Edman) to the Assistant Program Manager for Policy Application of the United States Information Agency (Zorthian), re: Developments in Poland, 24 October 1956, in *Foreign Relations of the United States, 1955–1957, Volume XXV: Eastern Europe* (Washington: US Government Printing Office, 1990), 270–1; NP 10110/148 'Report on Dulles Comments on the Polish Situation', 22 October 1956, 1–2, FO 371/122598.

60 Taubman, *Khrushchev*, 294; Machcewicz, *Rebellious Satellite*, 170, 210.

61 Kemp-Welch, *Poland under Communism*, 100, 102, 104; Kramer, 'The Soviet Union and the 1956 Crises', 170–3; Persak, 'The Polish–Soviet Confrontation', 1,297, 1,298–1,306; *Memoirs of Nikita Khrushchev, Volume 3*, 629; Machcewicz, *Rebellious Satellite*, 167–70; Granville, '1956 Reconsidered', 676–9.

17. UPRISING

1 'Kerepesi Cemetry: Budapest's Garden of History' at http://disappearing-budapest.blogspot.co.uk/2008/06/kerepesi-cemetery-budapests-garden-of.

html; Lisa Weil and Katrin Holt, 'Springtime in Budapest' at http://buda-
pesttimes.hu/2014/04/25/springtime-in-budapest-2/.

2 '200,000 Hungarians March by Rajk's Coffin as Hungary Honors
Ex-"Traitors"', *NYT*, 7 October 1956, 1, 16; Dean Koch, 'Special Report
on the Hungarian Revolution', 3 December 1956 [Electronic Record]. HU
OSA 300-8-3-3190; Records of Radio Free Europe/Radio Liberty Research
Institute: Publications Department: Background Reports; Open Society
Archives at Central European University, Budapest, at http://hdl.handle.
net/10891/osa:544450d7-413d-4cc2-9711-a61d52e04aae.

3 Telegram from Sir Leslie Fry, 12 October 1956, 1 (NH 10110/76) in FO
371/122376; 'Hungary Reburies "Martyrs"', *Observer*, 7 October 1956,
1; 'Dead "Titoists" Honoured', *The Times*, 8 October 1956, 8; Aczél and
Méray, *Revolt of the Mind*, 437.

4 '200,000 Hungarians March by Rajk's Coffin'; Aczél and Méray, *Revolt of
the Mind*, 437–8; Sebestyen, *Twelve Days*, 97, 98.

5 Applebaum, *Iron Curtain*, 484; Antal Apró's speech and 'Speech of Ferenc
Münnich' in *Szabad Nép*, 7 October 1956, in NH 10110/76, 6 (Hungarian
Press Summary), FO 371/122376; Aczél and Méray, *Revolt of the Mind*, 438.

6 Translation of a report in *Magyar Nemzet*, 7 October 1956, in NH
10110/76, 'Reports that the State Funeral of Messieurs Rajk, Szőnyi,
Palffy and Szalai, who were executed for treason and Titoism in 1949,
was held in Budapest on October 6', 9/a (Hungarian Press Summary),
FO 371/122376.

7 Aczél and Méray, *Revolt of the Mind*, 438–9; 'Ferment in Eastern Europe',
NYT, 8 October 1956, 26; 'Hungary Reburies "Martyrs"', 1; György Litván, ed., *The Hungarian Revolution of 1956: Reform, Revolt and Repression,
1953–1963* (Harlow: Longman, 1996), 48–9; Telegram from Sir Leslie Fry,
12 October 1956, 2 (NH 10110/76), *Szabad Nép*, 7 October 1956, in NH
10110/76, 8 (Hungarian Press Summary), and 'The People of Hungary
Take a Mute and Grief-Stricken Farewell from Their Great Dead', *Szabad
Nép*, 7 October 1956, NH 10110/76, 10 (Hungarian Press Summary), in
FO 371/122376; 'The Hungarian Explosion: An Analysis' (Department
of State: Office of Intelligence Research, 1957), 13–14, in *O.S.S./State
Department Intelligence and Research Reports, Europe: 1950-1961* (University
Publications of America, 1980), reel 9, RSC; Koch, 'Special Report on the
Hungarian Revolution', 4.

8 'Interview in the Hungarian Army Paper during the Uprising with Mrs.
László Rajk', 3 November 1956, 1 [electronic record]. HU OSA 398-0-1-
8613; Records of the UN Special Committee on the Problem of Hungary:
UN Documents; Open Society Archives at Central European University,
Budapest, at http://hdl.handle.net/10891/osa:6adeebc0-fbaa-4aa5-a72e-
cb8e3fafec61.

9 Applebaum, *Iron Curtain*, 484; Sebestyen, *Twelve Days*, 96–7; 'Record of

Conversation between Yuri Andropov and Ernő Gerő, October 12, 1956' in Békés, *The 1956 Hungarian Revolution*, 178–9.

10 Applebaum, *Iron Curtain*, 483; Cartledge, *Will to Survive*, 443; Zinner, *National Communism and Popular Revolt*, 388–9.

11 'Record of Conversation between Yuri Andropov and Ernő Gerő, October 12, 1956' in Békés, *The 1956 Hungarian Revolution*, 178–80.

12 Sebestyen, *Twelve Days*, 101; 'Anti-Soviet Inscriptions Adorn Gyor's Walls', 11 September 1956 [Electronic Resource]. HU OSA 300-1-2-74755; Records of Radio Free Europe/Radio Liberty Research Institute: General Records: Information Items; Open Society Archives at Central European University, Budapest. http://hdl.handle.net/10891/osa:047a5faa-664e-4883-b20f-079fcc3b521e.

13 Roger Gough, *A Good Comrade: Janos Kadar, Communism, and Hungary* (London: I. B. Tauris, 2006), 76; Sebestyen, *Twelve Days*, 99, 107–8.

14 Matthews, *Explosion*, 5; John MacCormac, 'Hungarians Urge Soviet Troops Go', *NYT*, 23 October 1956, 1, 15.

15 Matthews, *Explosion*, 5–7; Békés, *The 1956 Hungarian Revolution*, xxvi, 188; Sebestyen, *Twelve Days*, 102; Csaba Jancsák, 'The Spark of Revolution (1956) – The Association of Hungarian University and College Students (AHUCS)', 1, 5–9, 10–11, available at http://www.coldwar.hu/html/en/publications/JancsakCs_Thesparkofrevolution_1956_AHUCS.pdf; Leslie B. Bain, *The Reluctant Satellites: An Eyewitness Report on East Europe and the Hungarian Revolution* (New York: The Macmillan Company, 1960), 95–6.

16 Matthews, *Explosion*, 19, 20–3; Litván, *The Hungarian Revolution of 1956*, 53; Sebestyen, *Twelve Days*, 102, 303–4; 'The "Sixteen Points" Prepared by Hungarian Students, October 22–23, 1956' in Békés, *The 1956 Hungarian Revolution*, 188–9.

17 Lasky, *The Hungarian Revolution*, 49; 'The Hungarian Explosion: An Analysis', 18; Matthews, *Explosion*, 30–2.

18 Lasky, *The Hungarian Revolution*, 48, 50–1; Matthews, *Explosion*, 32–3, 36–8; Sebestyen, *Twelve Days*, 108–10; Litván, *The Hungarian Revolution of 1956*, 54–5.

19 Litván, *The Hungarian Revolution of 1956*, 55; Sebestyen, *Twelve Days*, 110–11; Matthews, *Explosion*, 39, 40–4.

20 Lasky, *The Hungarian Revolution*, 50.

21 Sebestyen, *Twelve Days*, 110; Matthews, *Explosion*, 45; Lendvai, *One Day*, 9.

22 Sebestyen, *Twelve Days*, 111; Matthews, *Explosion*, 49, 50–1; Lasky, *The Hungarian Revolution*, 50–1; Lendvai, *One Day*, 14; Mark Pittaway, *The Workers' State: Industrial Labor and the Making of Socialist Hungary, 1944–1958* (Pittsburgh: University of Pittsburgh Press, 2012), 206–14.

23 Lasky, *The Hungarian Revolution*, 49.

24 Lasky, *The Hungarian Revolution*, 55–6; Matthews, *Explosion*, 34, 47–55.

25 Sebestyen, *Twelve Days*, 113–14, 119; Matthews, *Explosion*, 56–7; Rainer, *Imre Nagy*, 101.

26 Sebestyen, *Twelve Days*, 68, 101, 108; 'A Strange Communist: Imre Nagy', *NYT*, 25 October 1956, 8; Rainer, *Imre Nagy*, 98, 100.

27 Sebestyen, *Twelve Days*, 68–78; Rainer, *Imre Nagy*, 29–30; Johanna Granville, 'Imre Nagy, aka "Volodya" – Dent in the Martyr's Halo?', *Cold War International History Project Bulletin*, 5 (Spring 1995), 34–7.

28 Rainer, *Imre Nagy*, 92–3, 98, 99, 100–2; Aczél and Méray, *Revolt of the Mind*, 396; Sebestyen, *Twelve Days*, 101, 108.

29 Rainer, *Imre Nagy*, 102–3; Sebestyen, *Twelve Days*, 12, 119–20; Matthews, *Explosion*, 62.

30 Zinner, ed. *National Communism and Popular Revolt*, 402–7; Sir Leslie Fry, NH10110/140, 'The Hungarian Revolution: analysis of its causes and assessment of its likely consequences', 3 January 1957, 5, FO 371/128670.

31 'When the Earth Moved', *Time*, 5 November 1956; Lasky, *The Hungarian Revolution*, 54; 'Police Open Fire in Budapest', *Manchester Guardian*, 24 October 1956, 1; Sebestyen, *Twelve Days*, 112, 118–19; Litván, *The Hungarian Revolution of 1956*, 57–8; David Lowe and Tony Joel, *Remembering the Cold War: Global Contest and National Stories* (Abingdon, Oxon: Routledge, 2013), 103–4.

32 Sebestyen, *Twelve Days*, 121–4; Matthews, *Explosion*, 111–20, 125–30; Litván, *The Hungarian Revolution of 1956*, 58; Cartledge, *Will to Survive*, 446; 'From Demonstrations to the Revolution' in Békés, *The 1956 Hungarian Revolution*, 193; Applebaum, *Iron Curtain*, 487; Miklós Molnár, *Budapest 1956: A History of the Hungarian Revolution* (London: George Allen & Unwin, Ltd, 1971), 118–21; Fry, 'The Hungarian Revolution: analysis of its causes and assessment of its likely consequences', 3–4; Lasky, *The Hungarian Revolution*, 57; 'The Hungarian Explosion: An Analysis', 22.

33 Lasky, *The Hungarian Revolution*, 58.

34 NH10110/204, FO 371/122379; Kramer, 'The Soviet Union and the 1956 Crises in Hungary and Poland, 184–5; NH10110/215(D), FO 371/122379; Sebestyen, *Twelve Days*, 126.

35 Kramer, 'The Soviet Union and the 1956 Crises', 183–4; Johanna Granville, '1956 Reconsidered', 667–9; Litván, *The Hungarian Revolution of 1956*, 58; Sebestyen, *Twelve Days*, 112–13.

36 'Working Notes from the Session of the CPSU CC Presidium, October 23, 1956' in Békés, *The 1956 Hungarian Revolution*, 217–18; Taubman, *Khrushchev*, 295; Kramer, 'The Soviet Union', 184.

37 Rainer, *Imre Nagy*, 103–4.

38 Ibid., 104–5; Gati, *Failed Illusions*, 148; Litván, *The Hungarian Revolution of 1956*, 58–9; 'From Demonstrations to the Revolution' in Békés, *The 1956 Hungarian Revolution*, 194–5.

39 Sebestyen, *Twelve Days*, 133.

40 NH10110/86, FO 371/122376.

41 NH10110/204, FO 371/122379; Sebestyen, *Twelve Days*, 129–31, 136; Kramer, 'The Soviet Union and the 1956 Crises', 185; 'From Demonstrations to Revolution' in Békés, *The 1956 Hungarian Revolution*, 195; Lendvai, *One Day*, 57–9; Matthews, *Explosion*, 172–3; NH10110/140, FO 371/128670.

42 Lendvai, *One Day*, 58, 63–4; 'CURPH Interview 64-M with a 1956 Hungarian Refugee: 19 Years Old, Male, Elevator Installation Worker', 1957 [Electronic Resource], 1, 3, 8, 9, 12, 14, HU OSA 414-0-2-62; Donald and Vera Blinken Collection on Hungarian Refugees of 1956: Transcripts of Refugee Interviews; Open Society Archives at Central European University, Budapest. http://hdl.handle.net/10891/osa:acd88d39-ac05-45c6-a87c-457750bb6171.

43 'From Demonstrations to the Revolution' in Békés, *The 1956 Hungarian Revolution*, 195; Matthews, *Explosion*, 161–2; 'Situation Report from Anastas Mikoyan and Mikhail Suslov in Budapest to the CPSU CC Presidium', October 24, 1956, in Békés, *The 1956 Hungarian Revolution*, 219–20.

44 'Jan Svoboda's Notes on the CPSU CC Presidium Meeting with Satellite Leaders, October 24, 1956', in Békés, *The 1956 Hungarian Revolution*, 226.

45 Lasky, *The Hungarian Revolution*, 70.

46 'Soviet Tank Fires on the Unarmed', *NYT*, 26 October 1956, 1; Matthews, *Explosion*, 174–6; Lendvai, *One Day*, 76; Gábor Jobbágyi, 'Bloody Thursday, 1956: The Anatomy of the Kossuth Square Massacre', *Hungarian Review*, vol. 5, no. 3 (January 2014); Sebestyen, *Twelve Days*, 144; 'From Demonstrations to the Revolution' in Békés, *The 1956 Hungarian Revolution*, 196; Bain, *The Reluctant Satellites*, 114–15.

47 'From Demonstrations to the Revolution' in Békés, *The 1956 Hungarian Revolution*, 196–7; Matthews, *Explosion*, 176–8; Sebestyen, *Twelve Days*, 144–5; Jobbágyi, 'Bloody Thursday, 1956'; Lendvai, *One Day*, 7; Lasky, *The Hungarian Revolution*, 71; Fry, 'The Hungarian Revolution: analysis of its causes and assessment of its likely consequences', 6.

48 Lendvai, *One Day*, 79; Rainer, *Imre Nagy*, 107.

49 Lasky, *The Hungarian Revolution*, 74–5; Matthews, *Explosion*, 180–1.

50 Lendvai, *One Day*, 1956, 78; Lasky, *The Hungarian Revolution*, 71–2, 76; 'Transcript of a Teletype Conversation Between the Legation in Hungary and the Department of State, October 25, 1956' in *FRUS, 1955–1957*, Volume XXV, 285.

51 NH10110/89 and NH10110/101, FO 371/122376.

52 NH10110/140, FO 371/128670; 'The Hungarian Explosion: An Analysis', 26–7, 33–6; 'Whole Country in Revolt', *The Times*, 29 October 1956, 8; Litván, *The Hungarian Revolution of 1956*, 66–7; Lendvai, *One Day*, 85–7; 'From Demonstrations to the Revolution' in Békés, *The 1956 Hungarian Revolution*, 199; Attila Szakolczai, 'The Main Provincial Centres of the 1956 Revolution: Győr and Miskolc', *Europe-Asia Studies*, vol. 58, no. 8

(December 2006), 1,311–28; author's interviews with Rozalia Kollar and Maria Szuhánszky on the revolution in Balassagyarmat, 25 January 2015.

53 Hannah Arendt, 'Reflections on the Hungarian Revolution' in Lee Congdon et al., *1956: The Hungarian Revolution and War for Independence* (Boulder, Colorado: Social Science monographs, 2006), 636; Peter Fryer, *Hungarian Tragedy* (London: Index Books, 1997), 50–2.

54 Pittaway, *The Workers' State*, 212–13, 218–20.

55 'CURPH Interview 10-M with a 1956 Hungarian Refugee: 25 years old Male, Construction technician', 1957, 7. HU OSA 414-0-2-3 [Electronic Resource] and 'CURPH Interview 12-M with a 1956 Hungarian Refugee: 28 Years Old, Male, Bank Teller Clerk', 1957, 4–6 [Electronic Record]. HU OSA 414-0-2-5; Donald and Vera Blinken Collection on Hungarian Refugees of 1956: Transcripts of Refugee Interviews; Open Society Archives at Central European University, Budapest, available at http://hdl.handle.net/10891/osa:bc65e3c6-00a4-409e-b205-2457acd98f00 and http://hdl.handle.net/10891/osa:ba65abc5-4bbc-4a9e-be34-c7146f785d5b; Litván, *Hungarian Revolution*, 67; Pittaway, *The Workers' State*, 222–9.

56 'Mass Shooting Avenged in Hungarian Town', *The Times*, 29 October 1956, 8; Sebestyen, *Twelve Days*, 163; Fryer, *Hungarian Tragedy*, 20, 21, 26; Matthews, *Explosion*, 200; Homer Bigart, 'Mass Burial Held for 85 Rebel Dead', *NYT*, 29 October 1956, 1; Lasky, *The Hungarian Revolution*, 83, 85.

57 Lasky, *The Hungarian Revolution*, 83; 'Mass Shooting Avenged in Hungarian Town', 8; Bigart, 'Mass Burial Held', 1, 9; Sebestyen, *Twelve Days*, 156; Matthews, *Explosion*, 197–8, 200.

58 Sebestyen, *Twelve Days*, 157; Matthews, *Explosion*, 199; Bigart, 'Mass Burial Held', 9; Lasky, *The Hungarian Revolution*, 83.

59 Litván, *The Hungarian Revolution*, 161; Mark, 'Society, Resistance and Revolution', 979; Cartledge, *The Will to Survive*, 333–412.

60 György Litván, 'A Forty-Year Perspective on 1956' in Terry Cox, ed., *Hungary 1956 – Forty Years On* (London: Frank Cass, 1997), 22–4; Bain, *Reluctant Satellites*, 128–34.

61 Lendvai, *One Day*, 60; Litván, *The Hungarian Revolution*, 60–2; Pittaway, *The Workers' State*, 205; Mark, 'Society, Resistance and Revolution', 979–86.

62 Rainer, *Imre Nagy*, 111–14; 'Radio Message from Imre Nagy Announcing the Formation of a New Government, October 28, 1956, 5:25 p.m.', in Békés, *The 1956 Hungarian Revolution*, 284–5; Granville, '1956 Reconsidered', 680.

63 'From Demonstrations to the Revolution' in Békés, *The 1956 Hungarian Revolution*, 204–5; Rainer, *Imre Nagy*, 116–18; Szakolczai, 'The Main Provincial Centres of the 1956 Revolution', 1,323.

64 'Proclamation by Imre Nagy on the Creation of a Multi-Party System, October 30, 1956' in Békés, *The 1956 Hungarian Revolution*, 290–1.

65 Litván, *The Hungarian Revolution of 1956*, 76.
66 'Working Notes from the Session of the CPSU CC Presidium on October 30, 1956', in Békés, *The 1956 Hungarian Revolution*, 295, 297, 299; Taubman, *Khrushchev*, 296.
67 'Declaration by the Government of the USSR', 30 October 1956, in Békés, *The 1956 Hungarian Revolution*, 300–2.

18. SUEZ

1 Kyle, *Suez*, 444.
2 Neillands, *A Fighting Retreat*, 337–8.
3 Kyle, *Suez*, 446–7; WO 288/74, Operation Musketeer – War Diary, 16 Independent Parachute Brigade Group, 5–6.
4 Kyle, *Suez*, 447; WO 288/74, 6.
5 WO 288/74, 6–7.
6 A casualty list is provided in WO 288/74, Annexe B, 2–3.
7 Kyle, *Suez*, 444, 448–9.
8 Ibid., 445, 449, 452, 454–5; WO 288/74, 7.
9 Ibid., 461.
10 Kyle, *Suez*, 461, 463; Neillands, *A Fighting Retreat*, 341; ADM 202/455, 'Operation Musketeer, Unit Report: 45 Commando Royal Marines', 2.
11 Neillands, *A Fighting Retreat*, 342.
12 ADM 202/455, '3 Commando Brigade Royal Marines, Operation Musketeer Report', 12, 13, Appendix L, 6.
13 Kyle, *Suez*, 462; ADM 202/455, 'Operation Musketeer, Unit Report' (45 Commando), 3, 4, 6; '3 Commando Brigade Report', Appendix L, 2, 5.
14 Neillands, *A Fighting Retreat*, 345.
15 Neillands, *A Fighting Retreat*, 343; WO 288/142, 'Civilian Battle Casualties', 1; FO 371/118908, E1094/125(A), Allied Commander-in-Chief to Chiefs of Staff, 12 November 1956.
16 Neillands, *A Fighting Retreat*, 338; ADM 202/455, 'Operation Musketeer, Unit Report' (45 Commando), 3, 4; Kyle, *Suez*, 462–3.
17 Kyle, *Suez*, 461–2.
18 ADM 202/455, '3 Commando Brigade Report', Appendix L, 3–5, 6; Kyle, *Suez*, 463–4.
19 Kyle, *Suez*, 476; Neillands, *A Fighting Retreat*, 345.
20 'Army Attacks Bases in Heart of Sinai', *Jerusalem Post*, 30 October 1956, 1.
21 Moshe Dayan, *Diary of the Sinai Campaign* (New York: Schocken Books, 1967), 77–88.
22 'Ultimatum to Israel and Egypt Expires', *The Times*, 31 October 1956, 8; 'Parliament', *The Times*, 31 October 1956, 4.
23 'Rejection by Col. Nasser', *The Times*, 31 October 1956, 8; Lucas, *Divided We Stand*, 261, 263.
24 ADM 116/6103, 'Summary of Operations During Operation Musketeer,

Flag Officer Aircraft Carriers No. 100/7' (HMS Eagle), 20 November 1956, 4, 5–6, Appendix C; ADM 116/6103, 'Operation Musketeer – Interim Report, No. 7/1956, 20 December 1956, 5; Kyle, *Suez*, 484.

25 Heikal, *Cutting the Lion's Tail*, 177–80; Mohamed Heikal, *The Cairo Documents: The Inside Story of Nasser and His Relationship with World Leaders, Rebels, and Statesmen* (New York: Doubleday, 1973), 105–11; James, *Nasser at War*, 37–42; Laura M. James, 'When Did Nasser Expect War? The Suez Nationalization and its Aftermath in Egypt', in Smith, ed., *Reassessing Suez 1956*, 159–64.

26 Lucas, *Divided We Stand*, 272–3; Lucas, *Britain and Suez*, 94–5.

27 James, *Nasser at War*, 43.

28 'Col. Nasser's Retort', *The Times*, 2 November 1956, 8; FO371/118904/JE1094/39, 1 November 1956; James, *Nasser at War*, 43.

29 Anne Alexander, *Nasser* (London: Haus Publishing, 2005), 93; Lucas, *Divided We Stand*, 273.

30 Alexander, *Nasser*, 94.

31 'Demonstrations and Disagreement', *Manchester Guardian*, 3 November 1956, 7; Jankowski, *Nasser's Egypt*, 85–6; Kyle, *Suez*, 397; Heikal, *Cutting the Lion's Tail*, 188–91.

32 CO 1035/21, Reaction in Certain Colonial Territories to Anglo-French Action in Suez, November 1956.

33 CO 1035/21, Joint Intelligence Committee, Far East, 16 November 1956, 1; CO 1035/21, Annex 3 to JIFC (56)709, 7 November 1956, 2–3.

34 'Demonstrations and Disagreement', 7; FO 371/118904/JE1094/50, Belgrade to London, 3 November 1956.

35 'Demonstrations and Disagreement', 7; Kyle, *Suez*, 396–7; Jung Chang and Jon Halliday, *Mao: The Unknown Story* (London: Jonathan Cape, 2005), 424.

36 CO 1035/21, Joint Intelligence Committee, Far East, 16 November 1956, 2; Chang and Halliday, *Mao*, 424–5.

37 PREM 11/1096, Prime Minister's Personal Telegram, Serial No. T 528/56, 5 November 1956; Kyle, *Suez*, 393–5.

38 'Demonstrations and Disagreement', 7; Kyle, *Suez*, 395–6.

39 FO 371/118904/JE1099/46, New Delhi to London, 1 November 1956.

40 PREM 11/1176, From Foreign Office to Washington, 1 September 1956.

41 Kyle, *Suez*, 258.

42 Nichols, *Eisenhower 1956*, 201–2; Eisenhower, *Waging Peace*, 71–2; Robert F. Dorr, *Air Force One* (St Paul, MN: MBI Publishing Company, 2002), 45.

43 Nichols, *Eisenhower 1956*, 203.

44 'Memorandum of a Conference with the President, White House, Washington, October 29, 7:15 p.m.', in *FRUS, 1955–1957, Volume XVI, Suez Crisis, July 26–December 31, 1956*, 836; Ricky-Dale Calhoun, 'The Musketeer's Cloak: Strategic Deception During the Suez Crisis 1956', *CIA Studies in Intelligence* (2007) 51:2.

45 Nichols, *Eisenhower 1956*, 207; 'Memorandum of a Conference with the

President, White House, Washington, October 30, 1956, 4:25 p.m.', in *FRUS-Suez*, 873.

46 'Memorandum of a Conference with the President, White House, Washington, October 30, 1956, 10:06–10:55 a.m.', in *FRUS-Suez*, 853–4.

47 Nichols, *Eisenhower 1956*, 204–5; Smith, 'Introduction' in Smith, ed., *Reassessing Suez 1956*, 5–8.

48 'Memorandum of Discussion at the 302d Meeting of the National Security Council, Washington, November 1, 1956, 9 a.m.', in *FRUS-Suez*, 906.

49 Thorpe, *Eden*, 525.

50 Lucas, *Divided We Stand*, 265, 269.

51 'Draft Message from President Eisenhower to Prime Minister Eden', in *FRUS-Suez*, 874–5.

52 Lucas, *Divided We Stand*, 270.

53 Lucas, *Divided We Stand*, 275.

54 Kyle, *Suez*, 374–5, 421–4; Lucas, *Divided We Stand*, 275, 280–1.

55 http://www.greatbuildings.com/buildings/United_Nations_Headquarter.html; Ingeborg Glambek, 'The Council Chambers in the UN Building in New York', *Scandinavian Journal of Design History*, vol. 15 (2005), 8–39.

56 *FRUS-Suez*, 881–2; Lucas, *Divided We Stand*, 263; Kyle, *Suez*, 363; Edward Johnson, 'The Suez Crisis at the United Nations: The Effects for the Foreign Office and British Foreign Policy', in Smith, ed., *Reassessing Suez 1956*, 171.

57 Johnson, 'The Suez Crisis at the United Nations', 171.

58 Gorst and Johnman, *The Suez Crisis*, 115; Lucas, *Britain and Suez*, 98.

59 Lucas, *Divided We Stand*, 280.

60 Kyle, *Suez*, 377–8, 388–9, 390.

61 Thorpe, *Eden*, 523; 'Christian Opinion Terribly Unhappy and Uneasy', *Manchester Guardian*, 2 November 1956, 3.

62 Gorst and Johnman, *The Suez Crisis*, 116.

63 'A Lack of Candour?', *The Times*, 2 November 1956, 9.

64 Sandbrook, *Never Had It So Good*, 18; Kyle, *Suez*, 404–5.

65 'Eden', *Observer*, 4 November 1956, 8.

66 Sandbrook, *Never Had It So Good*, 17.

67 'Fights at Universities During Anti-War Demonstrations', *Manchester Guardian*, 3 November 1956, 3; 'Protest Meeting in Manchester', *Manchester Guardian*, 6 November 1956, 14.

68 'Work Stopped for Protest over Suez Policy', *Manchester Guardian*, 7 November 1956, 4; 'Tories Walk Out Singing "Land of Hope and Glory"', *Manchester Guardian*, 8 November 1956, 4; 'Eighty Oxford Dons Attack Government Actions', *Manchester Guardian*, 2 November 1956, 16.

69 Demonstrators in Clash', *The Times*, 5 November 1956, 4; '20 Fined After London Scenes', *Manchester Guardian*, 6 November 1956, 3.

70 Gorst and Johnman, *The Suez Crisis*, 116–17; Kyle, *Suez*, 436–8.

71 Sandbrook, *Never Had It So Good*, 20.

72 Lloyd, *Suez 1956*, 207

73 A. J. Stockwell, 'Suez 1956 and the Moral Disarmament of the British Empire', in Smith, ed., *Reassessing Suez 1956*, 228–9.

74 CAB 134/1408, Cabinet Minutes, 4 November 1956, 2.

75 'Message from Prime Minister Eden to President Eisenhower', 5 November 1956, in *FRUS-Suez*, 984.

76 Gorst and Johnman, *The Suez Crisis*, 122–3.

77 'Letter from Prime Minister Bulganin to President Eisenhower', 5 November 1956, in *FRUS-Suez*, 993.

78 'Memorandum of a Conference With the President, White House, Washington, November 5, 1956, 5 p.m.', *FRUS-Suez*, 1,000–1; Nichols, *Eisenhower 1956*, 245–7; 'White House News Release', 5 November 1956, in *FRUS-Suez*, 1,007–8.

79 Nichols, *Eisenhower 1956*, 251; Lloyd, *Suez 1956*, 206, 209, 210–11; Lucas, *Divided We Stand*, 291–4; Sandbrook, *Never Had It So Good*, 21.

80 Nichols, *Eisenhower 1956*, 260–2; 'Memorandum of Discussion at the 303d Meeting of the National Security Council, Washington, November 8, 1956, 9–11:25 a.m.' in FRUS-Suez, 1,070–7; Lucas, *Divided We Stand*, 301–2.

19. OPERATION WHIRLWIND

1 'Memorandum of Discussion at the 302d Meeting of the National Security Council, Washington, November 1, 1956, 9–10:55 a.m.', in *FRUS, 1955–1957*, vol. XXV, 358–9.

2 Telegram, Spencer Barnes to State Department, 31 October 1956, 1, in Ann Whitman File, Dulles-Herter Series, Box 7, Dulles, John Foster Oct '56 (1), Eisenhower Library; Charles Bohelen, 'Telegram from the Embassy in the Soviet Union to the Department of State', 31 October 1956 – 1 p.m., in *FRUS, 1955–1957*, vol. XXV, 348–9.

3 Memorandum of Discussion at the 302d Meeting of the National Security Council', 358–9.

4 'Hungary: The Five Days of Freedom', *Time*, 12 November 1956; Henry Giniger, 'Hungary is Found Happy, Confused', *NYT*, 1 November 1956, 27; Fryer, *Hungarian Tragedy*, 64.

5 Matthews, *Explosion*, 301–2; Lasky, *The Hungarian Revolution*, 155.

6 Fryer, *Hungarian Tragedy*, 66–7; 'Hungary: The Five Days of Freedom'.

7 Lasky, *The Hungarian Revolution*, 166, 173–4; FO 371/122379/NH10110/202 – Fry, 31 October 1956.

8 Taubman, *Khrushchev*, 10, 296; Catherine Merridale, 'Behind Closed Doors: The secrets contained within the imposing walls of the Kremlin', *Independent*, 12 October 2013; 'Working Notes and Attached Extract from the Minutes of the CPSU CC Presidium Meeting, October 31, 1956' in

Békés, *The 1956 Hungarian Revolution*, 307–10.

9 'Situation Report from Anastas Mikoyan and Mikhail Suslov in Budapest, October 30, 1956', in Békés, *The 1956 Hungarian Revolution*, 292.

10 Rainer, Imre Nagy, 121; Sebestyen, *Twelve Days*, 201; Matthews, *Explosion*, 279–81, 296; Peter Fryer, *Hungarian Tragedy*, 64.

11 John Sadovy, 'People Were Dropping Like Flies', *Life*, 12 November 1956, 41.

12 'Working Notes and Attached Extract from the Minutes of the CPSU CC Presidium Meeting, October 31, 1956' in Békés, *The 1956 Hungarian Revolution*, 307–10.

13 Taubman, *Khrushchev*, 297; Chang and Halliday, *Mao*, 422.

14 Kramer, 'The Soviet Union and the 1956 Crises in Hungary and Poland', 192–8.

15 'From Demonstrations to the Revolution' in Békés, *The 1956 Hungarian Revolution*, 202; 'Information Report from Bulgarian State Security on the Activities of 'Hostile Elements', October 30, 1956', in Békés, *The 1956 Hungarian Revolution*, 305–6; Kramer, 'The Soviet Union and the 1956 Crises in Hungary and Poland', 194.

16 Johanna C. Granville, 'Temporary Triumph in Timişoara: Unrest among Romanian Students in 1956', *History* vol. 93, no. 309 (January 2008), 71; Welles Hangen, 'Rumania Arrests Unruly Magyars', *NYT*, 30 October 1956, 17; Dennis Deletant, 'Romania, 1945–1989: Resistance, Protest and Dissent' in Kevin McDermott and Matthew Stibbe, eds, *Revolution and Resistance in Eastern Europe: Challenges to Communist Rule* (Oxford: Berg, 2006), 81–99; Johanna C. Granville, '"We Have Wines of All Kinds: Red, White, and Green": Romanian Reactions to the Hungarian Uprising in 1956', *Australian Journal of Politics and History*, vol. 54, no. 2 (2008), 185–210; Zoltán Szász, 'Romania and the 1956 Hungarian Revolution' in Congdon et al., *1956: The Hungarian Revolution and War for Independence*, 129–30, 132–5.

17 Granville, 'Temporary Triumph', 74–7, 88–93; Deletant, 'Romania, 1945–1989', 87; Szász, 'Romania and the 1956 Hungarian Revolution', 134; 'Minutes of 58th Meeting of the Romanian Politburo, October 30, 1956', in Békés, *The 1956 Hungarian Revolution*, 303–4.

18 Taubman, *Khrushchev*, 297; Kramer, 'The Soviet Union and the 1956 Crises', 189–92; 'Working Notes and Attached Extract from the Minutes of the CPSU CC Presidium Meeting, October 31, 1956' in Békés, *The 1956 Hungarian Revolution*, 307.

19 Taubman, *Khrushchev*, 298; Kramer, 'The Soviet Union and the 1956 Crises in Hungary and Poland', 198–9.

20 Rainer, *Imre Nagy*, 125.

21 Lasky, *The Hungarian Revolution*, 154, 172–3, 175.

22 'Telegram from Imre Nagy to Kliment Voroshilov Proposing Negotiations

on the Withdrawal of Soviet Troops, October 31, 1956', in Békés, *The 1956 Hungarian Revolution*, 316.

23 'Imre Nagy's Declaration of Hungarian Neutrality (Radio Broadcast), November 1, 1956', in Békés, *The 1956 Hungarian Revolution*, 334; Rainer, *Imre Nagy*, 126–30.

24 'Telegram from Imre Nagy to U. N. Secretary General Dag Hammerskjöld, November 1 1956', in Békés, *The 1956 Hungarian Revolution*, 333.

25 Litván, *The Hungarian Revolution*, 96–9; Csaba Békés, 'Policies of the USA, Great Britain and France in 1956', in Congdon et al., *1956*, 494–512; Sebestyen, *Twelve Days*, 252; 'United Nations Resolutions adopted by the General Assembly during its second emergency special session from 4–10 November 1956', available at http://www.un.org/en/ga/search/view_doc.asp?symbol=A/3355&Lang=E.

26 Rainer, *Imre Nagy*, 133; Sebestyen, *Twelve Days*, 244–5, 249, 257–8, 261; Granville, *The First Domino*, 95.

27 Lendvai, *One Day*, 149; Kramer, 'The Soviet Union and the 1956 Crises', 206, 208; Litván, *The Hungarian Revolution*, 81–2.

28 Rainer, *Imre Nagy*, 134.

29 'Soviet Tanks Crush Resistance', *Manchester Guardian*, 5 November 1956, 1.

30 'Report from Georgii Zhukov to the CPSU CC, November 4, 1956, 12 a.m.', in Békés, *The 1956 Hungarian Revolution*, 384.

31 Kramer, 'The Soviet Union and the 1956 Crises in Hungary and Poland', 208; Litván, *The Hungarian Revolution*, 102; Lendvai, *One Day*, 149; FO 371/122385/NH10110/427.

32 Kramer, 'The Soviet Union and the 1956 Crises', 207–8; Lendvai, *One Day*, 150–1; Rainer, *Imre Nagy*, 134–5; Miklós Horváth, 'Introduction' in Congdon, *1956*, 452–3, 455–8; Béla K. Király, 'The Fighting of the National Guard Against Overwhelming Odds' in Congdon, *1956*, 465–75; author's interview with János Szuhánszki (Sr), 25 January 2015.

33 Lasky, *The Hungarian Revolution*, 228.

34 FO 371/122381 NH10110/301; Lendvai, *One Day*, 149; Sebestyen, *Twelve Days*, 268–9; 'Hungary: Death in Budapest', *Time*, 19 November 1956.

35 Lasky, *The Hungarian Revolution*, 249.

36 Fryer, *Hungarian Tragedy*, 80; FO 371/122380/NH10110/266–267.

37 Fryer, *Hungarian Tragedy*, 82–3; FO 371/122382/NH10110/318.

38 FO 371/122380/NH10110/264 (B)

39 FO 371/122382/NH 10110/316; FO 371/128670/NH10110/140, 15–16.

40 Fryer, *Hungarian Tragedy*, 81, 83; FO 371/122393/NH10110/635; Sebestyen, *Twelve Days*, 275.

41 Lendvai, *One Day*, 151; Litván, *The Hungarian Revolution*, 103; Kramer, 'The Soviet Union and the 1956 Crises', 210 note 187.

42 Kramer, 'The Soviet Union and the 1956 Crises', 199–200; Litván, *The Hungarian Revolution*, 104.

43 FO 371/122394/NH 10110/648.

44 Litván, *The Hungarian Revolution*, 108–11; FO 371/128670/NH10110/140, 20.

45 Hannah Arendt, *The Origins of Totalitarianism* (Cleveland: A Meridian Book, 1958), 480; Sebestyen, *Twelve Days*, 280; 'Foreign News: The Rivalry of Exhaustion', *Time*, 17 December 1956; FO 371/128670/NH10110/140, 22; 'Hungary: The Unvanquished', *Time*, 26 November 1956.

46 Litván, *The Hungarian Revolution*, 106–9; Sebestyen, *Twelve Days*, 278; Johanna Granville, 'In the Line of Fire: The Soviet Crackdown on Hungary, 1956–57' in Terry Cox, ed., *Hungary 1956 – Forty Years On*, 88.

47 Litván, *The Hungarian Revolution*, 110–14.

48 Sebestyen, *Twelve Days*, 286–8; Granville, 'In the Line of Fire', 88–9, 92–4; Litván, *The Hungarian Revolution*, 117–20.

49 Rainer, *Imre Nagy*, 137–8, 142, 154–65, 193.

50 Granville, 'In the Line of Fire', 89; Litván, *The Hungarian Revolution*, 143; 'Hungary in the Aftermath' in Békés, *The 1956 Hungarian Revolution*, 375.

51 Rupert Colville, 'A Matter of the Heart: How the Hungarian Crisis Changed the World of Refugees', *Refugees*, no. 144, issue 3 (2006) (UNHCR), 6, 10; Nador F. Dreisziger, 'The Hungarian Revolution of 1956: The Legacy of the Refugees', *Nationalities Papers*, 13:2 (1985), 198–208.

52 FO 371/122389/NH10110/547.

53 'Hungary: Freedom's Choice', *Time*, 7 January 1957.

54 'Melbourne Students Demonstrate', *Sydney Morning Herald*, 8 November 1956, 7; FO 371/122394/NH10110/662; FO 371/122382/NH10110/331; 'Thousands Protest in Salvador', *NYT*, 9 November 1956, 20; 'World Crisis: The Mark of Cain', *Time*, 19 November 1956.

55 Michael James, 'Marchers Depict Hungary's Cause', *NYT*, 5 November 1956, 29; Milton Bracker, '10,000 at Garden Back Up Hungary', *NYT*, 9 November 1956, 15.

56 'The Free World Condemns Russia', *Manchester Guardian*, 6 November 1956, 7; 'World Crisis: The Mark of Cain'; Big Protest in Brussels', *NYT*, 7 November 1956, 38; FO 371/122382/NH10110/349; 'More Protests on Hungary – and Offers of Help', *Manchester Guardian*, 9 November 1956, 4.

57 'Silence in Sympathy with Hungary', *Manchester Guardian*, 9 November 1956, 4; 'Salzburg Students Protest on Behalf of Their Hungarian Colleagues', 22 November 1956 [Electronic Resource]. HU OSA 300-1-2-76694; Records of Radio Free Europe/Radio Liberty Research Institute: General Records: Information Items; Open Society Archives at Central European University, Budapest, at http://hdl.handle.net/10891/osa:e0c7f148-fd28-43ba-af4c-8837fcd63aac.

58 FO 371/122385/NH10110/428; FO 371/122387/NH10110/486.

59 FO 371/122385/NH10110/425; FO 371/122385/NH10110/429; 'Luxembourg

Embassy Damaged', *NYT*, 7 November 1956, 38.

60 World Crisis: The Mark of Cain'; NH10110/495, 615, 629, 653 & 654 in
FO371/122393; various files in LAB 10/1510.

61 'Universities Prominent in Protests on Hungary', *Manchester Guardian*,
10 November 1956, 9; 'More Protests on Hungary – and Offers of Help',
Manchester Guardian, 9 November 1956, 4; 'Exiles Volunteer to Fight in
Hungary', *Manchester Guardian*, 6 November 1956, 2; 'Protests and Offers
of Help to Hungary', *Manchester Guardian*, 8 November 1956, 3.

62 Lasky, *The Hungarian Revolution*, 271.

63 Mark B. Smith, 'Peaceful coexistence at all costs: Cold War exchanges between
Britain and the Soviet Union in 1956', *Cold War History* (2011), 10, 16.

64 '"The Bloody Olympics Down Under": Sport, Politics and the 1956 Melbourne Games', Sport & Society: The Summer Olympics and Paralympics
through the lens of social science, at http://www.bl.uk/sportandsociety/
exploresocsci/politics/articles/melbourne.pdf; 'Blood in the Water: The
1956 Olympics in Melbourne', World News Australia Radio, 3 September
2013, at http://www.sbs.com.au/news/article/2012/07/25/blood-water-1956-
olympics-melbourne.

65 'Statement by the President on the Developments in Hungary', 25 October
1956, and 'Radio and Television Report to the American People on the
Developments in Eastern Europe and the Middle East', 31 October 1956,
in *Public Papers of the Presidents of the United States*, 1,018–19, 1,061–2.

66 'Memorandum of Discussion at the 301st Meeting of the National Security
Council, Washington, October 26, 1956, 9–10:42 a.m.', in *FRUS, 1955–57*,
vol. XXV, 299; 'Address by the Secretary of State Before the Dallas Council
on World Affairs, October 27, 1956' in *FRUS, 1955–57*, vol. XXV, 318; Documents 116 and 119–21 in *FRUS, 1955–57*, vol. XXV, 299, 305–7; Litván, *The
Hungarian Revolution of 1956*, 93; Gati, *Failed Illusions*, 163–4.

67 Eisenhower, *Waging Peace*, 88–9.

68 'Radio Free Europe and the Hungarian Uprising', p. 5, in C. D. Jackson
Papers, 1931–67, Box 54, Free Europe Committee (1), Eisenhower Library;
Kinzer, *The Brothers*, 213; 'Transcripts of Radio Free Europe Programs,
Advising on Military Tactics to Use Against a Superior Enemy', 28 Octo-
ber 1956 and William Griffith, 'Policy Review of Voice of Free Hungary
Programming, October 23–November 23, 1956', 5 December 1956, in
Békés, *The 1956 Hungarian Revolution*, 286–9, 481, 465, 466–8, 473, 479;
Arch Puddington, *Broadcasting Freedom: The Cold War Triumph of Radio
Free Europe and Radio Liberty* (Lexington: University Press of Kentucky,
2000), 99–114; Johanna Granville, '"Caught with Jam on Our Fingers":
Radio Free Europe and the Hungarian Revolution of 1956', *Diplomatic
History*, vol. 29, no. 5 (November 2005), 811–39.

69 'CURPH Interview 524 with a 1956 Hungarian Refugee: 21 Years Old,
Male, Miner', 1957 [Electronic Resource], 17. HU OSA 414-0-2-318; and

'CURPH Interview 78-M with a 1956 Hungarian Refugee: 19 Years Old, Male, Tailor', 1957 [Electronic Resource], 3, 8. HU OSA 414-0-2-77, Donald and Vera Blinken Collection on Hungarian Refugees of 1956: Transcripts of Refugee Interviews; Open Society Archives at Central European University, Budapest, http://hdl.handle.net/10891/osa:88711ac8-6c08-46b6-adeb-f08555150c0a and http://hdl.handle.net/10891/osa:f7c43020-a74a-4463-8acb-4d0dbc2fc282; author's interview with Maria Szuhánszky, 25 January 2015.

70 'Memorandum of a Telephone Conversation Between the Secretary of State in Washington and the Representative at the United Nations (Lodge) in New York, October 24, 1956, 6:07 p.m.', in *FRUS, 1955–57*, vol. XXV, 273.

71 Gati, *Failed Illusions*, 164–5; NSC 174 and NSC 5608 in Békés, *The 1956 Hungarian Revolution*, 34–53, 119–26.

72 Comments of Eisenhower and Allen Dulles in 'Bipartisan Legislative Meeting, November 9, 1956' 9:35am–11:45am, 2–3, in *The Diaries of Dwight D. Eisenhower*, reel 10, 0929 Miscellaneous (3). November 1956, RSC.

73 'The Hungarian Victory', *New York Times*, 7 November 1956, 30.

20. SIERRA MAESTRA

1 Herbert L. Matthews, *Revolution in Cuba: An Essay in Understanding* (New York: Charles Scribner's Sons, 1975), 71–2; Hugh Thomas, *Cuba: or The Pursuit of Freedom* (New York: DaCapo Press, 1998), 891, 894.

2 Thomas, *Cuba*, 888, 891; Carlos Franqui, *Diary of the Cuban Revolution* (New York: Viking Press, 1976), 121–2; Ernesto Che Guevara, *Reminiscences of the Cuban Revolutionary War* (London: Harper Perennial, 2009), 139; Julia E. Sweig, *Inside the Cuban Revolution: Fidel Castro and the Urban Underground* (Cambridge, MA: Harvard University Press, 2002).

3 Guevara, *Reminiscences*, 139.

4 Franqui, *Diary*, 122; Matthews, *Revolution*, 71–2.

5 Matthews, *Revolution*, 71–2; Thomas, *Cuba*, 891, 894–7; Franqui, *Diary*, 120, 124; 'Cuba: Hit-Run Revolt', *Time*, 10 December 1956; Enzo Infante, 'Santiago Uprising: A Harbinger of Victory', *The Militant*, vol. 60, no. 9 (4 March 1996).

6 Franqui, *Diary*, 123–4, 129; Guevara, *Reminiscences*, 9, 140–1; Thomas, *Cuba*, 897; Matthews, *Revolution*, 72; Max Boot, 'M-26-7: Castro's Improbable Comeback, 1952–1959' in Max Boot, *Invisible Armies: An Epic History of Guerrilla Warfare from Ancient Times to the Present* (Liveright, 2013), 427–8; Jorge Castañeda, *Compañero: The Life and Death of Che Guevara* (London: Bloomsbury, 1997), 99.

7 Guevara, *Reminiscences*, 9–10, 141; Thomas, *Cuba*, 897–8; Franqui, *Diary*, 124.

8 Guevara, *Reminiscences*, 10–12; Franqui, *Diary*, 125, 129; Fidel Castro and Ignacio Ramonet, *Fidel Castro: My Life. A Spoken Autobiography* (New York: Scribner, 2009), 182–3; Boot, 'M-26-7', 428; Thomas, *Cuba*, 898–9; 'July 26 Movement appealed to soldiers and youth in Cuba to join revolutionary struggle', *The Militant*, vol. 68, no. 3 (26 January 2004).

9 Castañeda, *Compañero*, 78, 80; Aviva Chomsky, *A History of the Cuban Revolution* (Chichester: Wiley-Blackwell, 2011), 24–5; http://history.state.gov/milestones/1899-1913/Platt; see also Thomas, *Cuba*, chapters xxxv–l.

10 Chomsky, *History of the Cuban Revolution*, 24.

11 Ibid., 24, 33–4; Castañeda, *Compañero*, 78–9; Thomas, *Cuba*, 893; Matthews, *Revolution in Cuba*, 34–9; James O'Connor, *The Origins of Socialism in Cuba* (Ithaca: Cornell University Press, 1970), esp. 1, 20; 'Memorandum from the Director of the Office of Middle American Affairs (Wieland) to the Assistant Secretary of State for Inter-American Affairs (Rubottom), 19 December 1957, re: Policy Recommendation for Restoration of Normalcy in Cuba' in *FRUS, 1955–1957, Vol. IV, American Republics: Multilateral; Mexico; Caribbean*, 870.

12 Castañeda, *Compañero*, 80, 81, 82; Chomsky, *History of the Cuban Revolution*, 28.

13 Chomsky, *History of the Cuban Revolution*, 28–33; Matthews, *Revolution*, 29–34; Boot, 'M-26-7', 430–1; Sweig, *Inside the Cuban Revolution*, 4.

14 'Another Dictatorship', *NYT*, 22 September 1955, 30.

15 Thomas, *Cuba*, 883–5, 889–90; Leycester Coltman, *The Real Fidel Castro* (New Haven: Yale University Press, 2003), 109; Chomsky, *History of the Cuban Revolution*, 34; 'Cuba: Hit-Run Revolt'; 'Student Disorders Have Cuba Worried', *NYT*, 7 December 1955, 10; 'Cuba Suppresses Plot for Revolt', *NYT*, 4 April 1956, 9; '17 Cubans Arrested; Revolt Data Seized', *NYT*, 4 May 1956, 9; Herbert L. Matthews, 'Cuba a Live Volcano of Political Unrest', *NYT*, 6 May 1956, 186; '17 Arrested in Cuba in Anti-Batista Plot', *NYT*, 27 June 1956, 2; 'Cuban Army Aide Slain by Gunmen', *NYT*, 29 October 1956, 6; Herbert L. Matthews, 'Cuba's Violence is Found Normal', *NYT*, 4 November 1956, 4.

16 Thomas, *Cuba*, 810–23; Boot, 'M-26-7', 429–31; Matthews, *Revolution*, 41–7; Castañeda, *Compañero*, 82; Coltman, *Real Fidel Castro*, 18; http://www.cubatechtravel.com/destination/extrahotel/9613/havana-university.

17 Thomas, *Cuba*, 817–21; Boot, 'M-26-7', 430–1; Sweig, *Inside the Cuban Revolution*, 5.

18 Thomas, *Cuba*, 835–41; Boot, 'M-26-7', 431–2; Matthews, *Revolution*, 49, 55–63; Coltman, *Real Fidel Castro*, 75–6, 82; http://www.pbs.org/wgbh/amex/castro/peopleevents/e_moncada.html; Chomsky, *History of the Cuban Revolution*, 36–7; Castro, *My Life*, 129. See also Herbert L. Matthews, 'Batista is Facing Fateful Decisions', *NYT*, 22 October 1953, 15.

19 Boot, 'M-26-7', 432; Matthews, *Revolution*, 64–5; Thomas, *Cuba*, 843; Coltman, *Real Fidel Castro*, 87–8, 90; Castro, 'History Will Absolve Me' available at http://www.marxists.org/history/cuba/archive/castro/1953/10/16.htm; 'Cuba Begins Trial of 100 for Revolt', *NYT*, 22 September 1953, 19.

20 Coltman, *Real Fidel Castro*, 93–101; Matthews, *Revolution*, 67–8; Thomas, *Cuba*, 862–3. See Castro's letters from prison (especially those of 18 December 1953, 22 December 1953 and 24 March 1955) in Franqui, *Diary*, 66, 68, 71, 73.

21 'Cuba: Creeping Revolt', *Time*, 7 January 1957; 'The Violent Cubans', *NYT*, 4 December 1956, 38; 'Cuba Rebels Take to the Hills', *The Times*, 6 December 1956, 9.

22 UPI News Release in Franqui, *Diary*, 126.

23 'The Cuban Revolt', *The Times*, 4 December 1956, 11.

24 Castro, *My Life*, 183–4.

25 Thomas, *Cuba*, 899–904; Matthews, *Revolution*, 77–8; Manuel Fajardo, 'Recollections' in Franqui, *Diary*, 134; http://peakery.com/pico-caracas/.

26 Thomas, *Cuba*, 904–8; Chomsky, *History of the Cuban Revolution*, 38–9; Boot, 'M-26-7', 436; Coltman, *Real Fidel Castro*, 118.

27 Sweig, *Inside the Cuban Revolution*, 1, 184; Chomsky, *History of the Cuban Revolution*, 39–40; Boot, 'M-26-7', 437; Thomas, *Cuba*, 925.

28 Sweig, *Inside the Cuban Revolution*, 184.

29 Boot, 'M-26-7', 437–8; Coltman, *Real Fidel Castro*, 120–2.

30 'Cuba: Creeping Revolt'; Thomas, *Cuba*, 909–10; Matthews, *Revolution*, 79.

31 Telegram from the Ambassador in Cuba (Gardner) to the Secretary of State, 15 February 1957, in *FRUS 1955–1957 Vol. IV*, 840–1; Boot, 'M-26-7', 438–9; Chomsky, *History of the Cuban Revolution*, 40; Thomas, *Cuba*, 947.

21. FREEDOM ON TRIAL

1 Nelson Mandela, *Long Walk to Freedom: The Autobiography of Nelson Mandela* (London: Abacus, 1995), 231.

2 Ibid., 232.

3 Ibid., 232; Lionel Forman and E. S. [Solly] Sachs, *The South African Treason Trial* (London, John Calder, 1957), 19; Helen Joseph, *If This Be Treason* (London: Andre Deutsch, 1963), 13–14; Karis and Carter, eds, *From Protest to Challenge*, 81; '140 Arrested in South Africa', *Manchester Guardian*, 6 December 1956, 1; 'Preparatory examination in the matter of Regina vs 153 individuals on a charge of high treason; Outline of Crown Case', 70, 1956 Treason Trial, AD1812, A1.a70, Historical Papers, University of the Witwatersrand, Johannesburg, available at http://www.historicalpapers.wits.ac.za/?inventory_enhanced/U/Collections&c=132398/R/AD1812-A1-a.

4 Mandela, *Long Walk*, 233.

5 Robert Cook, 'Awake, the Beloved Country: A Comparative Perspective on the Visionary Leadership of Martin Luther King and Albert Lutuli', *South African History Journal*, vol. 36, no. 1 (May 1997), 117–21, 127; 'Walter Ulyate Sisulu' at http://www.sahistory.org.za/people/walter-ul-yate-sisulu and 'Oliver Reginald Tambo' at http://www.sahistory.org.za/people/oliver-reginald-tambo; Dubow, *Apartheid*, 70; 'Biographical Sketches' in Forman and Sachs, *The South African Treason Trial*; 'Emil Solomon Sachs' at http://www.sahistory.org.za/people/emil-solo-mon-sachs; Ameen Akhalwaya, 'Obituary: Helen Joseph', *Independent* (London), 28 December 1992 available at http://www.independent.co.uk/news/people/obituary-helen-joseph-1565649.html; Joseph, *Side by Side*, 21–3, 24, 39–40.

6 Forman and Sachs, *The South African Treason Trial*, 24, 26, 36–40.

7 Ibid., 38–9, 41–2; Rusty Bernstein, *Memory Against Forgetting: Memoirs from a Life in South African Politics, 1938–1964* (London: Viking, 1999), 166.

8 Albert Luthuli, 'Foreword', in Joseph, *If This Be Treason*, 7.

9 Mandela, *Long Walk*, 233–4; Elaine Unterhalter, 'The Work of the Nation: Heroic Masculinity in South African Autobiographical Writing of the Anti-Apartheid Struggle', in *The European Journal of Development Research*, vol. 12, issue 2 (2000), 163.

10 Mandela, *Long Walk*, 234; Forman and Sachs, *The South African Treason Trial*, 37; Elinor Batezat Sisulu, *Walter and Albertina Sisulu: In Our Life-time* (London: Abacus, 2002), 157.

11 Mandela, *Long Walk*, 234–5.

12 Forman and Sachs, *The South African Treason Trial*, 27–8, 31–3; Sisulu, *Walter and Albertina Sisulu*, 157–8.

13 Joseph, *Side by Side*, 55; Forman and Sachs, *The South African Treason Trial*, 24, 28–9.

14 Mandela, *Long Walk*, 235; Forman and Sachs, *The South African Treason Trial*, 47–9; Joseph, *Side by Side*, 56; Bernstein, *Memory Against Forgetting*, 167–8.

15 Forman and Sachs, *The South African Treason Trial*, 49–50.

16 Mandela, *Long Walk*, 236–7.

17 Forman and Sachs, *The South African Treason Trial*, 52, 53–4.

18 'Preparatory examination in the matter of Regina vs 153 individuals on a charge of high treason'; 'Treason Trial Press Summaries, 1956–1961, nos. 1–58', 1–2, 1956 Treason Trial, AD1812, I1, available at http://www.histor-icalpapers.wits.ac.za/?inventory_enhanced/U/Collections&c=133739/R/AD1812-I1.

19 Mandela, *Long Walk*, 237; Forman and Sachs, *The South African Treason Trial*, 55.

20 Mary Rayner, 'Law, Politics, and Treason in South Africa', *Human Rights Quarterly*, vol. 8, no. 3 (August 1986), 474, 475, 477; Joseph, *If This Be Treason*, 18–20.

21 Garrow, *Bearing the Cross*, 82.

22 Hampton and Fayer, *Voices of Freedom*, 32.

23 'Seminars on Non-Violence', *MIA Newsletter*, vol. 1, no. 5 (26 November 1956), 1–2, in John H. Bracey, Jr, and August Meier, eds, *Papers of the NAACP, Part 20: White Resistance and Reprisals, 1956–1965* (Bethesda, MD: University Publications of America, 1996), reel 5, 'Alabama-Montgomery Bus Boycott, November 1956–1957, Emory University.

24 Garrow, *Bearing the Cross*, 81–2; Burns, *Daybreak of Freedom*, 325–7.

25 Garrow, *Bearing the Cross*, 82.

AFTERMATH

1 'The Talk of the Town', *New Yorker*, 29 December 1956, 15.

2 Richard Löwenthal, 'Retrospect and Prospect: Beyond the Circus', *Observer*, 30 December 1956, 5; 'A Londoner's Retrospect: Looking Back on a Year of Crisis and Controversy', *Manchester Guardian*, 31 December 1956, 3; 'Some Clues to a Smoldering World Crisis', *I. F. Stone's Weekly*, 10 December 1956, 1; 'Hungary: Freedom's Choice'.

3 Hobsbawm, *Interesting Times*, 201.

4 Tony Judt, *Postwar*, 321; Sandbrook, *Never Had It So Good*, 216.

5 C. Wright Mills, *The Power Elite* (New York: Oxford University Press, 1956); Van Gosse, *Rethinking the New Left: An Interpretative History* (New York: Palgrave, 2005); Hobsbawm, *Interesting Times*, 210–11; Service, *Comrades*, 366; Michael Kenny, *First New Left: British Intellectuals After Stalin* (London: Lawrence & Wishart, 1995).

6 Geoffrey Hosking, *A History of the Soviet Union* (London: Fontana, 1985), 346–60; Polly Jones, ed., *The Dilemmas of De-Stalinization: Negotiating Cultural and Social Change in the Khrushchev Era* (Routledge, 2006); Taubman, *Khrushchev*, 417, 648–50; Mark B. Smith, *Property of Communists: The Urban Housing Program from Stalin to Khrushchev* (Northern Illinois University Press, 2010); 303–10, 364–5, 382–8; James E. Cronin, *The World the Cold War Made: Order, Chaos, and the Return of History*, 129–31; Francis Spufford, *Red Plenty: Inside the Fifties' Soviet Dream* (London: Faber & Faber, 2011).

7 Feigon, *Mao*, 112; Victor Zorza, '800,000 Chinese Liquidated: Policy Now Reversed', *Manchester Guardian*, 15 June 1957, 5; János Rádvanyi, 'The Hungarian Revolution and the Hundred Flowers Campaign', *The China Quarterly* no. 43 (Jul.–Sep. 1970), 122–3; Taubman, *Khrushchev*, 297.

8 Lynch, *Mao*, 161–3; Feigon, *Mao*, 113–17.

9 Chang and Halliday, *Mao*, 435.

10 Lynch, *Mao*, 164–72; Feigon, *Mao*, 117.

11 Mark Moyar, *Triumph Forsaken: The Vietnam War, 1954–1965* (Cambridge: Cambridge University Press, 2006), 62–4; see also 'Hanoi Radio Reports Quelling of Uprisings', *NYT*, 17 November 1956, 13.

12 Moyar, *Triumph Forsaken*, 58–9, 64–7.

13 Lendvai, *One Day*, 226, 228–31; Litván, *The Hungarian Revolution of 1956*,
    147–8; Cartledge, *Will to Survive*, 467–85, 490–501; Bill Lomax, 'The Hun-
    garian Revolution of 1956 and the Origins of the Kádár Regime', *Studies
    in Comparative Communism*, vol. XVIII, no. 2/3 (Summer/Autumn 1956),
    105–6, 110–11; Karl P. Benziger, *Imre Nagy: Martyr of the Nation* (New
    York: Lexington Books, 2010), 18–26, 105–6; Padraic Kenney, *A Carnival
    of Revolution: Central Europe 1989* (Princeton: Princeton University Press,
    2002), 261–4.

14 Mark Kurlansky, *1968: The Year that Rocked the World* (New York: Ballan-
    tine Books, 2004), 238–50, 287–305, 375–7.

15 Chomsky, *History of the Cuban Revolution*, 97–105.

16 Manning Marable, 'Race and Revolution in Cuba: African American
    Perspectives' in Marable, *Dispatches From the Ebony Tower: Intellectuals
    Confront the African American Experience* (New York: Columbia University
    Press, 2000), 90–108 (97); Plummer, *Rising Wind*, 285–97; Julio García
    Luis, *Cuban Revolution Reader: A Documentary History of 40 Key Moments
    of the Cuban Revolution* (New York: Ocean Press, 2001), 57; Coltman, *Real
    Fidel Castro*, 174–5; Timothy B. Tyson, *Radio Free Dixie: Robert F. Williams
    and the Roots of Black Power* (Chapel Hill: University of North Carolina
    Press, 1999), 239–42; Alex Doherty, 'Mandela and Cuba: Another Memory
    Hole', *openDemocracy*, 21 December 2013 at http://www.opendemocracy.
    net/alex-doherty/mandela-and-cuba-another-memory-hole; 'Why Nelson
    Mandela Loved Fidel Castro', *Huffington Post*, 6 December 2013 at http://
    www.huffingtonpost.com/2013/12/06/nelson-mandela-castro_n_4400212.
    html; Piero Gleijeses, *Visions of Freedom: Havana, Washington, Pretoria, and
    the Struggle for Southern Africa, 1976–1991* (Chapel Hill: University of North
    Carolina Press, 2013).

17 Van Gosse, *Where the Boys Are: Cuba, Cold War America and the Making
    of a New Left* (London: Verso, 1993), 50–1, 83–4; Castañada, *Compañero*,
    391–5, 406–10.

18 Ibid.; Chomsky, *History of the Cuban Revolution*, 41–2; Arthur M.
    Schlesinger, Jr, *A Thousand Days: John F. Kennedy in the White House* (Bos-
    ton: Houghton Mifflin, 1965, 2002), 220.

19 Ruth First, 'Our New Age', *Fighting Talk*, vol. 12, no. 1, January 1956, 2.

20 Derek Ker, 'The New Trinidadian Parliament', *The Crisis*, January 1957,
    13–16, 63.

21 Nugent, *Africa Since Independence*, 166–77; Birmingham, *Kwame Nkru-
    mah*, 63–74, 77–81.

22 Birmingham, *Kwame Nkrumah*, 74–6, 81–8, 93.

23 Derek Ker, 'The New Trinidadian Parliament', *The Crisis*, January 1957,
    13–16, 63; Remarks of Dr Sukarno on the opening of the Asian African
    Students Conference, 7 June 1957, in 'Secretarial Report of the ANC
    Youth League (Transvaal), June 15–16, 1957' in Karis and Carter, *From*

Protest to Challenge, 406. Nkrumah's victory also caught the imagination of civil rights activists as they battled racism in the United States. (Martin Luther King was one of those who attended the independence celebrations in Accra, while the NAACP welcomed Ghana into the 'family of nations', declaring that she would 'give further inspiration and encouragement to peoples . . . yet to achieve their freedom' – see Birmingham, *Kwame Nkrumah*, 94–5, 98–101; Brendon, *Decline and Fall*, 538–9; Garrow, *Bearing the Cross*, 90–1; 'NAACP Board Resolution Hailing Ghana', *The Crisis*, vol. 64, no. 4 (April 1957), 208.)

24 Julius K. Nyerere, *Freedom and Unity/Uhuru na Umoja: A Selection from Writings and Speeches, 1952–65* (London: Oxford University Press, 1967), 1, 4–5, 40–4, 45–7; Julius Nyerere, speech at Mnazi Mmoja, 27 January 1957, FCO141/17775, and Special Branch sketch of Julius K. Nyerere, 6–7, FCO 141/17912.

25 See 'Nigeria: Cabinet Memorandum by Mr Lennox Boyd', 14 May 1957, in Martin Lynn, ed., *British Documents on the End of Empire, Series B, Volume 7: Nigeria, Part II: Moving to Independence, 1953–1960* (London: The Stationery Office, 2001), 423–5.

26 Remarks of Dr Sukarno on the opening of the Asian African Students Conference, 7 June 1957, in 'Secretarial Report of the ANC Youth League (Transvaal), June 15–16, 1957' in Karis and Carter, *From Protest to Challenge*, 406.

27 Frantz Fanon, *The Wretched of the Earth* (London: Penguin Classics, 2001), 69.

28 Horne, *Savage War of Peace*, 187; Evans, *Algeria*, 189; 'France: Algerian Bloodshed', *Time*, 14 January 1957.

29 Evans, *Algeria*, 205–15, 218–25; Connelly, *A Diplomatic Revolution*, 130–3; Clayton, *The Wars of French Decolonization*, 134. Both Evans and Connelly describe the French victory in the Battle of Algiers as 'pyrrhic'.

30 James F. McMillan, *Twentieth Century France: Politics and Society 1898–1991* (London: Arnold, 1992), 162–7; Evans, *Algeria*, 231–40, 261–312, 336–7; Boot, *Invisible Armies*, 369–77; Betts, *France and Decolonisation, 1900–1960*, 107–13; Conklin, *France and Its Empire*, 273–4, 279–84.

31 Evans, *Algeria*, 320, 340–1.

32 Holland, *Britain and the Revolt in Cyprus*, 158; Brendon, *Decline and Fall*, 622; Crawshaw, *The Cyprus Revolt*, 203; W. Byford-Jones, *Grivas and the Story of EOKA* (London: Robert Hale Limited, 1959), 91.

33 Holland, *Britain and the Revolt in Cyprus*, 133.

34 Crawshaw, *The Cyprus Revolt*, 340–1, 360; Hyam, *Britain's Declining Empire*, 270; Brendon, *Decline and Fall*, 622–5; Bölükbaşı, 'The Cyprus Dispute and the United Nations', 414–15.

35 David Tal, 'The 1956 Sinai War: A Watershed in the History of the Arab-Israeli Conflict', in Smith, ed., *Reassessing Suez 1956*, 132–3, 147; Kyle, *Suez*, 573; Dayan, *Diary of the Sinai Campaign*, 203–4.

36 Thomas, *The French North African Crisis*, 127–9; McMillan, *Twentieth Century France*, 162; Thomas, *Fight or Flight*, 185–7; Kyle, *Suez*, 467.

37 James, *Nasser at War*, 47–8; Kyle, *Suez*, 571–3.

38 Sandbrook, *Never Had It So Good*, 22–4.

39 Tore T. Petersen, 'Post-Suez Consequences: Anglo-American Relations in the Middle East from Eisenhower to Nixon' and Stockwell, 'Suez 1956 and the Moral Disarmament of the British Empire' in Smith, ed., *Reassessing Suez 1956*; Darwin, *The End of the British Empire*, 70; Thomas, *Fight or Flight*, 168, 188; Sandbrook, *Never Had It So Good*, 25.

40 Sandbrook, *Never Had It So Good*, 25; Lucas, *Divided We Stand*, 324; Darwin, *The End of the British Empire*, 71–3; Thomas, *Fight or Flight*, 184; Lucas, *Britain and Suez*, 114; Wm. Roger Louis, 'Public Enemy Number One: The British Empire in the Dock at the United Nations, 1957–71', in Lynn, *The British Empire in the 1950s*, 191–2; Louis, 'Suez and Decolonization: Scrambling Out of Africa and Asia' in Louis, *Ends of British Imperialism*, 5.

41 Hyam, *Britain's Declining Empire*, 239–40; Rebellato, 'Look Back at Empire' and Stuart Ward, '"No Nation Could Be Broker": the Satire Boom and the Demise of Britain's World Role' in Ward, ed., *British Culture and the End of Empire* (Manchester: Manchester University Press, 2001).

42 Lucas, *Britain and Suez*, 113.

43 Nichols, *Eisenhower 1956*, 275–6, 277, 286; Richard V. Damms, 'In Search of "Some Big, Imaginative Plan": The Eisenhower Administration and American Strategy in the Middle East after Suez', in Smith, ed., *Reassessing Suez 1956*, 179–94.

44 'Statement by Roy Wilkins, Executive Secretary, National Association for the Advancement of Colored People, for *Liberation* Magazine', 15 November 1956, 1–2 in NAACP Part 20, Reel 5, Alabama-Montgomery Bus Boycott, November 1956–1957.

45 J. Mills Thornton, *Dividing Lines*, 93–7; Jeanne Theoharis, *Rebellious Life of Mrs. Rosa Parks*, 135.

46 Randall Kennedy, 'Martin Luther King's Constitution: A Legal History of the Montgomery Bus Boycott', *The Yale Law Journal*, vol. 98, no. 6 (April 1989), 1,057; Thornton, *Dividing Lines*, 102.

47 Theoharis, *Rebellious Life of Mrs. Rosa Parks*, 137, 141–2.

48 Ling, *Martin Luther King, Jr*, 56, 58–9; Garrow, *Bearing the Cross*, 90–4, 97–104.

49 Burns, *Daybreak of Freedom*, 317; 'Professor Zachariah Keodirelang Matthews' at http://www.sahistory.org.za/people/professor-zachariah-keo-direlang-matthews.

50 Brooks, *Boycotts, Buses, and Passes*, 229–30; *Fighting Talk*, vol. 11, no. 3 (March 1957); Karis and Carter, *From Protest to Challenge*, 275–8.

51 Brooks, *Boycotts, Buses, and Passes*, 233–4.

52 Bernstein, *Memory Against Forgetting*, 176–81; Sisulu, *Walter and Albertina Sisulu*, 160.

53 Dubow, *Apartheid, 1948–1994*, 70–1.

54 Ibid., 52–3, 72–3; 'The International Aid and Defence Fund' at http://www.sahistory.org.za/topic/international-defence-and-aid-fund-idaf-3; a useful account of overseas press reaction is provided in Forman and Sachs, *The Treason Trial*, 184–90; Rob Skinner, *The Foundations of Anti-Apartheid: Liberal Humanitarianism and Transnational Activists in Britain and the United States, c.1919–1964* (Basingstoke: Palgrave Macmillan, 2010), 147–55.

55 George M. Houser, 'Meeting Africa's Challenge: The Story of the American Committee on Africa', *Issue: A Journal of Opinion*, vol. 6, no. 2/3 (Summer 1976), 16–17, 20.

56 Lodge, *Black Politics in South Africa Since 1945*, 76; Blanche La Guma with Martin Klammer, *In the Dark With My Dress on Fire: My Life in Cape Town, London, Havana and Home Again* (Aukland Park: Jacana, 2010), 58; Bernstein, *Memory Against Forgetting*, 176–7; Mandela, *Long Walk*, 242.

57 Dubow, *Apartheid, 1948–1994*, 72, 74; Joe Slovo, 'South Africa – No Middle Road', in Basil Davidson, Joe Slovo and Anthony R. Wilkinson, *Southern Africa: The New Politics of Revolution* (Harmondsworth: Penguin Books, 1976), 168–71; Sisulu, *Walter and Albertina Sisulu*, 183–5; Mandela, *Long Walk*, 320–40; Bernstein, *Memory Against Forgetting*, 174–6; Trevor Huddleston, 'The Treason Trial', *New Statesman and Nation*, 15 December 1956, 780.

58 Carole Fink, Frank Hadler and Tomasz Schramm, '1956: New Perspectives – An Introduction' in Fink, Hadler and Schramm, eds, *1956: European and Global Perspectives* (Leipzig: Leipziger Universitätsverlag, 2006), 10–11; 'The Alba Platform' in Knabb, *Situationist International Anthology* (Berkeley, CA: Bureau of Public Secrets, 2006), 22–3.

59 '"Federal Troops" Bugaboo', *Jackson Daily News* in *The Citizens' Council*, vol. 1, no. 11 (August 1956), 3.

60 Evans, *Algeria*, 184–5.

61 Machcewicz, *Rebellious Satellite*, 136.

62 Cecil Williams, 'African Awakening', *Fighting Talk*, vol. 12, no. 5 (May 1956), 5–6; Tabitha Petran, 'Behind the Lines', *Fighting Talk*, vol. 12, no. 7 (July 1956); 'Joint Statement of the Working Committee of the ANC, SAIC, South Africa Congress of Democrats, FEDSAW, SACPO, and SACTU', Collection Number: AD1812, Records Relating to the 'Treason Trial' (Regina v. F. Adams and others on Charge of High Treason, etc.), 1956–1961, Historical Papers, University of the Witwatersrand.

63 Alfred Hutchinson, 'Against the College Colour-bar', *Fighting Talk*, vol. 12, no. 5 (May 1956), 9.

64 'A Statement to the South and the Nation' issued by Southern Negro Leaders Conference on Transportation and Nonviolent Integration, 10–11

January 1957, Atlanta, GA, The Martin Luther King, Jr, Papers Project, available at http://mlk-kpp01.stanford.edu/primarydocuments/Vol4/11-Jan-1957_AStatementToTheSouth.pdf. Although issued on behalf of King's new organisation (later the SCLC), this passage mirrors the language used by King in a number of his earlier (and later) speeches.

INDEX

Numbers in *italics* show pages with
illustrations.

26th July Movement (M-26-7), 357,
   366–7, 368, 387

Abernathy, Ralph, 6, 17, 19, 22, 380
Aczél, Tamás, 183–4, 190, 191
AFL-CIO, 174
Africa, British colonies, 113–14
African National Congress (ANC):
   anthem, 226; banned, 397; Castro's
   influence, 386; 'defiance campaign',
   230; foundation, 230; Freedom
   Charter, 230–1; leadership, 373, 374,
   386; membership, 230; solidarity with
   freedom struggles elsewhere, 398;
   women's anti-pass movement, 225–6,
   232–3; Women's League, 227
Akka (ship scuttled in Suez Canal), 322
Alabama, University of: desegregation
   attempt, 74–9, 82–3; desegregation
   protests, *67*, 77–9, 80, 82, 249
Alabama Journal, 23
Albion, HMS, 322
Algeria: ANC perspective, 398; armed
   struggle against French rule, xi, 27–8,
   40–6; Battle of Algiers, 389–90; civil
   rights issues, 34–5, 72; French rule,
   33–5; independence, 390; Mollet's visit,
   29–31, 45–6; Muslim population, 34–5,
   43–4, 134; Palestro massacre, 131–3, 136–
   7; *pieds noirs*, 27–8, 30, 43, 45, 134, 136,
   389; settlers, 34, 43–5, 134, 390; warfare,
   134–5, 389–90
Algiers: bombings, 137–8; Casbah raid,
   136
Államvédelmi Osztálya (ÁVO, later
   ÁVH), 103
Altman, Phyllis, 225

America, *see* United States of America
American Committee on Africa, 397
Amis, Kingsley, 205
Anderson, Lindsay, 205
Andropov, Yuri, 101, 293, 300, 302, 344
'Angry Young Men', 205
Applebaum, Anne, 185
Arab League, 142, 213
Arbeiderbladet, 125
Arden-Clarke, Sir Charles, 115
Arendt, Hannah, 309
Arrow Cross Party, 312
Arvalov, R. G., 63
Association of Hungarian University and
   College Students (MEFESz), 295
Astor, David, 331
Athos (minesweeper), 265–6
Atlanta Journal Constitution, 73
Atlantic Charter, xiii, 27
Attlee, Earl, 124
Australia: responses to Hungarian
   uprising, 350, 351; Suez conferences,
   258–9; Suez policy, 325, 330
Auténtico Party, 362
ÁVH, *see* Hungary
Azbell, Joe, 18–19, 21, 22
el-Azhari, Ismail, xi

Baard, Frances, 226
Baghdad Pact, 213
Baker, Ella, 15
Baltimore Afro-American, 386
Bandung Conference (1955), 42, 149
Bar-On, Mordechai, 258, 268
Barnes, Spencer, 339
Bartók, Béla, 190
Batista, Fulgencio: background and
   career, 362; coup, 362–3, 364, 365;
   flight, 368; opposition to, 359, 363, 364,
   387; regime, 357, 362–3, 364, 366–7, 369

114, 115, 118; Ghana independence, 119,
388; imprisonment, 115; military coup
against, 388; NLM opposition, 116–18;
picture, *109*; prime minister, 116,
118–19, 388
Nok Lapja, 182
nonviolent resistance, 154–7
North Africa: Communist view of
liberation struggles, 398; rebellion
against French, xi, 35–6
Novotný, Antonín, 105, 106–7
Nowa Kultura, 276
Nuri es-Said, 217
Nutting, Anthony, 214–15, 267
Nyerere, Julius, 388

L'Observateur, 133
Observer, London, 61, 133, 205, 331
Ocean, HMS, 318–19
Ochab, Edward, 96, 100, 169, 279–81
Olympic Games (Melbourne), 352–3
Operation Musketeer, 262, 322, 328, 392
Operation Whirlwind, 345–6
Orlov, Yuri, 63
Ortodoxo Party, 364, 369
Osborne, John, 204–5
Overton, Richard, 200–1

País, Frank, 359
Pakistan, Suez policy, 326
Palestro massacre, 131–3, 136–7
Palomar Gardens, Fats Domino concert,
195–6
Parker, 'Colonel' Tom, 200
Parks, Frank, 83
Parks, Raymond, 15, 16
Parks, Rosa, 14–16, 19, 22, 380, 395
Parr, John, *315*
Partelet, 183
People's Daily, 217
Peres, Shimon, 257
Pérez, Faustino, 360
Pérez, Louis, 362
Péter, Gábor, 102
Petőfi, Sándor, 184, 291, 297
Petőfi Circle, *179*, 184–8, 189, 191
Phillips, Sam, 197, 199

pieds noirs, 27–8, 30, 43, 45, 134, 136, 389
Piłsudski, Józef, 273
Pineau, Christian, 219–20, *255*, 257, 259,
269
Piros, László, 296
Pisareva, Yefrosinia, 53
Pius XII, Pope, 350
Po prostu, 97–8, 99
'A Poem for Adults' (Ważyk), 203
Poland: anti-Soviet sentiment, 283–5;
Communist regime, 94–5; flag, 168;
Gomułka's return to power, 280–2,
294; history, 273; international response
to repression of protests, 174–5,
176–7, 189; political and economic
discontent, 57, 97–9, 105, 171–2, 275;
Poznań protests, *see* Poznań; Poznań
trials, 276–8; press, 276; religion, 99,
282, 285–6; religious nationalism,
275–6; response to Khrushchev's
'secret speech', 95–8, 172–3; response to
Makarios deportation, 125; Sejm, 276,
282; Soviet relations, 279–82, 286–7;
student unrest, 276; wave of dissent,
177–8; workers' councils, 283, 285;
writing, 203; youth culture, 202
Polish Communist Party (KPP), 274
Polish United Workers' Party (PZPR):
Central Committee, 169; economic
approach, 276, 279, 282; Eighth
Plenum, 279, 280–1, 282, 284;
headquarters, 164–6; leadership, 275,
279; response to Khrushchev's 'secret
speech', 96; Soviet relations, 97, 279
Pontecorvo, Gillo, 389
Port Said: battle for, *315*, 317–22; British
strategy, 218, 262; British withdrawal,
212; Suez Canal garrison, 211
Pound, Ezra, 242
Poznań: aftermath of protests,
175–8, 275; background to protests,
171–4; international parallels, 398;
international responses to suppression
of protests, 174–5, 176–7; protests, *161*,
163–8; trials, 276–8; violent suppression
of protests, 168–71, 174, 175
Pravda, 65, 217, 314